KNOWLEDGE AS PROPERTY

KNOWLEDGE AS PROPERTY
Issues in the Moral Grounding of
Intellectual Property Rights

RAJSHREE CHANDRA

OXFORD
UNIVERSITY PRESS

OXFORD
UNIVERSITY PRESS

Oxford University Press is a department of the University of Oxford.
It furthers the University's objective of excellence in research, scholarship,
and education by publishing worldwide. Oxford is a registered trademark of
Oxford University Press in the UK and in certain other countries

Published in India by
Oxford University Press
2/11 Ground Floor, Ansari Road, Daryaganj, New Delhi 110 002, India

First published 2010
Oxford India Paperbacks 2012

ISNB-13 (print edition): 978-0-19-808911-7
ISNB-10 (print edition): 0-19-808911-2

ISNB-13 (eBook): 978-0-19-908818-8
ISNB-10 (eBook): 0-19-908818-7

Typeset in Bember 10.5/12.6 by Jojy Philip

For
Nikhil and Niyati
and
their free thinking spirit

Contents

Abbreviations

ALF	Alternative Law Forum
ARV	Anti Retroviral
CAFC	Federal Circuit Court of Appeals
CBD	Convention of Biodiversity
CENTAD	Centre for Trade and Development
CIPIH	Commission on Intellectual Property Rights, Innovation and Public Health
CPAA	Cancer Patients Aids Association
DND	Drugs for Neglected Diseases
ECOSOC	United Nations Economic and Social Council
EMR	Exclusive Marketing Rights
EPA	Environmental Protection Agency
EPC	European Patent Convention
EPO	European Patent Office
FAO	Food and Agricultural Organization
FDC	Fixed Dose Combination
FTA	Free Trade Agreement
GATT	General Agreement on Trade and Tariffs
GE	Genetic Engineering
GFATM	Global Fund to Fight AIDS, Tuberculosis and Malaria
GIPAP	Glivec International Patient Assistance Program
GM	Genetic Modification
HTS	High Throughput Screening
IDA	International Dispensary Association
IPAB	Intellectual Property Appellate Board
I-MAK	Initiative for Medicines, Access and Knowledge
IP	Intellectual Property
LDC	Least Developed Countries
MSF	Medecins Sans Frontieres
ND	Neglected Diseases
PBR	Plant Breeders' Rights

PEPFA	President's Emergency Plan for AIDS
PGFRA	International Undertaking on Plant Genetic Resources for Food and Agriculture
PLRMA	Pharmaceuticals Research and Manufacture America
PPA	Plant Protection Act
PPVFRA	Protection of Plant Variety and Farmers' Rights Act
PVP	Plant Variety Protection
TKDL	Traditional Knowledge Digital Library
TRIPS	Trade Related Intellectual Property Rights
UDHR	Universal Declaration of Human Rights
UNESCR	United Nations Economic, Social and Cultural Rights
UNCED	United Nations Conference on Environment and Development
UNIDO	United Nations Industrial Development Organization
UNICEF	United Nations International Children's Emergency Fund
UPOV	Union for the Protection of New Varieties of Plants
USDA	United States Department of Agriculture
USPTO	United States Patent and Trade Mark Office
USTR	United States Trade Representative
WIPO	World Intellectual Property Organization
WMS	Western Modern Sciences
WTO	World Trade Organization

Acknowledgements

The issue of intellectual property rights (IPRs) has always presented itself as an emotive one, besides, of course, being deeply political. Few issues combine and yet reflect the schism between the political, cultural, social and the normative, as do intellectual property rights. Usually considered a preserve of legal scholars and science and technology policy makers, it was a challenge to shear the 'technical' persona that this issue had come to don and see it as an issue of rights—rights which are claimed; rights which are confronted. The exercise was challenging and at times daunting. A number of people contributed in big and small, but always important, ways to make this process easier than it would have been in their absence.

As all 'intellectual' endeavours necessarily are, this work too has been a collaborative exercise. This work emerges out of my doctoral dissertation and owes a lot to a number of people. Foremost, I would like to thank my supervisor, Niraja Gopal Jayal for her generosity, encouragement, patience, and guidance. Such was her support that I find it hard to not access her mentoring on an ongoing basis.

I would also like to thank my College, Janki Devi Memorial College, University of Delhi, for granting me leave without which this could not have been possible. Thanks are also due to Center for the Study of Law and Governance (CSLG), JNU, for its generosity in procuring books that were not otherwise available. Research for this thesis was carried primarily in the JNU Central Library, CSLG Library, and the Nehru memorial Library. The official websites of SARAI, RIS Center, Oxfam, were a source of valuable research material and their databases proved extremely useful. Special thanks are due to Research Foundation for Science, Technology and Ecology, Gene Campaign, Alternative Law Forum, Medicins Sans Frontieres (MSF) for sharing their perspectives and research resources with me.

My sincere thanks to Pratap Bhanu Mehta for his theoretical provocations and incisive comments on my dissertation, and for sparing time for a continued engagement. Thanks are also due to Upendra Baxi for being my examiner—the depth and the range of issues that he raised have helped refine this work. Useful comments on a paper presented at The Center for International and Public Law, Australian National University, by Katie Young, Kim Rubenstein and Matthew Rimmer, helped sharpen the focus of the chapter on health rights. Special thanks to Thomas Pogge whose writings and email discussions helped resolve the moral dilemmas that rights invariably seem to pose.

I extend my sincere thanks to the editors at Oxford University Press, New Delhi for showing interest in the work. They have been immensely supportive and helpful.

I owe profuse thanks to some of my friends who miraculously filled all kinds of shoes: to my resourceful friend Madhuparna Mitra, who would courier books, photocopy articles, chapters from the US, to meet a perpetual shortfall of available reading material here; to Kishore Singh, Navneeta Behera, Poonam Kanwal, Rekha Krishnan for mentoring, advising, inspiring, and much else; to Ruplekha Khullar, my fellow traveller, for being my sounding board.

The debt one owes to the family is seldom acknowledged. This is more a dedication than anything else: To my parents for being so liberal when all else was prescriptive; To my sister, Rashmi for her solidarity; And to my generous husband, Jaideep, the warmest thanks ever. In big and small ways they are all responsible for my interest and enthusiasm and not for my errors and conclusions.

Introduction

Intellectual property rights are commonly seen as a legal issue, not coextensive with ethical concerns. They are seen as complicated legal linkages that allow for the expansion and streamlining of innovation and other forms of knowledge production in society. However, like most 'legal' issues, Intellectual Property Rights (IPRs) too are related to matters of just claims and rights. Whether rights exist as claims for individual liberty, social equity, cultural autonomy and group differences, or as incentives, they are inexorably linked to normative issues. There is always a matter of ethics involved, whether they align themselves with issues of life, liberty and property, or with issues of equity and human rights. For this reason this work claims as its objective, the study of the moral premises of IPRs. I have regarded IPRs as fundamentally an ethical and moral issue for their ability to augment or confront conditions of liberty or of existing human rights. For instance, much of the unauthorized exploitation of indigenous and traditional peoples' resources is contrary to international law and ethical practice. It is also contrary to the practice of democracy, which increasingly tries to extend the grammar of political claims to include claims of social equality, cultural autonomy, and group rights. The ambition of 'rights' is a difficult stance to adopt for IPRs since this demands that IPRs rest, atleast, minimally on deontological and/or consequentialist premises.

This study aims to analyse the established legitimacy of IPRs through an inquiry into the philosophical and moral premises of IPRs. Moral philosophy cannot, of course, prove that one way of organizing society is objectively better than the other. However, it can make our ideas of justice more precise and reasoned. Intellectual Property Rights are both about distributional justice and rights. Rights discourses and rights practices have enormous implications for justice, since as structuring discourses they impact the manner in which resources and capacities are distributed in society and across societies.

Most existing critiques of IPRs are consequentialist critiques, that is, they assess IPRs from the perspective of whether they have led to economically more efficient outcomes,[1] catalyzed innovation, had a positive impact on ecology or biodiversity or the rights of the poor. In other words, the validity or the critique of IPRs is seen to be contingent on their consequences. One of the effects of consequentialist approaches is to see rights as dependent wholly on the valuation of outcomes, rather than being integrated with them. An integrated approach, as the one I adopt here, extends itself and sees rights as based on normative premises and as constructs which have far-reaching consequences. An evaluation of rights would therefore not be consequence-independent but one which is not wholly derived from the consequences. Consequences are therefore, in the present study, regarded as necessary for the evaluation of IPRs, but not sufficient in themselves to uphold or dismantle rights.

Consequence dependent explanations are of course necessary, for IPRs cannot be seen as independent of an evaluative exercise. After all, rights are functional entities meant to change or safeguard situations. However, it is equally imperative to evaluate IPRs not just in terms of the consequence (that is, in terms of innovations achieved, rights encroached upon or abrogated, fairness of benefit sharing mechanisms, or economic or biotechnological benefits), but also in terms of a larger debate on the deontological premises of rights within political philosophy. The aim is not to suggest that the conceptualization of rights should be consequence-independent, or that the valuation of outcomes is secondary, but simply to assert that there are a category of rights for which a normative defence can be advanced without an evaluation of the consequences.[2] For instance,

---

[1] The basic public policy rationale for intellectual property laws is that they protect the rights of the inventor, author, or creator. IPRs have been conceived as a tool to reward innovators and creators, for their contributions to society, for a statutory period of time. They are intended to provide the necessary incentives to the generation and dissemination of knowledge as well as to encourage the transfer and diffusion of technology. IPRs constitute exceptions to market mechanisms as competition and free access were not considered adequate enough to provide incentives for innovation and development. It is typically suggested, usually by IP theory, that free market with no exclusive rights will lead to too little production of intellectual works. The economic rationale for IPRs is that unless invention or creation is compensated, invention and creation will be underprovided and economic development, even the development of science, will suffer. It is also designed to combat the 'free rider' problem, given that recent changes in technology have made replication and duplication much simpler. Individuals and firms will hesitate to make costly investments in innovation if imitators can reproduce these at a fraction of the cost and technological progress will be hampered.

[2] Joel Feinberg, 1970, 'Justice and Personal Desert', *Doing and Deserving*, Princeton, NJ, Princeton University Press; Amartya Sen, 2002, *Rationality and Freedom*, Delhi, OUP.

the right to individual liberty or the right to cultural autonomy are rights which derive their moral claim independent of consequences. The space over which rights are exercised can become a further reason to claim or dispute a right.

In the present states, NGOs and activists are engaged in the process of fine-tuning the benefit-sharing mechanisms, and the legal and political processes involved in making the IPR regime more sensitive to the needs of the developing countries, traditional societies and indigenous communities. While these are necessary practices to democratize the functioning of the IPR regime, which make apparent the entitlements on which these rights are based, there is clearly a further need to question the basic assumptions and premises of the notion of IPRs as a rights–claims. Intellectual property laws have profoundly normative visions of progress. They reflect this, not just in their functioning, but also in their conceptualisation and assumptions related to who qualifies to be the rights-holder and what ought to constitute a right.

The central concern of the study is with what may be called the conception or the idea of IPRs—*the idea of knowledge as property*. The question of the idea of intellectual property precedes and governs the answer to the question of whether IPRs can be claimed as rights. In other words, the very idea of knowledge as property is a primary concern in grounding IPRs. Whether intellectual property legitimately stakes its claim as a right naturally follows from this concern. The aim therefore, would be firstly to evaluate the conception of IP in the context of the property rights discourse, to see how these rights play out, and the implications that they have for other rights. How rights proceed and are enacted is very often implied in the principles that underlie them. Theoretical explorations of rights, property, and other related concepts will then be correlated with empirical, contextual studies of rights–processes in order to evaluate IPRs as rights–claims.

The critique of IPRs benefits greatly from the extended scope of political theory. The span of political theory has been significantly extended by the insights provide by post-modern philosophy, hermeneutics, and anthropology; including the study of language use, the interpretation of texts, reflections on different modes of rationality, the study of science as social practice, culture and the interpretation of tradition, cultural dimensions of rights, and many other such areas of inquiry. A large number of these inquiries relate to the practice of rights, knowledge, and property practices. The acknowledgement in political theory and philosophy, of multiple cultural modes of rationalities

xvi   Introduction

and epistemologies, makes the study of universal categories of IPRs particularly pertinent, perhaps even necessary. Rights need embody notions of cultural relativism and heterogeneity within both its theory and practice. IPRs will be evaluated and examined in this context and assessed in terms of their capacity to augment or mitigate socially and culturally heterogeneous rights–claims.

II

Intellectual property is not a monolithic concept. It is an umbrella term for various legal entitlements which attach to certain types of information, ideas, or other intangibles in their expressed form. The holder of this legal entitlement is generally entitled to exercise various exclusive rights in relation to the subject matter of the IP. Intellectual Property is a broad concept that covers several types of legally recognized rights arising from some type of intellectual creativity. In today's legal systems, IP typically includes at least copy rights, trademarks, patents, and trade secrets.[3]

A *Copyright* provides legal protection for *original material* in literary, artistic, dramatic or musical works, films, broadcasts, multimedia, and computer programs. Copyright gives exclusive right to reproduce work, prepare derivative works or to perform or present the work publicly. 'Copyrights protect only the *form* or *expression* of ideas, not the underlying ideas themselves.'[4] While a copyright may be registered to obtain legal advantages, a copyright need not be registered to exist. Rather, a copyright comes into existence automatically the moment the work is 'fixed' in a 'tangible medium of expression', and lasts for the life of the author plus seventy years, or for a total of ninety-five years in cases in which the employer owns the copyright.

A *patent* is a right granted for any device, substance, method or process which is *new, inventive, and useful*. A patent for an invention grants a property right to the inventor that will prevent anyone else from making, using, or selling an invention. A patent, therefore, grants to the patentee the right to *exclude* (that is, to prevent others from practicing the patented invention); it does not grant to the patentee the exclusivity of *use* of the patented invention. A patent lasts for a limited amount of time, usually 20 years from the date the application was filed, and is only effective in the country in which it was filed. Since a patent is considered 'property,' it may be bought,

---

[3] A useful introduction to IP can be found in Arthur R. Miller and Michael H. Davies, 1990.

[4] Stephen Kinsella, 2001, 'Against Intellectual Property'. *Journal of Libertarian Studies* 15(2), Ludwig von Mises Institute, Spring, p. 10.

sold, mortgaged, or licensed by the owner. Not every innovation or discovery is patentable. The US Supreme Court has, for example, identified three categories of subject matter that are unpatentable, namely 'laws of nature, natural phenomena, and abstract ideas'.[5] Reducing abstract ideas to some type of 'practical application,' that is, 'a useful, concrete and tangible result,' is patentable. Article 52 of European Patent Convention (EPC), for instance, excludes 'programs for computers' from patentability (Article 52(2)).[6] Countries like India exclude from patentability incrementally improved drugs, unless they can demonstrate 'enhanced efficacy'.[7]

A trade secret consists of any confidential formula, device, or piece of information which gives its holder a competitive advantage so long as it remains secret. An example would be the formula for Coca-Cola. Trade secrets can include information that is not novel enough to be the subject of patent protection, or not original enough to be protected by copyright (for example, a database of seismic data or customer lists). Trade secret laws are used to prevent 'misappropriations' of the trade secret, or to award damages for such misappropriations. Usually a word, phrase, symbol, or design used to *identify* the source of goods or services sold, it is to distinguish them from the goods or services of others. Trademark law primarily prevents competitors from 'infringing' upon the trademark, i.e., using 'confusingly similar' marks to identify their own goods and services. Besides the above, IP covers a larger area which extends to plant varieties, geographical indications, circuit layout rights, and so on.

The Trade Related Aspects of Intellectual Property Rights (TRIPS) agreement as a legal regime, sponsored by the World Trade Organization (WTO), offers protection to intellectual advancements, and offers near absolute ownership of an idea, or a resource associated with the idea, for a stipulated period. In the context of global TRIPS compliant laws, IPRs acquire a reach beyond that sanctioned by conventional property rights. What is significant is that against the backdrop of the new generation of socio-economic rights and group rights, a thoroughly capitalist principle—the right to the protection of material interests from scientific, literary or artistic productions—has been entrenched. The TRIPS

[5] United States Code (USC) Title 35—Patents. Section 101 outlines the basic requirements for patentability. The Patent Act, 1952 does not expressly bar any subject matter from patentability, the Courts have held physical phenomenon, abstract ideas and products of nature to be outside the scope of patentability. Available at http://www.uspto.gov/web/offices/pac/mpep/consolidated_laws.pdf (last accessed on 25 January 2008).

[6] Available at http://www.epo.org/patents/law/legal-texts/html/epc/2000/e/ar52.html (last accessed on 25 January 2008).

[7] Section 3d, Patent (Amendment) Act, 2005 (No. 15 OF 2005).

provisions of patenting, copyrights, trade secrets, plant variety protection, etc., have become potent vehicles for subverting the changed perspectives of the rights discourse. Granting knowledge the status of property and then incorporating it as a right, is to eschew the minimalist notions of property and to reverse the downgrading of property right that had been accomplished with the emergence of second and third generation rights.

This work does not endeavour to explain every nuance in each doctrine—the multiplicity and variety of subsumed topics precludes such an endeavour. However, the study does regard the scope of patents to have more pernicious exclusionary premises than for example, trademarks and trade secrets. To that extent a number of conclusions drawn relate to patents specifically, more than other forms of IP which vary in the extent they exclude and therefore demand moral justifications. What is attempted is to pave the way for broader conclusions on the rights and defences in the sphere of IP. In particular, the study attempts to situate IPRs within the rights discourse and examine issues of IP in larger debates about human rights, distributional equalities, and social justice.

III

Over the years, there have been three large movements within the institution of property. The first of these was the movement from common property to private property. Before the seventeenth century property was conceived either as common or private, but during its course, the idea of common property dropped 'virtually out of sight'. There was a marked change in the idea of ownership in the seventeenth century.[8] G.E. Alymer discusses the emergence of absolute individual ownership and of the erosion of the distinction between real and personal property.[9] The development of the institution of private property was also matched by a concomitant movement in political philosophy, which sought to offer different justificatory premises for establishing the moral claim of private property.

The second movement was with respect to the changing conception of rights in general. In the aftermath of the collapse of communism and widespread disenchantment with the Marxist grand narratives of progress and emancipation, many liberals came to see welfarism in a more positive light, as positively empowering for securing the autonomy and freedom of the individual. On this was premised the positive conception of rights

[8] S.F.C. Milson, 1969, *Historical Foundations of the Common Law*, London: Butterworths.

[9] G.E. Aylmer, 1980, 'The Meaning and Definition of Property in 17th Century England', *Past and Present*, no. 86, February, pp. 87–97.

in which rights began to be seen as structures that enabled individual pursuits. The idea of socio-economic rights, which enable individuals in substantive ways, gained a great deal of ground. More recently there have been important moves to recognize the fundamental nature of socio-economic rights as human rights and to integrate them within human-rights documents.[10] Such rights are based on a wider understanding of human welfare and its economic, moral, psychological, as well as cultural requirements. The language of national and international communication reflects this shift in priorities and emphasis. A number of significant supranational pronouncements have acknowledged the significance of welfare, social justice and have tried to integrate it with the concept of rights. The Universal Declaration of Human Rights (UDHR) and United Nations Economic, Social and Cultural Rights (UNESCR) are perhaps the most important documents in this regard.

Rights were first theorized as defences erected around individuals to cordon off an unimpeded space into which the state was not allowed to enter, whether it was to protect the natural rights of an individual (Locke), derived from the need to preserve the moral autonomy of the individual (Kant), or to maximize net welfare or productivity in society (Adam Smith, Jeremy Bentham). Rights theory suggests that the individual is a good user of this unimpeded space, and that such arrangements provide benefits for society, thus putting a low premium on state directed activity, or any such coordinated efforts. Historically, this was the negative rights conception supported by natural rights theorists (seventeenth century), liberal individualists and utilitarians (eighteenth and nineteenth centuries), and libertarians (twentieth century). Rights at these junctures privileged the notion of liberty and autonomy. However, when the concept of rights got aligned with that of welfare, its interpretation profoundly changed. New interpretations revised the realm of the private, the locus of the rights-bearing individual, and the non-desirability of state intervention. As Kevin Floyd states, 'while rights may serve as a source of autonomy and individual self assertion at one point, they may also serve as an indisputable force of emancipation at another point; at another time they may become a regulatory discourse—a means of restricting or co-opting more radical political or social demands.'[11]

[10] See for Instance, International Covenant on Social, Economic and Cultural Rights 1966 (ICESCR), the Convention on the Elimination of All Forms of Discrimination against Women, 1979 (CEDAW), the European Convention on Human Rights, 1950 (ECHR) and the European Social Charter, 1961.

[11] Kevin Floyd, 1998, 'Making History: Marxism, Queer Theory, and Contradiction in

Conceptually, rights are rather like a capsule surrounded by other social and political concepts such as property, liberty, welfare, interest, self-determination, etc., which makes it impossible to disentangle the analysis of rights from these client concepts.[12] The social context of contemporary times, with its accent on 'welfarism', has led to the attachment of the concept of rights to the notion of social justice and welfare. The changing perspective on rights has become critical in shaping the scope and structure of property rights too.

In a sense, there are two opposite ideas of property: property as a commodity, and property open to social needs. In the construction of property rights, the social aspect, though it never completely fades away, can range from a very limited incidence to a large, broad influence.[13] When the social aspect is almost negligible, rights are typically deployed in their negative conception. Conversely, emphasis on the social aspect of ownership highlights the interests of society as a whole, as opposed to those of the owner alone. On the face of it, welfare rights cannot belong in the same system as unfettered private property rights. 'Welfare rights, it is acknowledged, presuppose a welfare principle according to which individuals are entitled to call on the efforts of society as a whole to achieve an acceptable welfare condition for all.'[14] The social and the individual are thus mutually restricting.

In the context of the goals of social justice and welfare, the right to property began to be notably downgraded as is evident in some of the international charters and covenants. The European Convention on Human Rights (ECHR)[15] invoked 'public interest' in order to permit divesting individuals of their possessions. The American Convention on Human Rights subordinated the use and enjoyment of individual property to the interest of society or public utility.[16] In political theory and philosophy, various strands, such as social democratic theories, positive liberal theories, and liberal democratic theories, have emerged within liberalism to make liberal theory more sensitive to issues of equality and democracy. In consonance with these, property as a private right, has begun

---

the Future of American Studies', *Cultural Critique*, No. 40, The Futures of American Studies (Autumn), pp. 167–201.

[12] Michael Freeden, 1998, *Rights*, Delhi: WorldView Publications, p. 43.

[13] See A.M. Honoré, 1970, 'Ownership,' in, *Law and Philosophy: Readings in Legal Philosophy*, E.A. Kent (ed.), New York: Appleton Century Crofts, pp. 594–95.

[14] Attracta Ingram, 1994, *A Political Theory of Rights*, Oxford: Clarendon Press, p. 44.

[15] Protocol 1, Article 1.

[16] American Convention on Human Rights, O.A.S. Treaty Series No. 36, 1144 UNTS 123. Article 21.

to be seen as an institution associated with injustice and exploitation, and embodying an inherent tendency towards inequity. In aligning the principle of liberty with equality, private property as an institution and as a right, underwent a downward revision.

A third movement has been with regard to additions and deletions in the list of things that count as property.[17] For instance, slaves no longer count as property; there is an ongoing debate, in the context of trade in body parts, of whether they comprise property. At the centre of the debate is also the conception of knowledge as Intellectual Property. Does intellectual labour comprise property? Can rights be morally claimed for Intellectual Property? These are contested and compelling issues which serve to imply not only a plurality of perceptions emanating from varied philosophical and political perspectives, but also imply a plurality of traditions and social organizations where different things can or do count as property. The difference in the list of things that count as property would serve to establish the heterogeneity of social and, therefore property arrangements. If knowledge as an item were to be anticipated as property, it would be useful to see if it is regarded as an object of property in non-western societies and specially, if it is seen as property of particular persons.

While the first two movements established the autonomy of the individual, and property as an expression of that autonomy, the third movement linked individual autonomy and liberty with forms of intellectual labour. The latter, that is, the development of IP as a form of private property, has been one of the most revolutionary legal changes in the past generation. Although there are many notions and types of property—'private property', 'common property', 'public ownership', and so on—the institution and the notion of private property is being considered here because that is what IPRs are protected as.

IV

There are obviously many ways in which the study of IPRs can be both approached and organized, since the notion and the regime traverse diverse disciplines of law, ethics, economics, politics, international relations, ethnographic studies, and cultural studies. My entry point is from the perspective of political philosophy which sees rights as normative, socially and culturally contextualized, and consequently sensitive enterprises. The study separates the idea of IPRs from its consequences, that is, the notion from the practice, only to bring them together in the end as necessary

[17] Andrew Reeves, 1986, *Property,* London: Macmillan.

corollaries for rights–claims to be ethical. IPRs are contextualized in their evolutionary history and in the theories in which they are embedded, in Section I. In Section II the consequential dimensions of IPRs are examined, with the suggestion that rights which conjoin well with other rights (rights of 'other' people) have a stronger moral claim than rights which do not. I return to this suggestion later in the book.

Chapter 1 seeks to contextualize IPRs in their historical and social settings, before examining the peculiar dilemmas that knowledge poses for propertisation. How different is this notion of property in immaterial entitities like knowledge, from the earlier notion of property in things, resources, and labour? Labour, which becomes the strongest foundational principle for property, like knowledge, is an intangible quantity. The distinction between the two lies in their source. Earlier forms of property, including labour, had a clearly identifiable source, that is, the individual body, and was therefore amenable to characterization as 'separate' and individually owned. Knowledge, by contrast, defies such a characterization; it is something that is incremental, contextual, cultural, and clearly not a product of an individual mind alone. The separate and the clearly divisible character of earlier forms of property seem absent here. This comes to have a significant bearing on the justificatory grounds of Intellectual Property.

Chapter 2 outlines two justificatory theories of property—self ownership and utility. The reason why these two premises have been selected for closer scrutiny is because they have proved, intuitively and historically, to be the most powerful and enduring of defences for private property. This chapter outlines the fundamental principles of these theories as reflected in the pioneering works of John Locke, Robert Nozick, and Jeremy Bentham. Chapter 2 examines these two often used justificatory premises before evaluating the relevance and the translatability into defences for Intellectual Property in Chapters 3 and 4. The assumption that underlies these chapters is that justificatory premises for tangible property may not hold good for intangibles like intellectual property.

There is an underlying assumption in the conception of private property rights that property rules cover people as well as other types of external items. Further, that each bundle of human resources—mental and physical, can be assigned as private property to particular individuals. It is a principle which regards each individual as possessing a right to private property in himself, that is, self-ownership. That each individual is the morally rightful owner of his person, powers and talents has been the foundational claim of liberal philosophy since Locke: 'every man has a Property in his own Person'. The principle of self-ownership, as a right over one's body and talents, is joined with a principle of right over material resources. Bodily or mental powers require an implement to act through and a material to act upon in order to create something. The thing that is created becomes the property of the person who has mixed his labour, powers or talents with it. Thinking about property, therefore, has been informed by considerations of the origin of the material. The creator was seen to be the legitimate holder of that property. Right-holding is thus linked to ownership, with a proprietary control over the domain specified as the object of right. Self-ownership is a concept that brings persons into the domain of private property. This needs to be noted because not every system regards property in persons.[18]

Another common argument for private property is provided by the Utilitarians. They argue that private property and its corollary, the free market, will lead to increased productivity and that it would be maximally efficient at increasing social wealth. Utilitarians favour the free market, since its efficiency allows for the greatest overall satisfaction of preferences. For Utilitarians, the creation of property rights is linked to the utility it generates. The Utilitarian defence of property is the defence of a legal recognition of ownership as an instrument in promoting and optimizing welfare.

These two strands of liberal theory offer different premises of justification of private property and for claiming it as a moral right. The attempt in Chapters 3 and 4 would be to examine these philosophical premises of private property and see if they hold good for IPRs. I have deliberately avoided a discussion on the validity of these premises for tangible property, for my endeavour is to evacuate the concept of IPRs of the very justifications that it bases itself on.

Chapter 3 picks up one of the foundational premises, self-ownership, and tests it in the context of IPRs. The notion of self-ownership allows the dissolution of the distinction between ideas and things. Ideas, knowledge, faculties of the mind are part of the 'self'. The self-owner of knowledge has full private property rights over its exercise. IPRs seem to flow out of this conception, endorsing the view that a man has property in his person.

---

[18] Contradictions in the concept of self-ownership emerged in the context of slavery, serfdom, and political absolutism. Viewed through the prism of self-ownership, these were regarded as a violation of rights. The slave owner or exploiter illegitimately claims rights of disposal over a person's services that belong morally to that person himself. Subsequently, self-ownership has become one of the foundational principles of liberty and legitimating arguments for private property.

Does self-ownership yield property rights over products of intellectual labour, is what this chapter seeks to examine.

Chapter 4 examines the consequentialist utilitarian defence for IPRs, which argues that the presence of strong IPRs spurs innovation, leading to higher economic growth and development of science and technology which benefits the society at large. Utilitarianism tends to be extensively used at the policy level. This chapter asserts that utilitarian cost benefit analysis falters, both in terms of quantifiable economic costs, and the non-quantifiable social costs. The costs of a strong IPR regime, when measured beyond a narrow utilitarian frame, often outweigh benefits.

Chapter 5 considers the cognitive hierarchies which are implied and structured by the IP regime. This chapter looks at the sociology of knowledge creation and the implications that it has for opening up epistemes. It takes the argument of social construction of knowledge and extends it to question the claimed scientificity and objectivity of Western Modern Sciences (WMS) in an endeavour to engage with the possibility of multiple constructions and representations of reality and question the claimed universality and hegemony of WMS. It regards the conception and the institution of IPRs as an enterprise which reinstates the particularistic perspectives of science and the universalistic notions of development. It regards this conceptualization of IPRs as a productive and a stratifying force and therefore as an exercise of power. Finally, the chapter engages with the issues of science citizenship, and the limits of existing measures for enlisting the participation of the marginalized citizens in the creation of knowledge.

Chapters 6, 7, and 8 are premised on the idea that rights need to communicate with other rights because rights need to be evaluated in terms of how well they conjoin with other rights. This may well constitute a consequentialist approach, but one that is rights-sensitive, which coheres with the idea that rights matter to—and as—consequences. These chapters utilize the consequence-sensitivity of utilitarianism, without being bound by its narrow view of relevant consequences. Compossibility with other rights becomes a necessary factor in deriving legitimacy for IPRs. Three case studies have been taken as illustrative of three fundamental rights, also aspects of human rights.

Chapter 6 examines IPRs in the context of the right to health. The Novartis patent claim for the anti-cancer drug 'Glivec' in India has been presented, as a case-study to highlight the infringement of health rights in the context of the high prices of patented drugs which make vital drugs inaccessible to a vast majority of people, particularly poor people.

The case brings to the fore issues of drug patenting, survival of generic drugs, and their impact on access to medicines, which are vital to the preservation of the right to health, an aspect of human rights, as well as a constitutional right in many countries.

Chapter 7 undertakes the study of the case *McFarling* v. *Monsanto* to draw attention to infringement of farmers' rights in the context of proprietary claims in agriculture and forms of IP protection to plant varieties. IPRs in plant varieties, which exist both as patents and as 'breeder's rights', have been created by a system that believes in private, monopolised control over plants and/or life forms for engendering innovation. These rights have the potential to result in the disruption of the traditional farming cultures which crucially impact livelihood concerns of farmers. The chapter also highlights the varied implications of IPRs for farmers in developed and poorer countries and communities.

Chapter 8 presents the bio-politics of Neem through two prominent cases that were fought against patent claims on Neem products in European Patent Office and the United States Patent Office. These two cases symbolize the vulnerability of knowledge or resources, which belong either to traditional peoples or lie in the public domain in poorer but bio-resource rich countries, to resource and knowledge piracy which constitutes an infringement of the knowledge rights of the traditional peoples. Knowledge rights are also aspects of human rights as declared by the UDHR. As co-equal rights, what are the bases for distinctions that can be drawn, such that we are able to employ a premise of moral adjudication and accord indigenous knowledge rights with higher claims as rights—this forms a part of discussion in the chapter.

IPRs are one of the sites which represent the encounter between indigenous knowledge and modern scientific knowledge. These are not just cognitive encounters but relate to the larger issue of intellectual and cultural domination of traditional knowledges and cultures. The perceived dichotomy between the two knowledge systems is not just about incompatible values, attitudes and practices but also relates to rights within a legal framework. The issue at stake is the right of different forms of knowledge, their associated practices and ways of being to co-exist and carry weight in the decisions that affect peoples' lives. Seeing knowledge as a relational concept provides a democratic frame for advancing democratic practice and for recognizing claims of communities and groups that may be articulated outside the realm of 'science'. This chapter argues that unacknowledged cultural contingencies of scientific knowledge need to be deployed in the framing, definition, and resolution of public-policy issues.

The concluding chapter returns to the question of legitimacy of IPRs with which this book begins. Can IPRs be legitimately claimed as rights? In the absence of moral principles that support such a claim, do IPRs derive any legitimacy at all from their ability to support or conjoin with other rights? Do IPRs fit in with a framework of rights, which unites welfare, well-being, equal access to advantage with autonomy? These are questions which emerge out of the contestations relating to intellectual property. These questions explore the broader challenges that collective claims pose to the liberal theory of rights. It is one thing for international covenants to recognize and felicitate these rights, and quite another for them to become justifiable tools for renegotiating both lost spaces of autonomy and protected future choices.

Section I

1 Contextualizing Intellectual Property Rights

The meaning, understanding, and theory of property have undergone many changes over time. So also has the notion of rights, often in relation to the concept of property. Any discussion of intellectual property, as an issue in political theory, must take into account both the conceptual problems involved and the historical dimensions of the theory and practice of property, since neither is the institution of property static nor is there a common attitude to the desirability of a particular form of property.

Notions of property are rooted in particular historical experience. For instance, western attitudes to property are associated with the development of capitalism and commodification, which generated the notion of private ownership. The whole idea of an individual actor having defined rights, however, may be alien in other historical settings. There are fundamental differences in the concepts of 'property' and 'persons' in different historical contexts and social groups. Property, therefore, needs to be understood both historically and contextually. Different historical and cultural settings which do not have defined or definite notions of individualistic rights have attempted, in recent times, to draw upon indigenous and human-rights traditions to establish their claims to livelihood resources, territories, and cultural survival. This has led to the genesis of notions of group rights, community rights, and cultural rights, all of which are underlined by the collective and communal nature of rights-claims.

Contextually, the idea of IPRs conforms to the western conceptions of individuated rights. It is important to contextualize the relation between property and persons as codified by IPRs as also to emphasize that this relationship has specificity in the western context and that this may not be the case in other intellectual or social traditions. It would be useful, therefore, to locate the genesis of IPRs in the evolving relations between persons and property in the western tradition.

CHANGING CONCEPTIONS OF PROPERTY

The classical conception of property did not exhibit the same identifying characteristics as property does today. Contingencies and contexts have brought about discernable changes, not only in determining who the legitimate property holder is, but also what comprises property. The beginning of upheavals in the conception of property began when the feudal notion of 'dominion' split into the two separate, consolidated domains of sovereignty and property. Separate bundles of political and economic rights were generated. Liberal-democratic revolutions, and the rise of constitutional liberalism counter-posed an absolutist definition of property to an absolutist definition of sovereignty. They advocated the notion of separation of property from personality, and made the latter alone the sufficient, and necessary condition of the extension of political rights. It was this displacement which led to the first reification of the concept of property.

Medieval conceptions of property had private rights co-existing with communal rights. This gave way, as noted by C.B. Macpherson, to an early idea of private individual ownership, which included life, liberty, as well as estate, which was narrowed once again to a right to alienate, as well as to use material things.[1] Until the seventeenth century, a great bulk of property was in land and was limited to certain uses often excluding the right to free alienation.[2] In the seventeenth century, a distinction began to emerge between private use and appropriation of common landed property and individuation of property rights in land which included the right to alienate land as a commodified object. The concept of divisible property was extended to land. It was the growing capitalist market that made the individuation of property complete. Limited rights in land, revenue, or office gave way to absolute ownership rights in freely disposable goods. Property moved from being a subject of ownership and right to being the subject of production and exchange. 'The concentration of property rights in post-feudal West was thus doubly predicated upon the individuation of the owning subject, and the extension of the scope of ownership itself, which came to *include not only rights of use and benefit, but also of rights of transfer by bequest and sale*' (emphasis mine).[3] As Macpherson

[1] C.B. MacPherson, 1973, *Democratic Theory: Essays in Retrieval*, Clarendon: Oxford, p. 3.

[2] Property also consisted in corporate charters, monopolies, tax-framing rights, political, and religious offices, etc. All of these were rights; albeit shared, limited or delegated, rather than tangible things.

[3] Dick Pels, 1998, *Property and Power in Social Theory*, London: Routledge, pp. 33–34.

states, previously unsaleable rights in things were now saleable.[4] Allocation of transfer rights was an important step towards the gradual reification of property into a concept of thing-ownership. There was a shift from rights as residing in a person over things to ownership of the thing itself.[5]

This divide emerged in Locke's writings that affirmed that rightful property resulted from the mixing of an individual's labour with unclaimed nature, thereby making the object his own, to use, dispose, and transfer. Pocock argues that this distinction gradually cemented, and that property instead of being a mere prerequisite to political relations between persons became a legally defined relationship between persons and things or between persons through things.[6] From an 'immaterial' relationship between people about things—a subject-subject relationship—property became an institution, and a concept which described the relationship between the subject and material object. In the seventeenth and eighteenth century, property acquired a 'thing-like' status, expressed as a shift from rights *in personam* to rights *in rem*. The first reification was thus represented by the physical externality, and materiality of the object owned.

The world of resources, and goods came to be delineated as material 'things' which could be owned, and become property. Immaterial entitities like individuals, skills, knowledge, and human rights formed a separate category—they could not alienated, and therefore could not be delineated as separate 'objectifiable' objects.[7] This divide was contingent upon the reification of ownership relations which regarded only that as an object of property which was separable, alienable, and divisible. A thing like status could only be conferred upon all items that fulfilled the criteria of 'sovereign completedness', alienability, etc.[8] However, things began to change with Locke. The language of Locke's natural rights philosophy suggests that it was possible to own one's self even when subjective rights were considered innate, and inalienable. It was thus possible to alienate one's self temporarily, in exchange for a wage, or by mixing one's labour with a 'thing', which was amenable to physical alienation. Physical tangibility, or intangibility began to emerge as having no great consequence.

[4] C.B. MacPherson, 1973, p. 128.

[5] For instance around the seventeenth century, property rights in land, which earlier consisted of rights over use and transfer of use, shifted to ownership rights involving not just use, but the transfer, and disposal of land itself.

[6] J.G.A. Pocock, 1985, *Virtue, Commerce and History: Essays on Political Thought and History Chiefly in the 18th Century*, Cambridge: Cambridge University Press, p. 104.

[7] This distinction formed the justification upon which the abolition of slavery was predicated.

[8] Dick Pels, 1998, p. 34.

This came to have an important bearing on the formulations around IPRs. The twentieth century saw the ontological connection between property and things break down further with property-like status being conferred on knowledge, ideas, and other forms of intellectual labour. The extension of property rights to intangibles like intellectual property, I argue, represents the second reification of the concept of property. A thing like status gets conferred on knowledge which when conjoined with the material world yields objects which can be regarded as 'exclusive' and 'alienable' products of the human minds and therefore, can be accorded the status of property. This development is to some extent related to the emergence of modern science in the seventeenth century. In more recent times, science has increasingly enmeshed itself with other social institutions, as discussed in chapter five of this work, raising new questions about intellectual property. These questions have been accompanied by efforts to both redefine the rights of ownership, and to extend them to new claimants, generating conflicts about the rights and responsibilities of property owners, and the extent to which these rights are observed in practice.

A fundamental reason for scepticism about the legitimacy of establishing property rights in the products of the mind is that consideration of intellectual property tends to be divorced from thoughts about tangible property. This is evident in the legal profession where both academicians and practitioners regard 'property' (that is, real property and other tangible goods) and 'intellectual property' as distinct topics with little cross-fertilization. The distinction seems to also hold in economic discussion and in general public discourse. The roots of this division go back to the origins of the different types of property in England, tangible property being a creature of common law, and copyright largely a creature of statute. It is clear that property in tangible form has a legitimacy that predates the charters and statutes that made property an institution which was under legal protection.

EVOLUTION OF INTELLECTUAL PROPERTY

Although there are references of chefs being granted year long monopolies over culinary delights in Greek colonies, and references in Roman law dwelling upon the problem of piracy of artistic work, these references are atypical for there were no known institutions or conventions of intellectual property protection in ancient times. The first patent instrument, in modern form, was a patent statute passed in the Venetian Republic in

1474, meant to protect inventions and discoveries of ingenious devices.[9] For the most part though, the institution of IP protection derives itself from the English system that began with the Statute of Monopolies (1624) and the Statute of Anne (1709).[10] The subject matter of intellectual property is largely codified in the Anglo American copyright, patent, and trade secret law and in the moral rights granted to authors and inventors within continental European doctrine. These systems encompass much of what is thought to count as intellectual property.

By about 1800s, with the expansion of international commerce, a number of European governments had negotiated a network of bilateral agreements protecting copyrights. British authors, including Charles Dickens, complained of the widespread piracy of British books abroad. The government realized this was robbing them of potential profits and a major export market.[11] Thus grew a demand for an international codification of regulatory copyright practices. Similarly, inventors, particularly the American and German inventors widely recognized as very innovative, raised similar concerns about the protection of their inventions within foreign countries. When the government of the Austria—Hungary empire invited several countries to participate in an international exhibition of inventions held in Vienna in 1873, many countries refused to display their inventions fearing inadequate legal protection.

This incident had a far-reaching impact. The Congress of Vienna for patent reforms was convened in 1873, to discuss the prospects of an international patent system. Following this, an international congress on industrial property was convened in Paris in 1878. A final draft proposing an 'international union' of laws was prepared by France and sent to other countries with an invitation to attend the international conference in Paris in 1880. The Paris Convention, as it was called, concluded in 1883. The main principles of the Paris Convention state that nationals of any country which is a signatory to the convention, will enjoy the same treatment (with respect to 'industrial property' laws) in other countries, as if they were nationals of the respective countries. The Paris Convention did not include the term 'intellectual property' but only 'industrial

---

[9] See Adam D. Moore, 2004, *Intellectual property and Information Control: Philosophic Foundations and Contemporary Issues,* London: Transaction, pp. 11.

[10] Ibid., p. 12.

[11] J. Feather, 1994, *Publishing, Piracy and Politics: A Historical Study of Copyright in Britain,* London: Mansell Publishing, p. 154. Quoted in Susan K. Sell, 2003, *Private Power, Public Law: The Globalisation of Intellectual Property Rights,* Cambridge: Cambridge University Press, p. 10.

property'. This necessitated an international convention to curb rampant piracy in the area of literary and artistic works. The Berne Convention for the protection of literary and artistic works was adopted in the year 1886 with an objective to facilitate uniformity in the level of protection granted in all the member countries. Since then both the conventions have been subject to several revisions. In 1967, in Stockholm, the last revision was made to the Paris Convention by which an international organization was formed to administer and promote intellectual property on an international level—the World Intellectual Property Organization (WIPO). States have responded by adopting national legislations on the basis of two conventions, the Paris Convention,1883 for protection of industrial property (covering patents, trademarks, and industrial designs), and the Berne Convention,1886 for protection of artistic works.

Until fairly recently, the law of intellectual property was something that did not occupy centre stage in either the field of rights or in economic theory and legal parlance. Of interest mostly to specialists within the field, it garnered little attention from the broader legal or economic community. It was certainly not a feature of the rights discourse. Within the last decade or two, however, due in large part, to the expanding role of high technology in our every day lives, this has changed. Recent decades have seen an explosion in the number of new ways of creating, recreating, transmitting, and manipulating ideal objects or non-tangible economic goods. Their arrival on the economic scene has led to the announcement of a new age—'the knowledge age'. New innovations and new technologies have radically altered the way economics and business is conceptualized and conducted. It has contributed to the explosive growth of a new 'industry' among economists and lawyers as well.

In the eighteenth century and again in the twentieth century, the changing economics of the book industry were a guide to courts and legislators trying to weigh the impact of liberalising copyrights—harm to information producers of liberalizing copyrights against the harm to society of restricting them. In the late seventies, US copyright reform had to contend with the additional complications of new technologies (for example, inexpensive copying, video, and computer technology) and new uses of older media (for example, educational uses of visual media and musical recordings). Current legal and public policy controversies over intellectual property have their origin in the development of xerography and electronic information technology during the sixties and seventies. Prior to this development, the most serious area of dispute concerned the fair handling of copyrights to music. The legislative trend toward expanding the rights of intellectual property owners accelerated with the enactment of such statutes as the Visual Artists Rights Act, 1990 the Architectural Works Protection Act, 1990, and the Federal Trademark Dilution Act, 1995, to name a few conventions. These conventions reflected a consensus among member states that was legitimated by domestic laws already in place.[12]

The Uruguay Round of the GATT (1994) negotiations ushered in a new era in multilateral trade policy, of which protection of IPRs were a vital aspect. The Uruguay round was unusual in so far as this agenda of new issues was driven almost entirely by the private sector, particularly by the activist elements of the US business community.[13] The Trade Related Intellectual Property Rights (TRIPS) agreement became obligatory for all the states who wished to join the World Trade Organization (WTO) and is part of the common institutional framework established under the WTO. The agreement covers all Intellectual property rights—patents, trademarks, copyrights, trade secrets, and includes several new rights such as semiconductor chip rights. It adopts the Berne Convention, 1886 and the Paris Convention, 1883 but substantially adds additional copyright and patent protection. Patents are extended to virtually all subject matter— plant varieties, pharmaceutical products, chemicals, pesticides, software, and *sui generis* (special or more specific) protection for semiconductor chips. Countries are expected to provide adequate and effective protection mechanisms for TRIPS enforcement. Failure to comply can lead to 'cross-sectoral' or bi-lateral retaliation for non-compliant states.[14]

Susan Sell divides the history of intellectual property protection into three broad phases: national, international, and global.[15] The Paris and the Berne conventions marked the beginning of the international period, while TRIPS agreement signals the launch of the global period. In the international era, the territorial bases of IP rights were preserved while being extended beyond the 'jurisdictional confines through contractual device of treaty making'.[16] The system launched by the Berne and the Paris Convention was more flexible permitting variations in scope and duration. For example, it was not considered a contravention of the treaty

[12] R. Gana, 1995, 'Has Creativity Died in the Third World? Some Implications of the Internationalization of Intellectual Property', *Denver Journal of International Law and Policy*, 24 (1), p. 138.

[13] Susan K. Sell, 2003, p. 7.

[14] Ibid., p. 9.

[15] Ibid., pp. 10–17.

[16] P. Drahos, 1997, 'Thinking Strategically About Intellectual Property Rights', *Telecommunications Policy*, 21(3), p. 202.

when many countries denied patents to pharmaceutical products to contain the medicine costs and prices. States had considerable autonomy in designing the patent laws, which were in consonance with their level of economic development. By contrast, she argues that the TRIPS agreement (belonging to the global period) is far less flexible. It is prescriptive in nature, prescribing a universal standard of patent laws for countries at varying levels of development. States are required to extend patentability to virtually all fields of technology recognized in developed patent systems. These new regulations reach deep into national territories in requiring respect for intellectual property from products destined for domestic markets, such as, pharmaceuticals, processes internal to production such as chemicals, and practices in local agriculture, medicine, and education which were outside market relations.[17] Furthermore, TRIPS requires states to adopt civil and criminal procedures for IP rights infringement. The old system, which recognized inherent variations in the development of various countries, has made way for a more universalistic binding and a less flexible regime.

The development of Intellectual property protection has had enormous implications for changes in the very conception of property— in not merely who the property holder can and ought to be, but also in what counts as property. The kinds of works to which copyright law may apply has also grown enormously. For example[18] in 1884, the US Supreme Court concluded that photographs could be copyrighted.[19] In 1971, Congress decided that musical recordings (not just musical compositions, but recorded performances thereof) should be shielded from copying.[20] In 1980, computer software was added to the list of protectable works.[21] The most recent major addition was architectural works.[22] Like copyright, patent law was gradually extended over the course of the nineteenth and twentieth centuries to an increasingly wide array of inventions. In

---

[17] Susan K. Sell, 2003, p. 12.

[18] The following examples and references to them have been borrowed from William W. Fisher III, 1999, 'The Growth of Intellectual Property: A History of the Ownership of Ideas in the United States'. Availaible at http://cyber.law.harvard.edu/people/tfisher/iphistory.pdf (last accessed on 12 April 2006).

[19] *Burrow-Giles Lithographic Co. v. Sarony*, 111 US 53 (1884).

[20] Sound Recording Amendment, P.L. 92–140, 85 Stat. 391 (1971). By its terms, the law was effective on 15 February 1972 and applies to sound recordings made on, or after that date.

[21] Copyright Amendments, Pub. L. No. 96–517, 94 Stat. 3015, 3028 (amending S. 101 and S. 117, title 17, *United States Code*, regarding computer programs, enacted on 12 December 1980).

[22] 17 USC, S. 201 (a).

1842, hoping to provide 'encouragement to the decorative arts', Congress extended the reach of the patent statute to cover 'new and original designs for articles of manufacture'. Recently a wide array of 'ornamental objects', from eyeglass display racks to containers, have been deemed protectable.[23] Until the early twentieth century, plants were considered products of nature and hence 'unpatentable'. The Plant Patent Act of 1930 overrode this principle, extending a modified form of patent protection to new plant varieties of asexually reproducing plants. In 1970, Congress went even further, reaching new and 'distinct' sexually reproducing plant varieties.[24] Until the Second World War, the Patent Office took the position that 'the methods or modes of treatment of physicians of certain diseases are not patentable.' In the 1950s, it abandoned this categorical rule, but the continued wariness of the courts combined with doctors' qualms concerning the monopolization of potentially life-saving processes kept the number of such patents low.[25] Recently, however, the rate has increased sharply. The Patent and Trademark Office now typically grants over a dozen medical procedure patents each week.[26]

The law, it appears, evolved so as to serve the changing needs of the global economy. The advocates of increased intellectual property protection have comprised, for the most part, businesses interested in protecting their trademarks, patent portfolios, or trade secrets. Most have had strong financial interests in statutory reform that would protect them against non-permissive use of their 'property'. The interests of persons who would benefit from reduced intellectual property protection, by contrast, have tended to be more diluted. The result is that lobbying efforts have repeatedly been biased in favour of the expansion of intellectual property.

The resurgence of IP rights in the 1980s saw a relaxation of formerly stringent anti-trust law in the US. Throughout the 1980s, the anti-trust law increasingly asserted that IPRs, including patent rights do not necessarily

---

[23] See Donald S. Chisum, 1992, *Patents*, Quoted in William. W. Fisher, Ibid., p. 4.

[24] Plant Variety Protection Act, 7 USC, sections 2321–582.

[25] See Edward Felsenthal, 1994, 'Medical Patents Trigger Debate Among Doctors', *Wall Street Journal*, 11 August.

[26] See Joel Garris, 1996, 'The Case for Patenting Medical Procedures', *American Journal of Law and Medicine*, 22(85); Jeffrey I.D. Lewis, 1997, 'No Protection for Medical Processes; International Posture May Be Hurt by New Law', *New York Law Journal*; Garris lists the following as examples of such patents: 'a method of diagnosing heartbeat disorders, US Patent No. 4,960,129; a method of treating arthritis, US Patent No. 5,026,538; a method of administering insulin, US Patent No. 5,320,094; and a method of treating diabetes, US Patent No. 5,321,009.'

'confer monopolies or even market power in any relevant market'.[27] Intellectual property licensing was removed from anti-trust scrutiny. It was believed that any propensity to induce monopolies by IPRs was offset by the advantages that accrued from increased economic incentives and advantages. IPRs became the legitimate means to extract full economic benefit from innovations. Thus gradually over the course of American history, the discourse of anti-trust and competition was supplanted by the notion that rights to control the use and dissemination of ideas, information, and knowledge are forms of 'property' and therefore, are exclusive to the holder.[28]

A significant feature in the expansion of IPRs has been a gradual shift in the terminology used by lawyers to describe and discuss these rights. In the eighteenth century, lawyers and politicians were more likely to refer to patents and copyrights as 'monopolies' than as forms of 'property'. Today, property is a standard term that lawyers and law teachers use to refer to the field. Specifically, the use of the term 'property' to describe copyrights, patents, trademarks, etc., conveys the impression that they are fundamentally like interests in land or tangible personal property—and should be protected on similar grounds. There has thus been a 'propertization' of the field. The earlier usage of the term 'monopolies' was based on the view that IPRs created monopolies and therefore conflicted with anti-trust laws in the US. In so far as IPRs confer monopoly privileges, there is a natural tendency between competition, or anti-trust policy, and IPRs. As Cornish suggests, 'exclusive rights to prevent other people from doing things are at least monopolistic in a legal sense, if not necessarily in an economic one'.[29]

Comparing 'Old' Tangible Property and 'New' Intellectual Property

The intangible nature of IP does create some real and significant differences between itself and older notions of property. The most obvious

---

[27] J. Webb, and L. Locke, 1991, 'Recent Development: Intellectual Property Misuse: Developments in Misuse Doctrine,' *Harvard Journal of Law and Technology*, vol. 4, p. 257.

[28] This transition can be seen most clearly in the context of trademark law. Until the middle of the nineteenth century, legal protection of trademarks was justified on the basis of the need to protect innocent sellers against 'fraud'. In other words, the law in this field was understood to be a branch of (what was gradually coming to be called) tort law, not property law. Tort and property concepts coexisted uneasily in the many subdivisions of the law of trademarks and unfair competition. But slowly, property discourse took precedence.

[29] W.R. Cornish, 1981, *Intellectual Property: Patents, Copyright, Trademarks and Allied Right*, London: Sweet and Maxwell, p. 47.

distinctions go under the rubric of 'non-exclusivity', 'non-exhaustion' and 'separability'. 'Non-exclusivity' means that possession and use of intellectual property are not limited to one person at a time. Only one entity can own a plot of land or drive a car at any point in time and multiple ownerships would result in irreconcilable conflicts. Whereas, if I sing a song, you can be singing it somewhere else at the same time, without interfering with my use. If I build a machine based on a novel idea, your construction of a similar machine based on the same idea does not at all affect mine. 'Non-exhaustion' means that the resource is not depleted by use. Even land, the quintessential symbol of permanence, loses its capacity to support crops and must be replenished. After all, depletion and exhaustion of natural resources leading to scarcity was the motivation for the Lockean proviso.[30] This depletion does not affect an intellectual capacity because an idea can exist forever and there is an infinite source of ideas. Your singing my song does not wear out the tune. Nor does your use of the idea underlying my patented invention destroy the idea. In other words, use neither depletes nor exhausts an idea. The intangibility of ideas also means that they are easily transferred and concurrently used, without diminishing the resources of the other users.

'Separability' denotes the capacity of a thing to be physically alienated from the 'owner'. Tangible property can be separated from the holder of the property and therefore, is easily amenable to transfer. Knowledge and ideas however, need to be materially embodied before they can be 'separated'. Penner uses a useful distinction between traits of the body to classify what can be 'propertized' and what cannot.[31] He presents a qualitative difference between rights in one's body—tangible (limbs, kidney, eyes, etc.) and intangible (ideas, intellect, and talents)—and rights in 'things' or objects. He uses his 'separability thesis', or the 'thinghood' of objects of property, to determine what things can be treated as property. Separability, for him, is a conceptual criterion for a thing to be held as property. According to him, we must not conceive of property as an aspect of ourselves.[32] Using Penner's distinction, I argue that every aspect of value that a person 'possesses' cannot be regarded as property. Some idea of 'separability' informs our understanding of what things can be called property. The difficulty in ascribing to all things the status of property lies in the fact that there are things that cannot be deemed to be separable from us in any straightforward way. 'We do not trade our talents, give away

---

[30] For an elaboration see, Chapter 5 of this work.

[31] J.E. Penner, 1997, *The Idea of Property in Law*, Oxford: Clarendon Press, p. 111.

[32] Ibid., p. 126.

our personalities, licence our friendship to others or pay taxes with our eyesight.'[33] Property denotes a right and a title in a 'thing'. It is through law that a title in a thing is conferred on a person. The law enables us to show, through our title, something that is only *contingently mine,* that is, it might well not have been mine. 'What distinguishes a property right is not just that they are contingently ours, *but that they might just as well be someone else's*' [emphasis mine].[34] This cannot be said about things 'with necessary links with particular persons', like our talents, personalities, our body parts, etc. They are not ours to hold or possess through a legal contract; they are ours in any case. Penner's thesis helps us to restrict the application of property to those items in the world which are contingently related to us, and this contingency changes with surrounding circumstances—personal, cultural as well as technological.

Over years there has been growth in forms of personal or 'self-owned' properties, and this has enabled the division between tangible and intangible property. This distinction is sometimes framed as the difference between 'choses in possession' and 'choses in action': things one owns because they can be physically held and things one owns only because one has a right to prosecute a legal relation by bringing a court action against some other person/persons.[35] Choses in possession denote rights *in rem* and choses in action denote rights *in personam,* held against specific individuals. Intellectual property rights are akin to choses in action because they are abstract legal rights.[36] The holder of intellectual property does not have an actual right in any specific property, but is granted a notional value on the use of his/her idea or knowledge, which can be conceived of as specific property. It will therefore be useful to understand what constitutes intellectual property rights and how they relate to tangible property.

Knowledge as a Public Good

Intellectual property is generally characterized as non-physical property, that is, a product of cognitive processes and whose value is based upon some idea or collection of ideas. The *res,* or the object of intellectual property, is an idea or a group of ideas. Typically, rights do not surround the abstract non-physical entity; rather IPRs surround the control of physical manifestations of expressions. Intellectual property rights protect ideas by

[33] Ibid., pp. 111–112.
[34] Ibid., p. 112.
[35] Ibid., p. 107.
[36] IPRs are however, in a different category than other choses of action like debts, bonds.

protecting, through rights, the physical manifestations or instantiations of those ideas. Tom Palmer explains that 'Intellectual Property rights are rights in ideal objects, which are distinguished from the material substrata in which they are instantiated.'[37] As another commentator notes, 'Intellectual Property may be defined as embracing rights to novel ideas as contained in tangible products of cognitive effort'.[38]

Knowledge is an intangible asset and it can generally be appropriated by several users at the same time without diminishing other users' enjoyment of it. This is a typical case of 'public good', which allows for consumption by several users at the same time, and in this case, without generally diminishing the availability of the good.[39] Classically, knowledge was given the status of an intangible public good. Both on grounds of indivisibility and simultaneous multiple use, it was never accorded the status of private property. It was never found consistent with the property prerequisites of 'freedom to dispose, use, and transfer'.[40] It was given the status of a public good, as a resource that is not owned by a single individual, household, or firm and its use did not exclude others from their use of it. The notion of IPRs, however, dramatically changes the character of knowledge, transforming it into property, bearing with it all the residential connotations of property and the 'active' or 'performative' ones of power.[41] IPRs divide and appropriate knowledge as private good, thereby creating private rights over that which is essentially public in nature.

[37] Tom G. Palmer, 1990, 'Are Patents and Copyrights Morally Justified? The Philosophy of Property Rights and Ideal Objects, in Symposium: Intellectual Property', *Harvard Journal of Law & Public Policy* 13(3), p. 818.

[38] Dale A. Nance, 'Foreword: Owning Ideas in Symposium: Intellectual Property', *Harvard Journal of Law & Public Policy* 13(3), p. 757.

[39] An examination of the two terms public and private—would be useful in order to highlight the 'public' character of knowledge and therefore, the difficulty that it poses for propertization without diminishing its social value. 'Public' typically refers to open, communal, commonly shared or accessible, non-proprietary, and non-appropriable yet still contestable precisely because of its openness to alternative discourse, claims, opinions, etc. 'Private' may refer to that which is closed, inaccessible, appropriated, and secured for private use and/or economic rent, and contestable only where its presumption of ownership is open to challenge by others. Public and private knowledge may also be distinguished in these broad terms. On public goods see, Chapter 4 of this work. Also see Peter Drahos, 2004, 'The Regulation of Public Goods', *The Journal of International Economic Law*, 7/2(321) and Keith E. Maskus and Jerome Reichman, 2004, 'The Globalization of Private Knowledge Goods and the Privatization of Global Public Goods', *The Journal of International Economic Law*, 7(2), pp. 279–320.

[40] For a discussion see Chapter 3 of this work.

[41] Dick Pels, 1998, p. 11. Pels distinguishes between two aspects of property to draw attention to the role of property in its residential capacity (it resides with someone and therefore generates benefit for that person) and its active capacity as a source of power.

Knowledge as a public good has a unique feature—unlike other public goods like water, forests, and meadows, knowledge as an asset is not subject to depletion or scarcity. As mentioned earlier, there is an infinite source of ideas making them bear the characteristic of non-exhaustion. It is thus not scarcity or an estimation of potential scarcity that informs the 'propertization' of knowledge. The starting point for introducing property rights is not the limited availability of the good but the inability to stop its multiple and simultaneous use by various users.[42] Unlike tangible property which, it can be argued, helped derive rules of allocation in a world of scarce resources, IPRs are rules which create scarcity to enable private appropriation.

The prevalent notion of intellectual property, therefore, is not definitionally dependent upon the physical externality, materiality or scarcity of the object owned. Knowledge, which is in the public domain, is freely available to all. The appropriation of intellectual property is thus derived not from its innate propensity to propertization, but from a politico-legal dispensation which conceives of IPRs as a reward structure which enables the social organization of research. Intellectual property rights thus constitute devices which enable the transformation of intangible assets into a tradable property to which there is private and restricted access. It comes to share with tangible property 'the mutual quality of exclusivity in the eyes of the law'.[43]

The idea of propertization of knowledge renders the classical distinction between tangible and intangible goods inconsequential in the determination of property rights. The nature of property rights is to be found, therefore, in institutionally defined rights and not in the physical externalities of the object. It is political and public opinion that makes some objects be regarded as liable for appropriation and others not. In reality, natural conditions do not render a large number of resources, such as land, forests, water or fishing, appropriable. Often these resources are not easy to fraction, divide, and sell.

A form of knowledge is either protected in the form of an intellectual property right or lies in the public domain. When knowledge is in the public domain, it can be claimed by anyone and access to it cannot be limited. The public domain would simply fluctuate according to

[42] Philippe Cullet, 2005, *Intellectual Property Protection and Sustainable Development*, Butterworths: Lexis Nexis, p. 24.
[43] Lippert Owen (ed.), 2000, *Competitive Strategies for the Protection of Intellectual Property*, The Fraser Institute, pp. 7–46.

the amount of knowledge which is protected through IPRs.[44] This distinction has important implications in determining the dimensions of politics of knowledge. Questions of how knowledge is categorized (as belonging either to the private or public domain) and who benefits from such categorizations, become crucial issues in the politics that surrounds knowledge.

Terms of Exclusion

Intellectual property rights, at least patents and copyrights may be considered rights in ideal objects.[45] It is important to point out that ownership of an idea, or an ideal object, effectively gives the intellectual property owners a property right in *every* physical embodiment of that work or invention. Here, I will focus on patents and copyrights because of all forms of IPRs they have been endowed with the maximum ability to exclude. Patents, for instance, seek to prevent owners of tangible property from the legitimate use of their owned property in the patented domain. Thus, for instance, I would not be able to use my tools and implements to make a three-legged wheelbarrow that is patented. I am prohibited by patent law to practice patented methods or fashion patented products (applying different methods), using my own tangible property.

Consider a copyrighted book. Copyright holder *A* has a right to the underlying ideal object, of which the book is but one example. The copyright system gives *A* the right in the sequence and the pattern of words in the book. By implication, therefore, *A* has a right to *every* tangible instantiation or embodiment of the book—that is, a right in every physical version of the book, within the legal jurisdiction of that copyright. 'Thus, if *A* writes a novel, he has a copyright in this 'work'. If he sells a physical copy of the novel to *B* in book form then *B* owns only that one physical copy of the novel; *B* does not own the "novel" itself, and is not entitled to make a copy of the novel, even using his own paper and ink. Thus, even if *B* owns the material property of paper and printing press, he cannot use his own property to create another copy of *A*'s book. Only *A* has the *right* to *copy* the book (hence, "copyright").'[46] Similarly, *A*'s ownership of a patent gives him the right to prevent a third party from using or practicing the patented invention, even if the third party uses his owned property. 'In this way, *A*'s ownership of ideal rights gives him a degree of control over the tangible property

[44] Phillipe Cullet, 2005, p. 24.
[45] Tom G. Palmer, 1990, p. 818.
[46] Stephen Kinsella, 2001, p. 15.

of innumerable others. Patent and copyright invariably transfer partial ownership of tangible property from its natural owner to innovators, inventors, and artists.'[47]

Forms of IP exclude, so do forms and versions of tangible property. However, causally the exclusionary premises of the two forms of property are not linked. While the latter emerges from conditions of scarcity, the former emerges more out of functional necessities of incentivizing innovation, increasing productivity, social welfare, to name a few.

Exclusion is implied in a world of scarce resources. Tangible resources are always finite. 'Natural scarcity is that which follows from the relationship between man and nature.'[48] The finitude is imposed upon them either because supplies are short of demand, or, for instance, when a good like land loses its productivity and therefore, its capacity to sustain or be desired (despite being 'available'). Scarcity gives rise to the possibility of conflict and therefore, to a need for ethical rules which govern allocation in a scarce world. As Hoppe notes:

…only because scarcity exists is there even a problem of formulating moral laws; in so far as goods are superabundant ('free' goods), no conflict over the use of goods is possible and no action-coordination is needed. Hence, it follows that any ethic, correctly conceived, must be formulated as a theory of property, that is, a theory of the assignment of rights of exclusive control over scarce means. Because only then does it become possible to avoid otherwise inescapable and unresolvable conflict.[49]

The logic of scarcity then leads to the evolution of and institutionalization of property rights. Their function is to devise just principles of allocation,[50] based on which rightful owners are assigned their property and are given the right to 'exclude' others from the use of their 'owned' property. The terms of exclusion are concomitantly implied in the world of tangible resources—if I am deemed to the owner of a particular house, that house cannot simultaneously belong to another; other's are automatically excluded from its ownership. Such is not the case with intangible property like knowledge or ideas. Ideas, as mentioned earlier, can be concurrently owned and used without interfering with each other's use. The 'first occupier', in this case the 'first knower' does not preclude occupation of an idea by another.

---

[47] Ibid.

[48] Boudewijn Bouckaert, 'What is Property?' in 'Symposium: Intellectual Property', *Harvard Journal of Law & Public Policy*, 13(3), p. 793.

[49] Hans-Hermann Hoppe, 1989, *A Theory of Socialism and Capitalism*, Boston: Kluwer Academic Publishers, p. 235n9.

[50] Principles of 'labour-desert' (Locke) 'Creation', 'first occupancy' (Nozick), have been the most accepted principles of allocation.

The world of ideas is not scarce. Therefore, a different kind of impulse is needed to generate property rights in ideas, for the causal connection between the scarce world of resources and ownership seems severed here. As Arnold Plant explains:

It is a peculiarity of property rights in patents (and copyrights) that they do not arise out of the scarcity of the objects which become appropriated. They are not a consequence of scarcity. They are the deliberate creation of statute law, and, whereas in general the institution of private property makes for the preservation of scarce goods, tending . . . to lead us 'to make the most of them,' property rights in patents and copyrights make possible the creation of a scarcity of the products appropriated which could not otherwise be maintained.[51]

Once property rights are recognized in non-scarce resources like ideas, the exclusionary tendencies of these property rights far outweigh the exclusionary implications of tangible property. If *A* holds a patent over an HIV drug *D*, it would mean:

a)   That *A* has the exclusive right to use, dispose, and transfer not only D but also of the patent,
b)   That other than *A* nobody else can use that idea to manufacture *D*,
c)   That other than *A* nobody can use another idea or process to manufacture *D*, and
d)   That everybody, other than *A*, are prohibited from using their legitimately owned manufacturing capacities and technology to manufacture *D*.

The last point alerts us to the fact that if property rights are recognized in ideal objects, which are not finite, it would imply that property rights in tangible resources are correspondingly diminished. For *A* to have an effective patent right over drug *D*—which is an offshoot of a right in an idea or pattern (not in a scarce resource)—means that *A* has some control over everyone else's (potentially) scarce resources. In a way *A* (and like *A* all IP holders) becomes a partial owner of other's property. *A* will have a say in how others use their tangible property. 'What IPRs do is not only grant the holder property rights over the product of his intellectual labour, but *also simultaneously take this right away from others,* by prohibiting others' free use of their self-owned mental labour to create the same product.'[52]

[51] Arnold Plant, 2001, 'The Economic Theory Concerning Patents for Inventions', p. 36. Quoted from Stephan Kinsella, p. 33.
[52] Rajshree Chandra, 2009, 'Intellectual Property Rights: Excluding Other Rights of Other People', EPW, XLIV(31), August 1–7, p. 88.

Intellectual property rights create incentives as well as monopolies; in fact, they produce incentives because they are monopolies. The approach embodied in the TRIPS agreement, extending property rights and requiring high levels of protection has far-reaching implications for innovation, research and development, future location of industry, the global division of labour, and most importantly for the concomitant rights of 'other' peoples, particularly in the developing and underdeveloped parts of the world. Environmental activists, farmers' rights lobbyists, health rights activists have been protesting against transfer of resources from developing countries, indigenous communities consumers, producers, biodiversity, and traditional knowledge resources to firms in industrialized countries. Often the inherent propensities—within the very conception of intellectual property—towards exclusion have tended to contradict the goals of sustainable, inclusive development.

The implications that IPRs have on liberty and autonomy and rights of others is dealt in greater detail in the next Chapters. For the time being it suffices to state that IPRs do not emerge out of scarcity but are more in the nature of statutory devices to protect monopoly rights and are more pernicious in their exclusionary impact than property rights in tangable goods.

2 Property Rights
Principles of Legitimation

Property is a notoriously indeterminate concept, defying agreement on general principles that underlie them, or on how to define or conceptualize them. Tawney puts it rather succinctly in this passage:

Property is the most ambiguous of categories. It covers a multitude of rights which have nothing in common except that they are exercised by persons and enforced by the state. Apart from these formal characteristics, they vary indefinitely in economic character, in social effect, and moral justification. They may be conditional like the grant of patent rights, terminable like copyright, or permanent like a freehold, as comprehensive as sovereignty or as restricted as an easement, as intimate and personal as the ownership of clothes and books, or as remote and intangible as shares in a goldmine or rubber plantation.[1]

As difficult as it is to articulate, one can arrive at a very minimalist conception and state that property is a general term for rules governing access to and control of land and other material, and now various forms of immaterial, resources. But, because these rules are disputed, both in regard to their general structure and in regard to their particular application, there are interesting philosophical issues that these 'property disputes' throw up. Most philosophical deliberations have tended to focus on the issue of *private* property rights, their alignment with the foundational principle of individual liberty, autonomy and freedom. Within the Marxist discourse too, the critical, analytical crux has been private property and its implications for inequity and social justice. In both these rather broad planes of discourse focus has tended to fall short of philosophical engagements with ideas and practices of common and collective property despite, references to the existence of such practice. It is only in recent times that, notions of 'collective' and 'common' property have begun to articulate themselves as cultural productions and are demanding more space within the liberal domain of rights.

Property rights are rights of ownership: the important sticks in bundle of rights governing the right to use, transfer, and the right to

---

[1] R. H. Tawney, 1978, in an extract from 'The Sickness of an Acquisitive Society' reprinted in C.B. Macpherson (ed.), *Property: Mainstream and Critical Positions*, Oxford: Basil Blackwell, p. 136.

exclude others from the thing owned. Philosophers have often argued that 'exclusion' is necessary for the ethical development of the individual, or for the creation of a social environment in which people can prosper as free and responsible agents. Consequentialist theorists argue that these exclusionary rules are necessary to set out rules of allocation in society. Whatever the justification, as Lawrence Becker states, 'the history of property acquisition is a sordid one…and inequity in the distribution of goods has always been visible. An institution which has to manage the results of much injustice, and which has so often been used to perpetuate inequity, has an understandable aversion to moral analysis.'[2]

Apart from resultant inequities and injustices that Becker draws our attention to, there is a sociological reason that makes the terrain of private property a contested one. The whole idea of an individual actor having defined rights may be alien in some historical settings. There are fundamental differences in the concepts of 'property' and 'persons' in social groups belonging to a non-western setting. Property, therefore, needs to be understood both historically and contextually. Both ideas about property and institutional arrangements concerned with it have changed over time, the rhythms and trajectories of change being different in different societies. Like most other rights, property too has a cultural core. Co-existing societies have different understandings and practices and there is a growing consensus that rights need to be responsive to these diverse practices. Hence, when I discuss the justificatory premises of private property in this chapter, it is by no means an attempt to privilege the notion of private property over others. The purpose here is to first examine the justificatory theories of private property, as they have been offered in some traditions, and then to see if similar justifications apply to intellectual property. The ambition is not to traverse a very wide range of private property justifications but to limit ourselves to a few intuitively powerful justifications—Locke's labour theory, Bentham's utilitarian thesis, and Nozick's theory of just entitlements—that are still used in property discourse, either by themselves or in tandem, to legitimate separate property claims.

JUSTIFICATORY ARGUMENTS

Justifications of desired property systems have usually been attached to a large range of assumptions and presuppositions about human nature and its consequences for social organization. Questions of justification

---

[2] Lawrence C. Becker, 1977.

and legitimacy thus involve a normative analysis of property. Very often, therefore, we find in theories of property concerns about the relationship between property and values, like liberty and justice.

Strictly speaking, property is a general term for the rules that govern people's access to and control of things like land, natural resources, the means of production, manufactured goods, and also in some accounts, texts, ideas, inventions, and other intellectual products. A property right can be defined as a legally enforceable power to exclude others from using an object without the need to contract with them. A.M. Honoré gives a detailed account of the 'full' or the liberal concept of ownership which he says is common to all mature legal systems. The bundle of sticks that make up full, liberal ownership are: the right to *possess*; the right to *use*; the right to *manage*; the right to *income*; the right to *capital*; the right to *security*; the power of *transmissibility*; the *absence of term*; the *prohibition of harmful use*; the *liabilty to execution*; *residuary character*. Property rights are, according to him, proprietary rights, or ownership rights that a person exercises over corporeal or incorporeal things [emphasis mine].[3]

Scholars have a plurality of ideas about which from the above bundle of entitlements are essential elements. Some, like Hayek,[4] regard the right to alienate as the most fundamental stick of the bundle. Some regard the 'right of exclusion' as an essential feature of property rights in general. It is the power that may be exercised to the exclusion of all others, freely and without restrictions. The extent to which an owner is 'free' to operate his property and the extent to which he is unencumbered by restrictions depends to a large extent on the institutionalization of property in a society at a particular juncture.

Disagreements about property-use are likely to be serious because resource-use matters to people. They are particularly serious where the objects in question are both scarce and necessary. Some have suggested that property relations only make sense under conditions of scarcity.[5] However, other grounds of conflict are possible. There may be disagreements about how a given piece of land should be used which may stem from for instance, the history or symbolic significance *of that piece of land* or whether land, in general, is scarce or not. Intellectual property provides an example

---

[3] A.M. Honoré, 1961, 'Ownership,' in *Oxford Essays in Jurisprudence*, A.G. Guest (ed.), Oxford: Clarendon Press, pp. 107–47.

[4] Fredrich Von Hayek, 1944, *The Road to Serfdom*, Chicago: University of Chicago Press.

[5] David Hume, 1975, *Treatise on Human Nature*, 3 vols, (London, 1739–1740), L.A. Selby-Bigge (ed.), Oxford: Clarendon Press, pp. 484–98.

of property rules that do not respond directly to scarcity; moreover, unlike material objects, the objects of intellectual property are not exclusive by implication, for their use by any one person does not preclude their use by any number of others.

Different concepts of property exist in different legal systems, as well as in legal theory. In a sense, opposite ideas of property exist and operate in both domains—property as a commodity on the one hand and on the other, property open to social needs.[6] In the construction of property rights, the social aspect, even though it never completely fades away, can range from a very limited incidence to a large, broad influence. When the social aspect is almost nonexistent, objects of property rights are deemed commodities and what is stressed is the power of the owner. Conversely, emphasis on the social aspect of ownership stresses the interests of society as a whole, as opposed to those of the owner alone.

In an effort to simplify a very complex reality, one can argue that different theories, with different contexts and premises, conform to a varying mix of the two ideas mentioned above. Locke's labour theory, for example, recognized that the power of the owner over what he creates as almost absolute (barring some egalitarian interpretations of Locke which have been discussed later); property in this theory serves an individual end and not a social function. Property only has the role of satisfying individual preferences. Hayek, who is very sceptical about the 'social function' of property rights (and highly hostile to IPRs)[7] argues that commodification of property to its maximum extent is a necessary prerequisite for individuals to pursue their own ends and in so doing, to pursue individual liberty.[8] Utilitarianism, in another instance, permits both an individualistic reading, as well as a reading which will permit property as performing a social function.[9] Socialist theories of property would unequivocally tend to favour social good, to the extent that in

---

[6] For some distinctions, see James Boyle, 2003, 'The Second Enclosure Movement and the Construction of the Public Domain', *Law & Contemporary*, 66(33). Boyle starts his analysis by asking whether public domain is 'the opposite of property' and stating that it is impossible to think about the public domain or commons without considering the two basic ideas of property. Available at http://www.law.duke.edu/shell/cite.pl?66+Law+&+Contemp.+Probs.+33+(Winter Spring+2003) (last accessed on 11 November 2006).

[7] Hayek regards governmental intervention, or any kind of policy science to be the greatest subverter of spontaneous exchanges in economic exchange. IPRs are not only a system that subverts free exchange but also a system that subverts the ideal of individual liberty which is the root ideal of Hayek's philosophy.

[8] Fredrich Von Hayek, 1994.

[9] For two interpretations of utilitarianism see Will Kymlicka, 2002, *Contemporary Political Philosophy*, Oxford: OUP, pp. 32–7.

some socialist theories there is a complete negation of the legitimacy of private property.

Any society with an interest in avoiding conflict needs a system of rules based on some moral justification. These justifications establish that there ought to be property rules of *some* kind: private property rules are one variety of such rules. Some human societies have existed for millennia, satisfying the needs and wants of all their members, without private property or anything like it in land or in the other major resources of economic life. The first step in sound argumentation about property is distinguishing those arguments which support the existence of property in general from arguments which support the existence of a system of a specific kind. This chapter looks into the justificatory premises of private property and specifically those that can be extended as a justification of intellectual property.

The changes in property rights which have come about in the last three or four decades are enormous. The modern industrial state has become so complex and vast, its basic institutions so interdependent and entrenched that changes in the concept and institution of property, are perhaps an inevitable outcome of the need of institutions to constantly adapt to the changing environs. However, while the milieux have altered significantly in western societies, the extent of change has been less pronounced in other parts of the developing world and even less in traditional societies. The relation between property and persons may vary with societies. There may be traditions committed to other notions of property and therefore, particular relationships between person and property may lack uniformity. What may vary from society to society is also the things that can count as property—moveable property, land, ideas, software, plant varieties, germplasm, etc., have all been propertized in different societies at different historical junctures, and are still absent in some. Thus, an exploration of property needs to encompass not only who may hold property but also to what may constitute property.[10]

Discrimination between persons who may hold property is clearly something that needs justification, as much as the inclusion of particular resources amongst objects that count as property. These justificatory

---

[10] Lawrence C. Becker suggests three levels of justifications provided by philosophical arguments for property: the *general* justification which gives answers to the question of why there ought to be any property rights at all; the *specific* justification which addresses itself to the question of why there ought to be specific property rights (eg. full, liberal ownership of land); and a *particular* justification which, more importantly, focuses on why particular persons ought to have a particular property right in a particular thing. Lawrence C. Becker, 1977, *Property Rights: Philosophic Foundations,* London: RKP, p. 23.

arguments, with respect to who may hold property as also what may count
as property, have been classified by Becker in the form of philosophical
arguments, both for and against private property, and his book remains
one of the best general analysis of justificatory arguments. Borrowing
from him, I argue that attempts to justify the institution of property can
based upon:

- Argument of first occupancy,
- Labour theory of property acquisition,
- Arguments from utility,
- Arguments from political liberty, and
- Considerations of moral character.[11]

The ambition in this chapter is not to present a complete terrain of
the justificatory arguments in favour of private property rights. It is rather
to elicit a set of principles that form the basis for a claim for intellectual
property. The focus here is on those theories of property that (a) have
either located property in the 'self' (the labour-desert theory as explicated
by Locke and Nozick) and have put forward a strong moral claim for
property rights based on 'self ownership' and protection of individual
liberty; or (b) seek to put forward a contingent claim for property rights
based on the benefits that accrue to an individual, economy, or society,
that is, based on the principle of productivity and utility drawn from
Bentham.

The premise of a third approach—derived loosely from the writings
of Kant[12] and Hegel[13]—is that private property rights are an extension of
the personality and are crucial to the protection and development of the
'self'. The object created is invested with the personality of the self, of
'personhood' and, therefore would be as much a claimant of protection as
the self is. Hegel's account of property centers on the contribution property
makes to the development of the self.[14] Kant began by emphasizing a
general connection between property and agency, maintaining that there
would be an affront to agency and thus to human personality if some
system was not arrived at which could permit useful objects to be owned

[11] Ibid.

[12] Immanuel Kant, 1991, *The Metaphysics of Morals* [1797], trans. Mary Gregor,
Cambridge: Cambridge University Press.

[13] G.W.F. Hegel, 2001, *Philosophy of Right*, trans. S.W. Dyde, Kitchener: Batoche Books,
pp. 7–46.

[14] Ibid., para. 41a. Available at http://www.marxists.org/reference/archive/hegel/
works/pr/property.htm. (last accessed on 10 October 2006).

and used. He inferred from this that 'it is a duty of right to act towards others so that what is external (usable) could also become someone's.'[15]

Policymakers should thus strive to create and allocate entitlements to resources in the fashion that best enables people to protect and develop their personality and autonomy. From this standpoint, intellectual property rights may be justified either on the ground that they shield from appropriation or modification, artefacts through which authors and artists have expressed their wills (an activity thought central to personhood) or on the ground that they create social and economic conditions conducive to creative intellectual activity, which in turn is important to human flourishing. While these form important philosophic inquiries into the legitimacy of private property, they do not form the core of the justificatory premises employed currently at policy and international law levels. Also they are loosely implied in the first approach outlined above and, therefore, will be subsumed under my discussion of this approach.

Two principles currently dominate the theoretical literature on IPRs—self ownership (a principle derived from labour theory) and utility. They form two of the strongest justificatory and intuitively most persuasive arguments for intellectual property to be claimed as a right. The principle of self-ownership draws from the proposition that a person, a 'self-owner', who labours upon resources that are either unowned or 'held in common', has a natural property right, stemming from self-ownership to the fruits of his or her efforts, and that the state has a duty to respect and enforce that natural right. These ideas, originating in the writings of John Locke, are widely thought to be especially applicable to the field of intellectual property, where the pertinent raw materials (facts and concepts) do seem in some sense to be held in common and where labour seems to contribute importantly to the value of finished products. A good illustration of this perspective is Robert Nozick's brief but influential discussion of patent law in *Anarchy, State, and Utopia*.[16] The second, very influential approach, especially employed in policy circles with regard to justifications for intellectual property rights, 'utility', employs the familiar utilitarian guideline that lawmakers' summon when shaping property rights, of 'maximization of net social welfare'. In the context of intellectual property, it is generally thought that lawmakers ought to strike an optimal balance between the power to stimulate the

[15] Immanuel Kant, 1991, *The Metaphysics of Morals* [1797], trans. Mary Gregor, Cambridge: Cambridge University Press and Ibid.

[16] Robert Nozick, 1974, *Anarchy, State, and Utopia*, New York: Basic Books, pp. 141, 182.

creation of inventions and works of art on the one hand, and the power of exclusive rights, which curtails widespread public enjoyment of those creations, on the other.

The meaning of self-ownership was shaped by its historical role against the doctrines of political absolutism in seventeenth century England, while that of utility was directed against the numerous collective privileges and powers of the landed aristocracy in the eighteenth century. Locke, for instance, was responding against the absolutist regime of his era. Feudal collective privileges and rights blocked individual liberties and were incompatible not only with the conception of autonomous agency but also with commercial mobility of real estate. The endeavour was to link the demand for individual liberty with the freedom to alienate, exchange, and capitalize one's resources wherever profitable opportunities were made available. While the principle of self-ownership was used to vindicate the claim for individual autonomy and rights, and therefore for property rights, the principle of utility was used to assert the rights and happiness, and welfare of the majority against the elite minority and feudal landownership.

In self-ownership and utility we find two radically different formulations of why property rights are desirable and legitimate. While the principle of self-ownership is concerned with the issues of moral legitimacy of property rights, the principle of utility focuses on the issue of morality from a different perspective—it contends that private property is desirable, beneficial and therefore, legitimate and moral. Both these are used in tandem, to legitimate intellectual property rights. This chapter will look at the justificatory arguments of John Locke, Robert Nozick, and Jeremy Bentham and see how the principles of utility and self-ownership have been employed by them to legitimate property rights. The objective is to eventually test whether the canonical grounds developed to legitimate traditional, tangible property rights hold good for IP rights.

THE PRINCIPLE OF SELF-OWNERSHIP

Self-ownership as a principle was employed to denote the sovereignty of the individual over his self, that is, over his body and mind which cannot be enslaved against his will. It was to discredit the practice of slavery that the principle of self-ownership first employed. There is an egalitarian premise in self-ownership, that each of us has equal rights over our bodies, skills, talents, etc. It is condition for the realization of a person's autonomy based on the belief that individuals have a distinctive moral position as self-governors of some sort. The best known historical expression of the doctrine is by John Locke: 'Every Man has Property in his Person....'[17] In a striking twentieth century repetition, Robert Nozick argues that rights are understood as being 'possessed', 'owned', or held as 'freehold' by individuals.

The principle of self-ownership links the individual's claim for freedom and autonomy with the claim that freedom requires separate property. To the extent that ownership postulates the individual's absolute command over things, the essential meaning of property is sought in each person's claim for freedom and autonomy. It is a moral claim for ownership of the entire domain that emanates from ownership of the self. This is the libertarian view that rights are a species of moral property in one's person, personal powers, and legitimately acquired external resources.[18]

A powerful way of expressing the principle of individual liberty is to claim that individuals have full 'property rights' over their body, skills, and labour, and anything, justly acquired, with which they mix these becomes theirs to own, use, and dispose freely. There are thus two components of ownership that are implied here; firstly that individuals own themselves in the sense of having private property in their own person, and secondly, that they can also have extra-personal property in external resources by virtue of an extension of the principle of self-ownership.

PRINCIPLE OF SELF-OWNERSHIP IN LOCKE

Though the Earth, and all inferior Creature be common to all Men, yet every man has Property in his own Person. This no Body has any Right to but himself. The Labour of his Body, and the Work of his hands, we may say, are properly his. Whatsoever then he removes out of the State that Nature hath provided, and left it in, he hath mixed his Labour with, and joined it to something that is his own, and thereby makes it his Property. It being by him removed from the common state Nature placed it in, hath by his Labour something annexed to it, that exclude the common right of other Men. For this Labour being the unquestionable Property of the Labourer, no Man but he can have a right to what that is once joined to, at least where there is enough, and as good left in common for others. (Locke, Treatise II, section 27)

Two central ideas emerge from the above passage and they form the core of Locke's argument. First, that individuals have property in their own

[17] John Locke, *Two Treatises of Government* (Treatise II, section 27) Text available at http://oregonstate.edu/instruct/phl302/texts/locke/locke2/locke2nd-a.html. (last accessed on 5 December 2008.

Note: All references in this section to the work of John Locke are to *Two Treatises of Government*. Hereafter, Treatise and Section numbers are indicated alongside quoted passages, and not separately footnoted.

[18] For a discussion of self-ownership, see Attracta Ingram, 1994, pp. 25–41.

person and therefore, in their labour, talents, skills, and other productive capacities. Second, that human beings generate much of what they want and need by mixing their productive capacities with other resources, producing objects and services of value. The belief is that people are entitled to hold as property whatever they produce by their own initiative, intelligence, and labour. As long as the resources with which people mix their productive capacities are justly acquired, they may legitimately own the product of the conjunction. It is through this 'workmanship ideal' of ownership, which has been extensively incorporated into western thinking, that matters pertaining to distribution are negotiated in Locke.[19] The relevance of Locke for contemporary discussions on property is indirect and it is useful to highlight the historical conditions under which Locke established property as a natural right, by way of a contrast to contemporary settings. Locke's ideas were enunciated in the context of the natural rights theories of the seventeenth century.[20] It must be remembered that property rights for him emerged naturally only from a particular historical construction of the state of nature in which all things were held in common.

The leading issue to which Locke responds to in the *Two Treatise* is the arbitrary and absolutist government of Charles II. Locke's immediate objective in ideological terms can be identified as justifying resistance to Charles II's efforts to impose continental style absolutism in place of the limited monarchy in England. In Chapter 5 of the *Treatise*, Locke offers a vehement rejection of the principle of divine right used to justify and cloak absolutism, to challenge the absolutism of Charles II. He mounts a blistering attack on its most popular defence: the political tracts of Sir Robert Filmer (1588–1652).[21] Locke supplies a critique of the Stuart policy as subordinating the interests of the masses to the interest of the ruler and asserts a radical constitutionalist theory and an individualist theory of resistance to arbitrary government.

[19] Ian Shapiro, 1991, 'Resources, Capacities, and Ownership: The Workmanship Ideal and Distributive Justice'. *Political Theory,* 19(1), pp. 47–8.

[20] Samuel Pufendorf, 1991, 'On the Duty of Man and Citizen according to Natural Law', in James Tully and Michael Silverthorne (eds), *On the Duty of Man and Citizen, Cambridge Texts in the History of Political Thought,* Cambridge: CUP and L.E. Van Holk and C.G. Roelofsen (eds) 1983, *Grotius Reader: A Reader for Students of International Law and Legal History,* The Hague: T.M.C. Asser Instituut. For a discussion on the natural law tradition of Grotius and Pufendorf, see Karl Olivecrona, 1971, *Law as Fact,* London: Stevens.

[21] Filmer's *Patriarcha* (1630) had advanced the case for absolute monarchy on the ground that the sole legitimate authority derives from God's donation of the world to Adam and thus to his lineal heirs who happen to be the current holders of thrones by hereditary divine right.

Locke's procedure for negating the basis of Filmer's argument involved a conceptualization of political society within the natural law framework. According to him, the very purpose for which society had been established is the protection of rights and property of members. The validity of this purpose rests on what Locke calls, 'the Fundamental Law of Nature' which 'willeth the Peace and Preservation of all Mankind' (Treatise II, Sections 6, 7, 16). For the preservation of mankind Locke envisages three natural rights—of 'life, liberty, and estate'. The third natural right, the right to estate (property) is derived logically from the right to preservation. Self-preservation was, for Locke, a foundational right and by definition entailed the preservation of one's life and therefore, of one's property. Thus, one had the right to all things, within reason, for the maintenance of himself and his possessions. These rights were his and his only by the law of nature. Through this natural right the individual establishes as his own what originally was potentially available to all men (Treatise II, Sections 25-6). This natural right to preserve oneself also becomes the foundation for the right to resist arbitrary government (Treatise II, Sections149).

Appropriation

Locke's starting point is that god's gift of the world to mankind in common and the need for individual appropriation before the bounty can serve the divine purpose of preserving men's lives. Reason prompts man to appropriate what he needs for self-preservation without waiting for others' consent. The problem, however, is to determine by what right or title the individual establishes as his own what originally was potentially available to all men (Treatise II, Sections 25-6). For Locke, the basis for this lies in the fact that 'every man has a *property* in his own *person*: this no body has any right to but himself. The *labour* of his body, and the *work* of his hands, we may say, are properly his. Whatsoever then he removes out of the state that nature hath provided, and left it in, he hath mixed his *labour* with, and joined to it something that is his own, and thereby makes it his *property*...that excludes the common right of other men.'[22]

Locke was the first classical political theorist to place such great emphasis on labour, making it the cornerstone of his edifice of political ideas. He uses labour to show how things can unquestioningly be made our own without a preceding compact between all men. Man could legitimately acquire property in the state of nature by means of the work of his own hands, by mixing his labour with anything in nature.

[22] John Locke, Treatise II, Section 27.

Labour was the original entitlement to private possessions and landed property as distinct from what was common. Man had property in his own person; anything with which he mixed his labour with became his property by natural right, property to which no one else was morally entitled. The expenditure of labour required no agreement, therefore, the right to property was pre-social and pre-political, and as a result he was able to characterize the development of property as a natural economic process and assert it as a natural right. The infringement of what rightfully belonged to a person was morally wrong because the object was an extension of his moral being or person through his labour.

In the state of nature, the natural right to property was conditional; at least initially it was subject to the moral limitations of the law of nature on individual appropriation from nature. Natural law entailed that man is subject to divine imperatives. Within limits set by the law of nature men can act. [23] The existence of natural law constraints on human autonomy meant that there were circumstances in which the exercise of otherwise legitimate rights appropriation would be curtailed; the right to appropriate from nature would be limited.

The exercise of this right is limited by the 'fundamental law of nature', called the 'sufficiency limitation', which requires man to preserve the rest of mankind as much as he can 'by leaving enough and as good for others'. It is also important to realize that God confers his bounty to mankind not merely for subsistence but in order to avail 'the best advantage of Life and Convenience'[24], 'God has given us all things richly…to enjoy'.[25] God apparently intends that the earth should become the property of the 'industrious and rational', who when appropriate and cultivate the land advance the common good by maximizing the utility of land. Private property would lead to greater and more productive use of resources, which would then meet the needs of the property-less. Locke believed that the foundational right, the right to subsistence would be better protected if individuals had exclusive possessions over some resources.[26] Through the institution of private property, Locke thus removes the sufficiency limitation. Not only does Locke justify the appropriation of

[23] Natural law, Locke tells us, is to be distinguished from natural right: while a right indicates a capacity for autonomous action, law refers to externally imposed obligatory constraints.

[24] John Locke, Treatise II, Section 26.

[25] John Locke, Treatise II, Section 31.

[26] Subsistence here is derived from a right to life, which was one of the three natural rights of man. The logic of the idea of preservation seems to indicate that subsistence was a foundational right for Locke.

land in terms of mixing one's labour with it, but he also seeks to justify its appropriation on the ground that doing so serves to advance the common good by maximising productivity.

The link, on the one hand, between labour as the original title to property (especially land), and on the other, as the source of utility value were significant in establishing a legitimate shift from notions of common property to the notion of private property. Differences in industry and rationality accounted for differences in the extent of property owned by individuals. However, these differences remained insignificant and still were constrained by the natural law operative: 'No Man's Labour could subdue, or appropriate all: nor could this Enjoyment consume more than a small part....'[27] But this changed dramatically with the introduction of money.

Money, in acting as a store of value, transcends the second limitation, that is, the 'spoilage' limitation (arising from prohibition of waste) and eventually leads to major differences in the distribution of property. The institution of money meant that it was possible for men to enlarge their possessions and establish a natural right to them without violating the spoilage limitation. After McPherson highlighted the magnitude of change brought about by the adoption of money, the role that money played in removing the natural law constraints and in establishing property as a natural right, is now fully appreciated.[25]

What Locke endeavours to do, within natural law constraints, of leaving enough and as good for others, is to establish property as a natural and as an unlimited right. Locke, thus devises a system which accomplishes two things. First, it renders the natural law proviso of 'sufficiency' and 'spoilage' ineffective and second, it embodies a measure of consent in the evolution of property from the unrestricted opportunities of the original state of nature to a situation in which some individual possesses extensive property and others considerably less or perhaps none at all. Locke thus shows that this inequity in property distribution is not a violation of the law of nature. Locke uses the foundational right of subsistence to regard land as a part of the commons, a gift from the creator (god) to be held in common by mankind. He then goes on to use the labour theory of appropriation to justify common property coming into private hands. Use of labour allows private property to get instituted from a position of common property.

[27] John Locke, Treatise II, Section 36.

Enclosure

In the seventeenth century, improvement of wastes and forests of 'unimproved' commons became a regular slogan, given a large population to feed and clothe and the increasing unemployment. Locke echoed the language of the 'agricultural improvers' by his continuous reference to the need to increase agricultural productivity.[28] Improvement in productivity meant improvement of the wastes and that meant, for the improvers, as it did for Locke, enclosure of the commons. The foremost argument for enclosure, shared and constantly stressed by Locke, was that it would lead to an increase in agricultural productivity, besides, of course relieving the unemployment situation. Enclosure was also thought to be a solution to the constant conflict over use-rights that threatened to disrupt the harmony of the countryside. All these Locke refers to as the 'inconveniences of the State of Nature'. The purpose of civil society was to remedy these inconveniences through enclosures. Chapter 5 of *Two Treatises* is a significant argument for justifying enclosure in seventeenth century England.

Locke is clear that property in land is acquired in much the same way as property in moveable things. This means that a piece of land becomes a man's own when he cultivates it, that is, mixes his labour, which is his property, with it. In this way land is removed from the state of nature and joined to the personality of the cultivator. 'He by his Labour does, as it were, inclose it from the Common'.[29] Here the work on the land is expressly equated to 'inclosing'. Locke identifies enclosing with appropriating: 'Whatsoever he enclosed, and could feed, and make use of, the Cattle and Product was also his.'[30] In the inland parts of America, where there could be no hope of commerce the land would not be worth 'the inclosing'.[31]

The interest of Locke's account lies in the way he combines the structure of a theory of first occupancy, with an account of the substantive moral significance of labour. This is partly because Locke identified the ownership of labour as something connected substantially to the primal ownership of self. However, it was also because he thought the productivity of labour would help answer some of the difficulties which he saw in 'first occupancy' theory.[32] Though the first occupier does not

[28] For a discussion see, Neal Wood, 1984, *John Locke and Agrarian Capitalism*, Berkley: University of California Press, p. 61.

[29] John Locke, Treatise II, Section 32.

[30] John Locke, Treatise II, Section 38.

[31] John Locke, Treatise II, Section 48.

[32] According to Samuel Pufendorf (1632–94), a natural rights theorist, 'first occupancy' theory proceeded on the basis that it did not particularly matter *how* the first human user took possession of a natural resource, or what sort of use he made of it. What mattered was

actually dispossess anyone, still his acquisition may prejudice other's interests of others if there is not, in Locke's words, 'enough and as good left in common' for them to enjoy.[33] Locke's answer to this difficulty was to emphasize that appropriation by *productive* labour actually increased the amount of goods available in society for others.[34]

Locke's labour theory of property is thus a basis for a theory of appropriation as well as of occupation, a means for defining rightful claim to previously unoccupied land. Locke's writings, writes Neal Wood, 'reflect basic structural changes in the social relation of production then occurring in the English countryside, especially those related to the development of agrarian capitalism that was coming to dominate the corn and mixed corn areas of the south and east. Each work reflects a fundamental concern with the agrarian sector and with agricultural productivity'.[35] Laslett points out that Locke is using the language of agrarian enclosure in England.[36] Enclosure was thought to be a solution to the constant conflict over use-rights, and it was anticipated that it would also would lead to an enormous advance in productivity. Wood identifies Locke as a theorist of early agrarian capitalism and not as a thinker who articulated the interests of a nascent mercantile and manufacturing bourgeoisie, as argued by C.B. Macpherson.[37]

ABSOLUTE RIGHTS TO PROPERTY IN LOCKEAN THOUGHT: REVISITING THE INTERPRETATION

Whether Locke's theory favours agrarian capitalism or ascendant bourgeois capitalism is only of academic interest to the present work. The key point of relevance here, is that Locke's theory supported

---

that he began acting as its owner without dispossessing anyone else. Now although Locke used the logic of this account, it *did* matter for him that the land was cultivated or in some other way used productively.

[33] John Locke, Treatise II, Section 27.

[34] John Locke, Treatise II, Section 37.

[35] Neal Wood, 1984, p.13.

[36] Peter Laslett (ed.), 1960, *Two Treatise of Government*, Cambridge, Cambridge University Press, pp. 306–8. Laslett, while admitting that Locke was born into the 'classical atmosphere of early capitalism' , professed that Locke was extremely mistrustful of commerce and commercial men. John Dunn too expressed agreement with Laslett's view by asserting that Locke at no point in his works extended moral enthusiasm to the role of the merchant or industrial producer. See, John Dunn, 1985, *Rethinking Modern Political Theory: Essays 1979–83*, Cambridge: Oxford University Press, p. 32.

[37] The widely held view of Locke as bourgeois philosopher and ideologist of early capitalism has been largely due to the scholarship of C.B. Macpherson. For Macpherson, Locke's insistence that a man's labour was his own and that it could be alienated for a wage provided the moral foundation for bourgeois appropriation.

natural entitlements in property. However, this is not to suggest that he regarded property entitlements as absolute or unlimited. As Waldron states, 'all entitlements, whether they are natural or conventional, are subject at all times to the general right of every man when his survival is threatened....'[38] Wood also argues that the natural right to property in a political society was not an absolute one, for it was subject to common good, the preservation of society being the first and fundamental law of nature. Locke regarded regulation of property to be justified provided it was for public good and was done in accordance with principle of consent, rule of law, and the law of nature.[39] Ian Shapiro, in the same vein, stresses that the existence of natural law constraints meant that not all rights had the same status; 'property rights occupied a circumscribed space in an hierarchical system'.[40]

The degree to which natural law requirements or social needs and conventions limit property rights in Locke is, to be sure, a matter of debate. There appears in Locke competing requirements; the first, of natural law which privileges 'subsistence' as a right above all other rights and which can actually be pressed into service to provide a radical critique of property rights; the second of claims of 'human workmanship' which uphold the right of human appropriation. Locke's theory has left these claims open to interpretation and political arguments. Richard Ashcraft terms the *Two Treatise* as 'janus faced, with both a conservative and a radical tenor. He argues that although Locke began with the radical language of equality, liberty, 'fellow Commoners', a labour theory of property, and natural right; it shifts to a more conservative vocabulary of landed property, property differentials, money, exchange production, wage labour; and ends with improvement and the problem of waste, the advances of enclosure, and agricultural productivity.[34] Locke, thus takes the radical slogans of liberty and equality against tyranny and transforms it into a more conservative justification of inequality in landed property against absolutism.

These debates have been pressed into reference to undermine the assumption that rights of human appropriation are absolute in Locke and always supersede claims of just distribution. It is important to note this reading of Locke because these welfare assumptions, acknowledged by some interpretations, are totally dropped in the neo-Lockean, neo-liberal formulations on property. The function of theory is to reflect and

[38] Jeremy Waldron, 1984, 'Locke, Tully, and the Regulation of Property', *Political Studies*, vol. 32, p. 105.
[39] Neal Wood, 1984, p. 54.
[40] Ian Shapiro, 1991, p. 50.

legitimate existing structures, and Locke's theory of property reflected the expansion on the ownership rights of individuals. G.E. Aylmer, in fact, talks about the emergence of absolute individual ownership.[41] Whether ownership was absolute or whether there was merely an extension of the owner's powers, this period can definitely be identified as one which led to a significant increase in the owners' powers and rights which began to be held privately and not commonly as earlier.

An enduring contribution of Locke's theory of property, and one which travels beyond the confines of seventeenth century property, is the principle of self-ownership which emerged as the core belief in the legitimation of private property. What man creates is what he rightly owns. This fact about human creativity has been incorporated into western thinking and is based on the conviction that as long as the resources with which people mix their labour are justly acquired, they are the legitimate holders/owners of that product. These are natural rights whose basis is in natural law and are inalienable because they are also in natural duties men bear to God. Inalienability also implied that the owner of an object is the person who does not require the consent of others to use it and whose consent others must seek if they want to have access to or control over it. The nature of property in Lockean thought is such that 'without a man's own consent it cannot be taken from him' (Treatise II, Section 93).

It is important to underscore the fact that Locke establishes a formal link between property and consent for two rather different reasons. The first one to which James Tully draws our attention: Locke's definition marks a departure in the history of rights—from the earlier notion of rights as deriving from duties, and as an arena protected from interference by others, based on the prescriptions of natural or divine law, to the modern concept which has them flowing out of our own moral sovereignty.[42] Property in self protects a person from interference by others but it does so 'by focussing on the agent's moral power to exercise his consent, his natural right to property, rather than granting primacy to others to perform their negative duties.' The second reason is to secure a system of individual rights whose principle is private ownership.[43] All rights that exist emanate from natural endowments, physical and mental,

---

[41] G.E. Aylmer also points out the erosion of the distinction between real *and personal property*. See G.E. Aylmer, 1980, 'The Meaning and Definition of "Property" in the Seventeenth Century England', *Past and Present*, pp. 87–97.

[42] James Tully, 1980, *A Discourse Concerning Property: John Locke and his Adversaries*, Cambridge: Cambridge University Press, p. 114, for a discussion also see, Ian Shapiro, 1986, *The Evolution of Rights in Liberal Theory*, Cambridge: Cambridge University Press.

[43] Ibid., p. 115.

with which people come into the world. The purpose of all rights is to
enable individuals to be in control of their lives. As Ingram writes, 'What
remains untroubled by any changes in the meaning of property is the
idea that private ownership yields the form of all rights, both in personal
powers and external resources.'[44]

The primary social role of self-ownership was in providing a moral
defence for resistance to political absolutism and then for the creation
of an alternative political authority. Subsequently, self-ownership has
become one of the foundational principles of liberty and legitimating
arguments for private property since the time of Locke. In the twentieth
century, it continues to be the foundational claim of libertarianism,
echoed in individual the works of Nozick (1974) and Hillel Steiner
(1994). In *An Essay on Rights,* Steiner begins by arguing that our bundle
of original property rights must include at least ourselves. 'We must
each be self owners…unencumbered self-ownership is one of our two
original rights'.[45] It is from this right that rights over fruits of our labour
are derived. Any attempt to deprive us of the fruits is an encroachment
of our self-ownership. Right holding is thus linked to ownership,
with a proprietary control over the domain specified as the object of
right. However, Steiner recognizes the various difficulties in justifying
unequal appropriation of the initially unowned world, and so accepts
nationalization or equalization of natural resources, or compensation for
those left propertyless.

The principle of self-ownership, as a right over one's body and talents,
is joined with a principle of right over material resources. Labour, physical
or mental needs to be conjoined with material objects for the labour
to yield 'property'. Property in one's mental and physical labour, in the
absence of material objects, is property only in a notional sense, for it
is always contingent on materialization, that something that is created
becomes the property of the person who mixes his labour, powers, or
talents with it. Thinking about property, therefore, has been informed
by considerations of the origin of the material. The creator was seen to
be the legitimate holder of that property. This relationship between the
creator and the material object is reflected in a property system and in
rival political theories on property. The principle of rights over material
resources will operate to validate existing property claims or to contest it
and sanction some redistribution. In the context of the study of property,

[44] Attracta Ingram, 1994, p. 70.
[45] Hillel Steiner, 1994, *An Essay on Rights,* Oxford: Blackwell, pp. 231–5.

and the doctrine of IPRs, one can hold that the meaning of property to a large extent influences the meaning of rights.

How to organize distribution and property so that the moral principles of self-ownership and the workmanship ideal are not violated has not only been a subject of intense contestation, but has also set the terms of the debate about ownership, just distribution, and even the definition of property. The enduring intensity of arguments about the principle of self-ownership or the workmanship ideal signifies that it still retains a powerful hold on the western political imagination. Locke's theological assumptions have long been abandoned in the dominant intellectual traditions of the west, but many scholars have tried to formulate secular variants of them in order to retain the powerful moral claims of the principle of self-ownership that can be used to bind legitimate property rights to the work of productive agents.

NOZICK'S DEFENCE OF ABSOLUTE PROPERTY

In *Anarchy, State and Utopia*, Robert Nozick's account of the 'entitlement conception of just holdings', occupies a central position in an argument for the minimal state. Within the account, the author's construction of the right to appropriate plays a primary role in determining what rightfully and inviolably belongs to a person. Nozick presents compelling arguments as to why justice involves inviolable entitlements to individuals and why 'patterned' or 'distributionist' allocative principles cannot be principles of justice.

Like Locke, Nozick retains an abiding commitment to the workmanship ideal—acts of labour create entitlements in the objects or services produced.[46] Nozick, however secularises the workmanship ideal and replaces the Lockean theology with a foundational appeal to the value of individual autonomy for more or less Kantian reasons, that is, like Kant, Nozick too links property rights over a person's productive capacities to the preservation of his autonomy and freedom.[47] His fundamental premise remains that we are born 'owning ourselves'. Where Locke had said that men have property in their own persons, Nozick's theory speaks

[46] See, Robert Nozick, 1974. Note: All references in this section to the work of Nozick are to *Anarchy, State and Utopia*, pp. 3–9. Hereafter, page numbers are indicated alongside quoted passages, and not separately footnoted.

[47] Kant's liberalism belongs to a moral and political creed that is committed, without reservation, to upholding the claims of full individual ownership. He links property rights over a person's productive capacities to the preservation of autonomy. The central premise of Kantian view on property is based on a simultaneous commitment to private property and equal original right.

of individuals as 'holdings'. Each of us possesses a 'freehold' in ourselves. Nozick presents the principle of self-ownership as an interpretation of treating people as 'ends in themselves', a Kantian formula, invoked for expressing our moral equality.[48]

The heart of Nozick's theory, laid out in the first sentence of his book, is that 'individuals have rights, and there are things that no individual or group can do to them (without violating these rights).' (Nozick, ix). Society must respect these rights because they 'reflect the underlying Kantian principle that individuals are ends and not merely means; they may not be sacrificed or used for the achieving of other ends without their consent' (Nozick,130-1). Each individual is distinct with a distinct claim and his claim cannot be sacrificed for the sake of others, nor can he be treated as a resource of the society. For Nozick, the most important rights are rights over oneself—the rights which constitute self-ownership. Nozick attempts to derive the idea of property-ownership from the idea of treating people as owners of themselves.

Entitlement

Nozick's conception of property begins with the notion of rights over one's self. An object maybe mine on grounds that I made it. If it is mine I am justly entitled to dispose of it as I wish and therefore the title to it may accrue to anyone to whom I donate or sell it. Nozick claims that everyone has an inviolable right to what one has produced or been freely given. An agent is entitled to dispose of what he has produced however he likes.

However, Nozick realizes that property ultimately involves more than self-produced objects and ideas. The classic example is land. I may have improved the land but it was by no means created by me. So my title in land cannot be grounded solely in the exercise of my self-owned powers. Besides one is also an owner of things not produced or created by oneself. In his theory, the entitlement to external goods like land, is in accordance with the principle of transfer. An entitlement to external goods like land,

---

[48] It is unclear whether treating 'people as ends in themselves' amounts to treating people as equals. Rawls ties the idea of treating people as ends in themselves to a principle of equality. See John Rawls, 1971, *A Theory of Justice*, Cambridge: Harvard University Press, pp. 251–7. While a principle of abstract equality, it may be said, lies at the heart of Nozick's theory of rights, one can argue that Nozick's entitlement theory is best defended by an appeal to liberty, rather than equality, equality being tied to a notion of an 'end state', a notion totally repudiated by Nozick. Nozick rejects the left libertarian and socialist theories because they tend to define justice in terms of 'end states' like the satisfaction of needs, promotion, of equality, etc.

comes from the fact that others have transferred the land to the individual, considered the owner. This ownership will be considered legitimate if the earlier owner had legitimately acquired the land. A transfer is just only if the initial acquisition had been just.

The world is divided into objects that are owned and objects that are yet unowned. All titles to produced or freely transferred goods must derive from titles to natural or previously unowned objects. No title to a manufactured or a transferred object can be considered legitimate if that object was manufactured or transferred by someone not entitled to acquire it in its natural unaltered state. If there was no legitimate initial acquisition then there can be no legitimate transfer. However, whatever has been legitimately transferred becomes an inviolable right of the owner. Thus according to Nozick, my legitimate property (freehold) comprises of: things not previously possessed by anyone that are *acquired* through the exercise of my self-owned powers, or objects that have been transferred to me from a legitimate owner. This position has been summed up in the three main principles of Nozick's 'entitlement theory' (Nozick, 151).

1. A principle of justice in acquisition—an account of how people came to initially own the things or what people create through the exercise of their self-owned powers which can be transferred in accordance with principle (2).
2. A principle of justice in transfer—whatever is justly acquired can be freely transferred; just acquisition being defined either by the exercise of self-ownership or by principle (2).
3. A principle of rectification of injustice—how to deal with holdings that have been unjustly acquired or transferred.

Taken together, they imply that if people's holdings are justly acquired, then the formula for just distribution is 'from each as they choose, to each as they are chosen' (Nozick, 160).[49] The question about the initial acquisition is prior to the question of legitimate transfer. If there was no legitimate initial acquisition, then there can be no legitimate transfer. The validity of property rights depends on the validity of previous property rights. This means, in Nozick's theory, going back to the chain

[49] This statement was a take-off from the Marxian slogan 'from each according to his ability to each according to his need.' Nozick explains his slogan, summing up the three principles, more clearly: 'From each according to what he chooses to do, to each according to what he makes for himself (perhaps with the contacted aid of others) and what others chose to do for him and choose to give him of what they been given previously (under this maxim) and haven't yet expended or transferred.' Robert Nozick, 1974, p. 160.

of transfers to a point when it was first appropriated as private property and ascertaining if the initial acquisition was legitimate.

The Lockean Proviso

The Lockean proviso of 'leaving as good and enough for others', essentially a safeguard for the general right to subsistence, was interpreted differently by Nozick. In his view, each person has an inviolable right to what he legitimately owns, provided it does not interfere with the like liberty of others. 'A process normally giving rise to permanent bequeathable property rights in a previously unowned thing will not do so if the position of others no longer at the liberty to use the thing is thereby worsened. (Nozick, 178)

Nozick is not concerned with the right to subsistence. The concern is not with material condition of the non-appropriators. In the Nozickean scheme of things, the only fetters that can limit absolute ownership right are the rights of others. Worsening the position of others refers to curtailment of their rights, which would mean in this case, a loss of liberty to use or appropriate that object. If there is enough left, as in the case of sand from 'Coney Island' then there are no legitimate grounds of complaint of loss of liberty (Nozick, 175). However, if appropriation or privatization worsens the position of the non-appropriators, as in the case of the appropriation of the total supply of medical drugs by either preventing him from appropriating or using the object in question to improve his situation, then they have to be compensated by counterbalancing their loss of liberty by an improvement in the overall situation from the time it was in common use. (Nozick, 181)

Nozick employs what he calls, the 'Lockean proviso', to mean that all initial acquisitions would pass the test of 'not worsening the situation of others' because all initial enclosures of the commons led to an increased productivity thereby compensating for the loss of access to land for the propertyless.[50] Therefore initial appropriation is legitimate because it does not make people worse off, in material terms, than they had been when it was in general use. Persons do not suffer thereby any 'net harm'. Construed in this fashion, the Lockean proviso is not violated in most situations.

Nozick's view launches the idea that all ownership is naturally ownership of an outright freehold.[51] Self-ownership yields absolute

---

[50] It has been argued that the only way to that we leave enough and as good for our children is to prevent the tragedy of the commons by allocating property rights over resources. David Schmidtz, 1990, quoted from Will Kymlicka, 2002, p. 115.

[51] Alan Ryan, 1987, *Property,* Milton Keynes: Open University Press, p. 68.

ownership rights over the external world. Since the latter includes the right of transfer it would form a legitimate basis for absolute ownership in all productive resources. For Nozick, this principle of self-ownership necessarily yields absolute property rights, an implication that conflicts with the theories of redistribution. The central claim of Nozick's theory is that if we assume that everyone is entitled to the 'holdings' they possess then a just distribution is one that results from people's free exchanges and a free play of market forces. Nozick wants to argue that the minimal state or 'minarchy' is not only compatible with people's rights to self-ownership, but also that a minimal state would arise naturally without violating anyone's rights.[52]

Nozick believes that individual rights are 'co-possible', that is, each person may exercise his rights as he chooses. The exercise of these rights fixes certain features in this world. These features act as constraints within which social choices and social ordering have to be made. Only those alternatives of social ordering can be legitimately instituted which do not exclude anyone's exercise of his rights. 'If entitlements to holdings are rights then the social choice must take place within the constraints of how people choose to exercise their rights' (Nozick, 166). 'Patterning' will always be constrained by people's rights; it will always interfere with people's actions and choices.

A major objection to everyone having a right to various things such as equality of opportunity, life, and so on, and enforcing this right, is that, according to Nozick, these rights require a sub-structure of things, materials, and actions, and other people may have entitlements over these. No one has a right to something whose realization requires certain uses of things and activities that other people have rights and entitlements over'. (Nozick, 237-8). Property rights act as constraints upon any principle of redistribution and reordering of material resources. 'Particular rights over things fill the space of rights, leaving no room for general rights to be in a certain material condition' (Nozick, 238). Nozick argues that this conception of absolute property rights is the unavoidable consequence of a commitment to a deeper principle, namely, the principle of self-ownership , which treats people as ends in themselves. End-state or pattern

[52] This puts Nozick's theory within the social contract/rational choice tradition, as it justifies government by rational choice, though it does not justify rights this way. Rights are seen as prior to government. Apart from securing rights from encroachment by the state, there is another reason why Nozick favours a minimal state. He argues that 'economically well- off persons desire greater political power in a non-minimal state'; the more extensive the state, the more extensive will the political clout of the wealthy become who can give themselves 'differential economic benefits'. Robert Nozick, 1974, p. 272.

principles generally give everyone a share of the social product, which is produced by individual's labour. Thus, end-state or pattern principles generally institute partial ownership by others of people, their actions, and labour. In a purely egalitarian world, everyone has partial ownership of everyone else. In the libertarian world, everyone has ownership only of him/her self.

SELF-OWNERSHIP AS A PREMISE FOR PROPERTY RIGHTS

Liberal political philosophy, represented classically by John Locke and contemporarily by Robert Nozick, defends great inequality of economic outcome on the basis that people own themselves and are entitled to establish private property over the external world by virtue of self-ownership. What remains an abiding commitment in the writings of both theorists is the idea that self-ownership yields the form of all rights, both in personal powers and in external resources. Self-ownership, in both the Lockean and Nozickean readings, endorses negative individual liberty that is, the freedom to do as one pleases as long as one does not harm others.

There is an apparent conjunction between the principle of self-ownership and property rights and an apparent conflict between self-ownership and equality. Self-ownership is a powerful way of expressing the principle of individual liberty. The view is that those rights, liberties, and powers that are associated with the ownership of property comprise the rightful sovereignty of each person over himself. The principle of self-ownership is a difficult sticking point for egalitarians who cannot but acknowledge the moral force of the principle. Some egalitarians, like John Rawls[53] and Ronald Dworkin,[54] point out the moral arbitrariness of differential talents and advocate a public ownership of skills, thereby denying the force of self-ownership. Others in the egalitarian tradition, like Cohen and John Christman acknowledge the undeniable intuitive force of the principle of self-ownership but deny they can be used to make a species of private property claim. This helps them to retain the principle sans the unegalitarian consequences.[55] The discussion surrounding the principle of self-ownership is an important one and one that would be pressed into service to argue that even as we retain the principle of self-

[53] John Rawls, 1971.

[54] Ronald Dworkin, 1977, *Taking Rights Seriously*, London: Duckworth; Ronald Dworkin, 2000, *Sovereign Virtue: The Theory and Practice of Equality*, Cambridge: Harvard University Press.

[55] G.A. Cohen, 1983, 'Self-Ownership, World Ownership and Equality, Part II', *Social Philosophy and Policy*, 3(2), and 1995, *Self-Ownership, Freedom and Equality*, Cambridge: Cambridge University Press.

ownership and the moral high ground that it demands, we can still argue for limited property rights or even restricted property rights to achieve more equitable and egalitarian consequences. This conclusion would be useful in laying the foundation for the central conclusion of Chapter 2 of this work, which will be to state that the principle of self-ownership can be retained but that it does not form the basis of a moral ground on which the claim for IPRs can be made.

Contemporary left–libertarian political philosophers, such as John Rawls and Ronald Dworkin achieve their relatively egalitarian positions by denying self-ownership as a premise. They question the Nozickean conclusion that inequalities that exist in society are ethically defensible; that justice is merely a matter of following the right procedures and not a matter of 'end states'. Private ownership of the initially unowned external world is established by virtue of the exercise of the agents' self-owning powers, subject to certain constraints on private appropriation that aim to respect the rights and welfare of others. If people start with very different skills, Nozick's theory licenses a fairly rapid development of inequality of income or welfare. Rawls and Dworkin however, deny that each person should be the sole owner of his talents, that is, a person should have all the rights to differential income due to his productive skills and talents. Rawls argues that natural talents like social circumstances are matters of brute luck, and people's moral claims should not depend on brute luck.[56] In fact, Dworkin asserts that the undeserved character of natural assets makes the whole notion of equality of opportunity fraudulent.[57] How then should we treat differences in natural assets? Rawls' answer is that 'the basic structure can be arranged so that these contingencies work for the good of the least fortunate.'[58] This argument of Rawls is in accordance to the difference principle, which says that those who are talented do not deserve their advantages and their higher expectations 'are just only if they work as a part of a scheme which improves the expectations of the least advantaged member of the society.'[59]

Ronald Dworkin, in his work *Sovereign Virtue*, puts forward his version of self-ownership in an equal society. 'A political community must treat all its members as equals, that is, with equal concern and respect, and it must respect that sovereign requirement not only in its design of economic

[56] John Rawls, 1971, pp. 74–5.
[57] R. Dworkin, 1985, *A Matter of Principle,* Cambridge, MA: Harvard University Press, p. 207.
[58] John Rawls, 1971, p. 102.
[59] Ibid., p. 75.

institutions and practices, but in its conception of freedom, of community, and of political democracy as well.'[60] In Dworkin's theory, the talented and the naturally advantaged have a moral obligation to the disadvantaged. This is met by the talented owing 'insurance premiums' (taxes) that get paid out to the disadvantaged. These are transfer payments that are paid to the disadvantaged to compensate for their natural disabilities or lack of talents. Because talents are undeserved, it is not a denial of moral equality for the government to consider it as a possible ground for claims to compensation. Thus in Dworkin's theory, the talented owe insurance premiums that get paid out to the disadvantaged, while in Rawls' theory the talented only benefit from their talents if it also benefits the disadvantaged. Both Rawls and Dworkin have offered us theories of redistribution which are premised on the idea that economic freedoms are needed to enforce the more general idea of equality itself. The same principle that allows market freedom also limits the market where it penalizes the people for their unchosen circumstances. 'The same conception of equality underlies both market freedom and its constraints.'[61]

Self-ownership of the Nozickean kind, which translates into only a formal notion of self-ownership and not a substantive idea of self-determination, is a problematic idea. Self-ownership, as Kymkicka argues, actually restricts the self-determination of the property worker and makes him a resource for others.[62] Those who enter the market after others have appropriated all the available property are forced to work for the benefit of others. This forced compliance with a property system constitutes a form of exploitation and violates self-ownership of the propertyless, limiting the exercise of their self-owned powers. Lack of property ownership by some is a denial of their self-ownership and is therefore inconsistent with Nozick's root idea itself, which regards self-ownership as a foundational principle. 'Since meaningful self-determination requires both resources and liberties, and since each of us has a separate existence, each person should have an equal claim to these resources and liberties.'[63]

G.A. Cohen, from the analytical Marxist perspective, challenges the Libertarian concept of self-ownership in his book *Self-Ownership, Freedom, and Equality*.[64] Cohen in this work attempts to defend an egalitarian distribution of income, which he considers to be compatible with the

[60] Ronald Dworkin, 2000, p. 106.
[61] Will Kymlicka, 2002, p. 88.
[62] Ibid., p. 121.
[63] Ibid., p. 124.
[64] G.A. Cohen, 1995.

principle of self-ownership. He asserts that a union of self-ownership and unequal distribution of worldly resources or 'world ownership', as he terms it, leads to an indefinitely great inequality of private property in external goods and hence to inequality of conditions.[65] In an attempt to delegitimize the appropriation of external resources by individuals or groups by which they come to have property in such resources that would exclude the rival claim of others, he targets the connection Nozick makes between each person's property and liberty. According to Cohen, a person who owns himself must be allowed to profit equally comprehensively from the control of his own mental and bodily resources. Cohen argues that the Lockean proviso, employed by Nozick, fails the test. He argues that any appropriation will make someone 'worse off', for the simple reason that no one will now be able to appropriate the already appropriated item. Even if a latecomer, finding no unappropriated resources left to appropriate, were to be compensated with greater material benefit, this compensation cannot undo the fact that there in a contravention of that individual's will (liberty). Cohen explains that even if property rights have been achieved fairly, they frequently lead to an unacceptable amount of power over others. Therefore, Cohen explains that capitalist libertarianism sacrifices the liberty of those who lack the conditions and power necessary for achieving true freedom between persons.[66]

Cohen claims that individual appropriation cannot meet a properly formulated Nozickean proviso against harm and the like liberty of others, so there can be no legitimate or individual appropriation from a condition of no-ownership. Cohen considers the world of people with unequal talents who enjoy the rights associated with self-ownership. He argues that to enforce a system of equality in distribution of external resources in such a world would inevitably conflict with self-ownership, if the latter is construed in merely a formal manner. A strictly formal sense of self-ownership is one where individuals retain rights over their bodies and talents but have no rights over those material resources that enable them

[65] Ibid, p. 69.

[66] Taking his cue from Nozick (1974) that taxation on earnings is a form of coerced labor, Cohen concludes that various egalitarian arrangements (like welfare paid for out of taxation) are incompatible with the self-ownership of the rich, just like inequalities are incompatible with the self-ownership of the unpropertied. We have to choose therefore between principles of equality and principles of self-ownership. Debate on this issue continues: some argue that what we owe to others must be figured out first before there can be any question of owning either our selves, our bodies, or other material resources; while for Nozick, any attempt to make the argument in that order will lead to counter-intuitive results. Nozick,1974, p. 234.

to lead a meaningful life. A more 'substantive self-ownership', a notion that Cohen employs, demands a certain equality of condition.[67] Cohen's own theory presents an alternative to 'Nozick's up for grabs hypothesis about the external world'.[68]

It is possible therefore to retain the powerful appeal to self-ownership and yet discard the inequitable consequences that it may generate. John Christman unpacks the principle into two different aspects of ownership— 'control rights' and 'income rights'—which ought to be considered separately and justified according to contrasting considerations.[69] While a case can be made to defend control rights based on the value of autonomy and individual liberty (although, he says, that even these will rest on a consideration of the consequences of these rights on the society), the principle of self-ownership cannot be extended to justify income rights, that is, the right to benefit from the exchange of my skills in any way available. The value of these skills and the income rights from them, is purely conditional on the contingencies of the market sector, in particular, others' endowments.[70] Preventing a person from reaping increased benefits from market exchanges does not, for him, prevent a person from controlling his life and therefore, is not a contravention of the principle of self-ownership. 'The belief that self-control can be trumped in favour of distributive processes, benefiting from one's endowments via the happenstance of the surrounding distribution, is not so intuitively supported'.[71] Christman thus bifurcates self-ownership in order to develop a robust egalitarian theory assuring that equality does not mean a denial of self-ownership.

Self-ownership, in its substantive implication, therefore, needs to be used, as Attracta Ingram states, as an expression of autonomy, which is a matter of being in control of our own lives and having the *positive freedom* to shape one's lives according to self chosen principles.[72] Self-ownership is inevitably connected with our self-conception and our judgement about the importance of certain liberties.[73] Autonomy, therefore admits

[67] G.A. Cohen, 1986, pp. 77–96.

[68] Ibid. Cohen's theory posits an external world jointly owned by everyone with each having a veto over its prospective use. He demonstrates that 'final equality of condition is assured when that egalitarian hypothesis about the ownership of the external world is conjoined with the thesis of self-ownership'. G.A. Cohen, 1995, p. 14.

[69] John Christman, 1991, 'Self-ownership, Equality and the Structure of Property Rights', *Political Theory*, 19(1), February, pp. 28–46.

[70] Ibid.

[71] Ibid., p. 40.

[72] Attracta Ingram, 1994, p. 19.

[73] Ibid., p. 20.

a plurality of people who differ in their substantive conceptions of good. This calls for a pluralistic culture based on the ability to *govern oneself* in accordance with self chosen principles, rather than to the right to *own oneself* in accordance with principles that endow one with the capacity to construct a meaningful life.[74]

THE PRINCIPLE OF UTILITY

If the principle of self-ownership established its connection with property in the seventeenth century, liberal conceptions of property are commonly associated with the ideas of utility (Jeremy Bentham, Adam Smith) and the idea of individual autonomy (Immanuel Kant and J.S Mill) in the eighteenth century. While Locke began the assault on the absolutist state and argued for a more responsible government and a diffusion of property rights, the eighteenth century liberal thinkers like Bentham, Adam Smith, Kant exhibited a determination to rid individual ownership of the last vestiges of communal and corporate control. Different political priorities stood behind the defence of individual property. It was now directed less against the encroachments of a tyrannical state than against the numerous collective powers and privileges of the aristocracy. Their 'liberal' campaign against 'feudalism' was specifically against the feudal land tenure and the system of family trust. The English land tenure was designed to preserve the aristocracy's territorial rights by rendering the family estate as inalienable as possible by conferring hereditary transfer rights so that ownership was fixed 'in perpetuity'.[75]

Eighteenth century liberal conceptions on property were based on two premises, first, that freedom requires separate property and second, that the rights which property confers upon individuals do not amount to a quasi-political right over others. Land laws, which restricted 'ownability' and commercial mobility of real estate, inheritance arrangements, and the very notion of trans-generational rights seemed antithetical to the core of the liberal doctrine based on the notion of an autonomous individual whose duties and obligations are self incurred. Inheritance arrangements conferred not only economic privileges on a small elite, but also a monopoly over public offices and honours which were denied to the owners of commercial wealth, thus perpetuating the old alliance between land and political domination. Land thus stood in a special moral and political relationship with the community. For both Kant and utilitarians,

[74] Ibid., p. 94.
[75] For details see E. Pollock, 1896, *Land Laws,* third edn, London: Macmillan.

this negated the maxim of 'equal starting chances'. They employed the egalitarian principle of substantive equality of claim, that all have at least an equal right to opportunities, to discredit feudal privileges and property laws and practices.

For Kant, it reiterated his moral position that freedom requires separate property and that all 'incidents' of ownership should be concentrated in a single person as an absolute individual right. Kant stated, 'An external object which, in respect of its substance, can be claimed by someone as his own, is called property (dominium) of that person to whom all rights in that thing belong, like the accidents inhering in a substance, and which, therefore, he as the proprietor (dominus) can dispose of at will.'[76] There was an intense aversion to the remnants of the past, entertained in the writings of liberal critics from Adam Smith to J.S. Mill. Property rights were thus re-conceptualized in order to free individual liberty as well as the economy.

Adam Smith's *The Wealth of Nations* (1776) is a good example of theorizing in the eighteenth century which advocated the thesis of commercial and industrial liberty. In the writings of Adam Smith, the purpose and the consequence of individual choices and liberty is of paramount importance. In the name of liberty, Smith pleads for the removal of all restrictions and demands a particular freedom: the right to property. Property was considered as an institution vital to the growth of industry and commerce, an idea linked more to utility than to liberty.[77] Typically, a utilitarian explanation makes only a contingent claim for individual liberty and its sub-set, property. While Halevy finds Smith a typical representative of the dawning utilitarian movement, there is also at the same time, a considerable debate about how much of Smith's work is infused with Locke's natural law/natural rights tradition—a lineage which the utilitarians, and in particular Bentham, would be quick to dismiss.[78]

In the 'freeing' of the economy as well as of the state from elitist minority, utilitarianism came to be employed as a central tenet in the defence of both private property as well as the democratic state.

[76] Immanuel Kant, 1887, *The Philosophy of Law: An Exposition of the Fundamental Principles of Jurisprudence as the Science of Right,* Edinburgh: T. and T. Clark, trans. by W. Hastie, p. 98 (HTML and PDF files at libertyfund.org).

[77] Adam Smith, 1904 [1776], *An Enquiry into the Nature and Causes of the Wealth of Nations,* Edwin Cannan (ed.), Fifth edn, London: Metheun and Co. Ltd.

[78] It is on the twin grounds of utility and 'naturalness' of progression that Adam Smith makes a case that the idea of property implies a complete freedom of choice and that it is a necessary condition of society's progress. Elie Halevy, 1928, *The Growth of Philosophical Radicalism,* London: Faber and Faber, pp. 118–120.

Classically, by utilities is meant the economic benefits that are derived from institutions rather than other abstract utilities (like happiness, justice, and well-being) which are important but difficult to measure. Also over time social policy has increasingly used utility to mean economic benefits like efficiency, productivity, optimal allocation of resources, and so on. Property rights are utilitarian in two ways: by performing an allocational function and by encouraging production. The allocational function for property rights facilitates social order. Property thus prevents constant struggle among people to hold on to their possessions in a Hobbesian state of nature, and the expending of resources on private enforcement of their claims. Second, it would lead to the 'tragedy of the commons' where no individual would have the incentive to preserve its value, given that the cost of not doing so will be spread among his co-owners, compared to his immediate private benefit gained from overgrazing. There is a second function that the institution of private property serves. Many of the goods we value are the products of human labour. Property rights result in not only in the ownership of the object created if it is made using one's initial entitlements, but also other objects secured through consensual transfers, thus improving the value of our property (for instance, agricultural land or capital equipment). This allows us to appropriate the increased value through subsequent sale or further production. Thus, property rights provide an incentive to increase production and productivity. The production and allocational benefits of property rights thus lead to greater productivity, efficiency, co-ordination, and optimal use of resources, in short to the maximization of utilities. A utilitarian theory of property rights links the establishment of property rights and prescriptions about how to define such rights with increase in welfare or well-being.

UTILITY AND THE STRUCTURE OF PROPERTY RIGHTS IN BENTHAM'S WRITINGS

Jeremy Bentham explicating his principle of utility in 'Introduction to the Principles of Morals and Legislation' wrote:

By the principle of utility is meant that principle which approves or disapproves of every action whatsoever according to the tendency it appears to have to augment or diminish the happiness of the party whose interest is in question: or, what is the same thing in other words to promote or to oppose that happiness. I say of every action whatsoever, and therefore not only of every action of a private individual, but of every measure of government ... By utility is meant that property in any object, whereby it tends to produce benefit, advantage, pleasure, good, or happiness, (all this in the present case comes to the same thing) or (what comes again to the same thing) to prevent the happening of mischief, pain, evil, or unhappiness to the party whose interest is considered: if that party be the community in general, then the happiness of the community: if a particular individual, then the happiness of that individual....[79]

The simplest defence of the existence of property rights over external objects is utilitarian. It would be impossible for the individuals to use the raw materials provided by nature for anything other than the simplest sort of consumption unless he is granted the right to appropriate, use, and transfer objects of value or interest. Bentham argued that the essence of property was the deriving of benefit (pleasure) from the use of that thing. Bentham connected property directly with human feelings, human desire, and individual will. 'Nature has placed mankind under the governance of two sovereign masters, pain and pleasure. It is for them alone to point out what we ought to do, as well as to determine what we shall do... They govern us in all we do, in all we say, in all we think...'[80] He further explains that the principle of utility 'approves or disapproves of every action whatsoever, according to the tendency which it appears to have to augment or diminish the happiness of the party whose interest is in question....'[81] He believes that the happiness principle applies equally to the actions of individuals and to governments, and when applied to governments it requires them to maximize 'the greatest happiness of the greatest numbers' in the community.

Utilitarianism emerged as a political and philosophical movement, in the context of feudal privileges, as a radical critique of the English society, to protect the interests and enhance the rights of the majority against the privileges of small privileged feudal elite. It was at that time associated with progressive reforms and political programmes—the extension of democracy, penal reforms, welfare provisions, etc. Arguing against monarchy, Bentham regarded a monarch as the least safe of all masters. '[F] or (the monarch) being, on this hypothesis, absolutely free to do what he wishes, he will follow his own interest and not the interest of the greatest number... The majority which becomes the sovereign power is the least fallible of masters: for since each individual is the best judge of his interests, it is the majority of the individuals which will be able to estimate the interest of the greatest number...the most numerous are the strongest.'[82]

[79] Jeremy Bentham, 1907 [1789], *An Introduction to the Principles of Morals and Legislation*, Oxford: Clarendon Press, Chapter 1, 1.II. Available at http://www.econlib.org/library/Bentham/bnthPML.html (last accessed on 11 December 2009).

[80] Ibid. 1.I.

[81] Ibid, 1.II.

[82] Jeremy Bentham, 1928, 'An Introduction to the Principles of Morals and Legislation', in Elie Halevy, p. 491.

Utilitarianism, in its simplest formulation, claims that a morally right act or policy is that which produces the greatest happiness for the members of society. This principle of 'political morality' ought to govern the basic structure of society. Elie Halevy distils two fundamental postulates of utilitarian philosophy, although he says that they are never formally enunciated. First, that pleasure and pain can be quantified and measured as objects of a calculus, and a rational mathematical science of pleasure is possible. This, he calls the 'rationalist postulate' of the Utilitarian doctrine. Second, that all individuals who constitute society have an equal capacity for happiness. This he calls the 'individualistic postulate' of the utilitarian doctrine.[83] The primary goal of the state is therefore to rationally identify the greatest interest of the greatest numbers and ensure it. In calculating the aggregate interests, each person's interest should count as one. This Halevy contends, is the Benthamite 'equalitarianism' which results from the individualistic principle.[84] It may be said of all laws that they are in essence equalitarian and individualistic; in so far as they are laws they tend to consider all individuals as equal.

This, however led to two different formulations of utilitarianism, and two radically divergent streams of utilitarian philosophy in the post-Bentham period—one which contests individualism and the other, equalitarianism.[85] According to the first interpretation, utilitarianism is a standard for aggregating individual interests and desires and in aggregating each individual's preference is to count as one. In doing so we maximize happiness. Maximization of happiness (utility) is not the direct goal but a by-product of the equal consideration standard. In the second, maximizing utility is the primary, not the derived goal. The primary goal is not to treat people as equal but to maximize happiness.

The utilitarian defence of property, in any form, is a defence of the legal recognition of ownership as an instrument of promoting greatest happiness. The background assumption of the utilitarian defence of property is that resources in the nature are scarce, and need ever-growing; we thus need to devise ways in which nature can be made to yield as much as possible. Most men are not altruistic creatures and will therefore need rules to govern the distribution of appropriated goods. Property rights emerge as useful guidelines in devising principles of benefit sharing. Property also satisfies the need for security and provides a natural incentive for labour to succeed; rules of ownership will ensure

[83] Ibid., p. 492.
[84] Ibid., p. 501.
[85] For a discussion see Will Kymlicka, 2002, Chapter 1.

that our desire for well-being will lead us to work.[86] Bentham sees the private actions of individuals, particularly in the production of wealth, as the main source of utility. The utility of property, for Bentham, has a naturalistic basis, for it was rooted in the human species' imperative for survival. However here, Bentham is not drawing from Locke's natural law paradigm; in fact, he is hostile to the doctrines of 'natural right'. Bentham holds that property is a legal right and all legal rights are a matter of positive law. These legal rights are moral in nature for 'they are explicable as liberties and powers that an individual ought to have in order to promote their most important interests.'[87]

Bentham's theory moves away from the Lockean formulation on another count. Bentham believed that property was essentially an external relationship. Property relations were subject-object relations. Hence no man should be described as having property in his own person. A man might be said to 'have a property' in a thing (that is, in a certain relationship to it) without having or possessing the thing itself. Physical appropriation, for Bentham, was not a necessary condition for property to exist. Bentham divided objects of property into 'real' or 'corporeal' and 'fictitious' or 'incorporeal'.[88] He divided real property into moveable and immoveable. The classification of incorporeal property is interesting. He considered it a mistake to regard one's own livelihood or skills as one's property, though they could be another's, and said that 'Integral property would subsist in things only'. Many important abstract notions, such as 'reputation', 'power', 'rights', 'liberties', 'duty', and 'obligation' were not subsumed by Bentham under the heading of property. These for him were 'fictitious moral goods', which were objects of desire, not because they were inherently virtuous but because possession of them is justified by its social consequence, these being measured in terms of pleasure or pain to the individual.[89]

Thus, for Bentham, property essentially was vested in real or corporeal objects; it was essentially a relationship, not an object. These relationships ought to be protected by law which 'transformed the field of property relationships, from a battlefield of conflicting desires into a chessboard of reciprocal rights and duties, powers and obligations.'[90] Bentham argued

---

[86] Alan Ryan, 1987, p. 56.

[87] Ibid., p. 53.

[88] J. Bowring, 1843, *The Works of Jeremy Bentham,* 389, Edinburgh: William Tait.

[89] Jeremy Bentham, 1970 [1789], Chapter XIV, pp. 210–12.

[90] R.D. Long, 1979, 'Bentham on Property,' in *Theories of Property: Aristotle to the Present,* Anthony Parel and Thomas Flanagan (ed.), Waterloo: Wilfrid Laurier University Press, p. 227.

that the essence of property was the deriving of pleasure and benefit from the use of property and as long as the use of property was a source of happiness, it was an institution which was morally defensible and desirable. 'The very adequacy of an individual's being, expressed through the purposeful and powerful nature of his desires, was measured by his capacity to acquire and enjoy property'.[91] Bentham's defence of private property hinges on the co-relation between independence of will and the independence of means, the latter becoming a precondition for individual autonomy and freedom of will and happiness. However, as Long states, '[Bentham] allows the methodological structure of the legal system and the science of political economy to dictate the structure of happiness itself...it is not man who develops but rather, utilitarian social planning itself...his legislative theory overwhelms his moral theory....'[92]

There is also an inherent conservative character about utilitarianism, according to Kymlicka. Utilitarianism makes morality a contingent factor. Classical utilitarianism is a radically consequentialist doctrine. According to utilitarian thought, even if a policy involves grave harm, this is no reason to object if the net effect is an increase in total utility. Finding the morally right answer is not based on arbitrary moral prohibitions, but a matter of measuring changes in human welfare. Consequentialism seems to provide a straightforward method for resolving moral questions. What ought to be a matter of personal or political commitment becomes a matter of consequence.[93] Ryan argues that it is characteristic of utilitarian arguments that they are reversible, that is, since all justification rests on a consideration of consequences, a reconsideration of consequences will force a reconsideration of what is being justified.[94] The grounds of morality thus keep shifting, as do the grounds of utility.

This perhaps is the reason that the justification of private property on merely utilitarian grounds is a lukewarm one, for it is forever hostage to the relativity of consequences. The institution of private property is only defensible on grounds that it maximizes welfare of the greatest numbers, an empirically contestable issue. Since property rights are to be justified in terms of general benefit, there doesn't appear a clear cut case against public and common property too, as long as they can be legally and unambiguously defined. Property may be more or less private, or more or less public; the only issue is how to define, legally, the rights of ownership.

[91] Ibid, p. 239.
[92] Ibid., p. 249.
[93] For a discussion see Will Kymlicka, 2009, p. 46-48.
[94] Alan Ryan, 1987, p. 59.

Classical Utilitarianism, thus, does not present a very emphatic defence of private property.[95]

Bentham is not an unambiguously, or even a consistent minimal state theorist. It seems clear that he sees the private actions of individuals, particularly the production of wealth, as the main source of utility. Bentham seems committed to a notion of private property as a necessary condition for maximizing utility. This is explicit in Bentham's *Principles of Civil Code*. 'Law does not say to man, Work and I will reward you but it says: Labour, and by stopping the hand that would take from you, I will ensure to you the fruits of your labour—its natural and sufficient reward which without me you cannot preserve[...].'[96] Bentham wrote:

'In the distribution of rights and obligations, the legislator, as we have said, should have for his end the happiness of society. Investigating more distinctly in what that happiness consists, we shall find four subordinate ends—*Subsistence; Abundance; Equality; Security*. The more perfect enjoyment is in all these respects, the greater is the sum of social happiness: and especially of that happiness which depends upon the laws.... Some persons may be astonished to find that Liberty is not ranked among the principal objects of law. But a clear idea of liberty will lead us to regard it as a branch of security. Personal liberty is security against a certain kind of injuries which affect the person. As to what is called *political liberty*, it is another branch of security, security against injuries from the ministers of government.'[emphasis mine].[97]

This passage clearly reflects Bentham's view that although the rule of law is essential to the pursuit of utility, law should limit itself to ensuring that people can pursue utility for themselves.[98] On the other hand, Bentham's utilitarianism, by implication, may also regard the merits of redistribution and consider redistribution from the rich to the poor as a net social improvement. Although wealth increases happiness, ten thousand times the quantity of wealth will not bring ten thousand times the quantity of happiness; the law of diminishing marginal utility would prevent a corresponding increase in satisfaction. It would, however, if redistributed among the needy, would lead to a greater production of happiness, both individual and aggregated. The logic of utilitarianism in this reading is thus not antithetical to the idea of redistribution through state intervention.

[95] Bentham tackles property rights in particular only in 1887, *Theory of Legislation*, Trubner: London, a work compiled from his manuscripts and not considered one his main works.

[96] Jeremy Bentham, 1843, *Principles of the Civil Code*, reprinted in *The Works of Jeremy Bentham*, Edinburgh: William Tait, vol. 1, p. 301.

[97] Ibid., Chapter 2.

[98] For a further discussion on law's fundamental emphasis as providing security, see Nancy Rosenblum, 1978, *Bentham's Theory of the Modern State*, Cambridge: Harvard University Press, p. 53.

Ian Shapiro however argues that '[N]o particular redistributive policy can be inferred from the principle of diminishing marginal utility[...] The principle says that the wealthier you are, the less new utility you will derive from each additional dollar. This suggests that the more money you have, the larger the dollar increments that will be required, at the margin, to increase your utility.'[99] While it can be inferred that there is a redistributive core of the theory it is doubtful that anyone professing to be a Benthamite utilitarian will commit to it. Bentham also argues only for *practical equality* where this is understood to mean that no approach to equality can undermine *abundance, subsistence and security—which are of superior necessity* [emphasis mine].[100] Bentham further clears any ambiguity with respect to privileging of the principles. He writes that 'Equality ought not to be favoured except in the cases in which it does not interfere with security...'[101] As for subsistence, which the principle of equality would imply, he clearly states that it not for law to take care of subsistence: 'All it can do is to create motives, that is, punishments or rewards, by the force of which men may be led to provide subsistence for themselves. But nature herself has created these motives, and has given them a sufficient energy.'[102]

Bentham's defence of security was primarily directed against the egalitarian pressures of the doctrine of diminishing marginal utility. Bentham claims that the abundance of wealth is the inevitable result of the security of property; without security there would be no property; without property, there would be no general guarantee of subsistence, without abundance there would be less certainty of subsistence for all.[103]

There are two central points that Bentham makes here.First, that there is nothing gained from limiting the rights of the wealthy; and second,that abundance of wealth is to be created and defended for it provides a resource for the whole community. The case for security clearly overwhelms the case for equality. Security (of property) is a highly desirable feature in the scheme of utility. Continuous redistributive upheavals can hamper it.The state may aid the non-propertied, but only to the extent that the security of property is not jeopardized, even if it means that general welfare is lessened.

[99] Ian Shapiro, 2004, *Moral Foundations of Politics,* New Delhi: Aakar Books, p. 31–2.

[100] Bentham, 1954, *Psychology of Economic Man,* London: George Allen and Unwin, p. 442. Quoted from Shapiro, 2004, 30.

[101] Jeremy Bentham, 1843, reprinted in *The Works of Jeremy Bentham,* Edinburgh: WIlliam Tait, Part I, Chapter 3.

[102] Ibid., Part I, Chapter 4.

[103] Ian, Shapiro, 2004, pp. 30–3.

Utilitarianism is as readily available to the critics of private property as to its defenders. One of the liveliest controversies in recent times has involved a debate on whether claims of community, vis-à-vis the rights of the individual, are supported by the utilitarianism. The debate interestingly illustrates varied positions, depending on a perception of rights from a negative or a positive perspective. It is a fairly common perception that the utilitarians were deeply committed to capitalism, and therefore to unfettered private property rights.[104] This reading is based on the premise that utility and private property are happy allies. William Godwin's discussion on property rights in Book VIII of his *Political Justice* presents an extreme version of utilitarianism where it becomes a doctrine of welfare and amounts to a denial of any thing that one can call property rights. Ritchie, acknowledged as a trenchant critic of natural rights, formulated an important synthesis between rights-theory and utilitarianism.[105] In Ritchie's arguments, utilitarianism survived as a dominant aspect of modern welfare thought as it shed its highly individualistic Benthamite aspects. His version of 'ethical utilitarianism' proposes that property rights are not only about the protection of individual rights; it is as much about the promotion of collective interest and welfare.

Robert Nozick, a forceful critic of utilitarianism, relies on the view that each of us, being a proprietor of his own person, has no general duty to promote any other person's welfare. Nozick argues that utilitarianism doesn't take into account rights (individual) and their violation and instead gives rights a 'derivative status', employing them only as 'side constraints on actions'—'the rights of others determine the constraints upon your actions'.[106] He is strongly critical of propensity of utilitarianism to enhance the vulnerability of separate individuals to considerations of general interest and of equal treatment of individuals.

In utilitarianism there is no prospect of settling the question of property rights by asking the question of what property really is. What interests in objects should be protected by law, so that they become property rights, is a question to be settled by law, property being a legal and not a moral question. Property is entirely a by-product of law. In essence, the claim is that there are no natural titles of ownership; they may be created in accordance with the law of the land. Rationally, the law should be so designed that utility is maximized. Utility is maximized, for Bentham, when almost anything can be bought and sold in a free market, at prices

[104] Karl Marx, 1976, *Capital*, vol. 1, Harmondsworth: Penguin, p. 280.
[105] D.G. Ritchie, 1952, *Natural Rights*, London: Allen and Unwin, p. 98.
[106] Robert Nozick, 1974, pp. 28–29.

mutually agreed upon by the buyers and sellers; profit and wealth creation being the incentive.[107]

Bentham's defense of the individual being allowed to pursue his own good, in his own way, has less to do with a respect for individuality and a moral position on individual liberty than with maximization of benefits. Elie Halevy's claim that Bentham is no respecter of individuality, but his principle of utility is an instrument of individualist *laissez faire*, is widely accepted.[108] The point of rights of ownership is that they increase general well being by allowing appropriate areas freedom of choice- from freedom to invest, to freedom of contract, and so on. The classical utilitarian argument is about the best way to allocate and control rights over the use of society's resources. How property rights came to be, whether these rights ought to be unfettered, whether the net outcome of these rights are markedly egalitarian or nonegalitarian, are issues on which the doctrine does not provide clear answers; in fact it chooses not to enter the realm of moral philosophy. Utilitarianism, in a nutshell, believes that giving people property rights is a good way of solving the problem of coordinating everyone's productive activities. The argument for property rights is therefore a contingent one, as is utilitarian morality.

UTILITY AS A PREMISE FOR PRIVATE PROPERTY

The consequentialist utilitarian argument argues that people in general are better off when a given class of resources is governed by a private property regime than by any alternative system. Under private property, it is said, the resources will be more wisely used, or used to satisfy a wider (and perhaps more varied) set of wants than under any alternative system, so that the overall enjoyment that humans derive from a given stock of resources will be increased.

The argument for markets is that in a complex society there are innumerable decisions to be made about the allocation of particular resources to particular production processes. Is a given ton of coal better used to generate electricity which will in turn be used to refine aluminum for manufacturing cooking pots or aircraft, or to produce steel which can be used to build railway tracks? In most economies there are hundreds of thousands of distinct factors of production, and it has proved impossible for efficient decisions about their allocation to be made by central agencies acting in the name of the community, and charged

[107] Jeremy Bentham, 1887, pp. 118–19.
[108] E. Halevy, 1928.

with overseeing the economy as a whole. In actually existing socialist
societies, central planning turned out to be a way of ensuring economic
paralysis, inefficiency, and waste. In market economies, decisions like these
are made on a decentralized basis by thousands of individuals and firms
responding to price signals, each seeking to maximize profits from the
use of the productive resources under its control, and such a system often
works efficiently. Motives to improve and to be efficient will occur only
if the resources are privately owned, so that the loss is theirs (or their
employer's) when a market signal is missed and the gain is theirs (or their
employer's) when a profitable allocation is secured.

Arguments of this sort are familiar and important, but like all
consequentialist arguments, they need to be treated with caution. In most
private property systems, there are some individuals who own little or
nothing, and who are entirely at the mercy of others. So when it is said
that 'people in general' are better off under private property arrangements,
we have to ask, which people? everyone? the majority? or just a small class
of owners whose prosperity is so great as to offset the consequent
immiseration of the others in an aggregative utilitarian calculus?
Alternatively, some consequentialists cast their justifications in the
language of what is called 'Pareto-optimality'. Here the consequentialist
has to show that everyone is better off under a private property system,
or at least that no-one is worse off. Maybe the privatization of previously
common land does not benefit everybody: but it benefits some and
it leaves others no worse off than they were before. The homelessness
and immiseration of the poor, on this account, is not a result of private
property; it is simply the natural predicament of mankind from which a
few energetic appropriators have managed to extricate themselves.

FROM PRIVATE PROPERTY TO INTELLECTUAL PROPERTY

In dealing with the pros and cons of private property as an institution,
it has sometimes been suggested that the general justification of private
property and the distribution of particular property rights can be treated
as separate issues.[109] However, it can be argued that the separation is an
artificial one. Distribution of property rights and the distribution that the
property rights effect lay the moral basis on which these rights can be
justly claimed.

Most theories, whether consequentialists like the utilitarian argument,
or the deontological like liberty argument, affect patterns of distribution of

[109] See Alan Ryan, 1987, p. 82; Waldron, 1984, p. 330.

resources and rights. They have direct or indirect distributive implications. Justificatory premises for property have to be tested in the context of the distributive implications and outcomes such as those of income, wealth resources, rights, among others. The idea that property-owning promotes virtue (Aristotle), upholds individual will and autonomy, (Kant), protects individual liberty (Locke, Nozick), promotes market efficiency (Adam Smith), aggregates general welfare(Bentham)—are all arguments which provide a defence for private propperty and discredit economic collectivism and redistribution on various grounds. Robert Nozick, for instance, argues that a theory of historical entitlement, along Lockean lines, provides both a complete justification of the institution of property and a set of strict criteria that govern its legitimate distribution. Property rights, according to Nozick, are an act of individual liberty and constrain the extent to which we are entitled to act on our intuitions and theories of distributive justice. In Kantian liberalism, property guarantees to the individual external freedom, or scope for making choices. Any reference to particular ends and tangible benefits is excluded from the strict notion of rights. Property is a right because it is one of the expressions of the moral autonomy and will of the individual.

The liberty and the moral autonomy arguments describe societies with private property as free societies. Part of what this means is that owners are free to use their property as they please; they are not bound by social or political decisions. (And correlatively, the role of government in economic decision-making is minimized.) But what it ignores is that there is simultaneously a social exclusion of people from resources that others own. The freedoms of some coexist along with the 'unfreedoms' of others. As T.H. Green observed, a person who owns nothing in a capitalist society 'might as well, in respect of the ethical purposes which the possession of property should serve, be denied rights of property altogether'.[110] All property systems distribute freedoms and unfreedoms; no system of property can be described, without qualification, as a system of liberty. Arguments from liberty commit the libertarians to a moralized conception of freedom. Libertarians generally defend the ideal of freedom from the perspective of how little one is constrained by authority, that is, how much one is allowed to do (negative liberty) distinguished from a view of freedom focused on how much one is able to do (positive liberty).

Most recent theoretical writings on property have been dominated by two approaches: the labour theory and the utilitarian theory of property.

---

[110] T.H. Green, 1941, *Lectures on the Principles of Political Obligation* [1895], London: Longmans Green & Co., p. 219.

In a large part, their prominence derives from the fact that they grow out of and draw support from lines of argument and justifications that have long figured in the defence of property institutions and forms of property. Whether it has been the shift from common property to private property, the inclusion of land in the list of things that count as property, or the recent extension of knowledge as a form of property, the principles of self-ownership and utility (culminating in the labour theory and utilitarianism respectively) have for long retained their appeal for defences of various forms of property, particularly in the private domain. From limited rights in land, to rights over moveable objects, enhanced rights in estates, body rights, copyrights, and now IPRs and knowledge rights; from a property right as being ownership of a thing to rights as defining the relation between people with respect to that thing, property rights have come a long way but retain as their core philosophical appeal, labour and utilitarian justificatory premises.

The dependence of modern-day theorists on Locke's labour theory and on utilitarianism, and the debt they owe to these theories is amply demonstrated in constitutional provisions, case reports, preambles to legislation, and so forth. References to the role of intellectual-property rights in stimulating the production of socially valuable works riddle American law.[111] Thus, for example, the constitutional provision upon which the copyright and patent statutes rest indicates that the purpose of those laws is to provide incentives for creative intellectual efforts that will benefit the society at large. The United States Supreme Court, when construing the copyright and patent statutes, has repeatedly insisted that their primary objective is inducing the production and dissemination of works of the intellect. Drawing from the labour theory, references to the importance of rewarding authors and inventors for their labour are almost as common. Proponents of legislative extensions of copyright or patent protection routinely make arguments like: 'Our American society is founded on the principle that the one who creates something of value is entitled to enjoy the fruits of his labour'.[112] In the *Harper and Row*[113] case, the US Supreme Court took a similar line: ' the rights conferred by

---

[111] See, for example, Article I, Section 8, Clause 8 of the United States Constitution empowers Congress 'to Promote the Progress of Science and useful Arts, by securing for limited Times to Authors and Inventors the exclusive Right to their respective Writings and Discoveries.'

[112] Testimony of Elizabeth Janeway, Copyright Law Revision (1965), reprinted in George S. Grossman, 1976, *Omnibus Copyright Revision Legislative History*, vol. 5, Hein, p. 100.

[113] *Harper & Row* v. *Nation Enterprises*, 471 US 539, 545–46 (1985).

copyright are designed to assure contributors to the store of knowledge a fair return for their labours....'

Words such as—'incentive', 'reward', 'desert', in these and countless other passages reflect the influence that the two sets of theories have exerted on contemporary ideas about property and its institutions. While earlier, in the hands of their original propounders and loyal followers, they were employed as both sufficient and necessary explanatory theses, in contemporary times, by contrast, such themes are typically juxtaposed and employed in tandem, especially by the policy makers. It is quite common for a single author to invoke a wide range of arguments to support private property rights. In policy and legal literature such arguments are often regarded as providing multiple reasons for justifying the rationale and the purpose of property rights in general and IPRs in particular. It is not surprising that theorists familiar with these debates should separate ideas about intellectual property into similar piles. This has been the rationale behind distilling, from the multiple standpoints and justificatory arguments, the basic precepts of these theories. The labour theory and the utilitarian theory, more than any other theory of property demonstrate their modern relevance. It is no surprise that they are replicated in the context of intellectual property.

Interestingly, the various leading arguments that normally buttress each other and converge in support of private property diverge widely when applied to the concept of intellectual property. For example, a theory wherein property is viewed as the just reward for labour (a 'desert theory') might well support intellectual property rights, while at the same time, a theory in which property is defined as the expression of liberty might not. Those who strongly favour liberty and property might well arrive at differing conclusions. This occurs because liberty and property in the context of IPRs may be irreconcilable; copyrights and patents seem to be property, but they also seem to restrict liberty. Those who prioritize utility over liberty might well fall prey to counter empirical validations or differing conceptions of utilities in a world of multiple normative concerns.

Intellectual property as an instance of reification of property, marks the extension of property rights to an intangible realm where scarcity is not naturally or potentially implied. Most property rights have their roots in scarcity of goods; it is scarcity, which in the first place, led to the privatization of property. Knowledge as a good is not scarce and therefore requires a different set of principles or a different application of the principles to justify and legitimate its private use. How this is done and the

problems that are posed for the justificatory premises is the subject matter
of the next two chapters. They examine the notions of self-ownership and
utility as underlying principles of intellectual property rights and will test
their validity against the distributive implications of both goods and rights
that IPRs may generate.

3 Intellectual Property Rights and the Principle of Self-Ownership

One approach is to treat property of an entity as an ontological question: whether something can be considered as property depends on the possession of certain key traits or characteristics, or upon being an entity of a particular kind. Natural law and labour theories are ontological approaches to the definition of property. This chapter proposes to examine the claim of intellectual property rights from the perspective of self-ownership, a theme that emerges strongly in the writings of Locke and Nozick as discussed in Chapter 2 of this work. The premise is that the self that 'owns' intellectual labour also owns the knowledge it creates. Can the self be owned and if so, in what sense and what kinds of rights does it yield? Can the Lockean proviso, which is taken as a measure that grants legitimacy to property rights, hold good when employed to test IPRs? These are some of the issues raised in this chapter.

SELF-OWNERSHIP AND BODILY RIGHTS

Most libertarians support rights in one's own body. These rights can be said to emerge from rights of 'self-ownership'. Libertarians universally hold that all tangible scarce resources, including our very bodies—are subject to rightful control, or 'ownership', by specified individuals. According to the natural-rights view of intellectual property held by some libertarians, creations of the mind are entitled to protection just as tangible property is.[1] Both are products of one's physical or mental labour. Because one owns one's labour one has a natural law right to the fruit of one's labour. According to this view, just as one has a right to the house one constructs, so also one has a right to the ideas one generates and the art one produces. This theory depends on the notion that one owns one's body and labour,

---

[1] Adam D. Moore (ed.), 1997, *Intellectual Property: Moral, Legal, and Intellectual Dilemmas,* Oxford: Rowman & Litllefield; Adam Moore, 2004; Ayn Rand, 1967, 'Patents and Copyrights', in *Capitalism: The Unknown Ideal,* New York: New American Library, p. 133.

and therefore its fruits, including intellectual creations are owned by the creating self. An individual who creates a song, a sculpture, by employing his own labour is thus entitled to 'own' these creations because they result from the primary ownership of the self.

The analogy of property to the relation one has with one's body is grounded in the fact that both involve exclusive use. One has the freedom and the exclusive right to determine what one will do with one's body and talents, just as one does with respect to those things that are one's property. The distinction between the two is that the owner is not necessarily connected to but is separable from the things he holds as (tangible) property. The owner exercises absolute control over tangible property and can dispose of a thing he holds as property. This is not the case with property rights that we exercise over our bodies. Our body parts, intellect, and talents are very much a part of that which defines our self. This is the distinction that Penner draws between the two forms of ownership in his 'separabilty thesis'. He argues that what distinguishes a property right in 'things' from similar rights that one can assert over one's body is not just that they are contingently ours, but that they might just as well be someone else's.[2] This cannot be said about things 'with necessary links with particular persons', like our talents, personalities, our body parts, etc. They are not ours to hold or possess through a legal contract; they are ours in any case. However, Penner's separability thesis comes under strain when technology comes to aid separation of body parts and organs making them transferable entities. One could argue that technology has rendered some body parts separable in modern times—kidneys, cornea, liver sections, stem cells—making these body parts tangible entities which are physically separable. Does this then fulfil Penner's separability criterion rendering yet another distinction between property rights in things and self valueless? Clearly there are other moral issues involved in regarding one's kidney or one's limb as property merely because they are technically 'separable'.

A helpful criterion has been provided by Munzer in this regard which enables us to distinguish between rights that individuals may have with respect to their bodies and body rights.[3] Body rights confer on individuals the right to use their body as they wish to (subject to basic prohibitions and moral norms—you cannot, for example consent to assault on your self; sell body parts; commit suicide, etc.), so long as they do not harm

---

[2] J.E. Penner, 1997, *The Idea of Property in Law,* Oxford: Clarendon Press, pp. 111–12. For an overview of Penner's argument refer to his Introduction, p. 9.

[3] Stephen R. Munzer, 1990, *A Theory of Property,* NY: CUP, pp. 43–56.

others. But this according to Munzer does not suggest that people have property rights in their bodies. Body rights are what Munzer terms, 'personal rights', that protect interests or choices other than the choice to transfer. Property rights in body, therefore by implication, are rights that protect the choice of transfer. For example, the right to donate an organ on death, the right to sell blood, etc. are those body rights that protect the choice of transfer and hence yield property rights. But these property rights are neither so numerous nor so central to suggest that people own themselves.[4] Too many incidents are lacking to say that persons own their bodies. Restrictions on transfer and the absence of the liberty to consume or destroy, for example, indicate that persons do not own their bodies in the way that they own automobiles or desks.[5] Debate over this issue manifests itself in differences over the issue of inalienability and with respect to the law of contract, that is, can we 'sell' or alienate our bodies in the same manner that we can alienate title to property in house? The issue is obviously embroiled in moral dilemmas and debates and does not unambiguously lead to property rights in one's self.[6]

As we move away from the tangible, corporeal body parts towards the intangibles of the 'body' (for instance, intellect), matters become fuzzier. Rights to reputations, laws against defamation and blackmail, for example, are rights in very intangible type of things. Some libertarians oppose laws against blackmail and many oppose the idea of a right to one's reputation. Also disputed is the concept of intellectual property. The debate over these issues invariably manifests themselves in debates over differences between bodies and things, and issues of inalienability and the rights that alienability can possibly yield. The ambiguity increases when we ascribe the status of property to that which is inseparable in all senses. Intellect clearly belongs to the domain that is unambiguously a non-separable entity. A second complexity arises when we take into account the multiple locations of ideas. Ideas cannot be said to belong only to 'one body'. They can co-exist in many bodies simultaneously. In that case, self-ownership alone does not guarantee ownership of the body or the idea that it houses; ownership here reflecting the right to exclusive use

---

[4] Ibid. p. 57.

[5] Ibid. p. 43.

[6] For arguments against body inalienability, see Stephen Kinsella, 1998–99, 'Inalienability and Punishment: A Reply to George Smith', *Journal of Libertarian Studies*, 14(1), pp. 79–93. For arguments favouring such alienability, see Walter Block, 2003, 'Toward a Libertarian Theory of Inalienability: A Critique of Rothbard, Barnett, Gordon, Smith, Kinsella, and Epstein', *Journal of Libertarian Studies*, 17(2), pp. 39–85.

with a right to exclude others.[7] Because ideas can be concurrently used without diminishing another's right to use the exclusionary premises of IPRs come to have problematic implications for self-owned rights of others. The rest of this Chapter aims to ground this argument while retaining the principle of self ownership but at the same time delinking it with the right to exclude others from free use of their self-owned ideas and expression.

SELF-OWNERSHIP AND KNOWLEDGE RIGHTS

A powerful way of asserting the principle of individual liberty is to claim that every individual has full property rights over her body, skills and labour. John Locke along with later libertarians held that agents are self-owners in the sense that they have private property rights over themselves in the same way that people can have private property rights over inanimate objects. An astrophysicist and a radical intellectual property proponent, Andrew Joseph Galambos believes that man has property rights in his own life (primordial property) and in all 'non-procreative derivatives of his life.'[8] Since the 'first derivatives' of a man's life are his thoughts and ideas, thoughts and ideas are 'primary property'. Since, action is based on primary property (ideas), actions are owned as well; this is referred to as 'liberty'. Secondary derivatives, such as land, televisions, and other tangible goods, are produced by ideas and action. Thus, property rights in tangible items are relegated to lowly secondary status, as compared with the 'primary' status of property rights in ideas.[9]

The relationship between ownership of knowledge and property rights over it is complex, both in theory and practice. The question of whether ownership rights can be asserted over knowledge would entail an examination the social constituency of knowledge and the difficulties in establishing rights claims over it. Far from being the achievement of a few men of genius, scientific knowledge is a result of a long, complex,

---

[7] One of the elements in the analysis of a right is the specification of the conditions under which a right-claim may be said to be sound. Intellectual property rights are what can be regarded as 'claim rights' in the Hohfeldian conception of rights. The existence of a claim right in one person entails the absence of a right on someone else's part to interfere. IPRs are ownership rights that are 'negative' claim rights with a right to exclude others from the thing owned, thereby going beyond simply the right to use. W.N. Hohfeld, 1923, *Fundamental Legal Conceptions*, New Haven: Yale University Press.

[8] See Andrew J. Galambos, *The Theory of Volition*, 1. Reference from Evan R. Soulé, Jr., 'What Is Volitional Science?' Available at www.tuspco.com (last accessed on 5 May 2006).

[9] Ayn Rand elevated patents over mere property rights in tangible goods. In her opinion 'patents are the heart and core of property rights'. Ayn Rand, 1967, pp. 69-71.

and irregular social process. Knowledge and the capabilities arising thereof are constituted both socially and culturally. They emerge out of a process of social interaction and are essentially products of encounter and fusion of horizons. They must therefore, be looked at relationally. The creation of an idea has an unmistakable social and historical component. Invention, writing, and thought do not happen in a vacuum. Edwin Hettinger argues that 'intellectual activity is not creation *ex nihilo*.'[10] Ideas, knowledge, and thoughts of a person are crucially dependent on ideas and thoughts of the preceding generation. Ideas are therefore fundamentally intergenerational with a social component. Thus, even if we assume that the value of a product is entirely the product of human labour, this value is not attributable to any person or a group of persons who have ostensibly lent their labour to the product. Separating the inventor from this social and historical component is not easy. Hence if we assume that the labourer is entitled to a market value of the resultant product then this market value ought to be shared by all contributors to the resultant product. The fact that most contributors may not be identifiable or even present is no reason why the entire market value should accrue to the last contributor.[11] To what extent individual labourers should be allowed to receive the market value of their products is a question of social policy, and not a natural rights claim to self created product.

A characteristic of intellectual objects is that the same knowledge can be used and possessed concurrently by many people, without diminishing or hindering personal use. In the past, when one bought rice one could eat it, throw it, or plant it to generate a rice crop. One could use the 'idea' of rice embodied in it to develop better rice varieties without excluding others of a similar right. Current law and the IPR regime allow producers of genetically modified seeds and plant varieties to take this freedom. A person's right to prohibit and exclude others from using it can be only justified on grounds that it is necessary for this person's own unhindered use. No such justification is available for exclusive possession and use of intellectual property. The concurrent or simultaneous use of an idea by more than one person does not inflict any limitation on any person. In fact, an attempt to prevent free use of ideas restricts the unhindered use of ideas by other persons who possess them. It infringes upon their rights of freedom of thought and expression. The fundamental value that our society places on freedom of thought and expression creates a

[10] Edwin C. Hettinger, 1989, 'Justifying Intellectual Property', *Philosophy and Public Affairs*, 18(1).
[11] Ibid., p. 38.

difficulty for the justification of intellectual property. It may be argued that the person who originated the information deserves ownership rights over it. However, information is not a concrete thing an individual can control; it is universal, existing in other people's minds and other people's property, and over these the originator has no legitimate sovereignty. One cannot own information without owning other people or curtailing the ownership of other people.

Intellectual property is built around a fundamental tension: ideas are non-exclusive, non-separable but creators want private returns for their use. To overcome this tension, a distinction developed between ideas and their expression. Ideas could not be patented or copyrighted but their expression could. This peculiar distinction was tied to the idealized notion of the autonomous creator who somehow contributes to the common pool of ideas without drawing from it. This package of concepts apparently justified authors in claiming residual rights—namely patents and copyright—in their ideas after leaving their hands, while not giving manual workers any rationale for claiming residual rights in their creations.[12]

An essential feature of IPRs is that intellectual agents must use natural and tangible resources to create patentable expressions of an idea. Munzer counts materiality as an essential feature of intellectual property. Property must, at some point, involve material objects.[13] The qualification, 'at some point', is crucial. This feature does not mandate that all property be material or that all property rights be in material things. However, what this feature does assert is that at some stage property in intangibles has to manifest itself in material or physical objects. At some stage the IPRs, for example, will involve the claim for ownership of a patented machine or process. Also the power to exclude would not be effective unless there could be rules pertaining to physical manifestations of tangible things. Self-ownership therefore, on its own, has no substantive implications. It is only when combined with assumptions about how the physical world is owned (and the consequences of violating those property rights) that substantive implications follow. Self-owned labour, when deployed in the physical world, yields IPRs in the tangible component that labour produces. The worker is said to deserve, as a reward, the physical object that results from his labour. Underlying the theory of intellectual property and emanating from the principle of self ownership is the principle of desert.

---

[12] James Boyle, 1996, *Shamans, Software, and Spleens: Law and the Social Construction of the Information Economy*, Cambridge, MA: Harvard University Press.
[13] S. Munzer, 1990, p. 72.

INTELLECTUAL PROPERTY RIGHTS AND
THE PRINCIPLE OF DESERT

Another major argument for property is based on the desert-labour principle. Here labour means the exercise of effort in order to make or physically appropriate something. Desert means worthiness of some compensation because of the labour exerted or undertaken. The argument is that people deserve property rights because they employ their self-owned labour. This brings up the general issue of what people deserve, a topic that has been analysed and debated at length by philosophers. Most contemporary proposals for desert-bases fit into one of three broad categories:[14]

1. Producitivity: People should be rewarded for their work activity with the product of their labour or a value thereof.[15]
2. Effort: People should be rewarded according to the effort they expend in contributing to a social product.[16]
3. Compensation: People should be rewarded according to the costs they incur in their work activity.[17]

It is commonly argued that a fitting reward for labour should be proportionate to the person's effort, the risks taken, and moral considerations. Hettinger argues that while this may sound all right, it is important to note that in effect the labour reward is proportionate to the value of the results of the labour, assessed through markets or by other criteria.[18] In other words, the value of intellectual work is affected by things not controlled by the worker—market, luck, and natural talent. Hettinger contends that a person who is born with extraordinary natural talents, or who is extremely lucky, deserves nothing on the basis of these characteristics.[19] Rawls and Dworkin both lay emphasis on the arbitrary

[14] The following three categories have been drawn from Julian Lamont, 2004, 'Distributive Justice', in *Handbook of Political Theory*, Gerald F. Gaus and Chandran Kukathas (eds), New Arizona University: Sage, p. 228.

[15] David Miller, 1989, *Market, State, and Community,* Oxford: Clarendon Press; Jonathan Riley, 1989, 'Justice Under Capitalism', in *Markets and Justice*; John W. Chapman (ed.), New York: New York University Press, pp. 122–162; See also, Julian Lamont, 1994, 'The Concept of Desert in Distributive Justice', *The Philosophical Quarterly*, vol. 44, pp. 45–64.

[16] Wojciech Sadurski, 1985, *Giving Desert Its Due,* Dordrecht, Holland: D. Reidel, pp. 221–58.

[17] Joel Feinberg, 1970, *Doing and Deserving: Essays in Theory of Responsibility,* Princeton, NJ, Princeton University Press, pp. 55–94.

[18] Edwin C. Hettinger, 1989, 'Justifying Intellectual Property', *Philosophy and Public Affairs,* 18(1), pp. 31–52.

[19] Ibid. p. 42.

nature of natural talents and deny that each person should be the sole owner of his talents. They refute the claim that a person should have all the rights to differential income due to his productive skills and talents. At the core of Rawls' argument is that distribution of traits, skills, or talents is morally arbitrary. Natural talents, like social circumstances, are matters of brute luck, and people's moral claims should not depend on brute luck. From a moral standpoint the two seem equally arbitrary.[20] A musical genius like Mozart may make enormous contributions to society. But being born with enormous musical talents does not provide a justification for owning rights to musical compositions or performances. Taking the argument further, what about a situation where one person works hard at a task and a second person with less talent works harder? Which of the two workers deserve more reward? Property rights do not provide a suitable mechanism for allocating rewards. The market can give great rewards to the person who successfully claims property rights for a discovery, with little or nothing for the person who just misses out.

The root idea of a labour-desert principle is, as Becker argues, a poor choice as a fundamental principle for yielding property rights. The obvious covering principle is that the worker deserves something for his labour. Becker calls this 'recipient rights'.[21] A bearer of such a right is entitled to some reward for their creativity, but it is problematic to determine the form of this reward and specifically identify the duty-bearers. In this case, the right bearer is entitled to some reward because creation of a certain amount of intellectual property is necessary to reach maximal social utility, and an incentive system is a requisite means in attaining this end. The principle of desert may in some cases justify recognizing a property right in the thing laboured on. In other cases it may not; it could simply be fee for the labour or even simply recognition, admiration, and gratitude of the people.[22]

The ambiguity and the contested nature of IPRs illustrates the point that all exercise of labour cannot be expected to yield property rights. It is a matter of debate whether people should have property in their ideas in the from of patents and copyrights. It is also generally agreed that patents and copyrights should lapse after a period of time, while ownership of land would not be expected to. All expenditure of labour therefore need not unequivocally lead to a property claim. Labour, as Becker argues, is a

---

[20] John Rawls, 1971, pp. 74–5.
[21] Lawrence C. Becker, 1977, pp. 14–15.
[22] Ibid., p. 47.

necessary condition for property but not a sufficient one.[23] All one can claim for expenditure of labour is compensation, which is to say that one deserves 'something'. Whether property is the only form of desert for labour is a matter of debate. The labour argument gives no unequivocal grounds for private ownership of the things produced unless there is no substitute for it acceptable in terms of the goals of labour. Labour theory, to use Becker's thesis, therefore does not provide sufficient justification for private ownership of things produced. Granting property rights does not emerge as an implied corollary of desert of the innovator.

A qualified justification for property rights founded on desert by labour (is the one provided by Stephen Munzer), preempts some of the objections to the desert theory by imposing two restrictions. In his theory, desert based on labour is still the anchor of *prima facie* moral property rights.[24] He however, combines the labour-desert principle with the effects that property rights might generate for society and qualifies it compendiously by restrictions:

1) If everyone has a right to life, and if workers have a duty not to waste, spoil, or accumulate beyond their needs, then their rights in the products of their labour are qualified.
2) Property rights are justifiable only if the net effect on others during the process of acquisition is justifiable.[25]

The restrictions imposed by Munzer turns a highly individualistic desert of the initial labour theory into a socially qualified desert. A salient feature of his revised labour theory is a concern with the consequences of the exercise of 'liberty' and 'rights' on others. 'Similarly the full social context that gives rise to the labour-desert principle attends to the impact of work and worker on others'.[26]

Labour desert principle therefore, by itself, may not be sufficient ground for property rights claim, specifically for intellectual property rights claim. They have to be judged for the effects that they generate for other people and their rights, an analysis of which has been undertaken in Chapters 6, 7, and 8 of this study. It suffices to state here that as a stand-alone conception it does not yield sufficient grounds for intellectual property claim. The principle of desert is totally inapplicable in cases where gains are gotten by violating or unjustifiably overriding the claims

[23] Ibid., p. 52.
[24] Stephen Munzer 1998, p. 283.
[25] Ibid., for a full summary see p. 284.
[26] Ibid., p. 288.

and rights of others. If intellectual property regime grants property rights to the 'first knower', it thereby reduces total opportunities or welfare and disadvantages the rest of the players.

Patent monopoly 'consists in protecting inventors against competition for a period long enough to extort from the people a reward enormously in excess of the labour measure of their services, in other words, in giving certain people a right of property for a term of years in laws and facts of Nature,' and the power to exact tribute from others for the use of this natural wealth, which should be open to all.[27] The fact that the exercise of IPRs severely diminishes and curtails the similar exercise of these rights by others, the fact that these rights are not 'compossible' makes intellectual property rights, as a claim right, (in the Hohfeldian sense) difficult to fit into a socially or individually qualified desert.[28]

The self-owning labourer, who can claim compensation for the product he has created, cannot morally claim IPRs especially (in the form of patents), over his intellectual property for two reasons. First, because the IP claimed by the labourer has the potential to deny another of his right to self-ownership. To enforce patent laws and the like is to prevent people from making peaceful use of the ideas and information they possess. Private intellectual property restricts the methods of acquiring ideas, the use of ideas, and the expression of ideas. These restrictions militate against the very notion of individual autonomy that IPRs set out to protect. IPRs are difficult to fit into any system of compossible rights, owing to their tendency to conflict with other's rights (the rights of the non patent holders) and other rights in the system (for instance, rights of subsistence, livelihood, community knowledge rights, etc.).

KNOWLEDGE RIGHTS AS CONTROL SELF-OWNERSHIP
Self-ownership, like private ownership in general, is a bundle of rights that can vary in strength. Full self-ownership involves a maximal set of property rights over oneself comparable to the maximal set involved in the private ownership of tangible objects. Partial forms of self-ownership

[27] Benjamin Tucker, 1893, *Instead of a Book, By a Man Too Busy to Write One: A Fragmentary Exposition of Philosophical Anarchism,* New York: Tucker, p. 13.

[28] According to Hohfeld, the existence of a claim right in one person entails the existence of duty in another. A duty may be defined as an act of forbearance and should the act (of forbearance) not be done, it would be legal for the right holder to use coercive measures and/or demand compensation. The Hohfeldian 'claim' is different from a moral claim—farmers have a claim to affordable, unprotected seeds; people have a claim to clean environment; the poor have a claim to welfare measures by the government—these claims emerge out of deprivation, neglect, exclusion, and demand inclusion.

leave out some of these rights. Ownership is commonly conceived as a bundle of rights, liberties, powers, immunities, and so on. A.M. Honoré, in his influential essay on this subject, lists no fewer than eleven 'standard incidents' or constituent elements of ownership.[29] Some of these incidents however, are more essential than others and are in, Honoré words, 'cardinal features': 'no doubt the concentration in the same person of the right...of using as one wishes, the right to exclude others, the power of alienating and an immunity from expropriation is a cardinal feature of the institution [of ownership].'[30] As applied to the ownership of the *self*, this conception yields a version of self-ownership that has been called 'control self-ownership'.

At the core of self-ownership is control self-ownership, the right to control the use of one's person (but not necessarily any right to transfer this right to others). Something like control self-ownership is arguably needed to account for the fact there are some things (for example, various forms of physical contact) that may not be done to a person without his/her consent. Full-self ownership is sometimes thought to guarantee that the agent has a certain basic liberty of action, but this is not so. If the rest of the world (natural resources and artefacts) is fully owned by others, one is not permitted to do anything, without their consent (since it involves the use of their property). The protection that self-ownership affords is a basic protection against others doing certain things to one, and not a guarantee of liberty.

It is often supposed that full self-ownership gives one property rights in ones' products, but this is so only if the products are part of oneself (for instance, an improvement in one's ability to do mental arithmetic). Any product that involves natural resources involves materials that may belong to others, and a person who makes something from materials owned by others may not legitimately own the product. It depends on how the rest of the world is owned. If the rest of world is owned by others, then anything one does without their consent violates their property rights, and as a result of such violations, one may lose some or all of one's rights of self-ownership.

In this chapter, I have tried to reconstitute the debate with regard to IPRs in terms of the distinction between 'control rights' and 'income rights', borrowing from John Christman's unbundling of self-owned rights, which asserts that while self ownership may lead to control rights

---

[29] A.M. Honoré, 1961, pp. 108–34.
[30] Ibid., p. 113.

in intellectual property, it would not lead to income rights which forms the crux of the operations and conflicts with regard to IPRs. Honore's discussion of the incidents of ownership is used here to divide the concept of self ownership into two major classes that require separate justifications. Control self ownership is the right to decide what you will do; it has to do with your autonomy and volition. Income self ownership is the right to the income you are capable of securing by selling your abilities. Using Christman's construction I argue that control self-ownership is part of the core of human liberty and self-determination, but that income self ownership is not. These are the four incidents of ownership—the rights of use and exclusion, the power of transfer, and immunity from expropriation—that can be termed as 'control incidents' or, more loosely, 'control rights'.[31] To have control rights over an object is to possess final authority regarding the disposition of that object and to be free from interference in the exercise of that authority unless of course, the rights of others are being threatened. It is in effect to enjoy a kind of sovereignty over the owned object vis-à-vis other citizens. Another way of expressing this is to say that the owner has, with respect to a material object, the 'primary functional control'[32] which is the 'right to use, possess, manage, modify, alienate, and destroy'. Control self-ownership consists of the rights of use and exclusion, the power of transfer, and an immunity from expropriation with respect to one's own body and labour power, with these incidents being held permanently and *in rem* (that is, against the world). They are 'aspects of the person's independent powers over the thing owned; that is 'these rights are not conditional on the consent of others, except perhaps the recipient to

---

[31] Control Self Ownership is arguably the complete liberal conception of self-ownership. The concept is either explicitly or implicitly endorsed by John Christman, James Grünebaum, Andrew Kernohan, and Ronald Dworkin, and by John Rawls himself. See, John Christman, 'Self-Ownership, Equality, and the Structure of Property Rights', p. 39; James Grünebaum, 1987, *Private Ownership*, London: Routledge & Kegan Paul, p. 171; Andrew Kernohan, 1990, 'Rawls and the Collective Ownership of Natural Abilities', *Canadian Journal of Philosophy*, vol. 20, pp. 19–28; Ronald Dworkin, 1983, 'In Defense of Equality', *Social Philosophy and Policy*, vol. 1, pp. 24–40; John Rawls, 1987, 'The Basic Liberties and Their Priority', in S.M. McMurrin (ed.), *Liberty, Equality and the Law: Selected Tanner Lectures on Moral Philosophy*, Salt Lake City: University of Utah Press, p. 50. Rawls's endorsement is the most oblique. In discussing 'freedom of the person'. He argues that it would be 'violated, for example, by slavery and serfdom, and by the denial of freedom of movement and occupation' He seems to be concerned here primarily with an individual's control rights over his own person.

[32] John Christman, 1994, *The Myth of Property: Toward an Egalitarian Theory of Ownership*, New York: Oxford University Press, pp. 125, 146.

whom one alienates something or any other persons with whom one wants to use one's property.'[33]

Income rights, or the right to income from assets, forms another class of property right. It is, for example, income which is derived from the sale of a thing or from the income by way of interests and dividends on shares and trusts, or from patent royalties, which accrues to the holder of the intellectual property by virtue of transfer of 'use' rights. The right to income is therefore, as Christman states, contingent on two things: one, that it is an increased income accruing from a holding by virtue of the productive use of that holding, involving most centrally, trade; two, that it is contingent on the prevalent institutions, systems, and market conditions. It is adapted from or dependent on prevalent price systems, systems of remuneration, and trading laws which will determine the income right that emanate from a particular holding. Therefore, there is nothing inherent in the structure of property rights that implies that income rights are an inferred and a moral outcome of the principle of self ownership. Income rights do not inhere in a person but in the state or some other entity that devises the terms of transfer.[34]

An alternative approach to defining a right to income is to think about this right as being a direct implication of a seller's power of transfer. After all, if the seller has the power to transfer a product, service, or factor to a buyer then does he not, as a necessary consequence, have a right to the fruit of that transfer, that is, to the price (income) paid by the buyer? Robert Taylor argues that 'the answer, somewhat surprisingly, is no'.[35] The price that a seller receives in an economic exchange is, strictly speaking, independent of his power of transfer; rather, it is dependent on the *buyer's* power of transfer. The seller's right to income is directly implied by the buyer's power of monetary transfer. In other words, all that a seller needs, to have a secure right to the income from the sale of some item is the protection of the power of potential buyers to transfer money to him.

Control Self-Ownership constitutes the core of the libertarian conception of self-ownership. It has a host of radical implications for

---

[33] Christman, 1991, p. 29. Such a view of property is also supported by Brenkert, who defines ownership of property as a 'purely instrumental relation' between an individual and material objects. To own something is here 'to have the rights to sell, use, control, manage or even destroy what one owns'. George G. Brenkert, 1998, 'Self-Ownership, Freedom, and Autonomy', *Journal of Ethics*, No. 2, p. 50.

[34] Christman, 1991, p. 29.

[35] Robert S. Taylor, 2005, 'Self-Ownership and the limits of Libertarianism', *Social Theory and Practice*, vol. 314, p. 469.

personal liberty issues, implications that are decidedly libertarian in flavor. Control rights can be justified through a reference to 'individualist interests' such as liberty, autonomy, and self-determination. The source of justification for income rights, however, will necessarily be principles that govern the pattern of distribution of goods in the economy, consideration which are not reducible to individual interests.[36] Drawing on Mill's reference to 'self-regarding' and 'other regarding' activities, it can be argued that private transactions of property, that is, self-regarding acts, can be defended on grounds of self-ownership and hence protection of individual liberty, but a public sale of a thing for profit or trade is a social act which affects the interests of other persons and of society in general.[37] The grounds on which personal consumption and control of a resource must be justified are significantly different from those that are needed to justify income rights from trade. Jeremy Waldron's rightfully asserts that 'there is no sense to the idea that there is a natural phenomenon called "reaping the benefits of one's talents" which is understood apart from the social arrangements and institutions that define one's relationships to other people'.[38]

Christman's distinctions between control rights and income rights have important implications for our analysis of IPRs. First, he argues that control rights need not be 'distribution specific'. An agent's right to control property is essentially a manifestation of his free will, a function of his preferences and can be specified without reference to the distribution of resources, or to prevailing political and social structures. On the other hand, the value of income rights is purely conditional on the contingencies of the market sector, in particular other's endowments.[39] For example, the potential income that a patent holder can draw is based on several market and market related factors: the absence or presence of other traders and their bargaining capacities; the terms of trade available to the patent holder and to their competitors or transacting partners; the presence of obstacles, barriers, and costs, etc. Favourable trades are a function of the terms of trade, barriers and costs faced by other actors participating in the market. The structure of income rights recognized in an economy serves to distribute the surplus generated through trading activities. It follows therefore that income rights are directly tied to the distribution

---

[36] Christman, 1991, p. 30.

[37] J.S. Mill, 1975 [1859], *On Liberty*, David Spitz (ed.), New York: Norton.

[38] Jeremy Waldron, 1990, *The Right to Private Property*, New York: Oxford University Press, p. 404.

[39] Christman, 1991, p. 40.

of resources both by the fact that they determine the direction of the resource flows (who gets what) and that they presuppose and reinforce the distribution already in place.

Income rights are conditional in another way. To have control rights is to imply that others have a duty not to interfere with my possessions and use of the resource. This element of ownership can be understood to be held in rem. However income rights cannot be considered as a right held in rem. Although the sale of a commodity yields an income, over which the seller has exclusive rights, no one has a duty to supply him with an income. He might have the commodity for sale but nobody has a duty to buy it; nobody need buy it if he does not want to. The seller does not have a claim against anyone in such a situation. It is thus not an unconditional right but a contingent right, contingent upon: a) the presence of rules that govern exchange and b) stable rules of cooperation. This is not the case with control rights where the consumption of my property is independent of others. 'In this way the right to possess and manage are a direct extension of the self control expressed by the liberty or autonomy of the agent…Rights to income, on the other hand, imply not only self-control, but "other control" in that my enjoyment of these rights depends on the actions of others…'[40]

Autonomy, as implied by the powerful principle of self ownership is only preserved through granting 'control rights' of property, limited to a quantity sufficient for 'autonomous living'. In the final analysis, individuals have a right to exercise their talents freely but not to retain a profit from the use of those talents.[41]

It is possible therefore to have a much narrower conception of self-ownership than the libertarian one. It is also possible to retain a narrower conception of self ownership—one which protects autonomy—and dispense with the full self-ownership which has implications for rights and autonomy of others. Property rights can be unbundled and 'income rights', that is, rights to profits can be not only conceptually but also legally separated from 'control rights' and that these 'income rights' should not or need not be privately owned in order to satisfy moral requirements of autonomy.

A variety of potential incidents of ownership have been referred to in this section including the rights of use, exclusion, income, the power of transfer, and immunity from expropriation. It is important to note that

---

[40] Christman, 1991, p. 34.
[41] Ibid., p. 40.

the right to income is the odd one out: the right of use, the power of transfer, and an immunity from expropriation form a coherent grouping with the right of exclusion (which serves a justificatory role for them), while the right to income stands apart due to its derivation from an entirely different source—namely, the monetary transfer powers of other people. This separation of control rights and a right to income can be implicitly exploited in the context of the ongoing debate to argue that IPRs belong to the domain of income rights and therefore lack the moral force that self-ownership as a principle assumes. Talents are fully and individually owned with respect to decision-making (control rights), but the associated income rights that accrue to an individual or corporation as rent, loyalities, licensing fees, profits and such like, are not. They are governed by political and market forces and therefore are not extension of rights emanating from self-ownership.

What initially appears to be a good match between property and self ownership falters in its implications when self-ownership is unbundled into control rights and income rights. The simplest possible justification for self ownership—and the one that probably motivates its adherents—is a desire to protect individual autonomy and, more narrowly, the inviolability of the person. This chapter seeks to argue that control rights protect the domain of the liberty and autonomy of intellectual-labour expending individual but income rights that TRIPS guarantee are actually violative of others' control rights. The specific motivation behind self-ownership involves the strong interest that a person has in running his own life; an individual's rights to control himself; to no intervention in use of one's talents. The principle of self ownership does not therefore lend itself to the currently used form of IPRs which are a form of monopoly rights, granted to protect a domain of exclusive use and transfer to the exclusion of others who might want to exercise their self-owned rights. Self-ownership not only fails to provide a basis for IPRs but actually can be pressed into service to argue that IPRs are violative of self-ownership rights of those outside the domain of intellectual property protection.

Critique of the Lockean Reading

This chapter argues that intellectual property rights fail where tangible property rights succeed. This failure occurs because Lockean theory which protects the institution of tangible property fails to defend the premises of IPRs in the same way. Any recognisance of justificatory premises of property, usually begins with Locke for the simple reason that he constructed a defence of property on libertarian premises but added, what seemed to be, an egalitarian 'proviso' in the state of nature. The more egalitarian its purpose in the state of nature, the less it would seem able to justify unequal property rights under conditions of scarcity. Locke examines the natural law justifications for property in one's own person and in tangible objects. He moves from self-ownership to absolute rights in the appropriation of the commons, with a proviso that 'enough and as good' should be left for the others. Variously interpreted, as an 'egalitarian condition' to a 'Paretian optimal condition' one can assume it means that unrestricted appropriation of the natural world is a natural right of the self-owners provided nobody is left worse off. The underlying rationale of Locke's proviso is that if no one's situation is worsened, then no one can complain about another individual appropriating part of the commons. It is thus a Lockean way of testing the legitimacy of a property system.

The principle of self-ownership is a difficult point to negotiate for the egalitarians. While they cannot deny the moral force of the principle they also do realize that an application of the principle to differential skills and talents in society will eventually lead to vast material inequalities. Two largely egalitarian perspectives respond to the principle differently. While left libertarians like Rawls and Dworkin deny the principle of self-ownership in order to combat the moral arbitrariness of differential skills,[42] and recommend public ownership of skills, theorists like Christman and Taylor try to resolve the impasse between self-ownership and equality by making the outcome of property rights more egalitarian, even while retaining the principle of self-ownership.[43] Hillel Steiner and Peter Vallentyre start from the premise of self-ownership but recognise the difficulties in justifying unequal appropriation of the initially unowned world and so accept nationalization and equalization of natural resources, or compensation for those left propertyless.[44]

So far the principle of self-ownership has been retained to see if it yields claim rights in intellectual property. The attempt here is to see (while retaining the principle of self ownership in the Lockean vein), whether the appropriation sanctioned by IPRs stands the test of the Lockean 'proviso'. Intuitively, stealing a car seems to be a bigger crime than copying expensive software without paying for it. The reason perhaps lies in the distinction

[42] John Rawls, 1971, p. 89. Ronald Dworkin, 2002, *Sovereign Virtue: The Theory and Practice of Equality*, Cambridge: Harvard University Press, p. 73.

[43] Christman, 1991; Robert S. Taylor, 2005, 'Self-Ownership and the Limits of Left Libertarianism', *Social Theory and Practice*, 31(4), October.

[44] Peter Vallentyre and Hillel Steiner (eds), 2000, *Left Libertarianism and its Critics: The Contemporary Debate*, London: Palgrave; Hillel Steiner 1994, *An Essay on Rights*, Oxford: Blackwell Publishers.

drawn earlier between real property (tangibles) and intangible property (ideas). A's use of her intellectual property does not interfere with B's or others' use of it; This is not the case with tangible goods. A's stealing of B's software still allows B's unhindered use of her software; however A's stealing B's car would prevent B's use of it. Justifying or critiquing intellectual property in light of this feature raises deep questions about 'self-ownership', 'labour mixing', and the rights emanating from them and therefore makes a Lockean reading of intellectual property rights imperative, even though the dilemmas posed by Locke have led many to abandon a philosophical reading of intellectual property rights through Locke in favour of incentive based utilitarian theories.

In one respect the intangible nature of intellectual property makes the Lockean case for recognizing it stronger than the case for recognizing physical property. Lockean philosophy has trouble with a world in which natural resources are scarce and not unlimited. Locke recognized that the moral claim for absolute property rights is limited by the situation in which there is 'enough and as good' of the natural resources left for others to mix their labour with and appropriate. Subsistence of mankind was conditioned on the availability of sufficient resources left for the non-appropriators to mix their labour with. Obviously, this is not a problem for intellectual property. 'The physical resources used to create it are not limited in any meaningful sense—there is no shortage of paper and ink, and much of the raw material of intellectual property is itself intellectual property, such as alphabets and systems of musical notation.'[45] Thus the enough-and-as-good dilemma does not exist. The realm of ideas and knowledge is not limited in the same way as the world of physical resources.

Intellectual works are 'non-rivalrous', they can be used concurrently by many individuals at the same time and cannot be destroyed. The original acquisition of intellectual property does not necessitate a loss for others. In fact such acquisitions benefit everyone.[46] Second, the frontier of intellectual property is practically infinite. It is only in a situation of scarcity or potential scarcity that the dilemma of 'enough and as good' can possibly hold. Not only does intellectual property not entail a loss for others, but the creation of intellectual property may bring about greater wealth and opportunities for the rest, compensating for any loss of opportunities that may have arisen. This, as argued forcefully by

[45] James de Long, *Defending Intellectual Property*, vol. 28. Available at http://www.pff.org/issues-pubs/books/020701defendingip.pdf (last accessed on 25 October 2008).

[46] Adam Moore, 'Towards a Lockean Theory of Intellectual Property', in Adam D. Moore (ed.), p. 86.

Adam Moore, takes care of the Lockean proviso and therefore provides a Lockean defence for IPRs. The underlying rationale of Locke's proviso is that if no one's situation is worsened, then no one can complain about another individual appropriating part of the commons. Adam Moore terms it as 'weak Pareto superiority', which permits individuals to better themselves so long as no one is worsened.[47] This 'no harms no foul' principle for Moore is a plausible moral principle which leaves 'little room for rational complaint'.[48] The structure of Moore's argument is as follows:

1. If the acquisition of an intangible work satisfies a Paretian based proviso, then the acquisition and exclusion are justified.
2. Some acts of intangible property creation and possession satisfy a Paretian based proviso.
3. So, some intangible property rights are justified.[49]

In the broadest terms, Moore's goal is to justify rights to intellectual and intangible property, both at the level of acts and at the level of institutions. At both levels his argument is based on the two features of intellectual property—it is non-rivalrous and infinite characters. He argues that intellectual property rights are not state created entities—they are prior to and independent of governments and social progress; in a sense he gives them the status of natural rights.[50] Its non-rivalrous and infinite character ensures that the Lockean proviso is not violated; 'enough and as good' is still left for the rest of the humanity.

It is clear, as James W. Child argues, that Locke's concern with appropriation of property in the state of nature is not egalitarian but Paretian.[51] If for instance, A is the appropriator and B a non-appropriating individual, Locke could not have meant by 'enough', that an equal amount is left for B (and for the rest of humanity) after A has appropriated. The question rather is—is B better off or same after A appropriates, or does A's appropriation make B worse off? So long as latter is not the case, Locke's

[47] Adam Moore, 1997, p. 85.

[48] Adam D. Moore, 2004, *Intellectual Property and Information Control,* Transaction Publishers: New Jersey, p. 114.

[49] Ibid.

[50] Moore discards the utilitarian defence of intellectual property which tries to argue the case because it provides incentives necessary for social progress—society ought to maximize social utility, therefore rights to intellectual works should be granted.

[51] James W. Child, 1997, 'The Moral Foundations of Tangible Property', in *Intellectual Property: Moral Legal and International Dilemmas,* Adam D. Moore (ed.), New York: Rowman and Littlefield, pp. 57–69.

proviso is taken care of. Locke is not concerned with the question—does B have as much as A? Transposing the argument to the realm of ideas and intellectual property: Ownership of a particular idea as such does not preclude others' ownership or use of that idea. It is not to say that there are fewer ideas out there that one can now think of and use. All forms of 'knowledge ownership' share the characteristic that while one can exclude another from using one's property there is not thereby a smaller amount upon which others can draw upon to use or own. 'Moreover as with Locke's real property in the state of nature, you have only to mix your labour with it (here, the mental labour) to appropriate it. It is otherwise free, as it should be, if there is an inexhaustible supply presently unclaimed.'[52] Since there are an infinite number of new ideas that can be thought of and appropriated, a zero-sum condition is not met in the case of patented ideas. According to Child, you are not deprived as long as you remain able and willing to exert mental labour.[53]

An altered interpretation of the Lockean proviso will however yield different conclusions. If ownership of ideas is to yield not just control rights—which would give someone the right to employ his mental labour to create a product, exclude others from its use, and sell the product at a price that it can command in the market—but monopoly income rights for a specified period (as does the current intellectual property regime) then the Lockean proviso may leave people worse off and fulfil Paretian optimality. If the crucial point is whether IPRs and the appropriations worsen the position of others, Ingram inquires, why should we assume a Nozikian premise (of the Lockean proviso), and restrict the range of comparison to conditions before and after a given appropriation?[54] G.A. Cohen forcefully maintains that any appropriation will make someone worse off for the reason that no one will be able to appropriate the already appropriated item. 'It is clear beyond doubt that an appropriation of private property can contradict an individual's will just as much as levying a tax on him can.'[55] If contradicting one's will is the criterion for a theory that is supposed to be based on liberty, then according to Cohen, no private appropriation could meet the requirements of a suitably formulated Nozikian proviso. As Cohen argues, 'Nozick disallows objectively paternalist use of people's private property. But he permits objectively paternalist treatment of people in other ways. For, since he

[52] Ibid., p. 69.
[53] Ibid.
[54] Ingram Attracta, 1994, p. 58.
[55] G.A. Cohen, 1995, p. 90.

permits appropriations that satisfy nothing but his proviso, he allows A to appropriate against B's will when B benefits as a result, or, rather, as long as B does not lose.'[56] According to Cohen, B does not seek a 'not-worse-than-before' situation for himself. He seeks an improvement in his assets. As long as any appropriation prevents him from potentially improving his assets, he is rendered 'worse off' in the Lockean sense.

Why is there an assessment of who is rendered worse off only against Paretian optimality? Each of us can be left worse off than we would be under a different selection. Besides, even if a person is not rendered worse off, how does this compensate for a loss of liberty to freely use a patented idea? Ingram goes a step ahead and argues that even if you were to benefit from a privatization of an object (or an idea), 'how can your loss of that liberty and the consequential risks to your independence in other areas be set against the benefit you enjoy?'[57] Even Nozick's interpretation of the Lockean proviso requires a non-interference with the 'like liberties of others'. For him, 'worsening the position of others' refers specifically to the curtailment of rights. If we were to remove the baseline condition for comparison as before and after the appropriation, then the Lockean proviso, and Nozick's or Moore's interpretation of it, would not be complied with.

But what if we the eschew the Lockean Pareto optimality in favour of Rawls' 'difference principle', which would justify incentives given to highly talented people on grounds that they work to the advantage of the worst off in society? Rawls' principle of justice commits itself to the betterment of the condition of the worst off in society rather than being content with maintaining a situation which is not worse off than before. From the standpoint of the 'difference principle', the talented in society ought to be rewarded in the form of incentives if they work towards the betterment of the worst-off. If research scientists work better with incentives and they will only invest in the research of life-saving medicines for instance, if there are incentives in the form of patents, then as per Rawls' 'difference principle' this is justified, for the worst off in the society is better off by having these medicines invented. However, as Cohen argues, there's a superior alternative available to the scientist: let the talented work at this productive employment without demanding, receive the incentive pay.[58] The difference principle would still be adhered

[56] Ibid., p. 89.

[57] Attracta Ingram, 1994, p. 58.

[58] For an elaboration of Cohen's position see, G.A. Cohen, 1995, 'The Pareto Argument for Inequality', *Social Philosophy and Policy*, 12. Also, 2005, *If You're an Egalitarian, How Come You're So Rich?*, Cambridge: Harvard Univ. Press.

to with superior moral returns. Superior because in the earlier case, the worst off were better in one sense—that is through availability of life-saving drugs—but would be worse off in another—that is, in having to pay higher prices for these patented medicines. 'Pay and save yourself' as a maxim does not seem to uphold the difference principle, for there is a superior alternative—'Save yourself without having to pay a premium for it'. Incentives are not needed in a society in which all members of society internalize Rawls' principles such that the difference principle in these circumstances would not justify inequalities via incentives. In a just society, of people with Cohen's 'egalitarian conscience' the difference principle would not justify incentive-based inequalities.

The issue needs to be addressed from yet another angle—one idea and two (or more) claimants to its ownership. What are the moral grounds of adjudication between two rival claims of ownership which have been rendered competitive through the mediation of the IPR regimes? Who is to be legitimately granted rights of appropriation and use, with a right to exclude the other from a claim of ownership? By limiting the frontiers of ownership of ideas, through patents and copyrights, and preventing their concurrent use, one party is made absolutely worse off while the other party is made absolutely better off. Property created in this way, and following Locke's proviso, denies ownership rights to other creators thereby rendering them worse off than they would have been, had they been granted to concurrently use their ownership rights. The 'enough and as good' condition is meant to protect Locke's labour justification from any attacks asserting that property introduces immoral inequalities. This condition is not met with in this instance, thereby rendering a Lockean defence of intellectual property rights problematic. Even if we were to interpret the condition as an 'equal opportunity provision', there is a denial of equal opportunity to exercise the right to own and use that which one's mental labour has created, on grounds that the rights to intellectual property has been claimed, on a 'first-come-first-served' basis, by someone else.[59] Although ideas are theoretically 'available' to people in their own thoughts even though the ideas have already become someone else's property these ideas cannot take the form of tangible expressions. And as pointed out earlier, Intellectual property rights are not so much rights over ideas as rights over their tangible expressions and instantiations.

[59] Justin Hughes, 1997, 'The Philosophy of Intellectual Property', in *Intellectual Property: Moral, Legal and International Dilemmas,* Adam Moore, (ed.), New York: Rowman and Littlefield, p. 114.

It is important to point out that ownership of an idea effectively gives intellectual property owners a property right in *every* physical embodiment of that work or invention. Not only are ideas patented but also the physical expressions and manifestations of it. If *A* patents a particular kind of plough, then it prohibits *B*'s use of it, and constrains *B*'s actions on his own land. If intellectual property is an otherwise legitimate form of property, then the fact that its recognition inhibits uses of other property may present difficult practical problems of defining rights. A fundamental objection arises when *B*, realizing the merits of a plough, decides to design a plough of his own. However, since plough number 1 was patented by *A* it curtails *B*'s right to own and use the product of his labour, the plough, even when it does not interfere with the *A*'s right to own and use his plough. *A*'s ownership of a patent gives him the right to prevent a third party from using or practicing the patented invention, even if the third party only uses his own property. In this way, *A*'s ownership of IPRs gives him some degree of control-ownership over the tangible property of innumerable others. Patent and copyright invariably transfer partial ownership of tangible property from its natural owner to innovators, inventors, and artists. Opponents of intellectual property may say that they fully recognize your right to use the products of your labour, whether these products are physical or mental. However, only in the case of physical property does my ownership right entail or require that others be excluded from using my property. Given that only one person can use physical property, the creator has the superior claim. A normative interpretation of labour theory (as against the instrumental justification of property which believes that we must provide rewards to get labour) says that labour should be rewarded. In the case of intellectual property all creators of an idea can be argued to have an equal claim. I am as much an employer of self-owned labour as you are and therefore, can logically claim equal rights. My ownership of an idea is consistent with your ownership of the same idea for it does not preclude you from your ownership rights. Intellectual property does not share the zero-sum characteristic of 'real property'. The relative positions of parties, with respect to real property are not equal for as one has gained the other has, of necessity, lost.

The intangible nature of intellecual property generates a complex dilemma. On the one hand, the IPR regime could constitute a direct infringement of rights of self-ownership. I may not be able to exercise full ownership rights over that which I have created because it violates some patent claim. Multiple uses are possible for intellectual property, so recognizing that the right of the creator to the fruits of his labour does not require that others be excluded. The labourer, after all, still has his creation undiminished. The creator has lost nothing. If it does indeed violate any rights, (as in case of B, the manufacturer of the second plough in the example above) then it is a violation of the principle of self ownership, so assiduously guarded by the libertarians.[60] The accumulation of property through intellectual labour by one person, in a patent regime, requires the denial of rights, of use and accumulation of property, through the use of the same intellectual labour by another person.

How does one employ Nozick's principle of 'just initial acquisition' to a realm of ideas and knowledge where the frontiers are not limited and where, thereby every idea can be held to be justly acquired? A Nozikian principle of justice in acquisition is an account of how people came to initially own the things or what people create through the exercise of their self-owned powers and what is justly acquired can be freely transferred. My holding the same idea as you does not affect your holding or your right of free transfer. Nozick contends that fidelity to Locke's theory would mandate two limitations on the inventor's entitlements. First, persons who subsequently invented the same device independently must be permitted to make and sell it. Otherwise the assignment of the patent to the first inventor would leave them worse off. Second, for the same reason, patents should not last longer than on average what it would have taken someone else to invent the same device had knowledge of the invention not disabled them from inventing it independently.[61] The current conception of IPRs disallows this. Even on Nozikian grounds, IPRs in their present garb seem troublesome. In fact one can employ the Lockean labour theory to argue that recognizing your dominion over an idea may curtail my self ownership rights, that is, the rights that I exercise over that which my mental labour creates. Recognizing your dominion over an idea can inhibit my use of my physical property or what I could potentially make my property. And this, in no uncertain terms, leaves me worse off than I would or could have been.

SUBSTANTIVE IMPLICATIONS OF SELF-OWNERSHIP

The purpose of this chapter was to re-canvass the defences based on self-ownership, that can be made for intellectual property. The principle of

[60] One of the most famous statements of this view is a quotation from Thomas Jefferson: 'He who receives an idea from me receives instruction himself without lessening mine—as he who lights his taper at mine, receives light without darkening me.'
[61] Robert Nozick, 1974, p. 182.

self-ownership was retained in evaluating the rights claim of IPRs because of its powerful moral appeal. The natural law justifications for property in one's own person is a powerful way of asserting one's autonomy. After all this was the very premise on which slavery was rejected as morally indefensible. The principle of self-ownership is a direct implication of the natural law premise, as has been employed by both Locke and Nozick to justify property rights.

Contemporary theorists like James DeLong, Adam Mossoff, and Adam Moore[62] see a good connection between natural law and intellectual property. An alternative approach to IPRs however, would see a disjunction between the two, and more specifically, between the principle of self-ownership and IP protection. There are many people who think that the current scope of the intellectual property laws sets up intellectual property in opposition to human liberty of speech and expression. Thus, Tom Bell, a devoted natural rights Lockean, writes, rather critically: 'More pointedly, copyright and patent protection contradict Locke's justification of property. By invoking state power, a copyright or patent owner can impose prior restraint, fines, imprisonment, and confiscation on those engaged in peaceful expression and the quiet enjoyment of their tangible property.'[63] There is also a strong undercurrent of discontent about the protection of intellectual property interests among those who purport to treat individual freedom as the highest good.[64]

The yoking together of liberty and property has an obvious appeal for individuals who operate within the classical liberal tradition and view private property in its various manifestations as consistent with a regime of personal liberty (freedom to own and dispose off property being a variant of the freedoms that comprise liberty). Self-ownership as a principle is one that seeks to establish parity between liberty and property. Self-ownership consequently has become one of the abiding principles in libertarian thought. However, the correspondence between

---

[62] James de Long, *Defending Intellectual Property*, available at http://www.pff.org/issues-pub/books/020701defendingip.pdf (last accessed on 9 December 2009); Adam Mossoff, 2001, 'Rethinking the Development of Patents: An Intellectual History, 1550–1800', *Hastings Law Journal*, 52(1255). See also, Adam Moore, 1997, pp. 81–98.

[63] Tom W. Bell, *Indelicate Imbalancing in Copyright and Patent Law*, in Copy Fights. Published Paper. available at http://www.tomwbell.com/writings/Indelicate.pdf (last accessed on 25 January 2008). Some believe the creation of the copyright and patent monopoly is one of the factors that prevents the proportionate return to labour. For an explanation see John Christman, 1988, 'Entrepreneurs, Profits and Deserving Market Shares', *Soc. Phil. & Policy*, vol. 6, p. 1.

[64] The free software and the free copyright models show that there is much that unites the libertarian right with the socialist or libertarian left.

the two is often uneasy. For example, the ostensible parity between liberty and property is difficult to establish when we deal with property in the tangible realm.[65] The doubts about the parity between the two are, if anything, even more insistent in the realm of intellectual property. The project of liberal theory has been, since the time of Locke, to mitigate the inherent tension between liberty and property. While there is an uneasy alliance between the two in the case of tangible property, the notion of IPRs end up placing liberty in opposition to property. There is a basic tension between IPRs and freedom of speech and expression and, to use a Nozikian phrase, 'the like liberties of others'. The foundations of intellectual property law in general are shaky if it is assumed that liberty and autonomy are of a higher order than property or, as in the Rawlsian scheme of things, enjoy a lexical priority over property.

    G.A. Cohen asserts the principle of self-ownership leads to a principle of 'world ownership'. Since the principle of self-ownership, in the case of intellectual property, attaches itself to the manifestations in the material world, the logical implication of self-ownership is private ownership of the material world. Self-ownership and the derivation of rights to external objects from self-ownership are vigorously criticized by G.A. Cohen. He argues that the union of self-ownership and private ownership readily leads to inequality of condition, on any view of what constitutes equality of condition.[66] Such inequality of condition, he alleges, is morally protected by the principle of self-ownership, particularly in its Nozikian reading. Cohen's project is thus to divorce self-ownership from private ownership. Even if one were to concede rights in one's own person, this would not justify what he terms 'capitalist inequality' or inequities in 'world ownership'. World ownership, is not an extension of the principle of self-ownership. Cohen attempts to establish the case for equality of condition by combining private ownership of our internal resources (self-ownership) with public ownership of external, worldly resources (world-ownership). In that case, for Cohen formal self ownership should give way to substantive self-determination that really matter to us.[67]

    [65] Property enjoys an easy alliance with a negative conception of liberty but not with a positive one.

    [66] G.A. Cohen, 1986, 'Self-ownership, World Ownership, and Equality', in *Justice and Equality: Here and Now,* F. Lucash (ed.), Ithaca, NY: Cornell University Press, pp. 108–35; G.A. Cohen, 1995, *Self-Ownership, Freedom, and Equality,* Cambridge: Cambridge University Press.

    [67] G.A. Cohen, 1986, 'Self-Ownership, World-Ownership and Equality: Part 2', *Social Philosophy and Policy,* 3/2, pp. 77–96; For a brief outline of Cohen's position. See, Will Kymlicka, 1990, *Contemporary Political Philosophy: An Introduction,* Oxford: Oxford University

In a world of people with different measures of talent, self-ownership is hostile to autonomy, for, in such a world as Cohen puts it, '… the self-seeking authorized by self-ownership generates propertyless proletarians whose life prospects are too confined for them to enjoy the control of a substantial kind over their lives that answers to the idea of autonomy.'[68] Once we start concerning ourselves with the value that incidents of ownership have for individuals (for instance, in their ability to enhance autonomy), we must eventually face the question of how value is to be distributed across individuals. In this regard, IPRs face a daunting challenge in getting the conception of self-ownership to cohere with a notion of individual autonomy and liberty, as values distributed across individuals.

Press, pp. 103–25, and Alan Haworth, 1994, *Anti-libertarianism: Markets, Philosophy and Myth*, London: Routledge.
    [68] G.A. Cohen, 1997, p. 237.

4 The Utility of Intellectual Property Rights

Human institutions have multiple roots and draw stability from a combination of justifications. A foundational root for the institution of property discussed in the last chapter is the Lockean natural rights framework. A major turning point, however, from a natural rights framework for American institutions of intellectual property came from a court decision in 1834.[1] It distanced American copyright law from natural law perspectives which were very much in evidence at the end of the eighteenth century, and moved towards a more utilitarian justification.[2] Laws related to intellectual property today are premised usually on overtly utilitarian concerns. Utilitarianism holds that utility, by some measure—such as wealth or its corollaries—creation and innovation, human welfare, efficiency, happiness[3]—should be 'maximized', and thus favour legislation that cause certain desired results or consequences to be produced. The utilitarian theory is based on the assumption that such creators would not invest the time or capital necessary to produce such products, if others could copy or reverse engineer them freely. Patents are, it is argued, needed to encourage inventors to invent.

The fundamental utilitarian premise for any property is that ownership creates incentives for productivity. As Alan Ryan states, 'People might garden for fun, or hunt, write symphonies, but eventually they would have to make a living. Giving the producer a property right in the output of his effort, or letting him earn in exchange for producing it is the only sure way to foster these activities, outside of compulsion. Unless individuals

---

[1] *Wheaton v. Peters*, 33 US (8 Pet.) 591, 1834.

[2] See Edward C. Waltercheid, 1995, 'Inherent or created Rights: Early views on IP Clause', *Hamline Law Review*, vol. 19, p. 245.

[3] In translating the Benthamite ideal of the 'greatest good of the greatest number' into a more precise and administrable standard, differing conceptions of utilities make the 'winds of utilitarian augmentation blow in too many directions' (Sher 1975, p. 159). Quoted from Will Kymlicka, 2002, p. 48.

have the right to appropriate, use, transfer, and bequeath objects of value or interest, it would be impossible to use the raw materials provided by nature for anything other than the simplest sort of immediate consumption.'[4] The creation of such rights is therefore dictated by utility.

Property law has long been viewed as serving two main utilitarian purposes: providing incentives for development and preventing the depletion of finite resources. The two rationales overlap, of course, in internalizing the effects of owners' activity. The first rationale, related to scarcity, typically arises in discussions of the 'tragedy of the commons'.[5] Garrett Hardin's recounting of the tragedy of the commons has inspired a search for solutions, the most popular of which is privatization of property. Many utilitarians argue that private ownership of physical goods is justified because of the tragedy of the commons.[6] This line of reasoning argues that possession of things by individuals is superior to individual use of common possessions.[7] It is also believed that systems of private property are more efficient. In order to put any resource to best use, it is optimal to make sure that somebody owns it in the full liberal sense. 'The legal recognition of property has evolved under the impulse of pressures towards efficiency...Property satisfies the need for security, and allows the natural incentive for labour to succeed'.[8] Owners of physical goods are given incentives to succeed. Rights, rules, laws, therefore have to recognize this feature and incorporate it in social policy in order to optimize social utility. The incentive-based rule utilitarian argument for intellectual property is very similar.

Harold Demsetz provides a famous exposition explaining that the right to exclude creates incentives for efficiently utilizing resources and that it internalizes many of the costs of communal ownership, such as transaction

[4] Alan Ryan, 1987, p. 53.

[5] The idea that resources held in common will tragically be depleted by overuse received its most famous elaboration from Professor Garrett Hardin. Hardin's story centers on a pasture open to all, upon which herdsmen let their cattle graze. Herdsmen have an incentive to put as many cattle as possible on the commons because they are able to appropriate the entire gain from the cattle that they add but suffer only a fraction of the loss from overgrazing. The herdsmen therefore add continually more cattle to the commons, leading to the 'destination of ruin.' See, Hardin Garrett, 'The Tragedy of the Commons', *Science* 162 (1968), pp. 1243–8.

[6] For details see, Adam Moore, 2004, p. 42.

[7] Aristotle too remarks that individual ownership creates a more thorough and stable community of interests and beeter promotes efficient, economical, and careful use of things than does common ownership. Aristotle, 1941, *Politics*, Book II, Chapter 5, in *The Basic Works of Aristotle*, Richard McKeon (ed.), New York: Random House, p. 1151.

[8] Alan Ryan, 1987, p. 55.

costs. His 1967 paper argues that the allocation of property rights was a precondition for the efficient functioning of markets.[9] If something is scarce, the best way to ensure that it is put to its most productive use is to assign it to an owner motivated to find this best use. Property rights are a keystone of a complex market system that allocates resources among myriad investment and production possibilities. If society declares that crops belong to the grower but that petroleum belongs to all in common, it will produce too many crops and no oil. If it denies economic returns to intellectual property, it will invest too little in creating it. Property rights are thus important for efficient allocation of resources.

The second rationale involves providing incentives so that people can appropriate the results of their labour. The right to exclude helps create such an incentive by ensuring that 'free riders' cannot enjoy the fruits of labourers' work. Similarly, property creates incentives for development by identifying those who have claims to particular resources and thereby ensuring that they can appropriate the fruits of their efforts to cultivate these resources. Property rights are thus beneficial in two ways, by performing an allocational function and by encouraging production. The production and allocational benefits of property rights together allow for greater marketing and production possibilities including more elaborate coordination of production. The security of holdings alone is likely to free up the resources previously expended on private enforcement costs. Thus the size of the 'social pie' representative of goods and services produced and consumed is likely to increase. In the unlikely event that one or more parties are worse off than they were under the commons, some of the gains from the transition to property rights can in principle be redistributed to the 'losers' to ensure that they are no worse off or are better off than before.

When we say that property serves largely a utilitarian function we often refer to the economic benefits that are derived from the institution rather than other abstract utilities which are important but difficult to measure. Different utilitarians, however, do understand utility differently—for example, as pleasure, happiness, welfare, productive and allocative efficiency, preference satisfaction, and so on. Over time social policy increasingly uses utility to mean economic benefits like efficiency, productivity, optimal allocation of resources, and so on. Broadly it can be reduced to a principle that deals with utility-maximization of greatest number of individuals

---

[9] Harold Demsetz, 1967, 'Toward a Theory of Property Rights', *The American Economic Review*, 57(2), pp. 347–59.

such that the aggregate welfare in society is maximized. Private property, its use, possession and transfer, is expected to foster individual preference satisfaction which in turn will maximize welfare. Utilitarianism, founded by Jeremy Bentham, argues that private property and its corollary, the free market will lead to increased productivity and that it would be maximally efficient at increasing social wealth. Utilitarians, generally, favour the free market, since its efficiency allows for the greatest overall satisfaction of preferences.[10] This is the essence of the common argument for private property provided by the utilitarians.

Utilitarian consequentialism aims to provide a straightforward method for resolving moral questions. Moral rules must be tested for their consequences on human well being. That which maximizes human well-being/utility is a morally right act and morally right actions are those that maximize utility.[11] Utilitarian arguments have a role to play in understanding the moral grounds of property rights. That people will be more productive if they have incentives is a well recognized point. As an empirical matter, there is good reason to believe that when individuals know what their property rights are, they will be more productive and prosperous than if such rights are uncertain. There is an expectation that intellectual property protection would lead to good consequences for the society as a whole has lead to the codification of intellectual property rules and regulations. Utilitarian defense of intellectual property assert that an absence of intellectual property laws, and the protection that it provides for information producers, would seriously harm the potential for knowledge creation and retard innovation and growth. Conversely, the presence of those institutions and legal mechanisms that recognize and

---

[10] The free market is only defensible on utilitarian grounds in so far that it maximizes welfare of the greatest numbers, and this is an empirically contestable issue. If it can be demonstrated that a common or public property system can maximize more welfare than an alternative free market economy then the former becomes justifiable on utilitarian grounds. Since property rights are to be justified in terms of general benefit, there doesn't appear a clear cut case *against* public and common property too, as long as they can be legally and unambiguously defined. Property may be more or less private, or more or less public; the only issue is how to define, legally, the rights of ownership. Many regard a purely utilitarian formula to have sufficiently egalitarian implications. According to them, even if the goal is promotion of welfare, not the promotion of welfare-plus-equality, there are some contingent but pervasive facts about human beings that push in the direction of equal distribution of material resources. For instance see, R.B. Brandt, 1979, *A Theory of the Good and the Right*, Oxford: Oxford University Press.

[11] Utilitarianism here is being treated as philosophy of political morality. In this view utilitarian principles apply to, what Rawls calls, 'the basic structure' of society, and not as a philosophy of hedonism applying to the personal conduct of the individuals.

protect a creator's claim to intellectual activity, would lead to increased incentives for intellectual activity leading to the net aggregation of social and economic welfare.

Institutions of intellectual property are commonly justified on utilitarian grounds. The rationales underlying intellectual property and property overlap to a significant extent. Providing incentives for development is the primary goal of intellectual property and a critical goal of property. The extension of legal protection to intellectual property has been justified by reference to both moral and utilitarian economic arguments, but in countries with a British legal heritage the latter have been the most influential, especially in relation to patents. The utilitarian justification of providing incentives to innovate is the predominant justification for intellectual property, one that is consistent with the Anglo-US constitutions, that courts have recognized, and academic literature has tested. Article 1, Section 8 of the US Constitution, for instance, empowers Congress to: 'To promote the Progress of Science and useful Arts, by securing for limited Times to Authors and Inventors the exclusive Right to their respective Writings and Discoveries'. This incorporates an exclusively instrumental justification for patent legislation. There is no doubt that today, intellectual property protection is regarded by policymakers at both national and international levels primarily as a means of stimulating technological innovation.

Utilitarianism, seemingly, offers a relatively straightforward method for deciding the morally right course of action. First, we identify the various courses of action and choices available to us. Then we identify the foreseeable benefits and harms that would result from each course of action for everyone concerned. In the calculation of harms and benefits, the present costs may often be weighed against the future benefits that are expected to accrue, and the present benefits against future costs. Second, in the assessment of the costs and benefits specific instances of harm may be weighed against the overall benefits that may accrue to the society as a whole. Utilitarianism thus, entails cost-benefit comparison, both spatially and temporally. This may not be possible, desirable or even ethically defensible. How does one compare benefits of biotechnological innovations with the loss of access to seeds for farmers? Are trade-offs possible? Utilitarian calculation requires that we assign values to the benefits and harms resulting from one set of actions and compare them with the benefits and harms that might result from another. Moreover it is important that we compare the benefits of one set of people with the benefits, potential or actual, with that of another set. It compels us to devise terms of commensuration which may not be in accordance with principles of justice. If our moral decisions are to take into account considerations of justice, then apparently utilitarianism cannot be the sole principle guiding our decisions.[12]

INTELLECTUAL PROPERTY RIGHTS AS A RULE UTILITARIAN MODEL

Full rule-consequentialism selects rules solely in terms of the goodness of their consequences and then claims that these rules determine which kinds of acts are morally wrong. George Berkeley, a pioneer rule-consequentialist, wrote, 'In framing the general laws of nature, it is granted we must be entirely guided by the public good of mankind, but not in the ordinary moral actions of our lives. ... The rule is framed with respect to the good of mankind; but our practice must be always shaped immediately by the rule.'[13] There are two central arguments here: (1) Rule-utilitarianism starts from a commitment to consequentialist assessment, and (2) argues that assessing acts *indirectly* for instance, by focusing on the consequences of communal acceptance of rules, will in fact produce better consequences than assessing acts directly in terms of their own consequences.[14] Rule-consequentialism is essentially the conjunction of two claims: (1) that rules are to be selected solely in terms of their consequences and (2) that these rules determine which kinds of acts are morally wrong or right. Actions are therefore tested against rules and not against the consequences. Of course the rules were in the first place formulated against the calculation of consequences.

Rules that govern intellectual property are endorsed by utilitarianism and by other moral theories as well. In the case of intellectual property they are endorsed by the natural law doctrine and to an extent by the Kantian doctrine of private property being an extension of individual will and autonomy. These are premises that give IPRs their initial plausibility. These moral principles specify an underlying unifying principle that provides impartial justification for such rules and lends coherence within our beliefs. Admittedly, coherence with our moral beliefs does not make

[12] *See*, Peter Singer, 1973, *Practical Ethics*, London: Cambridge University Press.

[13] G. Berkeley, 1972, *Passive Obedience, or the Christian Doctrine of Not Resisting the Supreme Power, Proved and Vindicated upon the Principles of the Law of Nature [1712]*, Reprinted in *A Guide to the British Moralists*, D.H. Monro (ed.), London: Fonatana, Section 31, pp. 217–27.

[14] Influential rule-utilitarian writings include R.B. Brandt, 1979; J. Harsanyi, 1977, 'Morality and the Theory of Rational Behaviour', *Social Research*, 44(4); J. Riley, 2000, 'Defending Rule Utilitarianism', in Hooker, Mason, and Miller (eds), *Morality, Rules and Consequences*, Edinburgh: University of Edinburgh, pp. 40–69.

a moral theory *true*, since our moral beliefs might of course be mistaken. Nevertheless, if a moral theory fails significantly to cohere with our moral beliefs, this undermines the theory's ability to be justified to us. Having begun from a commitment to the morally compelling principle of self-ownership, the intellectual property rules are then assessed indirectly, for example, by focusing on the consequences of communal acceptance of intellectual property rules which will, it is argued, produce better consequences than assessing acts directly in terms of their own consequences.[15]

Individual acts of conferring rights to each author are not tested to see if they maximize overall expected utility for everyone. One of the claims of rule-utilitarianism is that it is not possible to test individual acts for their moral validity and therefore rules are necessary in order to represent what are broadly supposed to be acts that will maximize utility. Joan Robinson argues that one of the reasons why rule-utilitarianism is the underlying principle of IPRs is because IPRs are rooted in a contradiction—long term benefits versus short term incentives. There can be no such thing as an ideally beneficial patent system as it is bound to produce negative results in particular instances, impeding progress unnecessarily even if its general effect is favourable on balance.[16] Typically, therefore, the individual acts of patent claims, or the contestations thereof, are evaluated as per the intellectual property rules and laws that govern them. They are not tested against the consequences that they might generate. If the consequences do not benefit the global constituency evenly, as they do not, the rules are either justified against the potential long term good consequences that will be generated, or as Posner says, they are reordered to attain particular ends. [17]

Rule-consequentialism's claim is that bringing about widespread acceptance of a simpler code, even if acceptance of that code does sometimes lead to sub-optimal consequences, has higher expected value in the long run than bringing about widespread acceptance of a much more complicated and demanding code, that is, of assessing individual acts against their consequences (act-utilitarianism). Because rule-consequentialism favours this simpler and less demanding code, it implies that an act can be morally wrong, though that act maximizes expected good, even if it does not conform to the rules which have been laid

---

[15] J. Riley, 2000 and Ibid., pp. 40–69.

[16] Joan Robinson, quoted in Adam Moore, *Intellectual Property and Information Control*, p. 40.

[17] R. Posner, 1986, *The Economics of Justice*, Oxford: Clarendon Press, pp. 48–87.

down. Rule-utilitarianism is based primarily on one assumption, that in order for a society to function, its citizens must all obey a universal set of laws. Therefore, in any situation where the course of action providing the greatest immediate utility runs counter to the law, the law must still be obeyed to achieve the greatest overall utility. The most important interpretation of this allowance is that it permits the establishment of a system of laws and rules whose preservation always takes precedence over utility.

In terms of justification, modern systems of intellectual property are easily modeled as rule-utilitarian.[18] In a typical rule-utilitarian mould it is argued that the adoption of intellectual property systems of trademark, copyrights, patents, trade secrets, etc. are needed because they will enhance social progress through the inventive activity they induce.[19] They lead to an optimal amount of intellectual activity being produced and a corresponding amount of social utility. In particular cases, conferring intellectual property might lead to bad consequences and may not optimize utility. However, intellectual property law is morally justifiable because, in general, adopting this system will lead to good consequences for the society as a whole.

The 'Common Good' Argument

In its most simple form, the argument in favor of intellectual property rights is that such rights provide reward mechanisms to compensate those who invest in innovation and that in turn spurs inventive activity and leads to an overall maximization of good. As Abraham Lincoln said, '[t]he Patent System added the fuel of interest to the fire of genius'.[20] Intellectual property laws encourage innovation by allowing individuals and firms to use IPRs to protect their investments in research and development.[21] An example often used to justify this position comes from the pharmaceutical industry. Researching and developing new drugs is a lengthy and incredibly costly process. Without the protection of patents, it is unlikely that pharmaceutical companies would be willing to invest in much Research and Development (R&D). In the absence of

[18] Ibid, p. 40.

[19] While it is argued that intellectual property institutions promote social utility or well being, different forms of IP such as patents, copyrights, trade-secrets, etc. often have specific and different rationales.

[20] Inventing Trivia: http://tenonline.org/art/usa/9902.html (last accessed on 28 September 2008).

[21] See John Benassi, and Noel Gillespie, 2004, 'Competition is Good: Despite What You May Have Hear, Patents Encourage Innovation', *The Recorder.*

patent protection, there would be nothing to prevent a competitor from reverse engineering a new drug in order to produce a generic version. Obviously, this would greatly reduce the price at which the drug would sell. Innovation would thus be discouraged and, as a direct consequence, economic growth would be restricted.

One of the features of information/knowledge/ideas is that they are non-rivalrous and non-excludable. Non-excludability prevents owners from excluding others from the possession of information (in contrast to tangible property, for which physical restraints are often sufficient). Non-rivalrousness magnifies this danger because one person's consumption does not diminish the amount of the good for others to consume, that is, multiple persons can use the information without depleting it. Since the amount of tangible matter in the world is fixed, innovation is the sole source of productivity growth and thus our ability to enhance the (material) quality of life. Innovation is subject to market failure, which may occur along two dimensions: either, firms may not allocate sufficient resources for the creation of the asset, or society may under- (or over-) use an asset. These market failures are directly attributable to the properties of non-excludability and non-rivalry. Non-excludability leads to a sub-optimal level of investment into the creation of capital goods and non-rivalry leads to a sub-optimal consumption of capital goods.[22] Most types of innovation have non-rivalry properties due to the ability to copy without loss of service to other users. As a consequence, the amount of innovative activity, in an unfettered market, is generally regarded as being less than socially optimal. Precisely because other people may be able to use your invention without your consent, once you have disclosed your invention, your incentive to invest in creating or disclosing it would be lower than it otherwise would be. To copy or reverse engineer someone else's invention costs less. The fact that knowledge is non-rivalrous means that there is a near-zero marginal cost from an additional individual enjoying the benefits of the knowledge. There may be some costs incurred in the cost of transmission, for instance, the cost of printing a book, but the costs of transmission that accrue in transmitting knowledge are negligible, as compared to the initial cost of innovating, and the process does not in any way affect the public good nature of knowledge itself. Thus there may be substantial incentive to 'free ride' on other's inventions. And this reduces the incentive to invent something new, because the inventor may

[22] For details of the argument see, Roger D. Blair, and Thomas Cotter, 2005, *IP: Economic and Legal dimensions of Rights and Remedies,* Cambridge: Cambridge University Press, p. 14.

be unable to recoup his sunk cost of invention and there would be no incentive to innovate.

This is fundamental problem that knowledge as a public good poses for innovators and for a society interested in unleashing innovative potential in society. Thus, rules are devised for transmission which try and change the fundamental nature of knowledge as a public good—rules which create an artificial, rule-driven scarcity which transform knowledge into a rivalrous, excludable good. IPRs require that everyone also has only paid access to these. The free rider problem may undermine the incentive to create, disclose and commercialize new inventions. To prevent this result, patent and copyright laws grant inventors a right to 'exclude'. This right permits them to charge prices in excess of the marginal cost of producing their inventions so that they can not only recover their initial expenditures but also derive profits. The right to exclude is designed to increase appropriability and consequently, the level of innovation in society. Given the nature of inventions and creative works as 'public goods', the incentive theory appears at least as necessary for intellectual property as it is for property.[23]

Inventions are public goods, similar to park, roads, education, etc.—almost everyone benefits from these. However, everyone also has only paid access to these. This means that every beneficiary would be financially better off if he were to take a free ride. If everyone acted like this however the intellectual good would not be created in the first place and everyone would lose out. The free rider problem may undermine the incentive to create, disclose, and commercialize new inventions. Intellectual property laws seek to address this dilemma—protecting the intellectual property of the inventor in order to induce invention and innovation in society, and at the same time ensuring that the knowledge thereof is disclosed and shared for larger public good. By assigning exclusive rights over the use and distribution of informational works to their creators, for a specified duration, individuals and firms can safely anticipate the potential rewards for their inventive endeavors. Thus, they will be led to engage in substantially more information generation activity than their private calculus would indicate they should in a regime lacking legal protection. The fundamental principle is to bring the private incentives to develop socially useful information in line with the social incentives, a goal that barely anyone would question. Simply put, the claimed goal of intellectual

[23] Michael Carrier, 2004, 'Cabining Intellectual Property Through a Property Paradigm', *Duke Law Journal*, 54(1), p. 32.

property tries to balance the creation of information with the diffusion of socially useful information, at a cost which is less than the social value created by the diffusion of information.

The law of intellectual property—particularly patents and copyrights, has generated a lot of interest and debate among legal experts, law professors, rights theorists and philosophers, and economists. Of particular significance here is economists who have taken up the challenge of modeling the consequences of high and low levels of protection and, to some extent testing these models against empirical evidence. These empirical evidences form the backbone of the utilitarian defense of IPRs and protection, demonstrating that IPRs lead to an overall increase in levels of productivity, efficiency, innovation, and therefore, social welfare. It is the consideration of the consequences which, in utilitarian philosophy determines the validity of a rights-claim. It is important to note that in this view rights are granted to authors and inventors, not because they deserve such rights or have mixed their labor in an appropriate way, but because this is the only way to ensure that an optimal amount of intellectual products will be available for society.

Utility arguments are not designed to justify the mere protection of possession, use, management, and so forth, but are meant to protect the corresponding rights. Lawrence C. Becker states that taken together the arguments are addressed to the justification of a set of rules, policies, principles, and practices constitutive of institutions which define the rights of ownership, as well as the conditions under which these rights may be secured.[24] The utilitarian defense of property is the defense of a legal recognition of ownership as an instrument in promoting common good/welfare. In order to pursue the 'common good' the government grants IPRs (patents, copyrights, trade secrets, trademarks) as an incentive for the production of intellectual works, and utilitarians argue that production of this sort, in turn, maximizes social progress. Far from protecting private interests at the expense of the common good, patent protection, it is argued, advances the common good by means of private interest. The common good is the end, private IPRs is the means.

These arguments form the backbone of the utilitarian position. Drawing from Adam Moore, the utilitarian justification for IPRs can be summed up as follows:

Premise 1. Society ought to adopt a system or institution if and only if it leads to or, given our best estimates, is expected to lead to the maximization of overall social utility.

[24] L.C. Becker, 1977, p. 59.

Premise 2. A system or institution that confers limited rights on authors and inventors over what they produce is expected to serve as incentive for the production of intellectual works.

Premise 3. Promoting the creation and dissemination of intellectual works produces an optimal amount of social progress.

Conclusion 1. Therefore, a system of intellectual property should be adopted. It also follows that the system of intellectual property be granted legal protection, by according it the status of rights.[25]

Utilitarianism based justifications of intellectual property are elegantly simple, Adam Moore sums up, '…coupled with the theoretical claim that society ought to maximize utility, we arrive at a simple yet powerful argument'.[26] Tom Palmer, outlining the utilitarian position on intellectual property rights, argues that the principle or even the sole criterion for evaluating intellectual property law is its contribution to aggregate utility and that the legal regime, governing ideal objects, should aim explicitly at a utilitarian result—maximizing net utility by balancing off the welfare gain from innovations introduced by IPRs against welfare losses resulting from the restrictions on the dissemination of such innovations.[27] He suggests that *Intellectual Property Rights law belongs to that branch of jurisprudence that claims to be based on 'law and economics' but also one that constructively assigns or rearranges rights as part of a strategy to achieve some pre-determined outcome* (maximization of utility or of wealth, for example).[28]

The 'Incentive' Argument

The literature dealing with economic justifications and critiques for intellectual property protection is enormous. Drawing from different economists, four general ways in which the utilitarian justification of IPRs may be fashioned can be outlined.

1. Incentive Theory: The 'incentive' or as Nelson and Mazzoleni term it, the invention–inducement theory, postulates that by conferring on the patentee, or his or her assignees, the exclusive right to commercially exploit an invention for a limited time, patent rights

---

[25] Adam Moore, 2003, 'Intellectual Property Innovation, and Social Progress: The case against Incentive Based Arguments', *Hamline Law Review*, 26(3), p. 612.

[26] Adam Moore, 2004, p. 38.

[27] Tom G. Palmer, 1997, 'A Non-Posnerian law and Economics Approach', in *Intellectual Property: Moral, Legal and International Dimensions*, Adam D. Moore (ed.), New York: Rowman and Littlefield, p. 180.

[28] Ibid, p. 210.

create a needed economic incentive to engage in the relevant phase of the innovation process.[29] William Fisher,[30] draws from Nordhaus' classic treatment of patent law and states that each increase in the duration or strength of patents stimulates an increase in inventive activity. The resultant gains to social welfare include the distribution of the intellectual products whose creation is thereby induced.[31]

2.   Optimizing Patterns of Productivity: In the 1960s Harold Demsetz argued that the copyright and patent systems play the important roles of letting potential producers of intellectual products know what consumers want and thus channeling productive efforts in directions most likely to enhance consumer welfare.[32] In the past decade, a growing group of theorists have argued that recognition of this function justifies expanding the copyright and patent systems. Paul Goldstein states that 'the logic of property rights dictates their extension into every corner in which people derive enjoyment and value from literary and artistic works. To stop short of these ends would deprive producers of the signals of consumer preference that trigger and direct their investments.'[33]

3.   Rivalrous Invention: Distinguishable from the second utilitarian justification, in this case the objective is seen as being to eliminate or reduce duplicative or uncoordinated inventive activity.

4.   Prospect Development Theory: In most versions of the invention-inducement theory, it is generally assumed that the social benefit of a particular invention is strictly its final use value. The issues of the consequences of social benefits are more complicated if an invention is not only useful as it is, but also provides the basis for second-generation inventions. This is the prospect development aspect of patents. The social benefit of patent protection stems, therefore, from the additional invention induced by the prospect of a patent. The prospect development theory treats the patent system not

[29] Richard D. Nelson and Roberts Mazzoleni, 1997, *Economic Theories about Costs and Benefits of Patents*, available at http://www.nap.edu/readingroom/books/property/3.html (last accessed on 10 December 2006).

[30] William FIsher, 2001, 'Theories of Intellectual Property', in S. Munzer (ed.), *New Essays in the Legal and Political Theory of Property*, Cambridge: CUP.

[31] William D. Nordhaus, 1969, *Invention, Growth, and Welfare: A Theoretical Treatment of Technological Change*, Cambridge: M.I.T. Press.

[32] See Harold Demsetz, 1969, 'Information and Efficiency: Another Viewpoint', *Journal of Law and Economics*, 12, p. 1.

[33] See Paul Goldstein, 1994, *Copyright's Highway*, New York: Hill & Wang, pp. 178–79; See also William Fisher, 'Theories of Intellectual Property'.

merely as a device to enable the reaping of returns on investment in innovation, but also as a system for efficiently allocating resources and coordinating resultant research. Introduced by Edmund W. Kitch in 1977, [34] the prospect development theory postulates that granting broad patents on early stage inventions allows patent holders to coordinate subsequent research and development within the area of the patent claim (the 'prospect'). If the patent holder has an exclusive right to exploit the new technological prospect, later arrivals will be unable to derive economic benefit from developing the prospect unless they negotiate directly with the patent holder to obtain licences to the underlying technology. Thus the patent holder becomes a link among all those working to develop the prospect, preventing wasteful duplication of effort and facilitating the transfer of information. In Kitch's view, the prospect function of the patent system enhances its public welfare effect. The issues of the consequences of social benefits get more complicated because the invention here is not only useful as is, but also provides the basis for second-generation inventions and their coordination.

Under what might be called the canonical versions of the invention-inducement theory—versions associated with the models of economists like Arrow, Nordhaus, and Scherer—concluded that optimal levels of innovation may not be achieved in a free market. [35] In his 1962 article, *Economic Welfare and the Allocation of Resources for Invention,* Kenneth Arrow explained why perfect competition might fail to allocate resources optimally in the case of invention. We expect a free enterprise economy to under-invest in invention and research (as compared with an ideal), because the product can be appropriated only to a limited extent, and because of increasing returns in use. [36] Arrow argued that the likelihood of profits generated by its innovation that the innovating firm may be able to capture, has a direct bearing on that firm's willingness to engage in the development of new ideas. Essentially, he argues that there exists a sort of

---

[34] E.W. Kitch, 1977, 'The Nature and Function of the Patent System', *Journal of Law and Economics*, vol. 20, pp. 265–90.

[35] Kenneth J. Arrow, 1962, 'Economic Welfare and the Allocation of Resources for Invention', in *The Rate and Direction of Inventive Activity*, Richard Nelson (ed.), Princeton, NJ: Princeton University Press, available at http://www.rand.org/pubs/papers/2006/p1856.pdf (last accessed on 5 December 2009); William D. Nordhaus, 1969, *Invention, Growth, and Welfare: A Theoretical Treatment of Technological Change,* Cambridge: M.I.T. Press.

[36] Ibid., pdf file–p.1856–RC–15–(last accessed on 5 December 2009).

'free-rider' problem. If an invention is not patentable, then it will likely be imitated by competing firms that have spent none of their own money in developing the product. Arrow also suggested that the risk inherent in innovation would discourage investment in R&D. He argues that IPRs help address all of these concerns.

A good example of scholarship in this vein is William Landes' and Richard Posner's essay on copyright law.[37] The distinctive characteristics of most intellectual products, Landes and Posner argue, are that they are easily replicated and that enjoyment of them by one person does not prevent enjoyment of them by other persons. Those characteristics in combination create a danger that the creators of such products will be unable to recoup their 'costs of expression'(the time and effort devoted to writing or composing and the author's cost of finding a publisher and the publisher's cost of editing and publishing the books), because they will be undercut by copyists who bear only the low 'costs of production' (the costs of manufacturing and distributing books or CDs) and thus can offer consumers identical products at very low prices. Awareness of that danger will deter creators from making socially valuable intellectual products in the first instance. We can avoid this economically inefficient outcome by allocating to the creators (for limited times) the exclusive right to make copies of their creations. The creators of works that consumers find valuable, that is, for which there are not in the opinion of consumers, equally attractive substitutes, will be empowered thereby to charge prices for access to those works substantially greater than they could in a competitive market. All of the various alternative ways in which creators might be empowered to recover their costs, Landes and Posner contend, are, for one reason or another, more wasteful of social resources. This utilitarian rationale, they argue, has been and should be used to shape specific doctrines within the field.

Sceptics might ask why literature flourished before there was copyright. One answer is that we do not know if there would be even more works produced if there had been copyright. Another is that technological conditions have changed since then. The cost of copying is lower than it was before and unauthorized copying is easier. According to the Landes-Posner model, if the cost of copying is lower because of improvements in copying technology, this would also mean that the price of a copy of an author's work would be bid down even more. This would

---

[37] Richard Posner and William Landes, 1989, 'An Economic Analysis of Copyright Law', *Journal of Legal Studies*, p. 17.

imply that the gap between this cost and the actual total cost of creation and expression would be wider and thus the 'underproduction' problem would be greater.

Patents are defended on the basis that they solve the appropriability problem whereby inventors may not be able to recoup the costs of an invention if information about the invention were widely available. This is because rivals would then be able to enter the market the inventor is in, by imitating her invention and competing away her profits. By requiring other inventors/firms to negotiate a licensing agreement first, the patent guarantees the inventor a financial incentive to induce the production of the invention. In the absence of patent laws which protect against reverse engineering, inventors may invest excessively in ways to keep their invention secret. For example, individual inventors might invest in private security devices to protect their holdings in the absence of physical property rights. Apart from the cost of such investment there would be a further cost in keeping the invention secret when all parties might be better off if information about the investment was diffused as widely as possible. A patent ensures that the patentee must make details of her invention publicly available, through licences of use, patent royalty, etc., as a condition of getting a patent. An additional benefit from having the innovation diffused earlier is that it may induce related innovations to be invented earlier as well. In other words, the investor must expect some degree of protection from competition, or some monopoly power. The patent holder's right to exclude imitating users is intended to create or strengthen that expectation.[38] Finally, patents give the first inventor incentives to coordinate the search for new applications through the use of licensing arrangements in order to enhance the value of her invention. This is similar to the facility provided to the copyright holder to manage derivative works. This coordinative function may be important in the field of high technology where duplication or independent discovery may involve very high costs.

Posner sees the function of the intellectual property law as that of 'wealth maximization', preferring the term to utility. Wealth maximization becomes the normative principle which justifies intellectual property rights. Copyrights, in particular, are explained as 'devices for promoting efficient allocation of resources'. The role of law is constructivist and interventionist, an attempt to reorder economic institutions to attain a

---

[38] F.M. Scherer and David Ross, 1990, *Industrial Market Structure and Economic Performance*, third edn, Boston: Houghton Mifflin.

particular end.[39] The law then is tested against the consequence, remodeled and fine-tuned to deliver better.

Almost all empirical work on the role of patents has been oriented by invention-inducement theory, and almost all patent policy issues are argued out on the same terms. Does intellectual property protection lead to innovation? To answer this core question, also the focus of the utilitarian justification for IP, we need to look at the evidence which may actually, while providing ambiguous or mixed answers, also suggest that there is no overwhelming truth to either side of the claim. There is a proliferation of empirical work on what patents are about, who uses them, and how important they are. The attempt is not to present an exhaustive array of empirical data which cut both ways. Rather it will to point in the general direction that would imply that the utilitarian case—that IPRs lead to innovation—is not overwhelmingly supported by empirical evidence.

The evidence should not only be clear, easily demonstrable, but should also establish that greater benefits cannot be derived from an alternative system. If it can be demonstrated that an alternative system, like the government rewards system, can maximize more welfare than the existent intellectual property system, then the former becomes justifiable on utilitarian grounds. Since IPRs are to be justified in terms of general benefit, there doesn't appear a clear cut case against public and common property too, as long as they can be legally and unambiguously defined. What is being argued here is that the benefits of the existing intellectual property system need to be clearly demonstrable, in the absence of which it loses the utilitarian moral appeal. A morally right action, in utilitarian reading, is one that maximizes utility.

The 'Innovation' Argument

The impact of IPRs on innovations is one of the most persistent questions in the field of justificatory premises of intellectual property rights, particularly when its utility is being probed. There is no doubt that there has been a surge in patents which have been filed and have been granted. The weakening of examination standards and the increase in patent applications has led to a dramatic increase in the number of patents granted in the United States. The number of patents granted in the United States, which increased at less than 1 per cent per year from

[39] R. Posner, 1981, *Economics of Justice*, Cambridge: Harvard University Press. Quoted in Tom Palmer, 1997, 'A Non-Posnerian Law and Economics Approach', in *Intellectual Property: Moral, Legal and International Dimensions*, Adam D. Moore (ed.), New York: Rowman and Littlefield, p. 180.

1930 until 1982 roughly tripled between 1983 and 2002 (from 62,000 per year to 1,77,000 per year, an annual rate of increase of about 5.7 per cent).[40] Applications too, have ballooned, to the point that there are now about 3,50,000 per year. However, as is discussed later, the surge in patent activity may or may not be an adequate indicator of the innovation in society.

That innovation is a primary driver of economic growth is an accepted fact. In a world of finite resources, it is innovation which forms critical productive means. What remains hotly contested, however, is whether IPRs are the best available mechanisms to encourage such innovation. Opponents of strong IPRs argue that such rights do far more to discourage innovation than they do to promote it. Recent criticism has focused primarily on patents, but the same arguments have been applied to all types of state-recognized intellectual property (that is, copyrights, trademark and trade secrets). The critical question, in other words is: Do IPRs actually lead to greater innovation—more than free trade and competition would? Theoretical understanding gives ambiguous answers. So does empirical evidence. Jaffe in a review study concludes: 'robust conclusions regarding the empirical consequences for technological innovations of changes in patent policy are few'.[41] Lack of conclusive evidence becomes a convincing case against IPRs precisely because its premises rest on the evidence being conclusive. In the utilitarian matrix the benefits must outweigh the costs, conclusively. Any ambiguity makes a strong case in favour of reconsideration of the premises on which the 'rule' rests. Utilitarian defenses are particularly vulnerable against counter empirical evidence and falter when shown that defense of IPRs seems to rest on flawed premises.

UTILITARIAN ARGUMENTS AGAINST INTELLECTUAL PROPERTY
On a utilitarian balance, the benefits and utility should outweigh the costs of implementation of intellectual property rights. The fundamental principle is to bring the private incentives to develop socially useful information in line with the social incentives, an intuitive goal that barely anyone would question. Simply put, information is to be created when its development cost is less than its social value, and intellectual property

---

[40] Adam B. Jaffe and Josh Lerner, 2004, *Innovation and Its Discontents: How Our Broken Patent System is Endangering Innovation and Progress, and What to Do About It,* Princeton University Press, p. 11.

[41] A.B. Jaffe, 2009, 'The U.S. Patent System in Transition: Policy Innovation and the Innovation Process', *Research Policy,* vol. 29, pp. 531–57; A.B. Jaffe and Josh Lerner, 2004.

rights should aim to serve that purpose. However, what is often not considered are its costs.

The desirability of awarding property rights in information depends upon whether their advantage of encouraging the generation of information outweighs their costs in terms of the restrictions placed upon the availability of that information. The usual utilitarian problems crop up, namely—how to quantify all social costs and benefits, since all benefits and costs may not be quantifiable, and how to bring in all the benefits and costs to weigh upon the decision of what the net utility derived is. A number of costs that emerge from the institutionalization of intellectual property—substantial social costs; high economic costs incurred in the implementation of the intellectual property regime; costs of exclusion which may be in the form of loss of rights of people over their self-owned intellectual property (ideas, knowledge, information), and over the tangible property created (over which, as per the earlier notion of property rights, they would have had the rights, use, transfer, exclusion, etc.). In the utilitarian calculus the benefits derived by way of increased inventive potential of the society and scientific development should outweigh the costs incurred. With IPRs the problem becomes how to measure and compare the costs incurred by the owner (the rights holder) and society (the community). For the purposes of this Chapter, I adopt a minimalist deployment of the category of utility (that is, one that does not take into account infringement of rights in the valuation of outcomes),[42] and I argue that even with this minimalist approach one can adopt a cost benefit argument against intellectual property rights.

Arguments Against 'Invention-Inducement'

The invention-inducement theory presumes that more inventive efforts and more inventors mean more useful inventing. The invention-inducement theory takes on a different look if, instead, all inventors are assumed to be focused on the same set of paths to invention. It is not uncommon that, given the market signals, a significantly high number of people are simultaneously engaged in the same inventive activity or on a limited pool of inventive activity. This assumption gives rise to the 'patent race' model of Dasgupta and Stiglitz[43] and, to the 'over-fishing' model of

---

[42] Any consequnetialist argument must take into account the effect of policy or 'rule' on the rights of people. For a broader consequentialist approach to the consequences of IPRs see, Chapters 6,7, and 8 of this work.

[43] P. Dasgupta and J.E. Stiglitz, 1980, 'Uncertainty: Industrial Structure and the Speed of R&D', *Bell Journal of Economics*, vol. 11, pp. 1–28; P. Dasgupta, and J.E. Stiglitz, 1980, 'Industrial Structure and the Nature of Innovative Activity', *Economic Journal*, vol. 90, pp. 266–93.

Barzel.[44] Under either model, patents no longer provide an unambiguous benefit when there are increases in the total inventive effort exerted at any one time or in the number of persons engaged in inventive activity. If inventors perceive that other inventors are in the game, they will see that their returns depend not simply on whether they achieve an invention, but on whether they achieve it first. That might induce them to invest their resources faster or more widely than would be appropriate if the objective were defined simply in terms of achieving a particular invention most efficiently. Even if inventors are unaware of, or ignore the presence of other inventors in the game, then the diktats of the market will ensure that the potentially profitable areas will have too many inventors playing the game. Under either model, patents will constitute a winner-take-all system. Another possibility suggested by Dasgupta and Stiglitz is that the recognition that others are likely to be running towards a particular objective will deter parties from engaging in inventive work in a given field.[45] The system of patents, in either case therefore, induces inefficient inventive effort in a competitive context.

Kanwar and Evanson, however, argue to the contrary. Using two five-year averages, for thirty one countries for the period 1981–90, they find support for the idea that higher protection leads to higher R&D, as a fraction of Gross Domestic Product (GDP).[46] They find that increasing intellectual property by one level (they categorize them into five levels of intellectual property) raises R&D as a fraction of GDP between 0.6 p cent er to 1.0 per cent. The most favourable interpretation of this is that countries which offer higher stronger patent protection spur on higher research spending and therefore lead to greater innovation. Boldrin and Levine contest this claim that a 1 per cent increase in the size of a country, as measured by GDP, increases the ratio of R&D to GDP by 0.3 per cent.. In other words, as market sizes increase, innovative effort will increase, with or without patent protection. They further add that in poorer countries with low intellectual property protection, increases in intellectual property levels bring in more foreign investment and raise R&D. In richer countries with high levels of intellectual property, foreign

[44] Y. Barzel, 1968, 'Optimal timing of Innovation', *Review of Economics and Statistics*, vol. 50, pp. 348–55.

[45] Partha Dasgupta and Joseph Stiglitz, 1980, 'Industrial Structure and the Nature of Innovative Activity', *Economic Journal*, 90(358), pp. 266–93.

[46] Sunil Kanwar and Robert Evenson, 2001, *Does Intellectual Property Protection Spur Technological Change?* Center Discussion Paper No. 831, Economic Growth Center: Yale University.

investment is not an issue, and increases in intellectual property have little or no effect on innovation.[47]

A number of studies have attempted to examine whether introducing or strengthening patent protection leads to greater innovation. Boldrin and Levine have identified seventeen economic studies that have examined this issue empirically.[48] These studies find weak or no evidence that strengthening patent regimes increases innovation. They do find evidence that strengthening the patent regime increases patenting! However, the connection between patenting and innovation is weak.[49] Nelson and Mazzoleni argue that patents would reduce the number of diverse inventors who would be induced to work on the prospect by the lure of a patent down the road, inasmuch as their ability to work on that patent would be constrained by their ability to negotiate a license with the holder of the original prospect-defining patent. As most innovations are cumulative and derive inputs from earlier innovations, their technical advance of innovations would be hindered over the long run.[50] A key concern regarding the impact of patents in cumulative technologies, such as bio-medical research, is that 'unless licensed easily and widely',

[47] Michele Boldrin, and David K. Levine, *Against Intellectual Monopoly*, chapter 8. Available at http://www.micheleboldrin.com/research/aim/anew.all.pdf (last accessed on 11 October 2007). Studies which have used aggregate cross-national data have found a positive and significant effect (Eaton and Kortum 1999, Kanwar and Evenson 2003, and Lederman and Maloney 2003). Sakakibara and Branstetter, 2001, however, find that there is only a small positive effect of increasing patent scope on R&D investments using a reduced-form model estimated with a panel dataset of Japanese firms. Quoted from Ashish Arora *et al.*, *R and D and the Patent Premium*, Durham, North Carolina and WBER: Duke University. See fn 2.

[48] A. Arundel, 2001; J. Bessen and R. Hunt, 2004; Gallini; Bronwyn and Rosemarie Ham Ziedonis, 2001; Hall and Zeidonis; A. Jaffe, 2000; Kanwar and Evenson; Kortum and Lerner; Lanjouw; Lanjouw and Cockburn; Josh Lerner; Licht and Zoz; Loc; Park; M. Sakakibara and L. Branstetter, 2004; Scherer and Weisbrod cited from Michele Boldrin, and David K. Levine, 2002, 'The Case against Intellectual Property', *American Economic Review*, 92(2).

[49] For details on these positions see Michele Boldrin, and David K. Levine, 2002, pp. 209–12; Arundel, A., 2001, 'The Relative Effectiveness of Patents and Secrecy for Appropriation', *Research Policy*, 30(4), pp. 611–24; W.M. Cohen, A. Goto, A. Nagata, R.R. Nelson, and J.P. Walsh, 2002, 'R&D Spillovers, Patents and the Incentives to Innovate in Japan and the United States', *Research Policy*, 31(8–9), pp. 1349–67; P. Dasgupta, and P.A. David, 1994, 'Toward a New Economics of Science', *Policy Research*, 23, pp. 487–521; N. Gallini, and S. Scotchmer, 2004, 'Intellectual Property: When Is It the Best Incentive System?' in *Innovation Policy and the Economy*, vol. 2, A. Jaffe, J. Lerner, and S. Stern (eds), Massachusetts: MIT Press.

[50] Mazzoleni, Roberto and Richard R. Nelson, 1998, 'The Benefits and Costs of Strong Patent Protection: A Contribution to the Current Debate', *Research Policy*, 27(273).

patents—especially broad patents—on early, foundational discoveries may limit the use of these discoveries in subsequent discovery and consequently limit the pace of innovation.[51] The 'prospect development' potential of the patent model thus stands weakened.

Higher Transaction costs

Operative products or processes can be seen as forming a *system*, in that they incorporate a number of components and draw upon a number of previous innovations. Ability to use the most advanced system might require access to a collection of innovated products. Some of the most important technologies have both attributes. For example, aircraft and computers may be called cumulative system technologies. Merges and Nelson propose that the historical records show that granting broad patents in cumulative-system technologies is often counterproductive (for instance, research tools). Unless licensed easily and widely, the presence of such patents tends to limit the range of potential users who have access to all components of the technology. In a number of instances, the consequence is to make technological advance difficult and costly.

Each individual innovator may earn more revenue from innovating if he has an intellectual monopoly. At the same time, he also faces a higher cost of innovating: he must pay off all those other 'monopolists' owing to their rights to existing innovations. Indeed, in the extreme case when each new innovation requires the use of lots of previous ideas, the presence of intellectual monopoly may bring innovation to a screeching halt. What can also be a possibility is when the patents have been eliminated, by reducing the cost of innovation, innovations show an increase. In theory, the effect of 'stronger' patents on firms' incentives to innovate are also not apparent once one recognizes that 'stronger' patents mean that not only any given firm's patents but also those of its rivals are stronger.[52] Merges and Nelson argue that broad patents may slow the rate of technical change by impeding subsequent innovations where technologies develop cumulatively.[53]

---

[51] R.P. Merges and R.R. Nelson, 1990, 'On the Complex Economics of Patent Scope', quoted in Joshua Lerner, 'The Impact of Patent Scope: An Empirical Examination of New Biotechnology Firms', *CSIA Discussion Paper*, 91–4 (Kennedy School of Government: Harvard University, July 1991), available at http://belfercenter.ksg.harvard.edu/publication/2923/impact-of-patent-scope.html (last accessed on 12 December 2007).

[52] A.B. Jaffe, 2000, 'The U.S. Patent System in Transition: Policy Innovation and the Innovation Process', *Research Policy*, p. 29. Nancy T. Gallini, 2002, 'The Economics of Patents: Lessons from Recent U.S. Patent Reform', *Journal of Economic Perspectives*.

[53] R.P. Merges and R.R. Nelson, 1990, 'On the Complex Economics of Patent Scope', *Columbia Law Review*, vol. 90, pp. 893–916.

Inventions tend to be cumulative and thus one consequence of the patent system is to raise the cost of creating follow-up inventions based on an earlier technology. In the United States, drug discovery is now more guided by prior scientific findings than previously, and those findings are now more likely to be patented after the 1980 passage of the Bayh–Dole Act[54] and related legislation, that simplified the patenting of federally supported research outputs that are often upstream to the development of drugs and other biomedical products. This could prove problematic, even if the follow-up inventor is willing to pay for permission to use the patent (which may not always be the case, due to budget constraints, uncertainty of the future payoff, and so on). If the follow up inventor must negotiate with a multiplicity of previous researchers, the mere cost of transacting could be enormous; critics argue that this problem is becoming acute in fields such as bio-technology.[55]

Heller and Eisenberg suggest that a proliferation of patents on research tools that have become essential inputs into the discovery of drugs, other therapies, and diagnostic methods.[56] They argue that the combining of multiple rights is susceptible to a breakdown in negotiations or, similarly, a stacking of license fees to the point of overwhelming the value of the ultimate product. Shapiro has raised similar concerns, using the image of the 'patent thicket'.[57] He notes that technologies that depend on the agreement of multiple parties are vulnerable to holdup by any one of them, making commercialization potentially difficult.

Advocates of research exemptions argue that since much research is cumulative in nature, there may be multiple licensing arrangements that need to be negotiated separately before any actual research can take place. These will probably involve significant transaction costs. These payments are deadweight losses from society's point of view and do not augment the incentive to invest for either party. Negotiating one's way through a minefield of contracts (or cross-licensing arrangements) can also lead to well-known contractual problems such as hold-ups. As a consequence, research will only be conducted upto the point where the transaction costs imposed are less than the total expected value of the research itself. Moreover, the more basic and fundamental the level of

[54] Bayh–Dole Act, 35 USC 200–12, 1980.

[55] Michael A. Heller, and Rebecca S. Eisenberg, 1998, 'Can Patents Deter Innovation? The Anticommons in Biomedical Research', *Science*, 280(5364), pp. 698–701.

[56] Ibid.

[57] C. Shapiro, 'Navigating the Patent Thicket: Cross Licenses, Patent Pools, and Standard-Setting', University of California Working Paper. Available at http://faculty.haas.berkele.edu/shapiro/thicket.pdf (last accessed on 8 December 2009).

research, the more uncertain and unpredictable the social uses for the new knowledge and accordingly, the greater the deterrence effect of an explicit price for investors.

The pernicious consequences of the evolving patent situation can be seen in legal interactions as well. Companies in the United States spend over 100 billion dollars on R&D each year, and billions more obtaining and defending intellectual property protection for their inventions.[58] These expenditures have been growing across almost every industry, from traditional manufacturing, to services, to high technology. Legal fees during the 14-year long, Kodak-Polaroid court battle cost Kodak 100 million dollars.[59]

For numerous large companies—including, notoriously, Digital Equipment, IBM, Texas Instruments, and Wang Laboratories—these types of patent enforcement activities have become a line of business in their own right. These firms have established patent licensing units, which have frequently been successful in extracting license agreements and/or past royalties from smaller rivals. For instance, Texas Instruments has in recent years netted close to US 1 billion dollars annually from patent licenses and settlements resulting from its general counsel's aggressive enforcement policy. In some years, revenue from these sources has exceeded net income from product sales.

In addition to being forced to pay royalties, small firms may reduce or alter their investment in R&D. Evidence from surveys and practitioner accounts suggests that the time and expense of intellectual property litigation is a major consideration when deciding whether to pursue an innovation, especially among smaller firms. Smaller firms tend to shy away from pursuing innovations in areas where large firms have established patent portfolios. The whole system works against the smaller players. Patent litigation costs, protracted court battles, production of extensive documentation and time-consuming depositions, various types of enforcement activities by large firms, etc. may have the effect of suppressing innovation by younger, more vibrant concerns. As the patent system becomes a distraction from innovation rather than a source of incentive, technological progress and economic growth begin to labour. Burgeoning patent litigation is increasingly making lawyers the key players in competitive struggles rather than entrepreneurs and researchers.

[58] Adam B. Jaffe and Josh Lerner, 2004.
[59] G. Kevin Rivette and David Kline, 2000, 'Discovering New Value in Intellectual Property', *Harvard Business Review*, vol. 78, p. 65.

Distortion of the Inventive Field

This kind of invention inefficiency induced by strong patents would shift the balance between the benefits and costs of patents so as to increase the costs. Because of the high costs, even the award of patents may not induce inventions because investment in a particular field may not be lucrative enough. For instance, globally there are a group of diseases, termed Neglected Diseases (NDs) by the World Health Organization (WHO), for which there is little or no research—R&D efforts have 'neglected' them. One of the primary reasons is that these are diseases located in the poorer parts of the global south and there exists, because of low purchasing power of these peoples, a low monetary demand for their cures and drugs. Conversely, spurred by the high monetary demand from a small population of the north, innovations related to sexual stimulants, anti-baldness drugs, anti-depressants, etc. is on the rise.[60] One aspect of this problem that does not receive adequate consideration is the fact that the existence of patents might distort incentives, diverting inventive activity toward more easily 'patentable' products, further still to more easily patentable products where the returns are lucrative. It is important to note that not all discoveries and innovations are patentable, even when they are highly beneficial. Intellectual property assignments should be assessed not only by the incentive/cost tradeoff, but by their effects on the decision architectures surrounding the property right—their effects on how firms make product innovation decisions.[61]

The question is important because different decisional structures for product development can be fundamental to the performance of firms, industries, and even the economy as a whole. They may be critical to the welfare of the society. For example, different architectures of product development were among the principal differences between the centrally planned economies of communist countries and market economies. Consider a case in point: The biotech firm, Genetics Institute, decides which version of a drug to develop partly based on which composition shows the best results in clinical trials but also according to which version can command the strongest patent protection. Genetics Institute patent counsel says the strength of the potential patent position is 'a leading factor' in deciding what research to pursue.[62] The point is that if science

---

[60] For a discussion see, Chapter 6 of this work.

[61] Julio H. Cole, 2001, 'Patents and Copyrights: Do benefits Exceed costs?' *Journal of Libertarian Studies*, 15(4), pp. 79–105.

[62] Kevin Rivet and David Cline, 2000, p. 58; Glynn Lunney, 1996, 'Reexamining Copyrights' Incentives–Access Paradigm', *Vanderbelt Law Review*, p. 483.

is guided by the hand of commercial interests, it will focus primarily on puzzles that have commercial significance and the strategy of intellectual property protection may temper the rate of technological progress or change the direction of technological progress.

A group of theorists point out that in virtually no field of economic activity are innovators empowered to collect the full social value of their innovations. The elementary schoolteacher who develops a new technique for teaching mathematics, the civil-rights activist who discovers a way to reduce racial tension, the physicist who finds a way to integrate our understandings of gravity and quantum mechanics—all of these confer on society benefits that vastly exceed the innovators' incomes. Enlarging the entitlements of intellectual-property owners and according them the full social value of their innovation, thus might send out signals about the commercially most viable area of research investment, but at the same time distort the investment pattern—an over-investment in areas of consumer preference as opposed to such things as education, community activism, and primary research. An optimal system thus would somehow have to take into account both the signaling power of strong intellectual-property rights and their tendency to distort the signals provided to creative persons of other sorts.

Duplicative Efforts and Trivial Patent Claims

Intellectual-property rights can sometimes stimulate too much innovation. In other words, they can sometimes give rise to socially wasteful duplicative or uncoordinated inventive activity. The foundation for this approach was laid by a group of economists, led by Yoram Barzel, who over the last three decades, have explored the ways in which competition among firms complicates the impact of the patent system upon inventive activity.[63] This body of literature has sensitized legal theorists to three stages in the inventive process at which economic waste can occur. First, the pot of gold represented by a patent on a pioneering, commercially valuable invention may lure an inefficiently large number of persons and organizations into the race to be the first to reach the invention in question. Second, the race to develop a lucrative improvement on an existing technology may generate a similar scramble for similar reasons at the 'secondary' level. Finally, firms may try to 'invent around' technologies patented by their rivals—that is, to develop functionally equivalent but non-infringing

[63] Yoram Barzel, 1968, 'Optimal Timing of Innovation', *Review of Economics and Statistic*, vol. 50, pp. 348–55.

technologies. These are efforts that although rational from the standpoint
of the individual firm, represent a waste of social resources. Heightened
awareness of these risks has prompted legal scholars to search for possible
reforms of intellectual property law—or of related doctrines, such as
antitrust law—that would mitigate the dissipation of resources at these
various sites.[64]

The rapid increase in the rate of patenting has been accompanied by a
proliferation of patent awards of dubious merit. In recent years, there has
been a quantum leap in the US, patents per R&D dollar which almost
doubled between 1985 and 1997, increasing from 0.18 to 0.34 patents
per million US dollars.[65] Figure worldwide may not match up but are
likely to exhibit the same trend, especially in the post TRIPS era. From
a management perspective, as mentioned earlier, concerns have been
raised that aggressive patenting in certain industries could crowd-out
investments in innovation rather than stimulate it, by absorbing time and
resources for patent prosecution and litigation.[66]

The existence of trivial patents induces wasteful expenditure of
resources by competitors trying to 'invent around the patent,' that is,
to develop competing products that are sufficiently differentiated so as
not to infringe on an existing patent. Nelson puts it this way: 'There
are incentives for a firm to duplicate the prevailing best technology
patented by another firm in a way that does not infringe on patents. More
generally, there are incentives for a firm to develop a technology even if
it is worse than the current best one, if it is better than the one it has and
the best is blocked by patents.'[67] Thus, although these activities increase
the level of research-and-development spending, from the social point
of view they are not necessarily an efficient use of available resources.
Worse still, patent owners also have incentives to invent around their own
patents to preclude potential competition. To the extent that the patent
system itself induces these activities, resources devoted to them (as well
as the associated legal expenses) are essentially wasted from the social

[64] Edmund Kitch, 1977, 'The Nature and Function of the Patent System', *Journal of Law and Economics*, vol. 20, p. 265; Edmund Kitch, 1980, 'Patents, Prospects, and Economic Surplus: A Reply', *Journal of Law and Economics*, vol. 23.

[65] National Research Council, 2004.

[66] Ashish Arora, Marco Ceccagnoli, and Wesley M. Cohen, January 2003, 'R&D and the Patent Premium', *NBER Working Paper*, No. W9431. Available at SSRN: http://ssrn.com/abstract=368187 (last accessed on 15 April 2007).

[67] Richard R. Nelson, Spring 1981, 'Assessing Private Enterprise: An Exegesis of Tangled Doctrine', *Bell Journal of Economics*, vol. 12, p. 107; See also, Adam Jaffe and Josh Lerner, 2004.

point of view, and should be regarded as another cost of the system. For example, to protect its monopoly position in the market for plain-paper copiers, Xerox patented every conceivable aspect of its technology, 'IBM had spent millions to "invent around" Xerox's major patents—with 25 percent of the budget going for patent counsel, not R&D.'[68]

The diminished quality of patents, it is argued, has an extremely negative effect on innovation (and hence on economic growth), because too many individuals and firms are seeking what are called 'blocking' patents that is, they seek patent coverage not to allow them to produce some new product but to preclude someone else from producing it. Most often, this is done to protect some existing product or technology.

This is one of the chief components of the surge in patenting activity. An increase in patents in no way is a clear demonstration that increased patenting activity is tantamount to increased innovative activity. The correlation between the two may not be as unambiguous as it is often assumed to be. The pharmaceutical and the software industry are two areas of most intense patenting activity but are replete with examples of minor modifications and 'ever-greening', posing as new products. Pharmaceutical innovations present a very complex picture. The number of 'new' drugs invented may not actually be an indication of genuine innovation but, on the contrary, may be a refurbishment of existing drugs in order to reap the patent advantages and monopoly profits. An increasing number of studies show that while patent protection has increased over the last fifteen years, the innovation rate has been falling, with an increase in the number of 'me-too drugs' of little or no therapeutic gain. A survey published in April 2005 by La Revue Prescrire, concluded that 68 per cent of the 3,096 new products approved in France between 1981 and 2004 brought 'nothing new' over previously available preparations.[69] Similarly, the British Medical Journal published a study rating barely 5 per cent of all newly-patented drugs in Canada as 'breakthrough.'[70] A breakdown of over one thousand new drugs approved by the US Food and Drug Administration between the years 1989 and 2000 revealed that over three quarters have no therapeutic benefit over existing products.[71]

[68] Timothy F. Bresnahan, May 1985, 'Post-Entry Competition in the Plain Paper Copier Market', American Economic Review, vol. 75, p. 16. Quoted in Julio Cole, Fall 2001, 'Patents and Copyrights: Do benefits exceed costs?', Journal of Libertarian Studies, 15(4), p. 91.

[69] Quoted from MSF website. Available at http://www.msf.org/msfinternational/invoke.cfm?objectidfull_html (last accessed on 8 December 2009).

[70] Morris L. Barer, et al., 2 September 2005, 'Breakthrough Drugs and Growth in Expenditure on Prescription Drugs in Canada', British Medical Journal, pp. 815–6.

[71] 'Changing Patterns of Pharmaceutical Innovation', The National Institute for Health

Adam Jaffe and Josh Lerner's *Innovation and Its Discontents* cites many examples of patent awards of dubious merit: Patents on inventions that are trivially obvious, such as the 'Method for Swinging on a Swing' ('invented' by a five-year-old), Patents that have become weapons for firms to harass competitors, ranging from Rambus' efforts to exploit a semiconductor industry standard-setting body to Smucker's steps to quash a small-time lunch caterer,[72] Patents in areas new to patenting, but covering purported discoveries familiar to practitioners and academics alike, such as the patents on previously well-known option pricing formulae.

Tension between rewarding some innovators while potentially inhibiting the activities of others is inherent in the patent system. Many people and companies have received patents for trivial or even non-existent inventions. Moreover, many awardees have exploited the enhanced legal strength of their patents by suing (or threatening to sue) the true innovators in their industries. Patents that enabled companies to win huge damages awards, and even put rivals out of business, such as Polaroid's instant photography patents.[73] As a result, valuable technologies have become snarled in a web of litigation and licensing negotiations.[74]

Patents and Monopolies

Although the term 'intellectual property' is commonly used in the legal field, it is rather problematic in economics, since it is difficult to justify this type of property right with the same arguments that are used to justify private property in tangible goods. According to the economic theory of property, (following the utilitarians), society benefits from the delimitation and protection of private property rights because goods are scarce. There is no point in defining property rights over abundant goods. On the other hand, when goods are scarce and property is communal, they are not used efficiently. The 'tragedy of the commons' is the biggest threat to productive and efficient use of communal property. Private property guarantees that scarce goods will be put to their most efficient and productive uses.

Julio Cole argues that it is difficult to justify intellectual property rights under this concept of property, since these rights do not arise from

Care Management Research and Educational Foundation (NIHCM), Washington, DC (May 2002). http://www.nihcm.org/innovations.pdf Jaffe Adam and Josh Lerner, *Innovation and Its Discontents: How Our Broken Patent System is Endangering Innovation and Progress, and What to Do About It*, p. 11.
[72] Ibid., pp. 2–3. Also see, Chapter 1 and 2.
[73] Ibid., p. 2. Also see, Chapter 4.
[74] Ibid., p. 4.

the scarcity of the appropriated objects; rather, their purpose is to *create* scarcity, thereby generating a monopoly rent for holders of such rights.[75] In such a case, the law does not protect property over a scarce good; rather, it is the intellectual property law which creates an artificial scarcity. This artificial scarcity generates the monopoly rents that confer value upon those rights. The big difference between patents and copyrights on the one hand, and tangible goods on the other, is that the latter will be scarce even if there are no well defined property rights. In the case of patents and copyrights, the scarcity arises only after the property right is defined. Cole argues that there is no contradiction or incompatibility between the notions of 'patent as property' and 'patent as monopoly', and, in practice, they are closely related, since the monopolistic nature of patents is precisely what confers economic value upon them.[76] Morally and socially, it is a reward for unusual inventive ability. It is when the state or some branch of private law grants patents as a right that it becomes a grant of a monopoly of use to the inventor. The monopoly conferred by the patent is the right to exclude others from manufacturing or selling the patented product, or from practicing the patented process. It is the monopoly grant that makes tangible the inventor's reward and converts a formal into a realistic property right.[77] Classifying Intellectual Property rights as monopoly rights, Hayek argues:

The problem of the prevention of monopoly and the prevention of competition is raised much more acutely in certain other fields to which the concept of property has been extended only in recent times. I am thinking here of the extension of the concept of property to such rights and privileges as patents for inventions, copyright, trademarks, and the like. It seems to me beyond doubt that in thee fields a slavish application of the concept of property, as it has been developed for material things, has done a great deal to foster the growth of monopoly and that here drastic reforms may be required if competition is to be made to work... Patents, in particular, are specially interesting from our point of view because they provide so clear an illustration of how it is necessary in all such instances not to apply a ready-made formula but to go back to the rationale of the market system and to decide for each class what the precise rights are to be which the government ought to protect.[78]

In effect, therefore, a patent is a limited monopoly: an opportunity to create a legally enforced market structure in which the patent holder can

[75] Julio Cole, 2001, p. 80.

[76] For a different position, one that argues that patents do not lead to monopolies, see Michael Novak, 1997, *The Fire of Invention,* Lanham, Maryland: Rowman & Littlefield, p. 69.

[77] Ibid., p. 81.

[78] F.A. von Hayek, 1948, *Individualism and Economic Order,* Chicago: University of Chicago Press, pp. 113–14.

charge more for his or her product than would be possible in a competitive market. When the law gives a creator a copyright or patent over her work, in effect a temporary monopoly over that piece of information is awarded. Monopoly rights give rise to monopoly prices. As such, there is the very real possibility that many individuals who value the good at prices below monopoly prices will be unable to obtain it if their valuation is above the monopoly price. The corresponding social loss may potentially be quite significant, especially in instances where the spread between marginal cost and monopoly price charged is rather large, for example, in the pharmaceutical and software industries.[79] The inflation of price over that which would be witnessed in a competitive market necessarily leads to restriction of use, and therefore, less than socially optimal dissemination of information. Because monopoly rights impose a cost on the community by way of increased prices and reduced output, patent laws should be designed to grant patents only for inventions which would not otherwise have been made, or which would not otherwise have been made available to the community through disclosure or development and commercialization.

Effects on Disclosure and Diffusion

Intellectual Property Rights nearly always reflect an inherent tension between creation and diffusion. On the one hand, diffusion through the spread of successful ideas and methods is fundamental to improving the material standard of living of a society. At the same time, however, diffusion undermines a firm's ability to appropriate the returns from the innovation and thus attenuates the incentive to invest in innovation. Intellectual property such as patents, trade marks, and copyrights attenuate the under-investment problem in the production of knowledge, but they exacerbate the diffusion problem. The question that arises is: Will not the adoption of intellectual property protection impede public dissemination of intellectual products? Advocates disagree and argue that IPRs facilitate wide knowledge about and use of inventions by inducing inventors to disclose their inventions when otherwise they would rely on secrecy.[80] It is therefore argued that patents promote diffusion through disclosure

[79] See F.M. Scherer, 1973, *Industrial Market Structure and Economic Performance,* Rand McNally & Co., pp. 390–1. Scherer notes that Pfizer Corporation, a large pharmaceutical manufacturer, charged pharmacists US 30 dollars for 100-capsule bottles of tetracycline while it held the patent on it, whereas production costs were roughly US 1.60 dollars to US 3.80 dollars.

[80] See Wendy J. Gordon, 1989, 'An Inquiry into the Merits of Copyright: The Challenges of Consistency, Consent, and Encouragement Theory', *Stanford Law Review,* vol. 41, pp. 1439–49.

since ideas, that may otherwise be lost to society are recorded for posterity through patent publication.

However, using the premise that Machlup and Penrose,[81] and Nelson[82] employ, one can argue that patents do not lead to diffusion. With the push for greater commercialization of output, there is greater pressure on researchers to keep their research a secret (in order to fulfill the patenting criteria) and to turn research output into proprietary knowledge. This has increasingly resulted in the privatization of the scientific commons and the creation of anti-commons, where knowledge is under-used relative to the social optimum. Heller and Eisenberg state that the 'tragedy of the commons' metaphor explained why people overused shared resources.[83] However, the recent proliferation of intellectual property rights in biomedical research suggests a different tragedy, an 'anti-commons', which can emerge when there are numerous property right claims. When these property rights are held by numerous claimants (especially if they are from different kinds of institutions), the negotiations necessary to their combination may fail, quashing the pursuit of otherwise promising lines of research or product development. The argument that an anti-commons may emerge to undercut innovation emphasizes factors that might frustrate private incentives to realize what should otherwise be mutually beneficial trades.[84]

Diminished Public Domain

Copyright protection and patents often have hindered the cumulative development of creative or innovative works. As the duration, subject matter, and exclusive rights of copyright expand, the public domain is diminished. Although the concept of the public domain has undergone many iterations, it can most broadly be defined as 'material that is unprotected by intellectual property rights, either as a whole or in a particular context, and is thus "free" for all to use.'

Since the creation of copyrightable works is a cumulative process, in which one work builds upon its predecessor, it vitally depends on access

[81] Machlup Fritz and Edith Penrose, 1950, 'The Patent Controversy in the Nineteenth Century', J. Econ. Hist., 10(1), pp. 1–29.

[82] Richard Nelson, April 2004, 'The Market Economy, and the Scientific Commons', Research Policy, Elsevier, 33(3) , pp. 455–71.

[83] Michael A. Heller and Rebecca S. Eisenberg, May 1998, pp. 698–701.

[84] Privatization of biomedical research especially, must be more carefully deployed to sustain both upstream research and downstream product development. Otherwise, more intellectual property rights may lead paradoxically to fewer useful products for improving human health.

to works in the public domain. Composers recombine sounds that they have heard; novelists draw on other plots; playwrights use other literary characters; multimedia artists combine many small pieces of existing works into new creations; software writers use logic and algorithms from other software; and cinematographers, actors, choreographers, architects, and sculptors transform currently existing works. Non-access to building blocks in the public domain, many works would not be created. Michael Carrier argues that the expansion of copyright has kept many works out of the public domain, thereby threatening grave consequences for multigenerational creation. In fact, evidence already demonstrates that many works are not created because of the difficulty of entering into licensing agreements with copyright holders.[85]

The expansion of copyright, as well as of trademark and the right of publicity also limits speech. Copyright holders have ever greater ability to block expression commenting on copyrighted works, including political commentary, news reporting, parody, cultural critique, church dissent, and historical scholarship. Carrier adds that the expansive copyright—and these conclusions easily hold good for the patent laws as well—also threatens the decentralization that is essential for democracy. As discussed in greater detail below, decentralization allows challenges to the prevailing orthodoxy and permits smaller entities to contribute to public discourse. Yet vertical and horizontal consolidation have swept through the entertainment industry in recent years, increasing the control possessed by the conglomerates and making it more difficult for outsiders to use copyrighted works controlled by these companies. In short, the expansion of copyright has ominous consequences for the public domain, free speech, and the decentralization and discourse that are crucial to democracy.[86] John Perry Barlow sums it up rather well when he says that 'The greatest constraint on your future liberties may come not from government but from corporate legal departments laboring to protect by force what can no longer be protected by practical efficiency or general social consent.'[87]

Incentive based rule-utilitarian arguments become even more strained when viewed from a global perspective. The claims of increased utility/

---

[85] Michael Carrier, 2004, 'Cabining Intellectual Property Through a Property Paradigm', 54, *Duke Law Journal*, 1(8), p. 50.

[86] Ibid.

[87] John Perry Barlow, March 1994, 'The Economy of Ideas: A Framework for Patents and Copyrights in the Digital Age (Everything You Know about Intellectual Property is Wrong)', *Wired*, 2.03, p. 3.

welfare, because of intellectual property rights, become even more contentious, in the context of transfer of technology from developed countries to developing countries, and in the context of traditional knowledge transfer from developing to the developed countries. Josh Lerner in an important paper examines the effects of over 100 patent policy changes in the world's sixty largest nations over 150 years.[88] He concludes that pro-patent holder changes sharply increases patenting by foreign entities. However, patenting by domestic entities *decreases*. These results imply that although pro-patent holder changes may have helped international trade by allowing foreign firms to protect their products, they appear to have had a negative effect on domestic innovation. Lerner's extensive analysis goes a long way towards challenging conventional wisdom about the historical role of the patent system, and to providing some understanding of the system's multi-sided effects.[89] Econometric analysis using both Japanese and US patent data on 307 Japanese firms finds no evidence of an increase in either R&D spending or innovative output that could plausibly be attributed to patent reform.[90] The effects would be different for different countries even for the same innovation. The social costs and benefits will differ from one country to another, so will the optimum term of the patent. Since monopoly profits will be transferred from developing to the developed countries the agreement would be more beneficial to the latter countries than to the former ones.[91]

To conclude, the benefits stressed by IPRs turn out, on closer inspection, to be smaller than conventionally assumed; there are many costs involved that are commonly overlooked. There is an uncertainty regarding the validity of granted intellectual property rights, imitation by rival firms is difficult to detect, and enforcement through the courts is costly. The general point against the incentive argument is that institutions of intellectual property do not conclusively act as incentives for intellectual production and 'even if some system is necessary, the argument still fails to justify anything remotely close to Anglo-American systems of intellectual property' which has become a model for IPRs the world over.[92]

[88] Josh Lerner, 2002, '150 Years of Patent Protection', *American Economic Review*, Papers and Proceedings, vol. 92, May, pp. 221–5.

[89] For details of his analysis and study see Josh Lerner, ibid.

[90] Sakakibara Mariko, and Lee Branstetter, 1999, 'Do Stronger Patents Reduce More Innovation? Evidence From The 1998 Japanese Patent Law Reforms', *Working Paper 7066*, Cambridge, April.

[91] For details see, Elhanan Helpman, 1993, 'Innovation, Imitation and IPR', *Econometrics*, 61(6), November, pp. 1247–80.

[92] Adam D. Moore, 2004, *Intellectual Property and Information Control*, p. 49.

The consequences of intellectual property law have been evaluated through references to benefits and costs. These consequences of acceptance of rules should be part of a cost-benefit analysis of prospective rules. Formulating rule-consequentialism in terms of the consequences of acceptance allows them to be part of this analysis. In fact, consideration of incentive effects has played such a large role in the development of rule-consequentialism. While there may be a debate on the cost benefit balance the objective has not been to conclusively determine whether costs are more or the benefits outweigh the costs. That is not the purpose of this section. Rather through reference to large costs, the intention is simply to point out that the intellectual property 'rules' need to be tested against these consequences. If utilitarian grounds are our only reasons for supporting a practice or a rule, these become considerably shakier when the practice is imperfect.[93]

THE QUESTION OF ALTERNATIVES

A rule interpretation of intellectual property would require that the rules, not the individual acts of rights exercise, be tested against the consequences. The first way of arguing for rule-consequentialism starts by showing that rule-consequentialism does better than any other moral theory at specifying an impartial justification for intuitively plausible moral rules. Arguably, rule-consequentialism will be sunk if it can be shown that rule-consequentialism does not fulfill the intention of the rule. Tim Mulgan states, 'If Rule Consequentialism is defended on the basis of an intuitive appeal of its judgments regarding particular cases, then the inability to discover those judgments would be a fatal blow.'[94] The intention and the projected telos of intellectual property rules is to promote innovation, which in turn, is expected to promote welfare. The assertion is that since the intellectual property 'rules' do not stand the test of 'incentive' consequences, this rule needs to restructured in the light of the substantial costs incurred. Also, the consequentialist argument needs to move beyond the narrow conception of costs, which so far has remained confined to intellectual property and its effects on innovation. The valuation of outcomes needs to move beyond to include rights, that is, the effect that intellectual property rules generate on rights. I leave that discussion for Section II of the book. However, a pertinent question needs to be raised in this regard.

[93] For a critique of Utilitarianism, see David Lyons, 1965, *Forms and Limits of Utilitarianism*, UK: Oxford University Press.

[94] Tim Mulgan, 2005, *The Demands of Philosophy*, New York: OUP, p. 55.

Until now the query has been what would happen if everyone followed a set of rules. After all, rule utilitarianism rests on the premise that welfare can be maximized if everyone followed a set of rules. It also follows that an optimal set of rules is one that can be shown to perform better than the consequences generated by an alternative set of rules. The previous section did indicate that there are alternative models available which have been set aside. This argument is based on the intuitive appeal of its judgment that intellectual property rules will foster innovative activity. It has to be shown that the rule fits our everyday moral judgment better than other competing moral theories.

There are many theorists whose studies indicate that there are mechanisms which can be employed to achieve the desired goals of efficiency without incurring the social and economic costs. Fritz Machlup, in *Production and Distribution of Knowledge* argues that patent protection is not needed as incentive for corporations in a competitive market to invest in the development of new products and processes. The 'first mover' advantage may be incentive enough.[95] In *The Case Against Intellectual property,* Michele Boldrin and David K. Levine provide a comprehensive overview of what they call the right of sale. This is the right of a legitimate owner of intellectual property to sell it. In copyright law, when applied to the creator this right is sometimes called the 'right of first sale', but the right of sale extends also to the legitimate rights of others, for example, licensees, to sell the idea. Boldrin and Levine emphasize that they favor the right of sale, which they distinguish from the 'right to control'.[96] It is crucial that producers of intellectual property be able to profit from their invention. It is with the right of the owner of intellectual property to control how the purchaser makes use of the idea or creation, after purchasing, that they disagree.[97] The second feature of the law, which is the right to control the use of the intellectual property after sale produces a monopoly, enforced by the obligation of the government to prosecute individuals or organizations that use the idea in ways prohibited by the copyright or patent holder. Intellectual property therefore, has come to mean not only the right to own and sell ideas but also the right to regulate their use. This creates a socially inefficient monopoly.

In another alternative model, The Health Impact Fund, pioneered by Thomas Pogge, adopts a mechanism that offers pharmaceutical

---

[95] For details see, Fritz Machlup, 1962, *Production and Distribution of Knowledge in the US,* Princeton, NJ: Princeton University Press, pp. 168–69.

[96] Ibid.

[97] Ibid, p. 209.

innovators a supplementary reward based on the health impact of their products, if they agree to sell those products at cost.[98] It is a reward-based system, rather than a user-pays system. The proposed fund is to be financed mainly by governments. Yet another alternative suggested is government support of intellectual labour which will act as an incentive for intellectual production. Michael Polyani advocated a system where people who invent intangible goods are paid by the government and receive no exclusionary rights to their works.[99] Arrow suggests that the 'first-best' policy is to publicly finance the production of under-produced intangible goods.[100] Such public-funding mechanisms may range from *ex ante* procurement through to *ex post* prizes.[101] These alternatives highlight not only the possibility of establishing equally powerful, if not better, incentives for intellectual production, but also the desirability of it which would prevent restricted use and the encroachments on the rights claims of others in the use of their intellectual or tangible property.

A holistic approach to incentives should incorporate the effects of rights over abstract ideas on the distribution of socio-economic power within a community and the costs of these effects, which are harder to measure in purely economic terms. The social costs of discovery and development are likely to be less, at least in terms of rights encroachment if there are no exclusionary rights, and would be one that would maximize diffusion. Gallini and Scotchmer, however argue that in abstraction, the intellectual property policies are less efficient, since the social welfare losses incurred through taxing a single market (via a monopoly price) are always greater than those incurred though broad-based taxation.[102]

History tells us that the connection between IPRs and scientific and technological development is contingent and local rather than necessary

[98] Thomas Pogge and Adrian Hollis, *The Health Impact Fund: Making New Medicines Accessible to All*, available at www.HealthImpactFund.org (last accessed on 8 December 2009).

[99] Michaels Polyani, 1944, 'Patent Reform', *Review of Economic Studies*, 61, quoted in Adam D. Moore (ed.), 1997, p. 67.

[100] Kenneth Arrow, 1962, 'Economic Welfare and the Allocation of Resources for Innovation', in *The Rate and Direction of Inventive Activity*, Richard Nelson (ed.), Princeton, NJ: Princeton University Press, p. 612.

[101] Government prizes were commonly used in the nineteenth century and since then invention and innovation awards have continued to stimulate intangible investments, in part by acting as signals to the market.

[102] Nancy Gallini and Suzanne Scotchmer, 2000, 'Intellectual Property: When Is It the Best Incentive System?', in *Innovation Policy and the Economy*, vol. 2, Jaffe Adam, Joshua Lerner, and Scott Stern (eds), MIT Press.

and universal.[103] In the ancient era, common law countries like Britain had IPRs and good technical progress. In a striking contrast, imperial China is an example of a society that achieved spectacular success in science, yet did not rely on IPRs or any equivalent of it. In the modern age, some socialist countries such as China and USSR achieved a lot of success in scientific endeavors without relying on intellectual property regime.

Studies by Arundel, Gallini and Jaffe suggest that there is little need to strengthen patent protection since alternative appropriation methods are available.[104] In two separate studies, Mansfield suggests *that patent*

[103] History is replete with examples of the contingent and the cumulative nature of inventions. James Watt's steam engine was not an invention but more of an improvement upon the existing inefficient Newcomen design, improvements borrowed substantially from researchers like Matthew Wasborough. More dramatically, in the 1790s, when the superior and independently designed Hornblower engine was put into production, Boulton and Watt went after Hornblower with the full force of the legal system. In contrast to Watt, who died a rich man, the inventor Jonathan Hornblower was not only forced to close his shop, but found himself ruined and in jail; It is to Lilienthal, in fact, that the idea of 'wing warping' is to be attributed. When the Wright brothers applied for the first patent in 1902, it was for the system of flight control obtained by the combined used of warping and the rudder—that is, a very marginal improvement over Lilienthal's warping technology. It should be noticed as well that modern airplanes are not controlled by 'wing warping' but rather by movable control surfaces—elevators and ailerons. These were invented not by the Wright brothers, but by Glenn Curtis, a fact that did not prevent the Wright brothers from suing Glenn Curtis based on their patent over 'wing warping.' (3) Brock, 1981 provides a detailed history of both the telegraph and the telephone industries. Brock reports that Bell's patent was filed two hours earlier of an equivalent one by Elisha Gray, describing the same 'invention'. Brock also refers to the reference that US Congress ruled that Bell stole the telephone invention from Antonio Meucci. (4) The radio, according to popular history, was invented by the great inventor Guglielmo Marconi (filed for a patent in 1896). There are many competitors, which is to say, many people who have claimed to have invented the radio in a form more or less similar, but functionally equivalent, to Marconi. They range from the British physicist Oliver Lodge in the United Kingdom, and the forgotten genius Nikola Tesla in the United States, to Russian Aleksander Popov who, it is now clearly documented, described his findings in a paper published in 1895 and demonstrated the functioning of his apparatus in front of the St Petersburg Physical Society in March 1896. This obviously makes the whole thing even more interesting in retrospect, as it proves once again that big simultaneous inventions are more the rule than the exception, and that big simultaneous stealing is also part of the feasible set. For a history of the Steam Engine see, University of Rochester, NY, *The Growth of the Steam Engine*, online history resource, Chapter 2, for a history of the telegraph industry see Gerald Brock, 1981, *The Telecommunication Industry*, Cambridge: Harvard University Press; for a history of the modern airplanes see, A.B. Zaffe, 2000, 'The US Patent System in Transition: Policy Innovation and the Innovation Process', *Research Policy*, vol. 29, pp. 531–57.

[104] A. Arundel and I. Kabla, 1998, 'What Percentage of Innovations are Patented? Empirical Estimates for European Firms', *Research Policy*, vol. 27, pp. 127–141; N. Gallini and S. Sctochmer, 2004, 'Intellectual Property: When is it the Best Incentive System?' in

protection may not be an essential stimulus for innovation in most industries.[105]
Sidney Winter and Nelson present a simulation study of an innovation
in industry model: the results suggest rather strongly that unimpeded
imitation need not yield inferior results from a social standpoint.[106] The
survey findings of Levin *et al.*[107] and, more recently, Cohen *et al.*[108] suggest
that in most industries patents are less featured than other means of
protecting innovations, such as, first mover advantages or secrecy. Patent
ownership is not the only way to obtain an economic return from new
inventions. For example, innovators may enjoy a pioneer advantage even
in the absence of patent protection. As sociological studies of science
show, economic incentives are not the only kinds of incentives which
motivate innovation.[109] While empirical evidence suggests that overall
levels of innovation do respond to economic stimuli, governments have at
their disposal a range of economic instruments for stimulating innovation
other than patents, including the provision of research funding or venture
capital, tax concessions, procurement policy, export development grants,
tariffs, and bounties.[110]

Adan Jaffe, Joshua Lerner and Scott Stern (eds), *Innovation Policy and the Economy*, vol. 2,
Cambridge: MIT Press, p. 7.

[105] E. Mansfield, 1986, 'Patent and Innovation: An Empirical Study', *Management Science*,
vol. 32, pp. 173–81.

[106] Sidney Winter, 1989, 'Patents in Complex Contexts', in *Owning Scientific and Technical
Information,* New Brunswick, NJ: Rutger University Press.

[107] R.C. Levin, A.K. Klevorick, R.R. Nelson, and S.G. Winter, 1987, 'Appropriating the
Returns from Industrial R&D', *Brookings Papers on Economic Activity*, pp. 783–820. Quoted
in Ashish Arora, Marco Ceccagnoli, and Wesley M. Cohen, 'R&D and the Patent Premium'.
Avaialble at http://www.nber.org/confer/2002/prods02/arora.pdf (last accessed on 27
September 2008).

[108] W.M. Cohen, R.R. Nelson, and J.P Walsh, 2000, 'Protecting Their Intellectual
Assets: Appropriability Conditions and Why U.S. Manufacturing Firms Patent or Not',
NBER Working Paper, no. 7552. Quoted in Ashish Arora, Marco Ceccagnoli, and Wesley M.
Cohen, 'R&D and the Patent Premium'.

[109] Note in this connection the comments of Chief Justice Burger delivering the
judgment of the court in *Diamond* v. *Chakrabarty*, (1980) 447 US 303, pp. 317–18: 'It
is argued that this Court should weigh...potential hazards in considering whether
respondent's invention is patentable subject matter...We disagree. The grant or denial of
patents on microorganisms is not likely to put an end to genetic research or to its attendant
risks. The large amount of research that has already occurred when no researcher had sure
knowledge that patent protection would be available suggests that legislative or judicial fiat
as to patentability will not deter the scientific mind from probing into the unknown any
more than Canute could command the tides.'

[110] For a detailed analysis on this position see, Steve P. Calandrillo, 1998, 'An Economic
Analysis of Intellectual Property Rights: Justifications and Problems of Exclusive Rights,
Incentives to Generate Information, and the Alternative of a Government-Run Reward
System', *Fordham Intell. Prop. Media and Ent. L.J.*, vol. 9, pp. 316–21; Steven Shavell, October

The Limits of Consequentialism

Consequences and utilities can be conceptualized in two ways—a narrow conception of utility would employ wealth maximization and its corollaries, as the intended consequence of a particular rule; a broader deployment of the term would include welfare, a notion so abstract that it permits a whole range of interpretations. In either case, consequentialism runs into problems. Even if one were to discard the more abstract criterion of 'welfare' and take wealth maximization/efficiency as the sole criterion for determining the efficacy of intellectual property rights, the problem of the standard of utility employed to compare efficiency of one firm (for one category of goods) with that of another (for another set of goods) arises. For example, patents may induce incentives for one firm but may lead to inefficient or wasteful expenditure for another. A property right in an invention might reduce aggregate welfare by limiting access. At the same time, limited access could maximize aggregate welfare through distributive effects ruled out by egalitarian accounts of justice. There may be many short term disadvantages which may be offset in the longer run. A property institution, like the patent law, might satisfy the specific principle, that intellectual production needs to be protected in order that it acts as an incentive for innovation, and yet be part of an overall situation in which net efficiency achieved is lower than it could be were the property arrangement changed. Wide differences in wealth produce preference dissatisfaction in those who miss the bus or those who bear the brunt in terms of increased costs. Rule conformity, therefore, becomes neither a necessary nor a sufficient criterion for attaining efficient allocation of intellectual resources and, therefore, of rightness, even by the utilitarian criterion of morality.

Utilitarian consequentialism demands that it is the goodness of the consequence that determines the validity and morality of an act or of a rights claim. Rule utilitarianism instructs that patent rules, even after they have been codified according to expected good that they will generate, still need to be constantly refashioned in light of the consequences. Utilitarian assessments need to be worked out in relation to the concrete social circumstances. If one accepts that consequentialism resolves moral questions then it follows that rule utilitarianism, which does not test acts against consequences for moral soundness but rather the rules that

---

2001, 'Rewards Versus Intellectual Property Rights', *Journal of Law and Economics*, vol. XLIV, which concludes that 'the intellectual property rights system does not enjoy any fundamental advantage over the reward system', that is, a system in which 'innovators are paid for innovations directly by the government (possibly on the basis of sales)…'

codify these acts, is more a 'decision procedure', rather than a standard for rightness. It is important that a distinction is made between the best procedure for making moral decisions about what to do, and the criteria of moral rightness and wrongness. This distinction compels us then to evaluate the act according to some agreed upon criteria of moral rightness. In fact, the evaluative exercise is embedded in the very description of an act. Adam Moore states, '[s]ince the evaluation of rules is dependent on the consequences, and acts alone, not rules, have consequences, we must decide how to describe actions in order to justify rules'.[111]

Act utilitarianism argues that if the goodness of the consequences of breaking a rule is greater than the goodness of consequences of adhering to the rule, then these are valid grounds for abandoning the rule. In the present context therefore, it is important to view 'acts' that govern intellectual property related policies against the consequences that they generate, rather than in terms of their compliance to Intellectual Property laws and rules. Utilitarian consequentialism, however, faces the problem of act description when actions are tested against varying moral premises. For instance, a particular action might be described in any of the following ways:

1. Reverse engineering a drug innovation of another;
2. Reverse engineering a drug innovation of another when no one else will; and
3. Reverse engineering a drug innovation of another when no one else will, and when doing so will save lives of a thousand children.

The same act can be performed with different motivations, under different circumstances and can have different consequences. Since utilitarians are concerned with the goodness of consequences, an act should be described in such a way that all the relevant consequences are included. The problem here is that Utilitarianism does not prioritize consequences. It does not, for example, say that wealth maximization, as a consequence, is superior to equal distribution of wealth. Thus in circumstances when different utilities are being maximized—for example in the given instances above a) might lead to increase in wealth, or it could an exercise in liberty b) might lead to improvement in the original work leading better utilization of the resource in question, and c) might lead to increased welfare for thousand children—all maximize some utility or the other. Utilitarianism remains unhelpful

[111] Adam Moore, 2004, pp. 56–7.

in distinguishing between fair and unfair preferences or in determining the standard of rightness.

In defense of utilitarian consequentialism, it is often proposed that there are many variants of utility which are recognized and used as the basis of policy making and that consequentialism does not foreclose 'just' or 'rightful' consequences as a consideration in utility calculations. Let us then test this broader conception of utility in the context of intellectual property rights. Quite clearly, the conception of utility that has been deployed in defense of IPRs is the principle of wealth maximization through creation of incentives by institutions, for the efficient or optimal use of intellectual resources. However, if we were to expand the intention to not just maximize wealth but also to, for instance, serve the rights of indigenous peoples over their knowledges, it would involve the deployment of, what can be termed as, 'preference equality'. It would involve giving equal preference to indigenous knowledge systems and to western modern sciences. Chapters 7 and 8 both highlight the epistemic superiority which has been assumed, through, intellectual property rights, by western modern sciences. In utilitarian philosophy, each person's and group's utility or preference is to count equally with the utility or preference of others. This necessarily entails interpersonal comparisons. The dilemma is how to move from individual welfare to a criterion of social choice where each community's or group's welfare is counted as equal. The general difficulty that exists in interpersonal/inter-group comparisons is that the principle of utility requires the maximization of utilities across all individuals and no standards exist of comparing the utility of one person with that of the other.[112]

Preference equality or the equal rights principle often presents a normative issue for utilitarian analysis, which has been often critiqued for ignoring how utility or welfare is distributed across society. In his analysis of arguments from utility Lawrence Becker reasons that most of the justificatory weight of the utility arguments must be borne by the non-economic or 'meta-economic' principles of a normative sort— principles of justice, for example.[113] This is to say that while economic analysis is an important aspect of designing intellectual property policy, its results cannot settle all questions by a social policy designed on utilitarian premises. Efficiency and justice can certainly be mutually conflicting when put forward as social goals. All economic systems are dynamic and

---

[112] Problems of measurement, quantification, varying experiences and discourses of people, etc. are some of the issues that forestall reliable assessments

[113] Lawrence C. Becker, 1977, p. 71.

the pull to move away from equality would be continuous. Inventions produce new wealth for some while some lose out. In new transactions some are net gainers while others are net losers (for example, in the case of intellectual property protection, the second inventor; sometimes even the first inventor which happens to be a community with an unprotected knowledge system) once inequality enters questions of justice arise.[114] Economic efficiency arguments are on very weak grounds when asked to determine and adjudicate who should have what rights.

It is here that recourse to other moral norms becomes necessary in policy making.[115] Eric D'Arcy and David Lyons state that the only way to adequately determine the appropriate act description is to appeal to moral norms.[116] For Rawls, the non-negotiable (primary) moral good is justice—'interests requiring the violation of justice have no value'.[117] Justice limits the admissible conceptions of good, so those pursuits which violate the principle of justice are ruled out. Unjust preferences never enter the calculus. For Utilitarians, on the other hand, no restrictions, founded on rights and justice, are imposed on the evaluation of consequences.[118] There are some acts that we intuitively know are wrong. Bernard Williams gives the example of shooting people in an area of London to stop parking illegally in the area. This would increase the happiness that thousands of Londoners would derive from the end of the menace. In such a case, Amartya Sen argues that we do not even need to calculate whether threatening to shoot people over parking offences would maximize good outcomes. We already know that threatening to shoot people over parking offences is wrong, and any system that requires us to make that calculation is a system we should reject because by forgetting we know that, it misunderstands and misrepresents moral reasoning.[119]

The utilitarian justification of IPRs thus needs to be informed by other moral premises of rights and justice. If morality is to be evaluated in terms of the consequences, the goodness of the outcome should be

[114] See Edwin Baker, 1974, 'Utility and Rights: Two justifications for State Action Increasing Equality', *Yale Law Journal*, vol. 84, p. 39.

[115] Utilitarianism does not regard moral norms outside of its own moral theory, which is derived from the goodness of the consequences. However, there are moral norms which inform our practices and decisions irrespective of the consequences generated.

[116] Eric D'Arcy, 'Human Acts: An Essay in Their Moral Evaluation', in *Intellectual Property and Information Control,* Adam Moore (ed.), p. 56.

[117] John Rawls, 1971, pp. 302–3.

[118] John Rawls, 1982, 'Social Utility and Primary Goods', in *Utilitarianism and Beyond*, A. Sen, and Bernard Wlliams (eds), Cambridge: CUP, pp. 182–84.

[119] Amartya Sen, and Bernard Williams (eds), 1982, *Utilitarianism and Beyond*, Cambridge: Cambridge University Press.

in conjunction with other principles of justice. IPRs cannot be solely judged in terms of wealth maximization, efficiency, and so on—these cannot become the basis for the grant of a right. They may enter the rights calculus as additional supports or as disclaimers, but as a stand-alone justificatory premise it falters when confronted with other moral premises. Will Kymlicka expresses this point rather succinctly when he writes that a society of non-utilitarians, who believe in the intrinsic importance of rights, will do better in terms of maximizing utility, than a society of act or rule utilitarians who view rights as devices for maximizing utility.[120]

MOVING BEYOND UTILITARIAN CONSEQUENTIALISM
Given its intuitive appeal and the initial plausibility of utilitarian consequentialism, that consequences matter in the formulation of rules—it is worth asking whether it provides a morally sustainable justificatory premise for intellectual property rights. There were two ways in which this analysis was approached—one was to delve into an internal critique by undertaking a cost-benefit analysis, so vital for the legitimation of any rule in the utilitarian framework. In a way, it provided us with a minimalist window to evaluate the political morality adjudged in utilitarian terms. The cost-benefit analysis served to bring to notice the costs incurred (even adjudged minimally in terms of innovation, efficiency, wealth maximization) that are large enough for us to conclude that there is no overwhelming truth to the claim that IPR led benefits outweigh costs. Consequence sensitivity demands that the utilitarian calculus takes into account both the quantum of costs and the nature of costs. This then brought into play the trade offs between liberty, rights, equal respect principle and the push for increased innovation (which itself is not unambiguously demonstrable).

IPRs are based on the profit maximizing potential, generated by the patents, which act as incentives for innovation. Several factors may weaken the connection between profit maximization and individual preference satisfaction, thus weakening the link between utility of one form and utility of another or aggregate utility and individual liberty. Even if, for public policy considerations, we ignore details of individual preferences and focus instead on all-purpose goods like liberties and resources which are useful to people whatever their specific preferences, we can still use the distribution of these all-purpose goods as a reasonable proxy for the distribution of preference satisfaction.[121] So we can measure increase

---

[120] Will Kymlicka, 1990, p. 30.
[121] Will Kymlicka, 2002, p. 19.

or decrease in the level of preference satisfaction of individuals, not by the increase or decrease in the level of preference satisfaction, 'but by measuring the increases or decreases in the level of all-purpose means they can use to satisfy their preferences'.[122] If utility calculations lead to a loss in some of these 'all-purpose means', for example, as in the patents case, the like liberty of others to pursue and use their research or innovation for maximization of their profits, then the claim that existing rights be used to block intellectual property rights, by those who lose from them, is very strong, both on grounds of utility as well as liberty.

Liberty was one of the originating principles for the right to private property. The principle of utility, preference satisfaction and efficiency all supported powers and rights to act freely with respect to one's property in order to satisfy preferences. The principle of liberty supported most utilitarian premises of property.[123] Moving from tangible property to intangible intellectual property, the premises of justification ought to change because of a fundamental difference between the two. Tangible goods are clearly scarce and give rise to conflicting uses. It is the scarcity of tangible property that gives rise to property rights. IPRs, however, do not rest on a natural scarcity of goods, but on 'artificial, self-created scarcity'. That is to say, legislation or legal fiat limits the use of ideal objects in such a way as to create an artificial scarcity that, it is hoped, will generate greater revenues for innovators. However, Tom Palmer argues that the attempt to generate profit opportunities by legislatively limiting access to certain ideal goods, and therefore to mimic the market processes governing the allocation of tangible goods contains a fatal contradiction. It violates the rights to tangible goods the very rights that provide the legal foundations with which markets begin.[124] To deny someone the right to improve upon another's creation, manifested in the former's personal property, is to contradictorily support IPRs over real and personal property rights, clearly a non-libertarian position. Liberty-based arguments for property rights are fundamentally hostile to intellectual property claims, for patent

---

[122] Ibid., p. 20.

[123] The case for tangible property is also supported by the labour-desert and self-ownership principles which justify property rights on natural rights grounds. In fact, it is often asserted that the principle of utility does not support property rights in many ways, are less as powerfully as other philosophical traditions, particularly the labour-desert principle. For an interesting example where property rights for which utility cannot account, see Stephen Munzer, 1990, p. 225.

[124] Tom Palmer, Summer 1990, 'Are Patents and Copyrights Morally Justified? The Philosophy of Property Rights and Ideal Objects', *Harvard Journal of Law and Public Policy*, 13(3), p. 865.

and copyright monopolies interfere with the freedom of others to use their self-owned labour or their own justly acquired property in certain ways, as has been discussed in greater detail in Chapter 3.

If liberty was one of the foundational principles for the right to private property, then rights have been one of the sustaining principles of liberal democracy. The issue of rights brings into sharp focus questions of 'nature of costs and the limits of utilitarian consequentialism in negotiating the equal rights principle. Some of the fundamental questions with respect to what 'costs' ought to be: what costs is a society willing to pay for increased innovation, now or as a future prospect? Who are to be the bearers of these costs? What is the cost-bearing capacity of these individuals, groups or a society? Whose 'preference satisfaction' are we talking about? These are important questions which raise issues of rights and justice.

According to a widely held moral principle, individual lives matter, and they matter equally. The claims individuals make for intellectual property protection may conflict with each other and the rules of adjudication are likely to have distributional impacts, in favour of one individual, group or society and/or against another individual, group or society. What distributions are made morally justifiable by the equal importance of each and every individual and society? One of the serious gaps in utilitarian morality is it's response to the equal rights principle. Utility is unhelpful in adjudicating between competing rights, which might lead to disparate consequences, as it has no standards of comparing disparate utilities. For instance, the prospect of patents may bring about increased innovation and better drugs, but there is no utility calculus which can compare these gains vis-à-vis the loss of access to affordable medicines by millions.

Adjudicating between competing rights premises would necessitate a move away from the 'linguistic framework' of utilitarianism. Duties and obligations cannot exclusively be grounded in wealth maximization, or even an abstract notion of welfare, without incorporating rights and justice in the valuation of outcomes. Practices and rules cannot demand abdication of rights and liberty and therefore, need to be grounded in a moral philosophy which bases the validity of a practice (IPRs in this instance) in justice and fairness. Rights are not, as in the utilitarian reading, intermediate institutional structures and laws which lead to optimum utility being created in society. While there is no clear evidence that the pie increases with intellectual property rights, the very talk of increasing the size of the pie as being the basis of rights is philosophically flawed. The principle of utility (in any form) is an insufficient sole-standard for testing the validity, or legal status of a rule or a law. The goal for law, in the ultimate analysis is justice and not wealth maximization.[125] The goal of intellectual property law thus needs to be based on conceptions of morality other than the one evaluated in terms of utility maximization.

Considerations of utility can never be weighty enough to become the sole moral force behind a social policy which has global ramifications. For instance, when it is argued that 'the right to control the initial disclosure of one's ideas is grounded in respect for the individual',[126] there is an adherence to a moral principle which upholds the liberty principle. Paine, who uses this justification to support the right to control disclosure, seems to be upholding a deontological position—individuals are worthy of a deep moral respect and may not be treated in certain ways. Individuals may not be sacrificed for social utility.[127] More minimally, within the bounds of individual rights to sovereignty and privacy, utility may be promoted—but only within these constraints. Constraints, within which utility can be defined and installed as a principle of rights, can be varied depending on the moral norm that informs one's belief patterns. There moral principles, outside of utilitarianism, inform our intuition about what constitutes the ethicality of an act—individual, collective, or institutional. Simply put, moral norms are necessary to determine appropriate act descriptions and that these moral norms need to be derived from a non-consequential morality.

Institutions rarely serve only one end. A holistic study of IPRs should incorporate the effects of Intellectual Property rights on the distribution of socio-economic power within a community and costs of these effects, which are difficult to measure purely in utilitarian terms. There are big utilitarian dilemmas regarding innovation of drugs or health rights of the poor, knowledge rights of the indigenous communities

[125] Laws are often assumed to be based on ethics and are expected to determine the boundaries of fair conduct and fair use. However law can, at times, run contrary to requirements of ethics. As Fricke points out in his analysis of the ethical basis of the Library Bill of Rights, laws can be unethical or wrong: slavery in America and the Holocaust in Nazi-Germany are two examples. Abortion or embryo-based researches are legally and ethically divisive issues in many countries. While clearly there ought to be an overlap between legality and ethics, there are often instances where a set of laws may be based on considerations other than moral. IPRs are a case in this point.

[126] Lynn Sharp Paine, 'Trade Secrets and the Justification of Intellectual Property: A Comment on Hettinger', in *Intellectual Property: Moral, Legal and International Dimensions*, Adam Moore (ed.), p. 42.

[127] Ibid.

or knowledge rights of the innovators, livelihood rights of the farmers, or biotechnological led innovations. The arbitration of these questions requires reference to moral criteria beyond that which is acccepted by utilitarian consequentialism. The utilitarian justification of intellectual property is that it does not fit in with other right-generating moral theories. Life rights, livelihood rights, privacy rights are typically given a deontic premise that dwarf utilitarian concerns. In the absence of other moral norms, utilitarianism is an insufficient standard for determining the appropriateness of social policy and institutions.

5   The Politics of Knowledge

Two defining features of knowledge were introduced earlier in the book (Chapter 1)—that knowledge generation is cumulative and therefore, a collective intergenerational enterprise; and consequently, that knowledge has an indivisible character which makes it difficult to apportion. If we establish that knowledge as a category has well defined collective claims, having the character of indivisibility and therefore of a public good, then individual rights' claims over knowledge and its instantiation becomes a matter of contestation. Moreover, if we establish the contextual, relativist and the social dimension of intellectual practices then the claimed epistemological privileges granted by the TRIPS regime to the enterprise of western sciences, also becomes a matter of contestation. The 'cultural turn in development', to use a phrase by Nederveen Pieterse,[1] has opened up the possibilities of multiple epistemes whose values are no longer a matter of commensuration by standards evolved by the rational scientific enterprises of knowledge creation. This chapter looks at the sociology and culture of knowledge creation, knowledge not just as representation and mind as a mirror reflecting reality but as action, as a political and social tool and the implications that it has for opening up new and effective locales of knowledges. This chapter takes the argument of social construction of knowledge and extends it to question the claimed scientificity and objectivity of western modern sciences embodied and institutionalized in the TRIPS framework, in an endeavour to engage with the possibility of multiple constructions and representations of reality and question the claimed universality and hegemony of western modern sciences. Rosemary Coombe states, 'pointing to social constructionism is not a form of intellectual or political critique, unless it is linked to an analysis of the forces that incite cultural collectivities, the conditions of their making, and the

---

[1] Nederveen Pieterse, 2001, *Development Theory: Deconstructions/Reconstructions*, London: Sage, p. 15.

social consequences of their emergence and entitlements'.[2] This is what the chapter aims to do.

KNOWLEDGE AS CULTURE

Theoretical developments in anthropology increasingly emphasize the cultural dimension of knowledge. '…knowledge is best conceived and studied as culture, and the various types of social knowledges communicate and constitute social meaning—such as meanings about power and pleasure, beauty and death, goodness and danger'.[3] These studies have long focused on discrete, identifiable communities frequently paying attention to the existence of multiple cultures, rationalities, knowledges, and multiple ways of being itself. This in a large measure, has contributed to the growing critique of universalism, generating an engagement with polycentrism, localisms, multi-polarity, and pluralism.[4]

Culture is a major marker of difference. It marks the differences between shared customs, worldviews, knowledges of particular groups or kinds of people. According to Lyotard, culture enables us to represent 'the pluralistic, contingent and local features of our existence', to stress 'difference over unity', to assert the idea of 'constructions over essences', and to 'wage war on totality'.[5] It is located in the need to evolve general principles and the desire to apply these principles within culturally specific circumstances and contexts. Wagner sees culture arising from the dialectic between the individual and the social world. His analysis is situated in the relation between invention and convention, innovation and control, meaning and context.[6]

Acknowledgment of the importance of culture has also seeped into national and international rhetoric of development. The UNESCO-sponsored 'World Decade on Culture and Development'[7] for example, led to a growing engagement with the cultural dimensions of development at

[2] Rosemary Coombe, Forthcoming, 'Intellectual Property in Regimes of Neoliberal Governmentality: Locating Community Subjects and their Traditions', submitted for inclusion in Mario Biagicoli, Peter Jaszi and Martha Woodmansee (eds), *Contexts of Invention*, Chicago: University of Chicago Press, p. 2.

[3] McCarthy Doyle, 1996, *Knowledge as Culture: The New Sociology of Knowledge,* London: Routledge, p. 1.

[4] For a discussion see, for instance, Samir Amin, 1989, *Eurocentrism,* New York: Monthly Review Press.

[5] Jean François Lyotard, 1984, *The Postmodern Condition: A Report on Knowledge,* Minneapolis: University of Minnesota Press, p. 82.

[6] Roy Wagner, 1981, *The Invention of Culture,* Chicago: University of Chicago Press.

[7] 1988–97.

the international level. Pieterse calls this 'the cultural turn in development.'[8] Culture came to be accepted as another dimension of development, which could no longer ignored or viewed as just an obstacle to objective world views, as in orthodox modernization thinking. Culture now figures in development talk in several ways; Nederveen Pieterse outlines two of them. One is the regard for cultural diversity. A second related theme is 'cultural capital', as both a human capacity and a form of human capital, and as a political currency (both in ethnic and religious mobilization and as an asset in economic relations).[9] Culture then becomes an epistemological tool which can be used to interpret peoples, groups and civilizations and not merely to represent them.

Knowledge, understood within the broad category of 'culture' includes various types of knowledge, symbols and images that people use in various domains of their everyday life. The new sociology of knowledge asks what kind of symbols and knowledges are used by whom. How are they produced and disseminated? How are they linked to strategies of action and opportunity? The focus in each of these cases is on knowledge that is not simply derived from the constituted social order, but is itself a major element in the constitution of the social order itself. It provides the language, or to use Raymond William's well known phrase, the 'signifying system' through which 'the social order is communicated, reproduced, experienced and explored'.[10]

Knowledge then refers to sets of ideas accepted by a social group or society in terms of what is real for them. Gernot Bohme, in his essay on *Midwifery as Science* writes that 'to arrive at sociology of knowledge we proceed from the concept of cultural reproduction of society. This refers to the reproduction of resources of social life not included in the material, biological reproduction of the human species...These cultural resources will be called "knowledge contents"; participation in their production will be called knowledge'.[11] Rather than being a specialized area of sociology, the sociology of knowledge deals with the broad, underlying questions about the extent and limits of social influences on people's lives, and the social-cultural foundations of our knowledge of the world.

[8] Pieterse Jan Nederveen, 2001; see also, Roy Wagner, 1981, *The Invention of Culture.* Revised edition, Chicago: University of Chicago Press.

[9] Ibid., p. 15.

[10] Raymond Williams, 1981, *Culture,* London: Fontana, pp. 12–13.

[11] Gernot Bohme, 1894, 'Midwifery as Science: An Essay on the Relation between Scientific and Everyday Knowledge', in *Society and Knowledge: Contemporary Perspectives in the Sociology of Knowledge,* Meja Volker and Nico Stehr (eds), New Brunswick: Transaction Books, p. 365.

Knowledge is not something that exists in its own right but one that is generated and communicated. It is created with reference to, and in the context of social worlds that people inhabit. These specific, varying, multiple social worlds define the utility of knowledge. As Florian Znaniecki argues, for the sociologist at least, a system of knowledge is 'what it is to people who participate in its construction, reproduction, application, and development'.[12] In this view, the primary concern is how social groups and forms of social organization have contributed to the production and dissemination of knowledges and how, in turn, the social organization is framed and reframed according to the production and distribution of knowledge. The constituency and utility of knowledge is then something relative and necessarily contextual. That it may have universal or trans-contextual utility is not the defining or a necessary condition at all.

The need to assert culture has led, by implication, to the assertion of the local and need to blend the universal and the local. The assertion of the 'cultural local' found one of its earliest expressions in the rights discourse and now has gone beyond to include legal discourse as well, particularly in the context of the tensions between Western positive law and Islamic law.[13] The conflict between indigenous 'local' knowledge and western 'universal' sciences is a recent addition to the site as the latter becomes juridified in international law, seeking universal status through the TRIPS agreement. The TRIPS regime and its conception of intellectual property seek to delineate the domain of scientificity and then, based on its conformity with scientific norms and principles, adjudicate on knowledge endeavours worthy of propertization and intellectual property protection. It is important to underscore the point that categorizing knowledges, and then assigning rights based on them, creates not only categories and hierarchies of knowledges, distinguishing between 'scientific' and 'non-scientific' knowledge regardless of their contribution, but also creates an unequal basis for rights.

THE SOCIOLOGY OF KNOWLEDGE
Sociology of knowledge claims that the discovery of truth, that is, knowledge, is socially and historically conditioned. Sociology of knowledge has at times been regarded as a kind of Copernican revolution in the analysis of cultural products. While the older sociology of knowledge epitomized

[12] Florian Znaniecki, 1940, Quoted in McCarthy Doyle, *Knowledge as Culture*, p. 16.
[13] See Clifford Geertz, 1993, *Local Knowledge*, London: Fontana Press.

by Karl Mannheim's *Ideology and Utopia*[14] asks how the social location of individuals and groups shapes their knowledge, more recent sociologies of knowledge examine how different kinds of social organization make the ordering of knowledge as a whole possible.[15] In general, however, many philosophers have attempted to demonstrate in their own different ways, that a sociology of knowledge is neither possible nor desirable. Immanuel Kant thus argued that while there cannot be perception without conception, the constitutive components of cognition are *a priori*. For him a priori forms of cognition are independent of, and prior to, experience and are therefore, not contingent on social factors.[16] Positivism denies the legitimacy of sociology of knowledge by regarding truth to be 'out there' in the real world waiting to be discovered. Positivists contend that the only authentic knowledge is scientific in nature, which is derived from the strict application of the scientific method. Empiricists of various persuasions have maintained that scientific knowledge, in particular, is generated by direct experience unaffected by social conditions. Different philosophies have often explicitly rejected sociological relativism that is associated with the modem sociology of knowledge. They have attempted to overcome doubts and skepticism by placing knowledge on a firm, uncontested foundation, even outside the realm of socio-historical experience.[17] They assume a factual world structured in a law like manner by the constant conjunction of events. Stehr and Meja, in their exhaustive work, argue that constant conjunctions can only result from laboratory work which function like closed systems in which unambiguous results are possible and repeatable. In practice, such constant conjunctions are exceptions—as is predictive success.[18] Laws of nature and society are not as immanent as they are assumed to be; there are various subjectivities that intervene between the existence of 'reality' and the understanding and interpretation of it. In fact, sociology of knowledge proposes that reality is nothing but as we see it and make sense of it. Seeking of truth or attaining knowledge

[14] Karl Mannheim, 1968 [1936], *Ideology and Utopia: An Introduction to the Sociology of Knowledge*, Louis Wirth and Edward Shils (trans.), New York: Harcourt, Brace & World.

[15] For a discussion see, Meja Volker, and Nico Stehr (eds), 1984, *Knowledge and Society: Contemporary Perspectives on the Sociology of Knowledge,* Transaction Books; Stehr and Meja's two large volumes put together a full critical outline of the central questions and methods of the sociology of knowledge, including prospects for its revival in sociological discourse.

[16] Immanuel Kant, 1787, *Critique of Pure Reason*, Norman Kemp Smith (ed.), Electronic version, Palgrave: Macmillan, available at http://arts. Cuhk.edu.hk/Philosophy/Kant/cpr/ (last accessed on 17 September 2008).

[17] Ibid.

[18] Volker Meja and Nico Stehr (eds), 1984, p. 224.

of reality then becomes decoding not of the objective world as it exists out there but is an interested activity mediated by the perceptions and subjectivities of the 'truth seeker'. Sociology of knowledge, investigates the interconnections between categories of thought, knowledge claims, and social reality, the Seinsverbundenheit (existential connectedness) of thought.[19]

What is known as the 'modern' sociology of knowledge was a reinvention of the old school represented by German- sociologists, notably Max Scheler and Karl Mannheim,[20] particularly by Peter L. Berger and Thomas Luckmann in *The Social Construction of Reality*.[21] Luckmann and Berger redirected the focus of sociology of knowledge from the study of social determination of ideas to the social construction of reality itself; an idea of knowledge that guides and is produced by everyday life. Knowledge is seen not merely as an off-shoot of culture and society or one as having links with them, but the social is instead constitutive of knowledge that is dialectically linked to the social. Knowledge and reality, they argued, 'existed in dialectical and reciprocal relationship of mutual construction'.[22] Berger and Luckmann assert that all knowledge—scientific, everyday, commonsensical, cultural—is derived is derived from and maintained by social interactions, as a result of which human typifications, significations, and institutions come to be presented as part of an objective reality. It is in this sense that they maintain that reality is socially constructed, constantly changing, and evolving as peoples' perceptions and understandings evolve. A major focus of social constructionism is to uncover the ways in which individuals and groups participate in the creation of their perceived social reality. It also focuses on how perceptions of reality are created, institutionalized, and made into tradition by humans.

What is the function of knowledge? Is the function of knowledge, as Berger and Luckmann would state, to reveal aspects of reality? Or are forms of knowledge mystifying representations of reality in the form of

[19] Karl Mannheim, 1968.

[20] Karl Marx was a significant precursor of the field, with his theory that under certain historical conditions, economic realities ultimately determine the ideological 'superstructure' (knowledge and ideas being a part of it). Marx and the classical sociologists after him argued that, in the final analysis, knowledges (including people's belief systems and ideas) are profoundly influenced by the predominant form of existing social organization. This conception remains a central issue in the sociology of knowledge, and it has directly inspired some exemplary analyses of problems of cultural production, for example, in the work of Georg Lukacs, 1989, *Theory, Culture and Politics*, New Jersey: Transaction.

[21] P.L. Berger and T. Luckmann, 1966, *The Social Construction of Reality: A Treatise in the Sociology of Knowledge*, NY: Anchor Books.

[22] Doyle McCarthy, 1996, p. 2.

ideologies, disguising powerful interests in society, as orthodox Marxism would tend to argue? The function of knowledge is an amalgamation of both—to mystify and to reveal. The ideological function of knowledge is compatible with representative and constitutive functions of knowledge. Although the sociology of knowledge is concerned with intellectual structures, as being socially, historically, and culturally determined, it would also encompass the function of knowledge as ideology—to distort, justify or mystify group positions and interest.

There is a need to restore and focus on the political atmosphere in which knowledges are generated. McCarthy Doyle, for instance, moves beyond the social constituency of knowledge, to suggest the function of knowledge in public life and in politics. [23] Mental attitudes, for her are always linked with action. Knowledge is a capacity for action; it can represent, separately or in conjunction, a consciousness, an experience, capabilities, power—all of which can manifest in individual or social acts. Taken in this 'pragmatic' perspective, knowledge represents a function— 'to integrate social order, to provide a coherent and meaningful sense of reality[…]to render and preserve a person or a group's identity and to legitimate action and authority'. [24]

So far, I have stressed on two aspects of knowledge—first, that it is a social and cultural production, and second that knowledge is an interested activity which serves, beyond truth-seeking, a number of vital socio-political functions. Flowing form these two assertions is a third one—that reality has multiple constructions and that the knowledge of it is essentially relative and particularistic in character. The idea of social determination of knowledge implies the ontological primacy of the social existence over mentality, consciousness, and mental life. This primary social reality stands opposed to a realm in which things are ontologically less real, including the entire realm of representations— what people know, think, perceive or understand. [25]

Since knowledge generation, systems of codification, and transmission are deeply value laden, they cannot be anything other than culture specific. It is important to show that the cognitive and the social interrelate else there is always the danger that the 'new' orientation towards knowledge would become cognitively one sided, as has become the case with the determination of what constitutes intellectual property. Intellectual property rights are, for most part, associated with forms of

[23] Ibid., p. 2.
[24] Ibid., p. 5.
[25] Ibid., p. 15.

scientific knowledge, which are usually assumed to be warranted by direct experience of the natural world, governed by immanent laws of nature, unaffected by social conditions. In the context of these perceptions, a pertinent question arises: is sociology of scientific knowledge possible? Can the idea of social determination, and all that it implies a persuasive way to understand scientific knowledge in general and Intellectual Property in particular.

Sociology of Scientific Knowledge

At the center of what is broadly referred to as the 'western civilization' is the two-fold idea of science and reason. The age of enlightenment advocated reason as the primary basis of authority. The enlightenment is often closely linked with the arrival of the scientific revolution, for both movements emphasized reason, science, and rationality. It is through the progressive employment of reason and the development of science that the progressive history of the West has been chartered, almost without interruption since the seventeenth century. Some philosophers use the concepts of progress and rationality synonymously: progressive steps in science are precisely those that are based on the scientists' rational choices. The representation of science as objective reason, it is widely believed, paves the way for social progress and individuals' freedom. The idea of scientific knowledge was central to the period that followed the enlightenment era and it continued to conceive of itself as a project of and for all humanity. Unity and universality of knowledge arising out of objectivity of science became the central narrative of the post enlightenment era. Science began to be seen as a universal truth, a 'practical embodiment of impersonal reason'.

Often referred to as 'social construction of science' or 'sociology of scientific knowledge', these perspectives claim that because science's methods, like any other way of knowing, are wholly relative to a theoretical framework and a world-view science amounts to a construction, *and not a discovery*, of reality, scientific knowledge has come to be seen as being constitutive of similar processes as other forms of knowledge. Arce and Long argue that knowledge is constituted by the ways in which people categorize, code, process, and impute meaning to their experiences, and this is as true of 'scientific' as of 'non-scientific', everyday forms of knowledge.[26]

[26] Alberto Arce and Norman Long, 1992, 'The Dynamics of Knowledge', in *Battlefields of Knowledge: The Interlocking of Theory and Practice in Social Research and Development*, Norman Long and Ann Long (eds), London and New York: Routledge, p. 211.

The re-orientation has also been in terms developing a sociology of scientific knowledge beyond merely uncovering the social and cultural linkages of science. Michael Mulkay,[27] examining the implications that knowledge and utility have for sociology of knowledge, outlines two contrasting perspectives on science. The dominant perspective which treats science as being epistemologically unique believes that the veracity of scientific knowledge is firmly established by 'controlled, rigorous procedures of scientific methods' which enables it to present an accurate representation of the physical world.[28] This perspective is pithily summed up by the Werner Stark: 'Social developments do not determine the content of scientific developments because they do not determine natural facts. It is an objective account of the real world and is concerned with social organization only to the extent that the latter enables scientists to observe and report the world accurately'.[29] Within this perspective, social influences can intrude into the actual intellectual content of science only when the latter has been distorted by non-scientific pressures. Cultural and social 'situatedness' are the marks of lower knowledge forms and science, as Durkheim announced, and was 'independent of any local context'.[30]

The second perspective, which presents both a contrast and an alternative, argues that the procedures and conclusions of science are like all other cultural products, contingent on the outcome of interpretative social acts. The central contention of this perspective is that although the physical world does constrain the decisions of science, it never uniquely determines those decisions. Scientific research is not merely an act of registering an objective world. It is an act of interpretation whereby the scientist generates meaning out of the complex set of clues generated by his action on the physical world. This is not done in a moral or social vacuum, 'rather the attribution of technical meaning is always inextricably bound with those processes of social interaction whereby the social attributes of participants and their claims are negotiated'.[31] Within this second perspective, Mulkay proposes that 'there are good grounds for including science fully within the sociology of knowledge'. Since the 1980s, interest in developing philosophical accounts of scientific

[27] Michael Mulkay, 1984, 'Knowledge and Utility: Implications for the Sociology of Knowledge', in Knowledge and Society, N. Stehr and V. Meja (eds), p. 79.

[28] Ibid., pp. 77–9.

[29] Werner Stark, 1958, The Sociology of Knowledge and Sociological Theory, London: RKP, quoted from Michael Mulkay, 1984, p. 78.

[30] E. Durkheim, 1972, Selected Writings [1899], A. Giddens (ed. and trans.), Cambridge: Cambridge University Press, p. 88.

[31] Michael Mulkay, 1984, p. 79.

knowledge that incorporate the social dimensions of scientific practice has been on the increase.[32] Practitioners include H.M. Collins,[33] Barry Barnes.[34] Michael Mulkay,[35] Barnes,[36] Shapin,[37] B. Latour,[38] and Sheila Jasanoff.[39] The 'social study of science' has developed into an influential, argumentative, as well as a vital terrain of sociological inquiry.

Several developments combined to make social and cultural dimensions salient to the contemporary philosophy of science. The emergence of social movements, environmentalism, feminism, the assertion of indigenous knowledge systems, in different ways expressed concerns about the social effects of science-based technologies; the dilemmas posed by the emergence of 'big science';[40] the repositioning of development discourse which mainstreamed the 'local'; epistemological questions made salient by deconstructionism, postmodernism, social constructivism, science, and technology studies—all signaled a shift away from the grand narrative of

[32] However this has not been without contestations. Some understand the 'social' as biasing or distorting, and hence see the social as opposed to or competing with the cognitive or epistemic field. Sociology of Scientific knowledge (SSK) has been viewed by some as anti-science, anti-rational. Relativism is attacked as an insidious threat to the fabric of social order. T.S. Kuhn dissociating himself from sociological appropriation of his work, proclaimed that SSK, or, more ambiguously, what 'has been widely understood' as its claims, is 'an example of deconstruction gone mad'. T.S. Kuhn, 1992, 'The Trouble with the Historical Philosophy of Science', Robert and Maurine Rothschild Distinguished Lecture, 19 November 1991, Cambridge: Occasional Publication of the Department of the History of Science, pp. 8–9. For details of the debate see Steven Shapin, 1995, 'Here and Everywhere: Sociology of Scientific Knowledge', *Annual Review of Sociology*, vol. 21, pp. 289–321.

[33] H.M. Collins, 1983, 'The Sociology of Scientific Knowledge: Studies of Contemporary Science', *Annual Review of Sociology*, vol. 9, pp. 265–85.

[34] B. Barnes (ed.), 1972, *Sociology of Science*, Harmondsworth: Penguin; B. Barnes, 1985, *About Science*, Oxford: Blackwell.

[35] M. Mulkay, 1979, *Science and the Sociology of Knowledge*, London: George Allen & Unwin; M. Mulkay, 1991, *Sociology of Science: A Sociological Pilgrimage*, Milton Keynes: Open Univ Press.

[36] B. Barnes, and S. Shapin (eds), 1979, *Natural Order: Historical Studies of Scientific Culture*, London: Sage.

[37] Steven Shapin, 1995, 'Here and Everywhere: Sociology of Scientific Knowledge', *Annual Review of Sociology*, vol. 21.

[38] B. Latour, 1987, *Science in Action: How to Follow Scientists and Engineers through Society*, Cambridge, MA: Harvard University Press.

[39] S. Jasanoff, et al. (eds), 1994, *Handbook of Science and Technology Studies*, Beverly Hills, CA: Sage.

[40] 'Big Science' refers to large scientific projects which thrive on the involvement of a large number of researchers, scientists, who bring different kinds of expertise to bear upon the final product. Each has a crucial bit of expertise not possessed by other members of the group or sub-group.

universal science, to a conception of science which was both constructed and driven by normative concerns.

Critical questions have been raised in the last fifty years or so about the biases and categories that have shaped our visions of rationality, science, and progress in our everyday lives. Science's recent history has also been marked by a inquiry into the very notion of scientific progress. For the last half a century, the idea of the universal, objective science has been slowly but decisively being challenged, both by socio-political movements and by intellectual movements. Social movements brought into focus the increasing dangers and risks of medical and technological developments which have led to protests against the abuse of technology—protests and movements of anti-nuclear groups, environmentalists, anti-displacement activists, movements for community property rights in knowledge, etc. Intellectual developments, directed against positivist conceptions of scientific and method in social science, in the field of hermeneutics, structuralism, post-structuralism, phenomenology, and deconstruction offer different and competing conceptualizations of knowledge and science and scientific method. They have raised questions about the objectivity and universality of science, notion of science as progress, and universal conceptions of rationality itself. They highlight the 'constructed' nature of reality and the mediated nature of consciousness. Hermeneutical philosophy insists that the human way of being in the world is one of understanding. Humans understand reality through the interpretation of the cultural and linguistic world in which they find themselves. In other words, the journey to understanding of reality, including the physical world, involves a 'detour of interpretation'.[41] Reality is explored through dimensions of human subjectivity. Given this, there is no immediate self-transparency of the 'objective' reality, that is, reality is not something that stands on its own, apart from our interpretation of it. What is 'real' is to be grasped through its relationship to specific discourses or to 'codes' and 'conventions' of thinking and acting.[42]

The 'imperative of universalism' is rooted deep in the principle idea of science and in the idea that science and progress are synonymous.[43] Social and intellectual movements may have challenged the grand narrative of

---

[41] Paul Ricouer, 1976, *Interpretation Theory: Discourse and the Surplus of Meaning,* Texas Christian University Press.

[42] M. Doyle, 1996, p. 87.

[43] R.K. Merton, 1973, 'The Normative Structure of Science', in, R.K. Merton, *The Sociology of Science: Theoretical and Empirical Investigations* [1942], Chicago: University of Chicago Press, p. 69.

rational science, but in collective consciousness, the picture of science is predominantly one of science as objective, universal, rational and is compatible with operations and standards of democratic process. It is this picture which informs policymaking, institution building and in fact notions of political justice. It is significant to note that the questions of the scientific objectivity and universality, in short about its legitimation, were raised precisely during the period of expansion and increasing influence of science in everyday life.

One of the main objectives of this section is to establish that there is no one 'scientific Science'— if how we apprehend nature is an interpretative and a mediated exercise then, it follows, that there can be multiple ways of apprehending and understanding nature. There are, therefore, no 'true' or 'false' scientific knowledges based on the extent of contamination by social influences. Science lends itself to multiple constructions and different and differing knowledge systems can lay equal claims to being scientific. These conclusions are significant for they seek their relevance in the context of intellectual property rights' claim.

Science and Objectivity

The word 'science' has its origins in the Latin verb *scire*, meaning 'to know.' Although one can 'know' through faith, intuition or science, the method of science, or the 'scientific method', is thought to be distinct in its notion of empirical testing and validation. Observation, empirical generalizations among observable entities, testing of these empirical generalizations through laboratory experiments and practical applications, validations, predictions based on test results yielded by generalization, all form the core of scientific method. Scientific research is designed not just to make descriptive or explanatory inferences on the basis of empirical information about the world, but to deduce laws and patterns that go beyond the particular observations collected. These inferences form the basis of empirical laws which govern the natural world. Empirical laws and theoretical propositions about science are designed to provide literal descriptions of the natural world. It is assumed that the facts and the empirical laws based on them, provide an objective account of the real world. Scientific accounts preserve the law like structure of the real. This is the foundational belief of objectivism—it assumes a factual world structured in a law like manner by the constant conjunction of events.[44]

---

[44] Karin Knorr-Cetina, 'The Fabrication of Facts: Towards a Microsociology of Scientific Knowledge', in Stehr, and Meja, *Knowledge and Society*, p. 224.

The process of scientific inquiry, the logic of scientific procedure, it is widely held, makes objectivism of reality possible. Scientific research adheres to a set of rules of inference on which its validity depends. The content of 'science' is primarily the methods and rules, not the subject matter, since we can use these methods to study virtually anything. This point was recognized over a century ago when Karl Pearson explained that '[t]he unity of all sciences consists alone in its method, not in its material'.[45] This is to say that although procedures vary from one field of inquiry to another, identifiable features distinguish scientific inquiry from other methodologies of knowledge. Among other facets shared by the various fields of inquiry is the conviction that the process must be objective to reduce a subjective or a biased interpretation of the results.

Most philosophers of science draw a sharp distinction between the 'context of discovery' by which they mean the specific historical circumstances in which a scientific result is first established and disseminated, and the 'context of justification', the epistemological assessment of the reasons we have for regarding those results as accurate, or correct. It follows from this distinction that while the practice of scientists may be of historical and sociological interest, it is not directly relevant to the appraisal of current scientific achievements. The context of discovery is independent of social or historical contingency. The appraisal or the context of validation or justification is governed by scientific laws and methods which makes the discovery of facts or the 'facticity' of science an unmediated reflection of reality.

The 'universality' of science comes to rest on the alleged non-contextuality of science. Since scientific facts, it is argued, are socially non-contingent and are a true representation of natural phenomena, they are universally applicable. These assertions are however, intensely contested. Recent developments in science and technology studies, social constructionism/constructivism refute the objective basis of scientific inquiry. Much of the theoretical development of sociology of scientific knowledge through the 1970s and early 1980s concentrated on elaborating a fully general sociological framework for interpreting knowledge-acquisition and concept-application. Karin Knorr Cetina,[46] in her extensive work on

[45] Karl Pearson, 1892, *The Grammar of Science*. Quoted from Robert S. Michael, *Inquiry & Scientific Method*, http://www.indiana.edu/~educy520/sec5982/week_1/inquiry_sci_method02.pdf (last accessed on 28 September 2008).

[46] Karin Knorr-Cetina, 1981, *The Manufacture of Knowledge: An Essay on the Constructivist and Contextual Nature of Science*, New York: Pergamon Press; and 1999, *Epistemic Cultures: How the Sciences Make Knowledge*, Cambridge: Harvard University Press.

epistemology and social constructionism argues that both the context of discovery and the constitution of scientific facts, through the logic of scientific procedure (the context of validation), provide enough subjective inputs to lend a fabricated and constituted character to scientific products. She argues that objectivism 'is oblivious to the constituted character' of scientific products.[47] Her work on laboratory procedures is particularly interesting, for here she shifts the subjective component of scientific activity from the context of discovery to the context of justification and validation. She takes the site of the laboratory which is an assumed space that 'decode(s) facts' as they exist out there. Is the creation of facts in a laboratory bereft of subjective mediation and manipulation? Are natural objects and fixed entities not *malleable*? Knorr Cetina argues that there are at least three features of natural objects that laboratory science replicates:

1) It need not put up an object *as it is* (it can substitute transformed or partial versions).
2) It need not accommodate the natural object *where it is* (it can take an object out of its natural environment).
3) It need not accommodate an event *when it happens* (it can make events happen frequently enough for continuous study).

These three therefore, present an altered and a diminished representation of reality. 'By detaching objects from their natural environments, scientists install them in a new phenomenal field defined by social agents. In other words, laboratories allow natural processes to be "brought home" and to be made subject only to the conditions of the local social order'.[48] Physicist Heisenberg, in a similar vein, views physical reality as a web of relationships. He observes that whenever we isolate a pattern in this network and define it as a part, or an object, we do so by cutting through some of its connections to the rest of the network, and that this may be done in different ways. 'What we observe is not nature itself, but nature exposed to our method of questioning'.[49]

Scientific products, therefore, can be seen as 'structured in terms of several orders of selectivity'[50]—selection of the problem, construction of

[47] Karin Knorr-Cetina, 1984, 'The Fabrication of Facts: Towards a Microsociology of Scientific Knowledge', in Meja Volker and Nico Stehr (eds), *Knowledge and Society*, p. 228.

[48] Karin Knorr-Cetina, 1999, 'What is a laboratory?' in *Epistemic Cultures: How the Sciences Make Knowledge*, Cambridge: Harvard University Press.

[49] Fritjof Capra, 1994, 'Systems Theory and the New Paradigm', in *Key Concepts in Critical Theory*, Carolyn Merchant (ed.), New Delhi: Rawat publications, p. 337.

[50] Karin Knorr-Cetina, 1984, p. 228.

the problem, selection of programmes, functions, experiments, tools, and so on. In other words, in the fabrication of reality in a laboratory, a chain of decisions and negotiations are undertaken through which outcomes are derived. The selections that a scientific inquiry incorporate therefore lends it a certain complexity as well as a specificity. Moreover, previous selections also affect subsequent selections by influencing decision-making. The selections that a scientific procedure incorporates suggests that they are unlikely to be reproduced in the same way, with similar selections and assumptions, under different circumstances. The space within which the scientist therefore makes the selection is a space that is historically and culturally conditioned. So also is the scientific result or the conclusions pertaining to the natural world.[51]

The social and cultural contingency of science has led to, as Fritjof Capra states, a shift from objective science to 'epistemic' science.[52] Products of science are contextually specific constructions which bear the mark of situational contingency and interest structure which generates it. This means that whatever happens in the process of construction is not irrelevant to the scientific product obtained. The nature of findings is therefore relative to the context. All this lends scientific knowledge with an indeterminacy, social relativity with multiple possibilities of alternate selections. 'If scientific objects are selectively carved from reality, they can be deconstructed by challenging the selections they incorporate'.[53] Thus, what is assumed to be the institutionalized norms of science, is part of the broader repertoire of social formulations.

Truth is therefore, not a straightforward product of human experience or a paradigm of a true system of beliefs. As Barry Barnes states, when people confront the experience of their senses they do so within an already existing structure of knowledge given to them by their community and within a structure of purposes sustained by their community. Something intervenes between the 'retinal image' and our perception of it.[54] Thus, when new experience is confronted, it is sorted out with respect to existing schemes. The pre-existing structure and formulations of science determine whether the new fact is to be counted as evidence confirming or disconfirming some theory, whether

[51] Critics of the constructivist school of course contend that we are left with an indeterminate contextual picture which hands over science to the reign of irrationality For a summary of this discussion see Lakatos Imre and Alan Musgrave (eds), 1970, *Criticism and the Growth of Knowledge,* Cambridge: CUP.

[52] Fritjof Capra, 1994, p. 337.

[53] Karin Knorr-Cetina, 1984, p. 228.

[54] Fritjof Capra, 1994, p. 337.

it is to be bracketed, subjected to taboo, or filed away, to be dealt with another time. It is people's goal-orientation—the pragmatic structure of the community to which they belong—that judges, among possible courses of action. Data or facts are nothing but theoretical assumptions, partly explaining our perceptions.[55]

Facts are both socially and cognitively institutionalized.[56] The social aspects concern, in particular, differences in the structuring of education and research, research allocation and the degree of organization within the scientific community. These arrangements function as a basis for the social identity and as an organizing principle for the activities.[57] The cognitive institutionalization refers to how main research areas, central concepts, and theories within the discipline are defined and ordered. The context of research is dominated by various cognitive structures which are continually mediated and oriented by various reference groups. These cognitive structures are comprised of interpenetrating hierarchy of levels—the theoretical, a level of subject concerns indicated by the aspired goals of research and the overall values and beliefs which serve to justify scientific activity, and a technical level of procedures and techniques which are used during research. These structures exist in scientific consciousness and provide a general world view which integrates scientific activity with other systems of production.[58] Tom Jagtenberg argues that even procedures, techniques of scientific inquiry, that is, the level of the technical is not 'fully separable from metaphysical, theoretical, and subject level concerns' of scientific inquiry and knowledge generation.[59] He adds that scientific action (including research, speculation, communication, etc.) is always dependent on technical knowledge which necessarily becomes sedimented into products of research.

It is implicit here that scientific research is actually constrained at all levels by structures which exist as a reality. A field exhibits a high degree of institutionalization when the researchers share a common attitude in terms of its aims, methods, and explanation ideals. The more consensus there is about the central ways of conceptualizing the field, its basic

[55] Barry Barnes, 1974, *Scientific Knowledge and Sociological Theory,* London: Routledge Kegan and Paul, p. 11.

[56] See R. Whitley, 1974, 'Cognitive and Social Institutionalization of Scientific Specialties and Research Areas', in *Social Processes of Scientific Development,* R. Whitley (ed.), London, Routledge & Kegan Paul.

[57] Ibid., p. 72.

[58] Ibid., p. 41.

[59] Tom Jagtenberg, 1983, *The Social Construction of Science,* Boston: D. Reidel Publishing Co., p. 104.

problems and methods, relevant solutions and results, the more cognitively institutionalized it is. For instance, he states that the organization of social life in modern settings around ideas of scientific progress, rationality or self interest is a 'convention' just as ancestor worship is.[60] Cognition, or the act of knowing and knowledge creation always reflects, as Tom Jagtenberg states, both prevalent cognitive structures and its intersection with the 'unique biographies' of individual subjectivity.[61] This involves, to use Alfred Schutz's phrase, the institutionalization of knowledge into 'shared inter-subjective stocks of knowledge'.

The 'strong programme' in sociology of scientific knowledge theory, professes that the presence of social factors alone is not enough to falsify a scientific theory. The social construction of science does not distort or make science irrational.[62] Bloor has contrasted this with the so-called 'weak programme', which merely gives social explanations for erroneous beliefs. The 'strong programme' on the other hand, considers sociological factors as influencing all beliefs. Sociology of knowledge, scientific knowledge, and everyday knowledge propose that both 'true' and 'false' scientific theories should be treated the same way.[63] Both are caused by social factors or conditions, such as cultural context and self-interest. All human knowledge, as something that exists in the human cognition, must contain some social components in its formation process. Scientific facts are therefore, not trans-historical essences independent of conscious beings that determine the categorical structure of reality. In its essence, the sociology of science involves the study of science as a social activity, especially dealing 'with the social conditions and effects of science, and with the social structures and processes of scientific activity.'[64]

From an ecological perspective, Vandana Shiva argues that the view that scientific knowledge is a purely factual description of nature is ecologically

[60] Ibid., pp. 69–95.

[61] Ibid., pp. 100–1.

[62] Practitioners associated with strong Programme in the Sociology of Scientific Knowledge include Barry Barnes, David Bloor, Harry Collins, Donald MacKenzie, Andrew Pickering, Steve Shapin etc. These thinkers (sociologists, philosophers of science, historians of science, anthropologists and computer scientists) have analyzed the role that social factors play in scientific development relative to rational, empirical, and other factors See for insance, Barry Barnes, 1974, *Scientific Knowledge and Sociological Theory*, London: Routledge and Kegan Paul, David Bloor, *Knowledge and Social Imagery*, University of Chicago Press, 1991, Steven Shapin, 1995, 'Here and Everywhere: Sociology of Scientific Knowledge', *Annual Review of Sociology*, vol. 21.

[63] David Bloor, 1991.

[64] Joseph Ben-David, and Teresa A. Sullivan, 1975, 'Sociology of Science', *Annual Review of Sociology*, vol. 1, pp. 203–22.

unfounded. 'Ecology perceives relationships between different elements of an eco-system. What properties of a particular element or resource are picked up for study...depends on the relationships that are taken as the context defining the properties. Selection of the context is a value-determined process and the selection, in turn, determines what properties are seen in nature. There is nothing like a neutral fact about nature.'[65]

Rules do not sufficiently explain scientific judgment; the way in which rules are identified and used is itself a topic for contextual inquiry. In short, all the cognitive structures, theoretical, technical, and social, provide an interlocking structural context for research. The precise content and form that emerges from context to context is necessarily variable since the element of subjectivity varies. Importantly, despite the variations there is an inter-related quality to the overall field of scientific consciousness. The sub-universes of meanings draw upon the existing pool of scientific consciousness in order to evolve new meanings and forms of consciousness. It is the contextuality of scientific enterprise that lends it a subjective and evaluative character.

Sociology of scientific knowledge sets out to construct an 'anti-epistemology' to break down the legitimacy of the distinction between 'contexts of discovery and context of justification,' and to develop an anti-individualistic and anti-empiricist framework for the sociology of knowledge. 'Social factors are counted not as contaminants but as constitutive of the very idea of scientific knowledge.'[66] Science is undeniably made in specific sites, and it discernibly carries the marks of those sites of production.

Sociology of scientific knowledge then sets out to construct an 'anti-epistomology', to break down the legitimacy of the distinction between context of discovery and context of justification, and to develop an anti-individualistic and anti-empiricist framework for the sociology of knowledge: 'Social factors are not counted as contaminants but as constitutive of the very idea of scientific knowledge'.[67] Science is undeniably made in specific sites and it discernably carries the marks of those sites of production.

To summarise the central conclusions this section: There are no grand narratives of unique scientific norms and unique scientific method; those theories have lost their compulsion. The narrative of scientific rationality

[65] Vandana Shiva, 1988, 'Reductionist Science as Epistemological Violence', in *Science, Hegemony and Violence*, Ashish Nandy (ed.), Delhi: OUP, p. 234.
[66] Steven Shapin, 'Sociology of Scientific Knowledge', p. 296.
[67] Steven Shapin, 1995, p. 296.

deflected attention away from of situatedness or the contextuality of science. Instead, contemporary empirical and theoretical works are incorporating physical situatedness of scientific knowledge-making as an assumed idea. The significance of this conclusion can be appreciated in reference to the relationship between the diverse knowledge claims and ideology behind intellectual property. It leads us to assert the multiplicity of subjectivities which translate into different and varied sciences. How are these different sciences—traditional knowledge and Western Modern Sciences (WMS) for instance—made to relate to each other when the terms of the relationship are preset by the IPR regime? What is presently implied when some knowledge claims are characterized as rights to patents, copyrights, etc. and some are excluded? Are IPRs a specific instance of a larger claim for cultural and epistemological domination? These questions suggest that there are ethical and political questions embedded in the project of science and technology. IPRs are a case in point. Unless attention is paid to the ways in which cognitive and social structures (or factors) are shown to inter-relate there is a danger that the 'new' orientation of science and technology will become cognitively one-sided.

Sociology of knowledge and sociology of scientific knowledge suggest that knowledge is constructed in the context of the different worlds people inhabit. Knowledge systems are ideas that describe these particular worlds. A relativistic perspective of knowledge claims is adhered to in order to assert the relativity and legitimacy of all forms of knowledge and to contest the claim and efforts to build a unified system of science and scientific assessment which validates and legitimizes knowledge forms. The extensive discussion on the sociology of scientific knowledge and the relativity of scientific knowledge has been undertaken in order to underscore the validity of traditional, indigenous, alternative, non-western sciences, and to establish that if the grounds of knowledge generation and constitution are different, then the system of validation ought to be one that is consistent with the culture in which a particular knowledge is generated. Universal categories of commensuration and validation, as provided by the IPR regime, may not be ethically defensible.

SCIENCE AND TRADITIONAL INDIGENOUS KNOWLEDGE
Many terms are used to signify alternative modes of knowing—traditional knowledge (TK), traditional indigenous knowledge (TIK), traditional ecological knowledge (TEK), local knowledge, indigenous science, folk

knowledge, farmers' knowledge, fishers' knowledge, tacit knowledge, and so on. Each of these terms carries different implications and there is an ensuing discussion about which one is the most appropriate. The term 'traditional', some allege, for example, obscures the dynamism and capacity of traditional societies to adapt and change. The now widely used word, 'indigenous', coined by Brokensha, in the early 80s, is meant to highlight the 'original' nature of this knowledge, but it might overlook knowledge from populations who are not officially recognized as indigenous.[68] The word 'local' can be applied to different geographic contexts, but it lacks specificity. TIK is interpreted as a cumulative body of knowledge, practices and representations that describes the relationships of living beings with one another and with their physical environment, which evolved through adaptive processes and has been handed down through generations by cultural transmission.[69] For our purpose here, the terms traditional knowledge, indigenous knowledge, traditional indigenous knowledge, traditional ecological knowledge, traditional indigenous knowledge, will be used interchangeably because different scholars' and researchers' preferences for different terms suggest that the implications and nuances of these descriptive categories are best circumvented, for they are not directly related to the conclusions the chapter hopes to reach.

TIK has been used for centuries by indigenous and local communities under local laws, customs, and traditions.[70] It has been transmitted and evolved from generation to generation. TIK is a central component for the daily life of millions of people in developing countries and plays an important role in the development of agriculture, ecology, medical treatment and in ensuring food security of millions in the developing world. Traditional medicine, for instance, serves the health needs of a vast majority of people in developing countries where access to 'modern' health care services and medicine is limited by economic and cultural reasons.[71]

[68] D.W. Brokensha, et al. (eds), 1980, *Indigenous Knowledge Systems and Development*, Lanham: University Press of America.

[69] F. Berkes, 1993, 'Traditional Ecological Knowledge In Perspective', in *Traditional Ecological Knowledge: Concept and Cases*. Inglis J.T. (ed.), Ottawa, Canada: International Program on Traditional Ecological Knowledge and International Development Research Centre, pp. 1–9.

[70] Traditional usually refers to some kind of a cultural continuity transmitted in the form of social attitudes, beliefs, practices etc. derived from historical experience which do evolve and change, at times dynamically. It does not denote something that is static or unevolving.

[71] For instance, the per capita consumption of Traditional medicine (TM) products is in Malaysia, more than double that of modern pharmaceuticals. TM is also significant in more advanced developing countries such as South Korea, where the per capita consumption

It is often the only affordable treatment available to poor people and in remote communities. Similarly, in many agricultural systems, seed supply fundamentally relies on the 'informal' system of seed production which operates on the basis of the diffusion of the best seed available within a community, and on its movement. Indigenous traditional knowledge systems contain a rich understanding of plant, crop, and tree species, medicines, animal breeds, and local ecological and biological resources. They may also include useful technologies and adaptations to local environments. They display aspects of multicultural science and pedagogy which describes a rich and well-documented branch of indigenous science known to biologists and ecologists as traditional ecological knowledge. Traditionally inaccessible traditional and indigenous science, as cost effective and ecologically relevant, is increasingly being integrated with the western sciences to become commercially and globally viable.

The vast body of literature on traditional and indigenous knowledge points out to, in general, the communal nature of both knowledge generation and transmission and communication, with exceptions, as in the case of witchcraft, healing practices for example, which may be possessed by individuals.[72] TIK is based on data generated by resource users themselves (as opposed to that by a specialized cadre of researchers as in 'expert' forms of knowledge). These resource users are not isolated individuals but communities, who have developed resources and techniques in response to the set of immediate circumstances. The knowledge generated, as a result, the shared meaning, is then transmitted largely through oral history. It is remembered, sensory information that is usually transmitted orally in descriptive names and in stories where abstract principles are encapsulated in stories and metaphor. This information consists of organized bodies of knowledge, or, in other words, coherent systems of knowledge, which several theorists have referred to as indigenous science.[73] Ogawa proposes

---

of TM products is about 36% more than modern drugs. Carlos M. Correa, November 2001, *Issues and Options Surrounding the Protection of Traditional Knowledge: A Discussion Paper.* Commissioned by The Quaker United Nations Office (QUNO), Geneva.

[72] See, for instance, R.E. Johannes (ed.), 1989, *Traditional Ecological Knowledge: A Collection of Essays,* Switzerland and Cambridge: IUCN; K. Ruddle, and R.E. Johannes (eds), 1989, *Traditional Marine Resource Management in the Pacific Basin: An Anthology,* Jakarta: Unesco/RPSTSEA; A. Tanner, 1979, *Bringing Home Animals,* London: Hurst; D.M. Warren, D. Brokensha, and L.J. Slikkerveer (eds), 1993, *Indigenous Knowledge Systems: The Cultural Dimension of Development,* London: Kegan Paul International; M. Gadgil, and F. Berkes, 1991, 'Traditional Resource Management Systems', *Resource Management and Optimization,* 18, pp. 127–41.

[73] Sometimes also referred to as ethno-science, TIK has been described as 'the study of systems of knowledge developed by a given culture to classify the objects, activities, and

that every culture has its own science and refers to the science in a given culture as its indigenous science.[74] According to Ogawa, we must distinguish between two levels of science—the individual or personal science and cultural or societal science. He defines indigenous science as 'a culture-dependent collective rational perceiving of reality', where 'collective means held in sufficiently similar form by many persons to allow effective communication, but independent of any particular mind or set of minds'.[75] This knowledge is thus seen as the expression of a particular means of apprehending reality; it is encoded in a culture, in the sense that it is a part of culturally-specific systems of representation, and it conveys values and a particular view of the world, of nature, and of life.[76] Further, TIK is an attribute of societies with historical continuity in resource-use practices. By and large, these are non-industrial or less technologically advanced societies, many of them indigenous or tribal.

TIK stands in complete contrast to western modern science, in terms of conceptualizations, the residential and proprietary status, generation, and communication. It encompasses the beliefs, knowledge, practices, innovations, arts, spirituality, and other forms of cultural experience and expression that belong to indigenous communities worldwide. TIK, contrary to common perception, incorporates its own explanations of the natural world and has its own distinct database, its own 'science'. Berkes, for example, refers to horticulturalists in Philippines who possessed exceptionally detailed knowledge of local plants and animals and their natural history, recognizing in one case some 1,600 plant species. Indigenous science interprets how the local world works through a particular cultural perspective. Expressions of scientific thinking are abundant throughout indigenous agriculture, astronomy, navigation, mathematics, medical practices, engineering, military science, architecture, and ecology. In addition, processes of science that include rational observation of natural events, classification, and problem solving are woven into all aspects of indigenous cultures.

What came to be known as TIK from the early 1970s has been in ambiguous relationship with western modern science.[77] TIK and western

events of its given universe', D.L. Hardesty, 1977, *Ecological Anthropology*, New York: Wiley.
[74] M. Ogawa, 1995, 'Science Education in a Multiscience Perspective', *Science Education*, 79(5), pp. 583–93.
[75] Ibid., p. 588.
[76] Carole Lévesque, 2001, 'Indigenous Knowledge: Questions, Issues and Challenges 1, 2', in *The Handing Down of Culture, Smaller Societies, and Globalization*, Jean-Paul Baillargeon (ed.), Grubstreet editions.
[77] M. Leach, I. Scoones, and B. Wynne (eds), 2005, *Science and Citizens: Globalization and the Challenge of Engagement*, London: Zed Press, p.19.

modern science present themselves as binaries—of modernity *versus* tradition; rational versus irrational; universal versus local, science versus' faith, myth, religion, etc. There is no doubt that there are fundamental dichotomies between the two knowledge systems. TIK is not merely a system of knowledge and practice. It is an a way of being which integrates systems of knowledge, practice and beliefs, integrated with cosmology, ecology and community. Unlike western modern science, TIK does not create a separation between the natural and the social—it is seen as the expression of a fundamental and unified understanding of the place of human beings in the universe. Relations are based on reciprocity and obligations towards both community members and other beings, and communal resource management institutions based on shared knowledge and meaning.[78] TIK represents a collective understanding attained over long periods, in particular places, of the relationship between a community and the earth. Thus, continual acts of reciprocity establish the collective consciousness which form the logical framework for linked resource systems and their accompanying institutions.

In laying down these dichotomies, the objective is to distinguish traditional knowledge by defining it as a very different and autonomous field of knowledge. However, while it is important to take note of these dichotomies, there is also a need to caution that these are more like idealized categories which may have a wide range of variations and differences within apparently homogenous communities. However, internal differentiation between cultures of traditional societies does not detract from the fact that these generalizations approximate the realities of epistemic cultures of traditional societies worldwide. The prime objective is not to draw attention to the accuracy of these divergences but to focus on the larger issue to which these dichotomies point—the issue of existence of these various types of knowledge and indeed their right to coexist.

Rooted in different worldviews and unequal in power dispensations, the two systems of knowledge, western and traditional/indigenous, stem from different epistemic cultures and in fact from different ways of being. Yet forced by the ecological and cultural limits of its progress science has been obligated to accept its own cultural boundaries and has been, in a way, forced to 'patronize the intellectual and moral substance of other ways of knowing [...] Thus, the institutions have been invited [...] to

---

[78] See F. Berkes (ed.), 1989, *Common Property Resources: Ecology and Community-based Sustainable Development,* London, Belhaven Press; D. Brokensha, Warren, and O. Werner (eds), 1980, *Indigenous Knowledge Systems and Development,* Washington, DC, University Press of America.

recognize other kinds of knowledge framed within other practical cultural assumptions, meanings and life worlds'.[79]

Since the adoption of the Universal Declaration of Human Rights in 1948, knowledge, its production, and the material interests arising thereof, have been considered a fundamental human right of all peoples.[80] However, the need to protect, preserve the cultural and intellectual property of traditional peoples has only recently claimed national and international interest. One of the primary reasons has been the exclusionary implications that the TRIPS regime has for traditional knowledges. Traditional knowledges are not amenable to propertization and IP claims in the same way as the western modern scientific endeavours are. They are claimed to be of some value but are often dubbed as 'intuitive', 'folk', 'unscientific', 'faith-ridden' and therefore outside the claim of IP. Also, of particular concern is the fact that forms of TIK lie in the open public domain and are therefore amenable to being easily exploited by commercial interests who then claim it as their intellectual property, thus transforming the 'commons' into a private property domain. Public domain in the intellectual property field generally includes any information not claimed as IPRs or for which IPRs have expired. Thus, to the extent that TIK is not protected as IP rights, it would belong to the public domain and be freely exploited. This view, of course, ignores the fact that TIK may be deemed subject to customary laws that recognize other forms of ownership or possession rights.[81]

Since the mid-1990s, as the TIK systems gained greater visibility and acquired greater legitimacy, perceptions have changed about its relationship with science. The emphasis is now on incorporating TIK into scientific studies. This accounts for the growing interest of transnational companies in the health benefits of local plant and herb species, agricultural and ecological practices of rural communities, and so on. For example, about one quarter of all prescription drugs come

[79] Ibid., p. 7.

[80] Article 27 of the Declaration provides that: 1) Everyone has the right freely to participate in the cultural life of the community, to enjoy the arts and to share in scientific advancement and its benefits. 2) Everyone has the right to the protection of the moral and material interests resulting from any scientific, literary or artistic production of which he is the author. Available at http://www.un.org/Overview/rights.html (last accessed on 28 September 2008).

[81] See, G. Dutfield, 2003, *Intellectual Property Rights and the Life Sciences Industries: A 20th Century History,* England: Ashgate; G. Dutfield, 2000, 'IPRs and Sustainable Development', Issue Paper No. 1. *Science Communication,* 21(3), pp. 274–95; Krystyna Swiderska, 4–5 May 2004, 'Traditional Knowledge Protection and Recognition of Customary Law: Policy Issues and Challenges', Background Paper for the Planning Workshop on *Protecting Community Rights Over Traditional Knowledge: Implications of Customary Laws and Practices,* London.

from rainforest plants and three quarters of these have been gathered from information provided by indigenous peoples. Over one hundred and twenty pharmaceutical products in use are plant-derived, and some 75 per cent of these were discovered by examining the use of these plants in traditional medicine.[82] One aspect of this newly emerging relationship has been defined by the need for a constructive integration, where the value of indigenous knowledge is remodeled in terms of modern science and made to yield value for modern societies. The focus seems to be ostensibly on integration but the integration is generally influenced by the positivistic dictates of science, which views western modern science as the universal, as the approved language of scientific communication. TIK, in this process assumes a secondary status, that of supplementary knowledge. At best, it is absorbed and assimilated into a particular type of data, generally empirical, or instead, reduced to simple geographic data or isolated bits of information. TIK is then judged and measured according to standard scientific indicators, robbing it of its defining identities.[83]

The interface between western modern science and TIK, even at its democratic best, has been cast in terms that are amenable to management and control by expert institutions like the WTO, World Intellectual Property Organization (WIPO), and the TRIPS institutions.

Leach, Wynne and Scoones take the example of data basing of TIK which is done by WIPO and UNESCO as a means to protect them from exploitation. This process itself involves a selection and translation—a selection of what is considered significant and a translation of knowledge from different epistemic cultures, 'into formal quasi-scientific terms stripped from the contexts in which they have practical enactment, human identity and cultural reality'.[84] Indigenous knowledges are thus rendered formally commensurate with forms of scientific knowledge which have granted a universally-valid-vector status. The concepts of indigenous knowledge are adopted through a selective reconstruction and prevalent modes of cognitive institutionalization, devoid of the context and culture that defined it. Repackaging TIK as a complementary resource in terms of modernizing expert institutions has problematic implications for the subjects or citizens of such knowledge.[85] It not only ignores the diversity

[82] N.R. Farnsworth, O. Akerele, A.S. Bingel, 1985, 'Medicinal Plants in Therapy', *Bull. World Health Org.*, vol. 63, pp. 965–81.

[83] See, Carole Lévesque, 2001, pp. 165–67.

[84] Melissa Leach, Ian Scoones, Brian Wynne, 2005, *Science and Citizens: Globalization and the Challenge of Engagement*, London/New York: Zed Books, p. 9.

[85] See, V. Shiva, 1997, 'Western Science and its Destruction of Local Knowledge', in *The Post-Development Reader*, M. Rahnema M. and V. Bawtree (eds), London: Zed Press.

of the ideologies and goals that drive this appropriation, but also removes agency from the local people themselves. The notion of disembodied knowledge is one of the biggest challenges to the sociology of knowledge. Scoones and Thompson, in the context of farming practices, have stressed the need for methodologies that encompass the social and political complexities inherent in knowledge generation, transmission and adaptation. They call for 'a leap of the imagination—the need to enter into the world of farmers' ideas, values, representations, and performances'.[86]

There is very little real engagement between the practices of western modern science and indigenous knowledge. The existing engagements are largely located in the enrollment of TIK as complementary assets in projects of science and technology. The terms and institutions of international trade validate and assign value to forms of TIK. As Foucault states, in his elaboration of the power of discourse, 'the criteria of what constitutes knowledge, what is to be excluded and who is designated as qualified to know, involves acts of power'.[87] Foucault labels this discursive subjection and proposes that the author of a statement is a function of the statement itself—power centers on the practices of assessment and examination prevalent in discipline. Drawing from Foucault's conception Norman and Ann Long highlight the need to look closely at the issue of whose interpretations or models (for example, those of agricultural scientists, politicians, farmers, etc.) prevail over those of other actors and under what conditions. 'Knowledge processes are embedded in social processes that imply aspects of power, authority, and legitimation'.[88] Knowledge encounters involve the struggle between actors who aim to enroll others in their 'projects', getting them to accept particular frames of meanings, winning over (or coercing) to their point of view. If they succeed then the other party delegates power to them. The struggles focus on fixing key points that have controlling influence over the exchanges and attribution of meaning.

THE TRIPS AGREEMENT AS A SYSTEM OF COMMENSURATION

Every system of knowledge has its own epistemology, its own theory of what constitutes and what counts as knowledge. The submergence of

[86] Scoones and J. Thompson, 1994, 'Knowledge, Power and Agriculture—Towards a Theoretical Understanding', London: Intermediate Technology Publications, p. 30.

[87] Michel Foucault, as explicated in *Beyond Farmer First: Rural People's Knowledge, Agricultural Research and Extension Practice*, I. Scoones, and J. Thompson (eds).

[88] Norman Long and Ann Long (eds), 1992, *Battlefields of Knowledge*, London: RKP, pp. 26–7.

TIK into frameworks of western modern science has led some analysts to portray the differences between the two sciences as acute and ultimately irreconcilable because the relationship of indigenous knowledge and western sciences is rooted in incommensurable concepts and framings.[89]

What western science management institutions like the TRIPS framework have done is to provide a standard for commensuration of these varied knowledge systems. We can get epistemological commensuration only when we already have agreed upon practices of inquiry, of discourse. As Kuhn's states, since no such agreed upon premises exists, there can be no commensurability between groups of scientists who have different paradigms of successful explanations.[90] Kuhn argues that the criteria of choice between theories, even within normal science, 'function not as rules, which determine choice, but as values which influence it'.[91] Does this then suggest, as Grille points out, that such thinking borders on 'cultural solipsism' with its implication that communication between the 'local' and 'western' knowledge is impossible; rationalities are not shared or shareable?[92] An answer to this question could well be that commensuration and communication are two different enterprises. In the present case, commensuration necessarily fulfils an ideological function—that of domination and subsumption of the 'other' in the image of the rational and hegemonic. Standards of commensuration, such as the one applied by IPRs, reflect the rationality and the dominance of science, and through it, of the West which considers itself the repository of 'scientific rationality'. Lines between epistemologies, disciplines, subject matters, parts of culture are endangered by the substantive suggestions of commensuration through a competitive ranking system.

Systematic attention also needs to be given to the broader anthropological concern for the relationship of cultural, epistemic traditions, and institutions with economic processes. The epistemological and cultural battles of these two differing conceptions and understandings of reality are played out primarily for economic benefits. This politics of knowledge is inextricably linked to the politics of trade. The enterprise of knowledge politics then demands an alternative politics, to establish

[89] I. Scoones and J. Thompson, 'Knowledge, Power and Agriculture—Towards a Theoretical Understanding', pp. 28–35.

[90] T.S. Kuhn, 1970, *The Structure of Scientific Revolutions*, Second edn, Chicago: University of Chicago Press, p. 206. Also see, R. Rorty, 1979, *Philosophy and the Mirror of Nature*, New Jersey: Princeton University Press, pp. 322–33.

[91] Ibid., p. 327.

[92] R. Grille, 1997, 'Discourses of Development: The View from Anthropology', in *Discourses of Development*, R. Grille and R. Stirrat (eds), Oxford: Berg, p. 14.

multiciplity of realities and modes of cognition. Establishing the validity of diverse knowledge claims has become one of the central concerns of this enterprise. A claim for epistemological parity is an assertion:

a)   An assertion of the 'equal respect principle' which holds that traditional knowledge systems have equal claims to being scientific, and therefore, to being accorded legitimate cognitive status (that is. not being dismissed as faith derived, totem based, spiritual knowledge, unscientific, etc.). This also extends into a utilitarian claim that since TIK has made significant contributions, it ought to be given cognitive status within the IPRs regime, and that there should be devised norms for equitable benefit sharing between the holders and users of TIK. The definition of 'science' should be broadened, thereby including TIK as science. This claim is then a demand for articulation of custom or norms-based systems of innovation into the legal system of intellectual property law.

b)   An assertion that any validation system, like TRIPS, requires representation of those knowledge holders who have a stake in the manner the validation system affects the distribution of rights—property, knowledge, subsistence, or cultural rights. These claims of intellectual parity challenge the modernist representation of scientific knowledge and call for a broader, more politicized democratization of science and citizenship.

These are key issues that emerge relating to the terms of integration of traditional indigenous peoples. Attempts at integration inevitably come up against issues of science and citizenship, which focus on the terms of power sharing and participation in decision-making. Issues of compensations, profit sharing, bio-piracy, collective property rights, knowledge rights, etc. get articulated in this encounter. These issues are addressed within globalized, institutional contexts, where power relation shape the terms of engagement. Recent attempts by the TRIPS regime have tried to devise spaces for participation and acknowledgement of the cultural attributes of knowledge.[93] These reflections have been forced by

[93] One of the earliest attempts to incorporate the issues of the developing countries and issues regarding the protection of traditional knowledge within the WTO framework was in the Doha Declaration, 2001. Paragraph 19 of the 2001 Doha Declaration has broadened the discussion. It states that the TRIPS Council should also look at the relationship between the TRIPS Agreement and the UN Convention on Biological Diversity, the protection of traditional knowledge and folklore. Available at http://www.wto.org/English/tratop_e/trips_e/art27_3b_e.htm (last accessed on 14 December 2007).

the issue, beginning to be raised globally, that the TRIPS framework is a body of law in which particular types of power dynamics have come to prevail, resulting in the exclusion of particular groups, knowledges, and tacit ontologies. It is this exclusion which has pushed forward the demands for 'prior informed consent for access and fair and equitable benefit-sharing' (known as the Convention on Biodiversity (CBD) Amendment) and the extension of higher levels of Geographical Indications (GIs), currently enjoyed only by wines and spirits, to other products. The GI extension and CBD issues do not have a clear mandate to be included in these negotiations, and opponents have signalled a firm unwillingness to consider them. Opponents include Argentina, Australia, Canada, Chile, Japan, New Zealand, and the United States. These are clearly issues of inclusion—inclusion of benefit sharing, issues of recognition through disclosure, issues of parity within the structure of TRIPS institutions. These issues emerge out of the boundary conditions imposed by the TRIPS agreement and are instantiations of the complex relationship between knowledge, communication, ownership, and control.

SCIENCE, CITIZENSHIP, AND INTELLECTUAL PROPERTY

Science technology agendas and networks are being increasingly pursued on a global scale, whether through international public policy and agreements or trade and commerce. Particular views of science, technology, and policy are embedded in these new global networks. IPRs regime is one such global policy that brings into sharp focus the prevailing perspectives on scientific knowledge and expertise. In institutionalizing knowledge claims as 'patentable', 'copyrightable', 'trade markable' or as a 'trade secret', IPRs classify and codify knowledge in terms of its 'materiality' or 'immateriality'. It thus endeavours to frame an ecology of knowledge premised on certain binaries: scientific/non-scientific, innovative/non-innovative, traditional/scientific, patentable/alternative systems of knowledge, and so on. This classification of knowledge clearly demarcates knowledge systems into that which can be used as a property right and that which cannot be. We thus need to ferret out the complex relationship between knowledge, communication, ownership, and control.

Multiplicity of knowledge systems does not necessarily make for conflictual relations between them. It is when they are forced to negotiate each other in an implied hierarchical frame, set by the TRIPS agreement, that binaries are posited which render the terms of negotiation conflictual and confrontational. Increasing number of products—from media images to software, to gene cloning are more ideas than things. For these ideas to become capacities for appropriation, for them to acquire materiality they need to be able to make a claim for being regarded as intellectual property—a claim for being scientific and a claim to being the 'first knower'. Both claims work against traditional societies and their forms of knowledges. The criterion of scientificity precludes TIK as they are derived from alternate system of logic, method, and validation. They may not be verifiable, testable entities within the bounds of western scientific rationality. The claim of being the 'first-knower' also becomes a discriminatory criterion. There seldom exists an individuated notion of knowledge creation whereby one individual gets to know before the others. Disclosure, open knowledge, free circulation of information ensure that creation of knowledge continues to be cumulative, intergenerational, and collective. Further, there are practical constraints (albeit arising out of structural conditions of backwardness)—societies that are not legalized find it difficult to register a legal claim to being first owners or establish objectivity and universality, necessary conditions for recognition as a modern scientific endeavour. A universal law, like the intellectual property regime, works against communities and societies that are traditional and hold knowledge collectively. Intellectual property rights strengthen visions of dominant modernity and its hegemonic scientific culture and are an issue of mutual construction of scientific knowledge with global and local forms of power.

It is important to identify that knowledge, as an interested activity, has a function—economic and ideological. Nowhere is this better orchestrated than in the realm and function of IP. Sociology of knowledge draws our attention to the social constituency and cultural determinants of knowledge and holds that all knowledge is a relative and a contextual claim to truth. IPRs are divergent with the claims of sociology of knowledge as they accord epistemological primacy to the project of western science and technology, in the process, creating tacit cognitive hierarchies. IPRs are granted to those forms of knowledge which claim to be novel, rigorous, codified, verified, tested, etc., in other words, conforming to that which is regarded to be 'scientific'. IPRs have emerged as a way to institutionalize and systematize the production of scientific knowledge in commercially and economically desirable areas. This is the ideological function of IP rights—the function of distributing knowledge rights, from which emanate rights to further appropriation. The concept of ideology provides the sociology of knowledge with rudiments of a theory of collective motives. There are collective motives behind the institutionalization of knowledge rights. Ideological distortions and mystifications involve political processes—they have to do with claims of power and with claims of being powerful.[94]

Sociologists and historians have become intensely interested in the specific processes of argumentation and political action whereby claims come to be accepted as true or rejected as false. The intellectual property regime is legal means and a mechanism which has been deployed to validate and settle knowledge claims. The TRIPS regime has the power to define what constitutes IP and consequently is worthy of protection. In other words, it decides which knowledge is powerful and which is not. The IP regime implements power relations that makes it possible to extract and constitute knowledge. Thus, the discourse of modern sciences identifies appropriate and legitimate ways of practicing a certain conception of knowledge through IP rights.

By many accounts, contemporary Western societies are becoming 'knowledge societies' which are run on expert processes and expert systems epitomized by science, which is structured into all areas of social life. Knowledge is classified into categories which then become key 'cognitive nodes' that bind different kinds of knowledge in a technological field.[95] In the context of intellectual property, the existence of different knowledge categories is signaled by the patent classification system. As Michael Lounsbury states, 'Patent classes represent important "cognitive nodes" that provide shorthand for organizing and processing vast amounts of information about new technologies quickly and efficiently. Such knowledge categories shape perception, interpretation, and attention, providing the default conditions for making sense of an otherwise fragmented socio-technical world.'[96]

A principal model of domination in the western world is through the accumulation of private property. It rarely matters if the property accumulated is considered an idea or a tangible commodity; the idea

[94] Paul Ricoeur, 1986, p. 161, quoted in Doyle McCarthy, 1996, p. 7.

[95] Michele Lamont and Virág Molnár, 2002, 'The Study of Boundaries Across the Social Sciences', *Annual Review of Sociology*, vol. 28, pp. 167–95. Increasingly, the social sciences use boundary concepts to examine interactions between individuals, groups and nations. Boundaries between different research disciplines have also been examined, as have the borders between 'hard' and social sciences. Lamont and Molnar draw a distinction between social and symbolic boundaries, describing social boundaries as manifested in unequal access to and unequal distribution of resources, while symbolic boundaries are based upon conceptual categorizations of objects, people and practices.

[96] Michael Doonesbury, 'Structuring Intellectual Property: The Case of Carbon Nanotubes', available at http://www-management.wharton.upenn.edu/kaplan/documents/panel%202-lounsbury%20and%20jennings-nanoconference.pdf (last accesesed on 8 December 2009).

is to bring property to the social and political core and to disseminate information about it from the core. A law like the IPR essentializes social categories and identities and creates a new hierarchy of knowing and the knowledgeable. This is keeping with the perspective that holds science to be authoritative, objective, and universal, and an unquestionable basis for 'expert' led decisions. Despite critiques from the early 1970s by academics, this perspective continued to dominate in many policy contexts. The theory of science is directed, almost exclusively, towards the paradigm of modern natural sciences. In following the paradigm of natural sciences, the theory of science has neglected the contextuality and the historical basis of knowledge creation.

There are two hegemonic metaphors intertwined in the conception of IP rights—that of property and power. Dick Pels, in his commentary on property and power, states that 'knowledge' in post industrial knowledge society signals the erasing of all inherited distinctions between the metaphors of property and power. Current controversies surrounding knowledge, culture and technology have theorized knowledge as both a productive and a stratifying force. It is this, according to Pels, which signals a 'convergence or even osmosis of the traditional property and power vocabularies'.[97]

This deep equivalence of knowledge and power, of power and property is reflected rather clearly in the notion of intellectual property. Intellectual property becomes a set or a bundle of competences that provide a generalized 'capacity for social action'.[98] And that capacity for action is their social power. IPRs formalize relations of social actors, things, and facts through these rights. IPRs are as much 'powers' as they are 'properties'. Intellectual property also reflects clearly the property idiom, as is exhibited by the conception of 'owning knowledge' and conception of property as a form of 'appropriation' of material, intellectual, and cultural resources of society. To use Barnes' phrase, the 'residential' and 'distributive' connotations of property are embedded in the notion of intellectual property rights.[99] It endows the 'possessors' with both a capacity, and potentiality, to do something or produce certain effects, as well as a capacity for appropriation. The distribution of what is regarded as knowledge, influences the distribution of material resources. It also imbues the owner, as with classical forms of property, with the power to exclude others from the employment of that idea for appropriation.

[97] Dick Pels, 1998, *Property and Power in Social Theory,* London: Routledge, p. 198.
[98] Barry Barnes, 1988, *The Nature of Power,* Cambridge: Polity, p. 57.
[99] Ibid.

IPRs have defined themselves by this ability to interpret, to place ideas in a context, by producing meaning for others. The meaning that is produced represents the salient elements of the socio-cultural structure of the society which has devised the IPR rules. One can presume an immediate relationship between TRIPS and the corpus of knowledge that it codifies and legitimates. If knowledge is capacity for social action, and the TRIPS regime is a body of law which identifies a corpus of knowledge and grants it the status of legally defensible 'intellectual property', then it also simultaneously delimits other capacities for action—use of knowledge for appropriation and/or for determining the use of economic goods, etc. Under IP laws, production and reproduction of intellectual competences are a matter of productive capacity—which knowledge form becomes structurally engaged with the institution of TRIPS, and which ones get left out is what constitutes the politics of knowledge.

A key issue in intellectual property rights, where multi-actor rights and obligations prevail and conflict (as in GM seeds, pharmaceutical patents, software patents and open software development, for example), is to develop protocols through which competing interests and rights can be stabilized. This is where the TRIPS agreement steps in. Adjudicating between competing claims and interests, the TRIPS regime resorts to a highly detailed codification of the procedures, forms, and processes through which information and data are processed to grant patents, copyrights, etc. All forms of knowledge creation are subjected to a universalized system of evaluation. Specific forms of knowledge claims are set free from the context in which they are embedded, and made explicit through a set of context-free claims about their meaning, utility and governance. Such rights act to disentangle knowledge claims from their local, tacit, and embedded origins.

What is regarded as scientific and proven knowledge has an effect on the way knowledge claims are assembled, what researchers search for, and how they seek to control and make information available to others. When knowledge is deployed as protected IP it takes on new characteristics. The ways in which 'novelty', 'non-obviousness' is defined (with regard to scientific claims for patents) determines the packaging of knowledge claims. What is 'novel' or what is 'non-obvious' are evaluative and subjective criteria. Yoga *asanas* may be novel in one society but belong to the public, obvious domain in another society. Neem, a symbol of indigenous knowledge, provides another useful resource for symbolic politics of knowledge. The Neem tree of India finds myriad uses in every home and every community throughout India. Recognizing its vast potential, Western science and industry has embarked on a flurry of patenting Neem's much-valued derivatives, while India, the plant's native land, has been reduced to playing the role of a challenger. Thus, there are strong cultural, social underpinnings, not just in knowledge generation, but also in knowledge claims for intellectual property rights status. Claims of validity always remain contingent on the context of justification, which must always rest upon negotiated conventions and shared exemplars.[100]

IPRs conform to a patterned way of public knowing which Sheila Jasanoff terms as 'civic epistemology'.[101] Civic epistemology forms an important element of political culture in modern knowledge societies. Scientific practice is taken as normal practice and any departure from this normal practice needs to be accounted for. Science thus locates a knowledge claim within a pattern of normal practice and then assesses it by the standards of that practice. The credibility of a knowledge claim will always be effectively undermined if it is shown to be in breach of that practice. Technological and scientific developments and their institutions, become structured by broader cognitive belief structures. If social causation is invoked to explain the breach, the general ongoing credibility of the knowledge source involved may be seriously weakened or even destroyed.[102] The legitimacy of a knowledge claim then depends on the capacity of national institutions and policy makers, in fact the entire legalistic culture, to discern and cater to the epistemologies of their intended constituencies.[103]

In all communities, including scientific ones, beliefs are judged as valid or well founded, according to culturally established precedents. These may vary temporally, as Barnes argues, but in a given community over a given period of time they are generally maintained by mechanisms of social control and transmitted successfully to new members.[104] These mechanisms of social control, like IPRs, do not blend in with the visions of contextual, culturally grounded sciences. The exploration of traditional and alternative knowledge systems, which have been submerged by the dominance of modern science, has more than any other branch of knowledge been created, held and used collectively and communally. It is a resource held by communities and is intergenerational in every sense

[100] Barry Barnes, 1974, p. 154.
[101] Sheila Jasanoff, 2005, 'Let them eat cake: GM foods and the Democratic Imagination', in *Science and Citizens: Globalization and the Challenge of Engagement*, Melissa Leach, Ian Scoones and Brian Wynne (eds), London: Zed Press, p. 195.
[102] Barry Barnes, 1974, p. 136.
[103] Sheila Jasanoff, 2005, p. 195.
[104] Barry Barnes, 1974, p. 130.

of the term. To subject them to an alien conception of science and to an individuated notion of ownership is to carry on the project of grand universalistic theory of development which highlights the need to fit and conjoin indigenous knowledge systems within dominant perspective of modern western sciences.

The realization, within the scientific community of the value of TIK has widened the scope of cognitive encounters between science and traditional indigenous knowledge but the terms of this encounter are governed by scientific standards of truth and rationality and by the individuated conception of property. Linking knowledge politics to globalization, Leach, Wynne, and Scoones express, 'North-world authored globalization and commodification cultures are developing new kinds of global knowledge culture and epistemic politics, as reflected, for example, in the proliferating attempts to enroll indigenous people in global scientific and commercial systems of research, with intellectual property rights to exploit these indigenous knowledges for profit'.[105]

It is important to point out that institutions like the WTO and the TRIPS institutions, are often orchestrated, and convened in terms set by their host institutions, whether these are particular governments, aid-agencies or powerful trade lobbies. Once the agenda has been defined, the participating citizens, including the ones representing the developing countries and their interests, have a preset structure within which their participation is circumscribed. Attempts therefore to make the TRIPS agreement more sensitive to traditional and indigenous knowledge systems are therefore, instances of citizens being enrolled in a set of institutionally predefined agendas where science and technology are understood particularistically. This makes these participatory processes vulnerable to framings in terms of knowledges and life-world of the contextually more powerful. As Chambers puts it, 'the reality of the powerful tends to dominate'.[106]

It is thus important to understand that the epistemic privilege granted to the western sciences has already set the terms and the boundary conditions for participation in that space, which seeks to bring about changes in the status of traditional and indigenous knowledges. Participation is not only the right to participate formally in a given space, but the right to define and to shape that space. Andrea Cornwall argues that participation should be treated as 'situated practice' that 'locates

---

[105] Melissa Leach, *et al.*, 2005, p. 7.

[106] Robert Chambers, November 2004, 'Ideas for Development: Reflecting Forwards', IDS Working Paper 238.

spaces for participation in the places in which they occur, framing their possibilities with reference to actual political, social, cultural and historical particularities, rather than idealized notions of democratic practice'.[107]

TRIPS agreement predetermines the terms of negotiations and their parameters through internationalized governance of intellectual property. These have important implications for understanding citizenship issues in the arena of science and technology, for re-conceptualizing the domain of 'lay' and 'expert' knowledge, of knowledge rights themselves, notions of rationality, objectivity of scientific method, and a host of issues seeking to question the fundamental premises of science-led development and progress itself. Development institutions generate their own form of discourse, creating an extremely efficient apparatus for producing knowledge about, and the exercise of power over, the poorer parts of the Global South. Escobar argues that institutionalization of international development regime 'brings the Third World into the politics of expert knowledge and western sciences in general.'[108] Experts discover an order or system that is no more than the order they have been trained to perceive or discover. They have devised 'a set of techniques, strategies and disciplinary practices that organize the generation, validation and diffusion of development knowledge' at various levels including the criteria of expertise, professional practices, and development institutions.[109]

QUESTIONING EPISTEMIC HIERARCHIES

This chapter has undertaken a critical examination of the assertion that western science is objective, presents a true picture of reality and, therefore, has the legitimacy to devise policies and institutions, in a globalized context, for the entire world. This chapter has argued that knowledge, and the capabilities arising from it, is constituted both socially, culturally, and cumulatively. It emerges out of a process of social interaction and is essentially a product of encounter and fusion of horizons. It must, therefore be looked at relationally. This also implies that there are different and plural cognitive realities; differing ways of knowing and understanding the world. Arguments for culturally grounded sciences, therefore ought to assume

[107] A. Cornwall, October 2002, 'Making Spaces, Changing Places: Situating Participation in Development', IDS Working Paper 170, IDS, p. 29.
[108] A. Escobar, 1995, *Encountering Development: The Making and Unmaking of the Third World*, Princeton: Princeton University Press, p. 45.
[109] Ibid.

the possibility of a plurality of knowledge systems. These knowledge systems are grounded in the history and culture of a particular place. For instance, Unani, Ayurveda, Homeopathy, Allopathy, are not just different medical systems, but different ways of treating ailments and also of looking at the human body. Science and technology issues are subject to variety of alternate, sometimes incompatible meanings. Sociology of scientific knowledge has since the 1980s battled against claims to objectivism and universalism. It has tried to encourage policy actors to recognize the cultural and social dimension of scientific knowledge, the limitations of expert knowledge and its interactions with lay public knowledge in areas of, for instance, environmental issues, agriculture, health, therapeutics and the like.

Science frequently underwrites the rationality of policy decisions, as is the case with IPRs. Particular views of science, technology and policy are embedded in the network of the TRIPS agreement. The intellectual property regime presents a striking encounter between what is regarded as 'scientific' and 'traditional-indigenous' knowledge. These debates, and contests positioned around it have been triggered off, in a large part, by the cultural turn in development. It has led to re-positioning of what is considered knowledge and the structure of knowledges—scientific, indigenous, traditional, ecological, lay, public, expert, and so on. What this recognizance has led to is an acceptance, across disciplines, of the relative, relational and fundamentally public character of knowledge and knowledge creation. It has led to an acceptance that all belief systems must be treated at par for purposes of sociological explanation and for notion of rights as well. Belief systems cannot be objectively ranked in terms of their proximity to one reality or rationality and it is not ethically possible to to develop devices of commensuration of knowledges by deploying external or universal standards of 'truths' and 'rationality'. That this is being done by the intellectual property regime, has implication for the engagement between science and citizens.

When we give intellectual property the conception as well as the institutions that support and protect it, a universal status, a conceptual separation of knowledge from culture takes place. Knowledge gets incorporated into the contemporary discourse as a component of power relations, beyond the notion of cultural division of labor, beyond race and ethnicity. The TRIPS regime adjudicates over what comprises 'innovative', 'novel', 'non-obvious' knowledge and therefore, what comprises intellectual property. The criteria of what constitutes knowledge, what is to be excluded and who is designated as a qualified knower, involves acts of power, as Foucault had argued.[110] IPRs are an instantiation of power relations that make it possible to extract and constitute knowledge. Intellectual property rights are part of a discourse that identifies appropriate and legitimate ways of practicing knowledge and universalizes the basis and the practice of it.

The dominance of discourse of intellectual property has resulted in the marginalization and subjugation of non-Western knowledge systems to the Western science-based knowledge system. Indigenous knowledge, even after its value is being acknowledged by the West that support the use of indigenous knowledge in planned social change, has an asymmetrical location within the international, intercultural, and interclass relations of power that define and legitimize social, political, ideological, and economic practices. Throughout critiques of development discourse there is an assertion of the relative, the local, the plural epistemologies as well as ontologies. Escobar suggests that to escape the hegemony of the development discourse, we must move away from western modes of knowing to make room for other types of knowledge and experience.[111] Kloppenburg argues for the reconstruction of a 'successor science'— 'Material resources for the reconstruction of a 'successor science' are to be found in the 'local knowledge' that is continually produced and reproduced by farmers and agricultural workers'.[112] He proposes the deconstruction of modern knowledge systems or modern science and the inclusion not only of the well known 'science for the people' but 'science by the people' including the traditional or indigenous systems of knowledge. Shiv Visvanathan's puts forward a case for 'cognitive justice' which would entail a more dialogical engagement between dominant/ modernizing/western knowledge structures on the one hand, and indigenous/traditional knowledge formations, on the other.[113] That there is a need for a dialogue, and for preservation of diversity of knowledges, has been amply demonstrated by the limits of science led development

---

[110] Michel Foucault, 1972, cited in *Beyond Farmer First: Rural Knowledge in Agricultural Research and Extension Practices*, I. Scoones, and J. Thompson, (eds), London: IT Publications, pp. 61–64.

[111] Arturo Escobar, December 1997, 'Anthropology and Development', *International Social Science Journal*, 154, pp. 497–516; Arturo Escobar, 1995, *Encountering Development: The Making and Unmaking of the Third World*, Princeton: Princeton University Press.

[112] Jack Kloppenburg, 1991, 'Social Theory And The De/Reconstruction Of Agricultural Science: Local Knowledge For An Alternative Agriculture', *Rural Sociology*, 56(4), p. 519.

[113] See, Shiv Visvanathan, 'Knowledge and Information in the Network Society', available at http://www.india-seminar.com/2001/503/503%20shiv%20visvanathan.htm (last accessed on 11 November 2007).

practices. A dialogue between differing epistemic realities is not about 'tolerating' other knowledges. A dialogue can only take place when it is affirmed that different knowledges and knowers are treated equally. These dialogues will inform the politics of knowledge and technology surrounding new designs for communication and information sharing.

What deifies the principle of cognitive justice is when a legal regime like IPRs confers an epistemic superiority to western science and technology. The current intellectual property regime legitimizes a particular mode of knowledge production and innovation that challenges and transforms the traditional forms of knowledge rights. Traditional knowledge rights, and even the earlier legal doctrine of intellectual property rights, made it possible to delineate and distribute rights to different claims. However, the new patent regime makes varied knowledge rights non-compossible, creating knowledge enclaves with rights conferred to them, divesting others with similar claims.

There is, to conclude, no one objectively constructed reality, no one, true reality. As Bauman proclaims, 'the problem of truth is easy because there are so many truths, no one better than the other, and each one remaining truthful only within the framework of an ideology. The inequality of ideologies in the practice of fixing social reality […]is to be offset the easy way—by proclaiming intellectual equality'.[114] Knowledge politics, like all forms of politics, is a play in which there are players, each with its own characteristic vantage point. None can be legitimately selected, on intellectual grounds alone, as privileged or more truthful than the rest.

---

[114] Zygmut Bauman, 1976, *Towards a Critical Sociology: An Essay on Common-Sense and Emancipation*, London: RKP, p. 97.

Section **II**

Section II

Intellectual Property Rights and Aspects of Human Rights

In Section I, I have attempted to question the deontological premises of intellectual property rights. Two intuitively powerful arguments in defense of property—self-ownership and utility—have been examined as justificatory premises for intellectual property. I have argued that both self-ownership and utility yield insufficient moral premises, by themselves or in conjunction, for claiming rights in intellectual property. I have also argued knowledge has well defined collective claims and therefore, individuated rights' claims become contestable. These conclusions have been arrived at both by questioning the philosophical claim behind intellectual property rights and by examining its claimed utility.

Section II moves beyond the analysis of the justificatory premises of IPRs to another dimension of rights' claims. I argue that rights ought to be established, not merely on grounds of utility, natural rights, liberty, etc., but also for the effects that they may generate for other rights or, to put it differently, in terms of their compossibility with other rights. A right which conjoins well with other rights has a stronger claim than a right which infringes upon other rights. There are inherent tensions between some rights, for instance, between the right to liberty and the right to equality or between individual rights and collective rights in general. Which right is accorded primacy, or to use Rawls' phrase, 'a lexical priority', largely depends on the discourse that dominates social policy nationally, socially, and/or globally. The last two decades in particular have thrown up concerns of human rights. Rights of farmers, indigenous peoples, health rights, environmental rights, multicultural rights and a whole host of other rights, are beginning to be conceptualized and institutionalized, albeit with varying degrees of determinacy and juridical protection. There is a lot of 'rights talk' by collectivities of various dispensations—United Nations, Food and Agricultural Organization, States, Non-governmental organizations, civil society organizations to name a few. One of the primary reasons has been the inability of civil and political rights to mitigate conditions of the poor of the world. There has been a growing realization that rights need to be conceived increasingly as 'positive rights' and also as rights which call upon the 'negative duty' of the infringing party to refrain from encroaching upon these rights.

Positive rights draw their justification from the idea that people should have access, as a matter of moral right, to certain welfare conditions (as distinct from the notion that people should have access rights to external resources, and on their own persons and powers). This notion, in fact, became the grounds on which group rights and human rights were claimed. This idea underlies various provisions relating to economic, social, and cultural of international covenants and declarations, as well as the European Social Charter.[1] Socio-economic rights, it is acknowledged, presume a welfare principle according to which individuals are entitled to call on the efforts of society as a whole to achieve an acceptable welfare condition for all.[2] These rights presuppose that the powers and talents of more able members be treated as common resources, to be used to bring about collective welfare. This principle is in clear contravention of the libertarian principle according to which individual powers and talents cannot be used to alter conditions for the sake of greater good.

Together with this positive rights claim, there is also the negative rights claim which argues that world poverty has been a result of the violation of the negative duty not to contribute to the imposition of a global institutional order that foreseeably and avoidably renders the basic socio-economic rights of other human beings unfulfilled. Forcefully argued by Thomas Pogge, this argument shifts the premise of socio-economic rights from good-will, charity, sincerity to a far stronger claim of a 'duty' on part of the global order. Pogge relates socio-economic rights to the concepts of harm and justice and conceives harm in terms of an 'independently specified conception of social justice: we are harming the global poor if and insofar as we collaborate in imposing an unjust global institutional order upon them'.[3] This gives rise to *entitlements* to better conditions in place of a *plea* for amelioration of conditions. It makes for a stronger claim for socio-economic rights.

[1] See for instance, UDHR, articles 22–7 ICESCR, articles.7, 9, 15; European Social Charter, articles. 2, 12.

[2] Attracta Ingram, 1994, p. 44.

[3] Thomas Pogge, 2005, 'World Poverty and Human Rights', *Ethics & International Affairs*, 19(1), p. 5.

Socio-economic rights' claims, most of which are also conceived as human rights, are fundamental human claims which are increasingly demanding more representation and institutionalization. Foregrounding these rights I probe the question I had raised earlier: How and where do intellectual property rights fit in within this emerging discourse of socio-economic and human rights? Intellectual property rights are a domain of rights that are both 'universalistic' in conception as well in application. It is based on the assumption that property practices and associated rights need not be culture specific or contextual in nature. They are advanced as globally defined set of rules which need to be adopted universally, by national governments, regardless of variations in prevalent property and knowledge institutions and practices. The contention here would be to argue that universalistic conceptions of property rights, particularly intellectual property rights, bring into sharp focus the tension between the cultural and contextual nature of intellectual practices and a universalistic IPR regime. Some communities may, for instance, uphold collective ownership of knowledge resources. Most of these communities may, in fact, lack the very conception of self-owned knowledge rights. The self and the self that 'knows' and, in fact, even the natural world with which the self interacts, may not even exist in a subject-object relationship. The cultural and intellectual domination that is implied by intellectual property rights leads to an impingement of not just knowledge rights of traditional communities but a whole range of rights, as knowledge exists in a close relationship with ways and means of livelihood, well-being, health, and so on for diverse communities and peoples. The rights in question could be livelihood rights, right to subsistence, health rights, right to life, all of which have become important dimensions of human rights discourse which has gained acceptability across the globe in official, quasi-official protocols, social movements, intellectual debates, and policy forums to name some areas of human rights' practices and protocols.

In the past few decades, there has been a dramatic increase in negotiations between social groups of different kinds and political institutions, whether at the local, national or supra national level, phrased in the language of 'rights'. Processes of globalization have led to the rights discourses being adopted widely through the world. New domains of political struggle have been framed, such as reproductive rights, animal rights, ecological rights, health rights, and so on. There is a never-ending struggle to establish as legitimate, the ideas and rights of specific individuals or groups or societies against others. Since intellectual property is both claimed and also contested as a right, it forms yet another domain of struggle. The ubiquity and the diversity of rights discourses and rights practices made the exploration of the philosophical and ethical premises of IPRs, in the earlier chapters, particularly pertinent. Equally pertinent, especially in the context of globalization of intellectual property rights, is the question of how intellectual property rights relate to 'other' rights of 'other' peoples.

Three case studies have been taken to illustrate the point that IPRs are not sufficiently attentive to the moral claims or rights of diverse communities or societies. The range of rights that intellectual property rights seek to infringe, either directly or by implication are diverse. Three rights—the Right to Health; Farmers' Rights; and Knowledge Rights—that have been violated have been taken and illustrated through case studies. All three case studies have in some sense become symbolic of the politics and conflict over intellectual property rights. These three rights by no means form a comprehensive list of rights that intellectual property Rights seek to impinge upon, but they are nevertheless three significant and illustrative rights which reflect aspects of other human rights and rights infringement as well:

IPRs and Right to Health—A Case Study of the Glivec Patent Claim in India
IPRs and Farmers' Rights—*McFarling* v. *Monsanto*: A Case Study
IPRs and Knowledge Rights—Patent claims for Neem

This section aims to examine the different aspects of the relationship between intellectual property and the different categories of rights that have been affected in the process of intellectual property protection. The group of rights referred to above is crucially linked to the evolution of the field of Human Rights. What is significant is that though Human rights and IPRs are 'rights', they belong to two distinct fields that have largely evolved separately. How they relate to each other ought to be a subject of examination. The impact of rights on the realization of human rights, such as the right to health and livelihood rights/subsistence rights will provide an opportunity to judge the co-existence of intellectual property rights with three different categories of rights, all of which have been granted salience as human rights.

6 Intellectual Property Rights and the Right to Health
The Glivec Patent Claim in India

Health is a fundamental need of all human beings. Human rights treaties recognize the right to the 'enjoyment of the highest attainable standard of physical and mental health'.[1] Health is now beginning to be seen in the context of human rights protection in response to debilitating, life threatening and life altering diseases like HIV/AIDS (Human Immuno-deficiency Virus/Acquired Immuno Deficiency Syndrome), cancer, tuberculosis, malaria and a whole host of infectious disease which are seriously neglected in terms of international attention and research. Denying the rights of people living with these diseases imperils not only their well-being, but life itself. Across the globe more than 40 million people live with HIV, half of whom are women, and half the new infections are occurring in young people under the age of 25.[2] Many millions more are affected by other life threatening diseases. World Health Organization (WHO) identifies a select group of thirteen tropical diseases that afflict the poor and powerless in the developing regions of sub-Saharan Africa, Asia, and the Americas, broadly termed as 'neglected diseases' (NDs). Together, they cause an estimated 5,00,000 to 1 million deaths annually and cause a global disease burden equivalent to that of HIV-AIDS.[3] However, the overall toll of diseases cannot be measured by mortality

[1] See, article 12 International Covenant on Economic, Social and Cultural Rights,(ICESCR), New York, 15 December 1966.
[2] International Council of AIDS Service Organizations, 'The International Guidelines on HIV/AIDS and Human Rights: How Are They Being Used and Applied?', Toronto: International Council of AIDS Service Organizations, 2002.
[3] The George Washington University Neglected Tropical Diseases Initiative, 'Developing New Health Products; (Drugs, Diagnostics, and Vaccines) To Control The Ancient Afflictions of Stigma and Poverty'. Available at http://gstudynet.org/docs/The%20GWU%20Neglected%20Tropical%20Diseases%20Initiative.doc (last accessed on 13 July 2007).

alone. Generally speaking, NDs cause more chronic life-long disabilities and morbidity rather than death. For instance, Chagas disease causes a chronic and disabling heart condition; hookworm, chronic intestinal blood loss and anemia; onchocerciasis, blindness and intense itching that results in chronic skin changes; guinea worm, localized pain that prevents temporary disuse of a lower limb, and so on. NDs also have a huge social impact due to lost educational potential, reduced economic productivity, and stigma. Schistosomiasis and hookworm impair the ability of school-aged children to learn in school, while guinea worm and river blindness result in missed days of work for adults, especially the family breadwinner. Many diseases in general and NDs in particular, not only occur in the context of poverty, but through their adverse social impact may also promote poverty.

Addressing health needs is increasingly seen as critical for poverty alleviation and human development. Globalization, and its scale, has ensured that these problems are no longer viewed as mere local health concerns. There is an awareness of both the plight of the affected people and the global and epidemic nature of these diseases. The sheer scale of the problems and its endemic link with poverty has been a prime stimulus in the linking of health needs of peoples with the human rights discourse.

THE RIGHT TO HEALTH AS A RIGHT TO LIFE

The right to health has come to be critically linked to the right to life itself. Most significant, in this regard, is the connections that are drawn between life and human dignity and flourishing. It is an explicit shift away from notions of life as biological survival to include a disability free life existence. Health rights, conceptualized so, are based on mankind's increasing demand for a decent civilized life in which the inherent dignity of each human being is well-respected and protected. They are regarded fundamental to our very existence without which we cannot live as human beings. As former UN Secretary General, Kofi Annan said: 'Human rights are what makes us human. They are principles by which we create the sacred home for human dignity.' The alignment of the notion of human dignity and flourishing, with the right to life, has been a big leap forward in the rights entitlements for it has enabled rights like health, which are not constitutionally sanctioned in many countries, to draw juridical sustenance from it.

That health is as fundamental as the right to life is, finds an echo in various international documents, covenants—Universal Declaration of

Human Rights (UDHR)[4], International Covenant on Economic, Social and Cultural Rights (ICESCR), Convention on the Elimination of All Forms of Discrimination Against Women (CEDAW), the Convention on the Elimination of All Forms of Racial Discrimination (CERD), and the Convention on the Rights of the Child (CRC). Human Rights relating to health, set out in basic human rights treaties, include the human right to: the highest attainable standard of physical and mental health, reproductive and sexual health; equal access to adequate health care and health-related services, regardless of sex, race, or other status; equitable distribution of food; access to safe drinking water and sanitation; an adequate standard of living and adequate housing; a safe and healthy environment; a safe and healthy workplace, and to adequate protection for pregnant women in work proven to be harmful to them; freedom from discrimination and discriminatory social practices, including female genital mutilation, prenatal gender selection, and female infanticide; to education and access to information relating to health; the human right of the child to an environment appropriate for physical and mental development.

The expanded conceptualization of the right to health is welcome as it explicates the principles that ought to govern the right and the requirements of the right itself. However, some scholars, such as Tara Melish argue, that this expansion detracts from the minimum core of 'survival' and focuses instead on more elevated conceptions of life as linked to dignity, human flourishing, well-being, etc., which become like 'free for all provision, implicated by default in all human rights abuses that that affect a person's "dignity" or "life prospects".'[5] However, what this enables us to do is to disaggregate the right into more meaningful components. It provides, as Henry Shue states, 'the rational basis for a justified demand', and provides 'that the actual enjoyment of a substance be socially guaranteed against standard threats'.[6] The expanded concept may also play a role in setting out baselines and normative standards for constitutional democracies who can use it to add a more determinate content to the various sub-categories of the right to health. It can, for instance, allow a broad interpretation of the right to health as right to life itself, through which it gains justifiability, as in India. To say that health

[4] See, Universal Declaration of Human Rights, Article 25, available at http://www. udhr.org/UDHR/ART25.HTM (last accessed on 25 September 2008).

[5] Tara Melish, 2006, 'Rethinking the "Less as More" Thesis: Supranational Litigationof the Economic, Social and Cultural Rights in Americas', *NYU Journal of International Law and Politics*, vol. 39, p. 326.

[6] Henry Shue, 1996, *Basic Rights: Subsistence, Affluence and U.S. Foreign Policy*, Second edition, p. 23.

is linked to provisioning of clean drinking water, to levels of education, to working conditions, and so on, is to disaggregate the right in terms of the factors which critically affect health conditions in poorer parts of the world. That they are implicated in other human rights as well, does not detract from their efficacy for the right to health. It only adds to a determinate core to an otherwise nebulous right. To invoke a connection between the right to health and the right to life is also, as Katherine Young states, 'strategically sound' because it focuses attention on the most urgent steps necessary for the satisfaction of the 'basic rights'.[7]

'Basic rights' are moral minimums, in Shue's analysis,[8] for they precondition the enjoyment of all other rights. The right to health is one such right, premised on the fact that ill health leaves a person incapable of engaging in independent, self-directed activity and therefore of enjoying any right that protects such activity. The classification of health as a basic right is useful in order to qualify this right as vital to a minimally adequate existence and, in doing so, justify the priority of this right over rights that are based on want-fulfilment. I draw this distinction so as to assert the primacy of the right to health vis-à-vis innovators' rights protected by the TRIPS regime, which are more in the nature of economic rewards stimulating innovation and not, generally, preconditioning survival. The legal terms of adjudication between these two oft competing rights ought to be based on a cognizance of this distinction.

In recent times, the expanding TRIPS regime has ensured that rights of the innovators have become more well defined, more institutionalized and with enough legal teeth to trump rights which are vital to and, are in a sense, prior rights of people. The effects that IPRs generate for rights like health are significant for the latter is linked to issues of survival and dignified, disability-free existence. How they relate to each other, the way these rights are given content and are upheld juridically is always a subject of examination and concern. Rights that IPRs confront, for instance health rights, have remained stuck at the first level of articulation, that is, they exist more in statements of intent or remain relegated to the purpose and objectives sections of documents. They lack the juridical attention that IPRs have grabbed. The discourse on health rights has largely been under-inclusive as it has been unable to lend a conceptual

---

[7] Katherine Young, 2008, 'The Minimum Core of Economic and Social Rights: A Concept in Search of Content', *Yale Journal of International Law*, 33(1) , p. 129.

[8] This term used by Henry Shue to qualify these rights as entitlements to basic needs, that is, food, shelter, clothing, clean water, health care and minimal standards of education. Henry Shue, 1996.

and institutional content to claims for health interests, interests which are central to an emancipated life.

There are slow beginnings however—attempts are being made both at the national and international levels to institutionalize the right to health and lend it more legal teeth. Some national apex court judgments in India,[9] Venezuela,[10] Bangladesh,[11] South Africa,[12] Ecuador,[13] for instance, convey a broad interpretation of the right to health as a right to life. Some countries, like South Africa, for instance, adopt the normative standards of the ICESCR as the basis for constitutional, justiciable health rights. However, countries like India depend rather heavily on progressive and creative interpretations of the right to life in the absence of well grounded constitutional right to health. New levels of articulation of health rights are also beginning to prefigure in the ways in which intellectual property laws, pertaining to rights of innovators in pharmaceuticals, are being conceptualized and interpreted at national levels. National patent laws, particularly of developing countries like India, Thailand, Brazil, invoke the right to health either to delimit patentability of pharmaceuticals

[9] The Supreme Court of India has held in a number of cases that the right to life, enshrined in article 21 under the Constitution does not stand for animal existence but the right to life with human dignity. Right to health is now recognized as the fundamental right India. In the *Bandhua Mukti Morcha* v. *Union of India*, AIR 1984 SC 802 the Supreme Court held that article 21 closely linked Directive Principles of State Policy, particularly clause (e) and (f) of article 39, article 41 and article 42. 'It must include protection of the health and strength of workers, men and women, and tender age children against abuse, opportunities and facilities for children to develop in a healthy manner and in conditions of freedom and dignity, educational facilities, just and human conditions of work and maternity relief.' These are minimum requirements which must exist in order to enable a person live with dignity. In case of *State of Punjab* v. *Mahindrasingh Chawla*, AIR 1997 SC 1225, the Supreme Court of India held that right to life includes the right to health: 'It is now settled that the right to health is integral to the right to life…'. Similarly, in *Paschim Banga Khet Mazdoor Society* v. *State of West Bengal*, AIR 1996 SC 2426, the Supreme Court held that the timely medical treatment in Govt. hospital is fundamental right.

[10] For instance, *Cruz Bermude, et al.*, v. *Ministerio de Sanidad y Asistencia Social*, 17 July 1999. The Supreme Court of Justice of Venezuela in its ruling maintained that the rights to health, to life and to have access to scientific and technological advances are closely related.

[11] Refer to *Dr Mohinuddin Farooque* v. *Bangladesh & Ors*, Writ Petition No.1576, 1994 where the Supreme Court of Bangladesh compelled an importer to send a radiation affected milk consignment back to the importer as it was violative of the constitutional right to life.

[12] For instance, *Treatment Action Campaign* v. *Ministers of Health*, Constitutional Court of South Africa, 5 July 2002.

[13] *Mendoza and Others* v. *Minister of Public Health and the Director of the National AIDS-HIV-STI Programme*, (2004) Tribunal Constitucional, 3ra Sala, Equador, Resolution no. 0749-2003-RA, 28 January 2004.

drugs (section 3(d) of Indian Patents Act, 1970[14] for instance) or interpret TRIPS provisions of compulsory licensing more liberally to address health needs. More than anything else these laws reflect the dilemmas of developing countries as they struggle between the claims of public health and intellectual property protection.

I have outlined three varied conceptualizations and locations of the right to health: right to health as a right to life (South Africa); right to life as *also* right to health (India); and Right to health as a human right. All three conceptualizations establish a connection between 'rights' and 'life' (understood as human flourishing and well being). The linkage with life endows the right to health with a core which needs no other justification. Protection of life relies on no other foundation. However, variations in the way they are instituted—as constitutional rights in South Africa, as a derivative of the right to life in India, demonstrate that while the chain of reasoning that accompanies the rights argument remains largely the same, there is a definite possibility of varied efficacy in the way the rights are realized. The extent to which the right to health is 'realisable' and 'accruable', in the face of instituted and legalized IPRs, is a function of how entrenched health rights are in the legal framework of a society.

The WTO and the TRIPS regime have become important tools in the globalization of trade and institutionalization of globalized norms of trade. The TRIPS regime has brought about definitive changes in the dynamics of drug trade and research and has had far reaching impact on issues of drug access, availability, research, prices, disease control, and so on. Until recently, providing patent protection for pharmaceuticals was a choice made by individual governments according to their level of industrial development. Today, pharmaceutical patents are globalized through the WTO on TRIPS Agreement, and then further reinforced through bilateral and regional arrangements (the so-called TRIPS-Plus agreements).[15] This chapter raises the issue of health rights in this context.

TRIPS AGREEMENT AND THE RIGHT TO HEALTH
WHO estimates that currently one third of the world's population lacks access to essential drugs.[16] Over fifty percent of people in the developing

---

[14] Clause (d) added to Section 3 of the Indian Patent Act, 1970 by the 2005 Amendment. The Patents (Amendment) Act, 2005, no. 15 of 2005.

[15] J. Replogle, 2004, 'Central American Trade Pact May Limit Access to Generics,' *Lancet*, 363, pp. 1612–13.

[16] WHO Infectious Diseases Report, 1999, Chapter 1. Available at http://www.who.int/infectious-disease-report/pages/ch1text.html (last accessed on 12 September 2007).

world especially in Africa and Asia do not have access to even the most basic essential drugs.[17] A group of international organizations recently estimated that less than 10 per cent of people living with HIV/AIDS in developing countries have access to antiretroviral (ARV) therapy.[18]

The TRIPS agreement is one of the treaties administered by the WTO and is meant to generally provide enhanced opportunities for international trade by laying down conditions under which IP, like patents, can be claimed and monopoly over use and distribution established. Patents, it is believed, constitute an incentive for research and innovation in general, as also for the development of research by the pharmaceutical industry. The rationale for granting exclusive rights on patented medicines is that the development of new drugs has a very high research and development component, has a usually high gestation period and is a costly process. At the same time, it is relatively easy to reverse engineer and copy an existing drug. Thus, in order to promote innovation and research in developing drugs for a world afflicted with disease and challenged by new strains of virus and bacteria, innovation needs to be promoted and rewarded. Patents are forms of reward that accrue to the patent holder for his investment of resources in the innovation of a product. And these rewards are in the form of monopoly of use and exchange at monopoly prices, that is, at prices that are significantly higher than the generic (non-patented) counterparts. Patents, thus in a way, constitute a pre-condition for the involvement of the private sector in the development and production of new medicines. By obliging all governments to grant minimum twenty-year patents, the TRIPS framework shields pharmaceutical companies from generic competition globally. The end result is that patented drugs are usually significantly more expensive than generic drugs. Because patents are the primary rewards that provide research incentives, it logically follows that the patent system would stimulate innovation only where industry sees the opportunity for increasing sales and market share.

TRIPS has brought about two major implications for the health industry. The first is the R&D orientation of the pharmaceuticals industry comes to be dominated by commercial interests rather than need. A dimension of the health industry being driven by commercial interest is the lack of requisite R&D for a group of diseases which are broadly called

---

[17] Ibid. Chapter 16.

[18] ARV's are anti HIV treatment drugs. See for instance, 'Sources and Prices of Selected Drugs and Diagnostics for People Living with HIV/AIDS,' UNICEF-UNAIDS-WHO/HTP/MSF (May 2001). Available at http://www.who.int/hiv/topics/arv/en/who_edm_par_2002.pdf (last accessed on 8 December 2009).

'Neglected Diseases' (ND). The cost of development of drugs for tropical diseases seems to suffer from the syndrome of 'high-input costs into research' and weak monetary demand which translates into prospects for low returns. In theory, this could be addressed through the patent system which delivers commercial incentives for the costly process of developing vaccines and other drugs, but the prices that a firm would have to charge would prevent access by millions of people. The patent regime has still not been implemented in the Least Developed Countries (LDCs) which further reduce patent incentives for the pharmaceutical companies to invest in research of tropical and neglected diseases. On the other hand, there has been a significant growth in the research and development of lifestyle drugs. The growth in lifestyle drugs, research, development, and sales is significantly higher than for neglected diseases only because there is a strong monetary demand for the former.[19] Troullier noted that 1,393 new medicines were launched globally between 1975 and 1999, but only sixteen were for tropical diseases of which thirteen drugs (1 per cent) were for tropical infectious diseases, and three for tuberculosis.[20] Ten of the thirteen drugs (for tropical infectious diseases) were developed for veterinary or military purposes, leaving only three that were the result of genuine efforts to create drugs for neglected diseases. This enormous discrepancy is captured by the notion of the '10/90 gap': 90 per cent of the global disease burden attracts ten per cent of research investments.[21]

There is no indication that drug development for the most neglected diseases by pharmaceutical companies will significantly improve in the near future. A recent study by the DNDi (Drugs for Neglected Diseases) working group and the Harvard School of Public Health questioned the world's top twenty pharmaceutical companies on their

[19] Anti-baldness drugs generated 180 million dollars in sales in 1998, the anti-wrinkle drug Botox earned $90 million in sales in 1997, and Viagra's sales approached 800 million dollars in its first year. One industry analyst projected that with more than 20 billion dollars now being invested in developing drugs for lifestyle conditions, annual sales of lifestyle drugs will soon reach 11 billion dollars. 'Discretionary drug dollars,' *Journal of Business Strategy Publication* 1 July 2002. Available at http://www.accessmylibrary.com/coms2/summary_0286-25645998_ITM (last accessed on 26 June 2007).

[20] P. Troviller, *et al.*, 2002, 'Drug Development for Neglected Diseases: A Deficient Market and a Public Policy Failure', *Lancet*, vol. 359, pp. 2188–94, see also, WHO Report, 2003, 'Intellectual Property Rights, Innovation and Public Health', 56th World Health Assembly, A56/17, 12 May.

[21] L. Currat, 'The 10/90 Report on Health Research 2001–2002', (Geneva: Global Forum for Health Research., 2002), pp. 1–224. Available at http://www.globalforumhealth.org/Site/002__What%20we%20do/005__Publications/001__10%2090%20reports.php (last accessed on 21 April 2007).

R&D activities for malaria, tuberculosis, African trypanosomiasis, Chagas disease and leishmaniasis (five of the thirteen NDs listed by the WHO). Eleven companies responded, representing 29 per cent of the worldwide pharmaceutical market for 2002. Of these companies, seven reported spending less than 1 per cent of their R&D budget over the previous year on any of those five diseases, and eight spent nothing on the most neglected diseases (African trypanosomiasis, Chagas disease and leishmaniasis). None of the responding companies has brought a drug to market for any of the most neglected diseases included in the survey.[22]

The patent system stimulates innovation only where industry sees the opportunity for increasing sales and market shares. The poorest are hardest hit. While R&D of new therapies against tropical diseases has ground to a standstill, 14 million people die from infectious diseases each year, predominantly in developing countries.[23] It implies that NDs, which are areas of weak monetary demand, remain outside the interest of patent seeking drug companies.[24]

The second implication of the TRIPS framework has been reduced access to affordable drugs. Access to medicines depends on many critical elements: R&D, affordable prices, distribution and dispensing of drugs, legal and policy instruments that the government can use to regulate prices, government support of research, sustainable financing and reliable supply systems, and so on. There are a host of factors that play a significant role in shaping people's access to medicines, but drug prices remain a crucial factor in restricting or allowing access. This is particularly true of developing countries and LDCs where, in the context of limited financial resources and persistent poverty, drug pricing becomes the most important factor in restricting access to medicines. There are many determinants of drug pricing. While all aspects are important, the link between high patents and high priced drugs acquires prominence in the context of the TRIPS agreement. Drugs which are patented are priced high for they form the monopoly returns on investment in R&D in pharmaceuticals projects and hence, also the rationale behind R&D in the first place. Patenting of drugs has huge ramifications for drug access

[22] Von Christian Burri, April 2004, 'High Time to Take Action: Research on Neglected Diseases,' *Bulletin von Medicus Mundi Schweiz* Nr. 92. Available at http://www.medicusmundi.ch/mms/services/bulletin/bulletin200401/kap01/08burri.html (last accessed on 3 September 2007).

[23] P. Trouiller, *et al.*, 2002, 'Drug Development for Neglected Diseases: A Deficient Market and a Public-health Policy Failure', *Lancet*, vol. 359, pp. 2188–94.

[24] J. Gilbert, P. Henske, and A. Singh, 'Rebuilding Big Pharma's Business Model', *Vivo: The Business and Medicine Report*, vol. 21, p. 73.

and consequently, have enormous implications for access to health. The comparative price advantages that generic drugs have in comparison to patented drugs become associated with greater access to medicines and therefore, align with issues of health rights.

Two cases, the Brazilian and the South African, became international health rights campaigns linking the supply of generic drugs (reverse-engineered versions of patented drugs which may be disallowed to operate in the market under intellectual property laws) with issues of drug access. These campaigns highlighted the sovereign right of a nation to grant the right to health a higher priority than IPRs. In 1997, South Africa legislated Medicines and Related Substances Control Amendment Act in order to override the TRIPS agreement's provisions and facilitate the import of generic antiretroviral (ARV) drugs for HIV/AIDS treatment under a practice termed 'parallel importing'.[25] The law also allowed compulsory licensing, giving the minister powers to permit local companies to manufacture generic versions of patented drugs. Compulsory licensing is a measure in the TRIPS agreement that allows the government to permit domestic production or import of a patented product or process (in this case ARV drugs) without a necessary consent of the patent owner.[26] It is one of the flexibilities on patent protection included in the WTO's agreement on intellectual property, the TRIPS (Article 31).[27] This amendment was a reaction to the severe HIV/AIDS crisis that the country had been facing, with 4.3 million of the country's

[25] See, Section 15C of the 'Medicines and Related Substance Control Amendment Act', 1997, Republic of South Africa, *Government Gazette*, 12 December.

[26] Many patent law systems provide for the granting of compulsory licenses in a variety of situations. Specific situations in which compulsory licenses may be issued are set out in the legislation of each patent system and vary between systems. Developing countries, with low or non-existent levels of intellectual property protection, and limited access to new pharmaceutical products, are more likely than other countries to implement legislation permitting compulsory licensing under a broad range of circumstances, including to meet loosely defined 'national requirements'. Some examples of situations in which a compulsory license may be granted include health emergencies, particular cases of national emergency or extreme urgency or in cases of public non-commercial use. In cases of health emergencies where it has acquired significant application, the endeavour is to allow the import or domestic production of cheaper generic drugs improve access to prescription medicine which otherwise could not have been possible under the terms of the patented drug.

[27] It is significant to note that Article 31of the TRIPS agreement, does not use the term compulsory licensing; instead it refers to it as 'Other Use Without Authorization of the Right Holder'. The TRIPS agreement thus leaves members free to determine grounds for granting compulsory licences, provided that the conditions and procedures imposed by article 31 are met, and taking into account the other provisions of the TRIPS agreement.

40 million people (more than 10 per cent) estimated to be HIV-positive, making it one of the worst affected countries, and the need to provide affordable treatment and drugs to them. Less than 1 per cent of the 25 million people infected with HIV/AIDS in Africa were in year 2000 receiving ARVs, yet there were medicines available, proven effective in prolonging lives of those who could afford the prevalent market prices. The South African amendment was designed to facilitate the import of generic versions of the ARV drugs, available 30–40 per cent cheaper.[28] Lack of access to ARVs was precipitating a serious health crisis within the country.[29] This law sought to override patent rights to facilitate the availability and affordability of medicines in the interest of public health. The Amendment was vigorously challenged by a group of pharmaceutical companies. As many as 39 pharmaceutical companies challenged the South African legislation on grounds that it was in contravention of the non-discrimination clause of Article 27 of the TRIPS agreement.[30] The petition was eventually abandoned in April 2001 in the face of strong public opposition and mounting international pressures. What this case highlighted was the ability of patented drugs to delimit the scope of the right to health, as did the Brazilian case.

In 2001, Brazil was involved in international disputes related to its program of access to AIDS medicines. At the core of the controversy was Brazil's need to provide cheaper ARV therapy (drugs used in HIV/AIDS treatment) by allowing its own generic drug capacity to function and by allowing parallel import of generic drugs.[31] Constrained by the laws related

---

[28] The cost of annual treatment with the triple-therapy cocktails, which have proven effective in inhibiting the development of HIV into AIDS, was between US 10,000–15,000 dollars per person in the United States. Cipla, an Indian pharmaceutical company, offered to sell generic versions of a triple-therapy drug cocktail for 350 dollars per annual treatment to 20 programmes in Africa run by the International non-governmental organizations, Doctors Without Borders (Médecins Sans Frontières, known by its French acronym MSF). Cipla said it would be willing to sell the drugs to African governments for US 600 dollars per person. Gumisai Mutume, 9 February 2001, *Pressure mounts for cheaper anti-AIDS drugs,* Washington: Third World Network.

[29] See for instance Patrick Bond, 1999, 'Globalization, Pharmaceutical Pricing and South African Health Policy—Managing Confrontation with US Firms and Politicians', *International Journal of Health Services,* 29(4).

[30] See *The Pharmaceutical Manufacturers' Association of South Africa, et al.* v. *The President of the Republic of South Africa and others,* Notice of Motion, High Court of South Africa (Transvaal Provincial Division), 18 February 1998. See also, Varells, Marcelo Dias, 'The WTO, Intellectual Property and AIDs—Case Studies from Brazil and South Africa,' 7/4, *J World Intellectual Property,* 523 (2004).

[31] J. Galvão, December 2002, 'Access to antiretroviral drugs in Brazil', *Lancet,* pp. 1862–65.

to the TRIPS agreement, the Brazilian government adopted a decree establishing rules concerning the granting of compulsory licenses in cases of national emergency and public interest. In that year, the WTO accepted a request for a panel by the United States, which was challenging Brazil's patent laws, particularly, the provisions that permitted the compulsory license of patents under special conditions. At its heart, the US challenge questioned Brazil's commitment to producing ARVs nationally. Explicitly, however, the United States was challenging the prospective patent violations that would occur as a result of Brazil's program. In June 2001, the US withdrew its complaint before the WTO. In September 2003, a presidential decree was issued in Brazil that facilitated the importation of generic medicines.

The Brazilian and the South African experience played a key role in changing expectations in the interpretation of the WTO's TRIPS agreement. The two cases generated a vast surge in international public awareness on the impact of patents on the prices and drug access in developing countries and LDCs and eventually led to ministerial conference culminating in the Doha Declaration on Public Health in November 2001. When the Doha Health Declaration, at the end of 2001, declared that the TRIPS agreement ought not to stand in the way of AIDS responses, it in effect acknowledged the ethical and practical imperatives represented by South Africa and Brazil.

The Doha Health Declaration[32] was a response to the public concerns. A huge public upsurge was generated following the Brazilian and South African cases. NGOs campaigned vigorously on the issue arguing that the global patent rules would exacerbate the health crisis ravaging poor countries. International debate culminated in the Doha Health Declaration on TRIPS and Public Health,(the Doha Declaration), agreed at the WTO Ministerial in Doha in November 2001. This was an important step forward in the campaign for affordable medicines. It affirmed the primacy of public health over IPRs and the rights of governments to make full use of the public health safeguards in the TRIPS agreement.[33] The Declaration reaffirmed and clarified the flexibilities available under TRIPS agreement, and proclaimed:

---

[32] Doha Declaration, WTO Ministerial Conference 14 November 2001. Available at http://www.wto.org/English/thewto_e/minist_e/min01_e/mindecl_trips_e.htm (last accessed on 20 September 2007).

[33] See paragraphs 4, 5 and 6 of the Doha Health Declaration, 2001. Available at http://www.wto.org/English/thewto_e/minist_e/min01_e/mindecl_trips_e.htm (last accessed on 28 September 2008).

We agree that the TRIPS agreement does not and should not prevent Members from taking measures to protect public health ....We affirm that the agreement can and should be interpreted in a manner supportive of Members' right to protect public health and in particular, to promote access to medicines for all.

It spelt out several flexibilities that WTO members can use to the full, such as the right to grant compulsory licenses and the freedom to determine the grounds for these. The Declaration clearly outlines all the key flexibilities available in the TRIPS framework, including:

1. The right of countries to use compulsory licensing and to determine the grounds on which to grant them;
2. The right of countries to determine what constitutes a national emergency or urgency, which can ease the granting of compulsory licenses;
3. The right of countries to determine their own parallel import regimes; and
4. The right of LDCs to postpone implementing pharmaceutical patents until *at least* 2016, and possibly longer.

Significantly, the Doha Declaration does not define the term 'public health'. A narrow interpretation of the term would clearly render many public health initiatives futile. It does recognize the obvious problems faced by developing countries in promoting public health, especially in the wake of epidemics like AIDS, malaria, tuberculosis, etc. However, the very fact that the document restricts itself to certain specific epidemics creates a problem as the flexibility may be allowed only in the case of these particular diseases, if at all. The pharmaceutical industry would certainly like to interpret this provision restrictively, leaving out certain diseases prevalent in member countries which may not be internationally recognized as epidemics. For example, diabetes, coronary heart diseases, certain tropical diseases that are endemic in the developing world may not be given the same importance even though they represent serious public health concerns in many countries.[34]

Another inherent defect is built into the system through the stipulation that member countries can make use of options such as the compulsory license mechanism to promote public health *only when a health crisis has*

---

[34] Stevens Philip, (Director of Health Projects, International Policy Network), 'Diseases of poverty and the 10/90 Gap', November 2004. Available at www.policynetwork.net (last acessed on 21 July 2007); Also see, Alternative Law Forum 'TRIPS and Public Health,'. Available at http://www.altlawforum.org/PUBLICATIONS/document.2004-12-18.5846929564 (last accessed on 26 July 2007).

arisen, especially in the form of an epidemic affecting the populace at large. This limitation clearly weakens their right to take preventive and precautionary action before a disease becomes a full-blown crisis. The Declaration does recognize the problems posed by the pricing of drugs and the impact of this on access. At the same time, it accepts the importance of IPRs for the development of new medicines. But a commitment to the latter renders the former as an insufficient protective mechanism, particularly when seen in the context of endemic public health issues which are not explicit 'emergencies'.

Interestingly, the Doha Declaration does not restrict patentability in the field of health even in the context of national emergencies.[35] It only reaffirms the flexibility in the TRIPS agreement. It specifically focuses on compulsory licenses as a means to improve drug access. It reiterates that countries have a right to determine the grounds on which compulsory licenses can be granted. Paragraph 5(b), 5(c) of the Doha Health Declaration states:[36]

5(b) Each member has the right to grant compulsory licences and the freedom to determine the grounds upon which such licences are granted. 5 (c) Each member has the right to determine what constitutes a national emergency or other circumstances of extreme urgency, it being understood that public health crises, including those relating to HIV/AIDS, tuberculosis, malaria and other epidemics, can represent a national emergency or other circumstances of extreme urgency.

The provisions of compulsory licensing are an extremely complex. For instance, Article 31(f) of the TRIPS framework initially ruled that licenses can be used mainly to supply to domestic market. This posed a challenge to those countries with health emergencies but with no generic production capacity of their own. Doha Health Declaration recognized in paragraph 6 that LDCs, who do not have generic production capacities of their own are curtailed by Article 31(f) of the TRIPS agreement.[37] In other words, licenses could not be used to import generic drugs from other countries. This was a serious practical hurdle. Countries, in particular LDCs, who didn't have domestic manufacturing capacity, would continue to be denied access to affordable drugs, if this interpretation of Article 31(f) were to continue.

[35] Philippe Cullet, 2005, p. 85.
[36] DOHA, WTO Ministerial. Available at http://www.wto.org/English/theWTOe/ministe/min01emindecl.trips.e.htm (last accessed on 8 July 2009).
[37] 'The use without authorization of the right holder' permissible under article 31 of the TRIPS agreement, is subject to being authorized 'predominantly for the supply of the domestic market of the Member authorizing such use.' This conditionality continues to prevail and exports from countries having generic production are barred.

This clause also restricted developing countries that do have domestic drug production capacity (for instance, India) from exporting sufficient quantities of medicines to those that do not (for instance, Togo), making compulsory licensing a meaningless measure for many LDCs. A United Nations Industrial Development Organization (UNIDO) study, in 1992, indicated that 60 countries do not have the capacity for either active ingredients or formulation.[38] Cognizant of the problem posed by Article 31(f) Paragraph 6 of the Doha Declaration instructed the TRIPS Council to 'find an expeditious solution' to this issue by the end of 2002. Negotiations on Article 31 (f) continued, with a lot of resistance from the US to the review of Article 31(f). In August 2003, a waiver, known as the 'August 30th decision',[39] to Article 31(f) was implied with a number of riders and provisos, allowing export through licenses. A country could import a generic version of the patented product by issuing a compulsory license to a company or agency to import the drug, and the government could exercise the freedom to determine the grounds upon which such licenses are given. The imported drug can be from a country in which the drug is not patented, or in which the drug is patented, in which case the exporting country has also to issue a compulsory license. The applicant has to first negotiate to obtain a voluntary license from the patent holder (except in cases of public non-commercial use, situations of extreme urgency and national emergency), and if that fails, then a compulsory license can be granted. Adequate compensation must be paid to the patent holder.[40]

The August 30th decision is needlessly complex, says Ellen t'Hoen of the Médecins Sans Frontières (MSF) Access to Medicines Campaign, and is not likely to remove the real threat of dwindling generic production in countries such as India.[41] The potential role of compulsory

[38] UNIDO, 1980, *Appropriate Industrial Technology for Drugs and Phramaceuticals, United Nations Industrial Development Organization* (UNIDO), New York: NY Monograph on Appropriate Industrial Technology, p. 10.

[39] See, WTO General Council Amendment of 30 August 2003, 'Implementation of para 8 of the Doha Declaration on the TRIPS Agreement and Public Health', WT/L/ 540 and Corr. 1.

[40] For details refer Khor Martin, *Patents, Compulsory License and Access to Medicines: Some Recent Experiences*, TWN: February 2007. Available at http://www.twnside.org.sg.title2/ IPR/pdf/pr10.pdf (last accessed on 5 December 2009).

[41] For details of the argument see, t'Hoen, Ellen 'TRIPS, R&D and Access to Medicines: A Guide to the Post 2005 World' External briefing document, (Médecins Sans Frontières (MSF) Campaign for Access to Essential Medicines, February 2005) Based on a 18 January 2005 presentation to Members of European Parliament. Especially see footnote 4 of the presentation for a synopsis of how the compulsory licensing system works; See also, Correa, C., 'Access to drugs under TRIPS: A Not so Expeditious Solution', *Bridges* 8 (1), pp. 21–2.

licensing in promoting access to medicines is replete with compelling issues. The issue of compulsory licenses is also mired in the politics of bilateral relations and has not proved the most uncontentious way to address critical public health concerns. In the absence of national patent legislations which protect public health concerns, compulsory licensing may not be the best strategy. Martin Khor of Third World Network (TWN) states, 'If the Doha Declaration is to benefit patients of AIDS and other ailments in developing countries, these countries now have to establish appropriate provisions in their national patent legislation by using 'to the full' the flexibilities in the TRIPS agreement…In other words, whilst in recent years the goal for access to medicines had been significantly fought at the international level, action is now equally or even more important at the national level, where policy makers should focus on policy and practical measures to get medicines to poor patients.'[42]

A number of developing countries including Indonesia, Malaysia, Mozambique, Zambia and more recently in 2005, Thailand, have made use of compulsory licensing or government use orders to enable the supply of more affordable generic drugs in recent years. However, access to medicines is being affected by new developments such as bilateral free trade agreements (FTA), 'TRIPS Plus' agreements, and the coming into force of India's new patent laws in 2005. Two factors in recent times have and will ensure that compulsory licensing will not be the most effective tool to facilitate the supply of generic drugs.

Mogha Kamal Smith of Oxfam states that the space given to developing countries by the August 2003 agreement, is being taken away by bilateral and regional free trade agreements (FTAs) with developed countries, especially the United States.[43] The US also seeks worldwide harmonization of intellectual property rules on a level at or above US law, which is stricter than TRIPS, known as TRIPS Plus agreements. According to the Report of the Industry Trade Advisory Committee on Intellectual Property Rights (ITAC 15), which is part of the United States Trade Representative's (USTR) formal advisory committee structure and represents the pharmaceutical industry, 'The Committee seeks to establish

[42] Martin Khor, 2007, *Patents, Compulsory License and Access to Medicines: Some Recent Experiences,* Penang, TWN.
[43] For a perspective on FTAs, see, 2006, GRAIN Summary Report on 'Fighting FTAS: An International Strategy Workshop, Bangkok. Available at www.grain.org/nfg/?id=433 (last accessed on 2 March 2009). Also see, Sangeeta Shashikant, 2004, 'The Politics of US Free Trade Agreements', *Third World Resurgence,* pp. 167–8.

strong precedents in these FTAs in order to raise the level of protection and enforcement globally, nationally and in regional and in multilateral agreements. The FTA process has become the principal process through which the IPR-based industries are able to ensure that the standards of protection and enforcement keep pace with new developments.'[44]

A central element of the recent set of bilateral FTAs is the establishment of strong rules for the protection of intellectual property rights (IPRs). There are many restrictions that FTAs impose. For instance, to effectively make use of compulsory licenses, generic drug manufacturers need to be able to obtain regulatory permission to enter the market. Provisions in the bilateral agreements impose an obstacle in this respect. All but two agreements (US-Vietnam and US-Jordan) prevent marketing approval of a generic drug during the patent term without the consent of the patent holder—an issue on which the TRIPS framework does not impose any obligation. In other words, compulsory licenses may become ineffective in introducing competition from generic drug makers. The FTAs require developing countries to undertake commitments beyond those in the TRIPS agreement. For example, some FTAs require that countries can not make use of 'parallel imports' while others restrict the grounds for compulsory license. Many of the FTAs also impose 'data exclusivity' clauses which restrict the use of the patent holder's test data as the basis for granting safety approval of the generic versions of the same drug.[45] FTAs are routinely used by the branded-drug manufacturing companies to prevent or delay competition from generic drugs thus adversely affecting patient's access to medicine.

Section 301 of the United States Trade Act of 1974, is another tool employed by the pharmacy companies to bring about TRIPS compliance[46] throughout the Uruguay Round (September, 1986) the USA repeatedly put on its 'Special 301 watch list' countries that

[44] Report of the ITAC 15, The U.S. Colombia Trade Promotion Agreement (TPA) The Intellectual Property Provisions. Available at http://ustraderep.gov/assets/Trade-agreement/bilateral/Columbia-FTA/Reports/asset_upload_file605_9835 (last accessed on 5 November 2009).

[45] For details on FTA and IP protection see, World Bank Group Trade note, 'Tightening TRIPS: The Intellectual Property Provisions of Recent US Free Trade Agreements', 7 February 2005, Available at http://www.cptech.org/ip/health/trade/worldbank02072005.pdf (last accessed on 28 September 2008); Also see, J. Replogle, 2004, 'Central American Trade Pact May Limit Access to Generics', *Lancet*, 363, pp. 1612–13.

[46] Under Section 301, the US may impose trade sanctions against foreign countries that maintain acts, policies and practices that violate or deny US rights or benefits under trade agreements and burden or restrict US Commerce.

supposedly did not provide the kind of IP protection it wanted.[47] In 2001, Pfizer, a USA based pharmaceutical company, fought a long process of attrition against the generic manufacture and sale of Fluconazole (a vital drug for meningitis associated with HIV/AIDS infection) at prices well below the Pfizer price (Pfizer price 12 US dollars a tablet; generic price 50 cents), frequently threatening legal action for alleged infringements of its patent on the drug. It also lobbied successfully through the powerful industry organization, the Pharmaceuticals Research and Manufacture America (PhRMA) to have Thailand notified under Section 301 of the Trade Act as a country that provided inadequate standards of protection for intellectual property. If Pfizer was stopped in its tracks and deterred from following up on its threats, it was a tribute to the global mobilization on access to essential medicines. In its 2001 Report, Oxfam cautions us against bilateral and TRIPS plus agreements which severely restrict access to medicines.[48]

A second factor that seriously threatens to affect supply and production of generic drugs is full TRIPS compliance by India from December 2005. India, known as the pharmacy of the world, is a leading supplier of generic drugs to the world. Generic drugs have not only been supplied under compulsory licensing to various countries (HIV drug, Efavirenz to Thailand being a recent instance in 2005), but have been instrumental and invaluable in providing competition leading to reduction of prices of patented drugs.[49] Ellen t'Hoen of MSF, expressed concerns that the main source of affordable generic versions of new medicines may dry up in future as India allows for patents on medicines from 2005 to comply with its TRIPS obligations.[50]

Both the TRIPS Plus agreement and India's TRIPS compatibility ensure that promoting access to medicines is replete with compelling

[47] Anna Lanoszka, 2003, 'The Global Politics of Intellectual Property Rights and Pharmaceutical Drug Policies in Developing Countries', *International Political Science Review*, 24 (2), p. 188.

[48] Oxfam briefing Paper—Make Trade Fair. Available at www.Oxfam.org.uk/resources/policy/health/downloads/bp33_bullying.pdf (last accessed on 14 October 2009).

[49] See, Sangeeta Shashikant, 19 May 2005, 'More Countries Use Compulsory License, but New Problems Emerge', *TWN Info Service on Health Issues,* vol. 4, Geneva: TWN, available at http://www.twnside.org.sg/title2/health.info/twninfohealth004.htm (last accesed on 24 October 2007).

[50] See Ellen t' Hoen, 2002, 'TRIPS, Pharmaceutical Patents, and Access to Essential Medicines: A Long Way From Seattle to Doha', *Chicago Journal of International Law,* 3(27), Ellen t' Hoen, February 2005, 'TRIPS, R&D and Access to Medicines: A Guide to the Post 2005 World' External briefing document, Médecins Sans Frontières Campaign for Access to Essential Medicines.

issues. There is a need, therefore, to secure a domain for health safeguards outside of global politics but within the realms of national laws where it can receive sovereign protection. It is in this context, that the Glivec patent case is reviewed here to highlight the conflict between the imperatives of health and of IP protection.

The Glivec patent case demonstrates the threat that the TRIPS regime holds for production of generic drugs, the restricted space that the Doha Health Declaration provides for countries to legislate in order to protect their health concerns, and the polarized terms of debate within the legal wrangles that ensue when a country attempts to build in safeguards even within the broad framework of TRIPS. The case (hereafter referred to as the Novartis/Glivec case) is significant because it became the global face of a battle to allow the supply of generic drugs and to protect the sovereign right of a nation to legislate in order to check the implications of IPRs in health related products. Before Novartis/Glivec case study is undertaken, it is relevant that we briefly understand the key provisions and amendments related to health in Indian patent laws.

HEALTH RELATED PROVISIONS IN INDIAN PATENT LAW

The pharmaceutical industry views the patent system as essential to its business model. Under the basic concept of the patent system, an inventor is entitled to a limited monopoly (technically, a right to exclude) for a period of time, typically twenty years. Such exclusivity may permit high prices during the patent term; the consequent profit incentives provide the basis for the pharmaceutical industry to invest in the very costly development process that is necessary to bring new drugs to market. When a patent expires, the price normally falls as generic competitors enter the market. Generic production of drugs is, as demonstrated earlier, one of the prime market forces that regulate drug prices.

Initially a number of developing countries like India, however, viewed patent law quite differently and deliberately decided to deny patent protection to pharmaceutical products and to grant protection only to *processes* for producing pharmaceuticals. These countries believed that access to pharmaceutical products is so important that the products themselves should not be patented. In its 1970 patent law—The Patents Act, 1970, India excluded drugs from product patent protection, effectively choosing to provide low-cost drugs for its people at the expense of perhaps eliminating incentives to create new products.[51] The Act specially

[51] Section 5 of the Patents Act, 1970 covered only 'methods or processes of manufacture' in case of 'substances intended for use, or capable of being used, as food or as medicine or

indicated that patents are granted to encourage innovation and not merely to enable patentees to enjoy a monopoly for the importation of the patented articles.[52]

This law was one of the reasons that the Indian generic drug industry was able to evolve to make and market copies of drugs still on patent in wealthier countries. India became a major international supplier of drugs to countries where these products can be marketed legally because they have not been patented locally. India began to be known as the pharmacy to the developing world. This situation changed when India agreed to switch over to the product patent regime after becoming a member of the WTO in 1995. Though India became a member of the WTO in 1995, it was given a 10-year transition period to bring into effect the change in regime from granting process patents to product patents for drugs. The TRIPS agreement being a minimum standard agreement requires its members to grant patents for inventions in all fields of technology for a period of 20 years if it satisfies the universally accepted criterion of patentability.

In order to harmonize its patent law with other patent regimes by implementing the provisions of the TRIPS agreement, amendments in The Patents Act, 1970 (the 1970 Act) were carried out by India through legislation in three stages–changes effective from 1 January 1995 by the Patents (Amendment) Act 1999, changes effective from 20 May 2003 by the Patents (Amendment) Act, 2002, and changes effective from 1 January, 2005 by the Patents (Amendment) Act, 2005.

The 1999 amendment (retrospectively effective from 1995) brought one significant change from the perspective of drug patents. It left prohibition of product patent on food and health untouched, but added a 'Chapter IV A' to Section 5 of the 1970 Act, which permitted the filing of a patent claim. It provided for receipt of product patent applications and for granting Exclusive Marketing Rights (EMRs) on such applications in the fields of pharmaceuticals and agricultural chemicals, till final patent is granted or the patent application is rejected. Product patents were to be filed only for products developed/ invented/innovated after 1995, the year in which India became a member of the WTO. The Amendment of 2002, under pressure from the US and the WTO to hasten compatibility with the TRIPS framework, included the main TRIPS requirements such as a 20-year uniform duration (earlier the process patent in the field of health and nutrition was only 7 years). In the field of compulsory licensing,

---

drug'. It stated 'no patent shall be granted in respect of claim for the substances themselves, but claims for the methods or processes of manufacture shall be patentable'.

[52] Section 83, Patents Act, 1970.

safeguards continued to be strengthened. However, Section 83 mentions that patents granted should not 'impede protection of public health'.[53]

India was required to introduce product patent protection in these sectors from 1 January 2005 in accordance with the obligation under the TRIPS agreement of the WTO. The Patents (Amendment) Act, 2005 (Act No. 15 of 2005) was passed in March 2005, with retrospective effect from 1 January 2005. From the perspective of this chapter, the following were some of the significant changes brought about by the amendment.

1. The Patents (Amendment) Act 2005 introduced product patent regime for food, chemicals and pharmaceuticals.
2. Provision (section 92A) for enabling grant of compulsory license for export of medicines to countries which have insufficient or no manufacturing capacity to meet emergent public health situations (in accordance with the Doha Declaration on TRIPS and Public Health).
3. Changes in section 3, were made listing out the exceptions to patentability, that is, what are not considered to be inventions.

The changes made in section 3, especially the addition of sub-section (d) is significant for it is a first effort by a national government to expand the interpretative framework of inventiveness for pharmaceutical patents. While the internationally recognized criteria of patentability—novelty, non-obviousness and utility—were retained, the amendment introduced some additional requirements. First, it defines what is required of a patent application to meet the inventive step criteria. To meet the 'inventive step' criteria, the patentee will either have to show that the invention includes a technical advance or has economic significance, or both. Second, it defines an invention to include 'any invention or technology which has not been anticipated by publication in any document or used in the country or elsewhere in the world before the date of filing of a patent application…'. And finally, it prescribed a new criterion for patentability—'enhanced efficacy', embodied in section 3(d) of the IPA.[54] The fundamental yardsticks to measure and determine an inventive step essentially remain the same as the TRIPS framework. It appears that the intent behind these provisions is to define a 'novelty' standard—which, along with 'non-obviousness' (or 'inventive step') and 'utility' (economic significance), are the three prerequisites for 'patentability'. In essence,

[53] Section 83 (d), (e), (g) of the Patents (Amendments) Act, 2002.
[54] There is considerable debate on both counts, most of which centers around the ambiguity of various criteria listed and the subjective interpretations and increased litigational impact that they will generate.

therefore, they adhere to the broad norms of patentability.[55] The significant departure seems to be the 'efficacy' standard, which adds a nuance to the content of inventiveness.

Efficacy Standards

Section 3(d) of the amended IPA, stipulates that a new form of a known substance is excluded from patent coverage if it does not show significantly enhanced efficacy, as compared to the known substance.[56] The enhancement in efficacy is further qualified in the 'Explanation' to the sub-section, which states that derivatives of a known substance ('salts, esters, ethers, polymorphs, metabolites, pure form, particle size, isomers, mixtures of isomers, complexes, combinations, and other derivatives of a known substance) shall be considered to be the same substance unless they differ significantly in properties with regard to efficacy.' Efficacy is thus the dividing line between a substance being, or not being an eligible subject matter for the grant of a patent.

The efficacy clause, it is important to stress, is not a product of Indian patent law jurisprudence. This provision, interestingly, has been taken from a directive of the European Parliament relating to drug regulation of medicinal products for human use.[57] The provision also relates to a class of patents, known as 'selection patents' in English jurisprudence, where a patentee is granted a patent for selected substances from an entire class of chemical compounds. To grant a patent to the whole class, comprising several 'related' chemical compounds, may result in a broad monopoly. Patent protection is thus granted only to those members of the class that can demonstrate a new use or form. It needs to be emphasized that novelty

[55] For a view that the definition of inventiveness definition dilutes the requirements of an inventive step and broadens the existing provision to the benefit of patent holders, See, for example, K.M. Gopakumar and Tahir Amin, 9 April 2005, *Patents (Amendment) Bill 2005: A Critique*, 40(15), *Economic & Political Weekly*. 1503, 1504.

[56] Section 3 (d), IPA states: 'the mere discovery of a new form of a known substance which does not result in the enhancement of the known efficacy of that substance or the mere discovery of any new property or new use for a known substance or of the mere use of a known process, machine or apparatus unless such known process results in a new product or employs at least one new reactant'. The enhancement to efficacy in further qualified in 'Expanation' to the Section 3(d): 'Salts, esters, ethers, polymorphs, metabolites, pure form, particle size, isomers, mixtures of isomers, complexes, combinations, and other derivatives of known substance shall be considered to be the same substance, *unless they differ significantly in properties with regard to efficacy.'* (Emphasis mine)

[57] Article 10(2) (b) of Directive 2004/27/EC of the European Parliament states that: 'The different salts, esters, ethers, isomers, mixtures of isomers, complexes or derivatives of an active substance shall be considered to be the same active substance, unless they differ significantly in properties with regard to safety and/or efficacy.'

is derived from the use, not the product.[58] In other words, for the purposes of a selection patent, the novelty, or inventive step involved in preparing a substance, may be located in the demonstration of a new use.[59]

Section 3(d), locating itself in this interpretative framework, is an endeavour to ensure the 'novelty of use', emphasizing use as an inventive step in the absence of newness of form. Section 3(d) makes it clear that those technical creations which are not truly inventive (that is, are only incremental improvement over existing formulations), are not patentable unless they present a significant increase in efficacy. The IPA, as a statute of India, therefore relies upon utility as the criterion for patentability to transform non-patentable inventions into patentable invention.

Besides, serving as a technical requirement delineating grounds for patentability of pharmaceutical drugs, section 3(d) also functions as an important public health safeguard. The objective of the section 3(d) patentability criteria is to prevent 'evergreening' and tweaking of old medicines to make or extend patent claims. Making patent claims conditional on the novelty or the efficacy of the new innovation is significant, for it ensures that patents for drugs are not claimed for mere incremental improvements over existing drugs. The term efficacy is being used in a 'drug regulatory' sense. In effect, section 3(d) delimits claims of patentability thereby ensuring the continued supplies of generics at cheaper prices.

The product patent regime that India became a part of, has had significant implications for the Indian health industry and importantly, for the supply of affordable drugs to the rest of the world. Safeguards introduced keeping in mind India's pharmaceutical export potential and public health concerns. The concern was, and is, based on the fact that over a period of time Indian drug companies will lose the opportunity to develop processes for patent protected drugs, and therefore will cease to be a supplier of affordable generic drugs to millions across the world.

It is in the background of these changes and amendments to the Indian patent law that the Novartis patent claim for Glivec needs to be evaluated.

[58] For a discussion see, Catherine Colston and Kristy Hiddleton, 2005, *Modern Intellectual Property Law*, London: Cavendish Publishing Ltd., pp. 163–4.

[59] This provision does not, apply to a case where the new form is found to have a completely different use (and not just an increased efficacy vis-à-vis the known use). Such claims are entertained as 'Swiss Claims'. E. Jochen Buhling, *et al.*, Working Guidelines, Question Q 209, Selection Inventions—The Inventive Step Requirement, Other Patentability Criteria and Scope of Protection. AIPPI. Available at http://www.aippi.ord/download/comitees/209/WG209English.pdf (last accessed on 12 January 2008).

I aim to highlight two issues that are brought to the fore by this case: First, the right of a sovereign country to build in safeguards in its patent laws in order to protect the interest of its people. A related issue is also the viability and the *de facto* acceptability of the Doha provisions, especially paragraphs 4 and 5, which recognizes this right of states, and affirms the rights of nations to use the exception clauses to the TRIPS regime.[60] The second issue relates to the issue of drug access, vital for the realization of health as a right. Both these issues explicate themselves clearly through the Glivec/Novartis patent case in India.

THE GLIVEC PATENT CASE

Imatinib mesylate (Glivec) is a cancer drug critical in prolonging the life of patients suffering from Chronic Myeloid Leukemia (CML, a form of blood cancer). Imatinib Mesylate controls the cellular action that allows the cancer to grow but does not cure the disease. This means that patients must take it for the rest of their lives, unless another type of treatment or cure is available. Glivec is produced and marketed internationally by the Swiss pharmaceutical company Novartis, and domestically by various Indian generic producers like Cipla, Ranbaxy, Natco, and Hetero. Novartis sells Glivec at Rs 1.44 million (US 26,000 dollars) per patient per year. Generic versions of the drug Glivec in the Indian market are priced at about Rs 96,000 (US 2100 dollars) per patient per year. Novartis charges high prices for Glivec worldwide: from about US 25,000 dollars to more than US 50,000 dollars per patient per year (50,000 CHF per patient per year in Switzerland).

THE PATENT CLAIM BY NOVARTIS

In 1998, Novartis filed a mailbox application in India for imatinib mesylate (Glivec) in crystalline form, in accordance with India's provisions for obtaining patents.[61] In November 2003, based on the patent application

---

[60] This provision is in conformity with the Doha Health Declaration and one that is endorsed by the CIPIH report. Each country can introduce a patent regime that is more suited to its socio-economic context. This is also in keeping with the 2001 Doha Declaration on the TRIPS agreement and public health. Paragraph 4(d) of the Doha Decl. states: The effect of the provisions in the TRIPS agreement that are relevant to the exhaustion of intellectual property rights is to leave each member free to establish its own regime for such exhaustion without challenge, subject to the MFN and national treatment provisions of articles 3 and 4. See, 'Public Health, Innovation and Intellectual Property Rights', CIPIH, Geneva: April 2006. Available at www.who.int/intellectualproperty/documents/thereport/en/index.html (last accessed on 28 December 2007).

[61] See, Novartis website for a 'History of Glinec in India' available at www.novartis.com/downloads/about-novartis/glivec-history-india.pdf (last accessed on 16 December 2007).

and section 92A of the Patents Act, Novartis obtained exclusive marketing rights (EMR) for Glivec, pending a final decision on the patent, subject to the condition that in case the patent was rejected EMR would be cancelled.[62] The EMR operated like a patent monopoly preventing Indian pharmaceutical companies from producing affordable generic versions of the drug imatinib mesylate. Indian courts specifically forbade six out of nine generic manufactures to market imatinib mesylate. Indian generic manufactures had to withdraw production and sale of generic versions of the drug from the domestic market and from export to other developing countries. With an over ten-fold increase in the price of the drug, Cancer Patients Aid Association (CPAA) and some other non-governmental organizations (NGOs) who provided affordable generic versions to cancer patients, had to withdraw their medical support. Patients of other developing countries who were importing generic versions of the drug were also seriously affected by the unavailability of the affordable versions. CPAA moved the Supreme Court of India against granting EMR to Novartis.[63]

Novartis' patent application on Glivec came up for examination in 2005. Armed with section 3 (d), pre-grant opposition was filed by Natco Pharmaceuticals, CIPLA, Alternative Law Forum (ALF) and Lawyers Collective, acting on behalf of the CPAA.[64] These bodies claimed that this application only concerned a modification of an already existing drug that did not improve its efficacy as required by Section 3(d) of the IPA. In addition, they claimed that the non-availability and non-affordability of any form of imatinib mesylate to Chronic Myeloid Leukemia (CML) patients is violative of these patients' rights under Article 14 (right to

---

[62] India amended her regime in 1999 to provide for exclusive marketing rights (EMRs). See Chapter IVA of The Patents (Amendment) Act 1999.

[63] CPAA also contested the fact that there were only around 7000 CML patients, 99 per cent of who were covered by Novartis GIPAP and provided Glivec free of charge. According to CPAA there are 30,000 CML patients detected every year most of who are not covered by Novartis drug donation program. Quoted from *The Times of India*, Sunday Mailbox, 22 April 2007. Available at http://www.cptech.org/ip/health/Glivec/amtc08072004.html (last accessed on 25 September 2008).

[64] Pre-grant opposition by Cipla and Cancer Patients group against Novartis's application for beta crystalline form of imatinib mesylate (marketed as Glivec) to treat achronic myeloid leukemia. *Novartis AG* (Application No. 1602/MAS/1998) v. *Cipla Ltd*, Chennai Patent Office (2006) and *Novartis AG* (Application No 1602/MAS/1998) v. *Cancer Patients AJ Association*, Chennai Patent Office (2006). As did several pharmaceutical companies—Cipla, Natco Pharma, Sun Pharmaceuticals and Ranbaxy in their own right. Natco Pharma, which launched a generic version of Glivec under the brand 'Veenat', had also challenged the grant of EMRs to Novartis.

equality before law), and Article 21 (right to life and personal liberty) of the Constitution of India.[65]

Two points in the Novartis patent claim are particularly worthy of attention, for they are instructive on how the criteria of novelty and non-obviousness are often manipulated. Imatinib as a 'free base' molecule was invented by Novartis in 1992, and patented in the US in 1993 and nearly forty other countries including China, Russia, and Taiwan.[66] In 1998, in its application before the CPO, Novartis applied for a patent for a beta crystalline form of imatinib mesylate, a salt which was claimed to be 'a new form of a known substance'. Since this beta crystalline form—Glivec—of imatinib mesylate, was the most thermodynamically stable, and also the form that the salt normally assumes, therefore it was an arguably 'obvious' form of the substance. This was asserted by the opponents to patent application, through evidence of multiple tests performed by the Indian Institute of Chemical Technology, Hyderabad and Indian Institute of Technology, Delhi. Further, this 'new' salt was a beta-isomer of the already disclosed Imatinib Mesylate and isomers were, as per the Explanation to section 3 (d) of the 1970 Act, 'considered to be the same substance, unless they differ significantly in properties with regard to efficacy'.[67]

Since imatinib mesylate was already known from prior publications, it therefore, needed to demonstrate enhanced efficacy in order to fulfill the section 3(d) patentability criterion. In full knowledge of this requirement, Novartis tried to demonstrate before the Controller that there was an enhancement of efficacy. It submitted that there was an enhanced 'bioavailability' of 30 per cent in studies conducted on rats. Bioavailability is one of the indicators of efficacy of a drug. However, the explanation to section 3(d) requires enhancement be 'significant'. Novartis' case suffered as they had produced a bioavailability study conducted on rats only, even though the drug was admittedly in the market for many years and was consumed by humans. Then again, it was not shown how the 30 per cent

[65] Text of the Writ petition No. 24759 OF 2006 in The High Court of Judicature at Madras. Paragraph 16, p. 12.

[66] See Novartis website at http://www.novartis.com/downloads/about-novartis/facts-vs-fiction-india-glivec-patent-case.pdf (last accessed on 25 December 2007).

Invention of the base compound, called imatinib had already been disclosed in the European Patent publication no. EP-A-056409, published on 6 October 1993, and its equivalent US Patent no. 5521184, etc. [IP-health]. The patent term extension certificate granted by US Patent Office for the 1993 Patent explicitly mentions imatinib mesylate (Glivec R)as the product. For details see Text of Indian Decisions on Glivec Patent Application <http://lists.essential.org/pipermail/ip-health/2006-March/009200.htm> (last accessed on 5 October 2009).

[67] Refer 'Explanation' to section 3(d) of the Patents Act, 1970.

increase was critical in the performance of the drug and how this increase made a difference when compared to the known efficacy of other forms of Imatinib Mesylate.[68]

Following these grounds of pre-grant oppositions, the Assistant Controller of Patents and Designs, V. Rengasamy, in his ruling, said that he was not convinced with the contention of Novartis that its patent claim was for a new substance.[69] He ruled, in effect, that Glivec was only a new form of a known substance. In his words, 'It is found that this patent application claims only a new form of a known substance without having any significant improvement in efficacy'.[70] Further, stating that Novartis had failed to prove enhanced efficacy of the beta-isomer over the known substance, the Assistant Controller concluded that, 'the subject matter of this application is not patentable under Section 3(d) of the Patents Act 1970 as amended by the Patents (Amendment) Act, 2005.' Novartis's application to patent the beta crystalline form of Imatinib mesylate was thus rejected by CPO in 25 January 2006.

The Novartis Appeal and Constitutional Challenge

Aggrieved by the order of the Controller, on 17 May 2006, Novartis filed two cases before the Madras (Chennai) High Court.[71] It not only appealed the patent office decision, but, in a rather controversial move, it also challenged section 3(d) on the grounds of lack of TRIPS compatibility and unconstitutionality. Its writ petition alleged the following:[72]

1. That section 3(d) of The Patents Act is unconstitutional on the ground that it violates Article 14 (Right to Equality) of the Constitution of India as it discriminates against the pharmaceutical sector vis-à-vis other technology sectors.
2. The 'new' Section 3(d) is in violation of India's obligation as a signatory to the TRIPS agreement under Article 1(1), Article 27 of the TRIPS agreement.

[68] Technical challenges were submitted to the Controller about the enhanced efficacy of the new compound by Natco Pharma Ltd. See Pre-grant opposition by Cipla and CPAA at note 64.

[69] Chennai Patent Office order in the matter of an application for patent no. 1602/MAS/98 filed on 17 July 1998 (Glivec). Text of the decision available at http://www.gnaipr.com/Articles/Glivec%20Order.pdf (last accessed on 25 September 2008).

[70] Ibid.

[71] Writ Petition No. 24759 and 24760 of 2006 in the High Court of Madras.

[72] Adapted from the petition filed by Novartis in Writ Petition.no.24759 of 2006 before The High Court of Madras (Special Original Jurisdiction) *Novartis AG & Anothers* v. *Union of India & Others.*

3.   Section 3(d) is vague and arbitrary. Its formulation, that a discovery
     becomes an invention if the substance in question results in
     enhancement of known efficacy is a very 'ingenious concept'…and
     'defies logic'.[73]

The three main issues raised actually bifurcated the case into three
parts: patentability of Glivec; section 3(d)'s compliance with the TRIPS
agreement; and constitutional validity of section 3(d).

On 23 February 2007, the Madras High court, in accordance with
IPA, converted one part of the Glivec case—the challenge to the patent
office's decision to not grant a patent for Glivec—from a writ petition
to an appeal and transferred it to the IPAB, the appellate body which has
statutory jurisdiction over appeals against orders of the patent office, to
assess the technical aspects of the patent claim. To win, Novartis needed
to convince the IPAB that: (a) in relation to section 3(d) the 30 per
cent increase in bioavailability is an enhanced efficacy and so the beta
crystalline form is patentable, and (b) the beta crystalline form of the
mesylate salt is not an 'obvious' form of the free base form. The IPAB, in
26 June 2009, ruled that the application of Glivec did not pass the hurdle
of section 3(d), and was consequently not patentable.

On the compatibility of section 3(d), with the TRIPS agreement, the
court considered the WTO's Dispute Settlement Board a more appropriate
forum. It further stated that it was outside the purview of the Court to
adjudicate on this matter.

Consequently, the decision in the Court hinged on—the third of the
issues urged by the petitioners, that is, section 3(d) and its constitutionality.
The Madras High Court, in its judgment of 6 August 2007, upheld
the validity and constitutionality of section 3(d). The court stated that
'India, being welfare and a developing country, which is predominantly
occupied by people below poverty line, has a constitutional duty to
provide good health care to its citizens by giving them easy access to
life saving drugs. In so doing, the Union of India would be right to take
into account the various factual aspects prevailing in this big country
and prevent evergreening by allowing generic medicine to be available
in the market'.[74]

It further ruled that there is no ambiguity or vagueness in the
expressions under attack as found incorporated in the amended section

[73] Novartis petition in Writ Petition no. 24759 of 2006 (Special Original Jurisdiction)
before The High Court of Madras (Special Original Jurisdiction).
    [74] *Novartis AG & Another v. Union of India & Others*, (2007) 4 MLJ 1153.

and the explanation attached to it. Also, section 3(d) sets an 'obviousness' standard, which member states (signatories to WTO agreement on TRIPS) are free to define the same in a manner consistent with their national policy. It added that while one of the fears of the petitioners was that the amended section 3(d) could lead to arbitrary interpretations and misuse, 'no law can be declared illegal because there is a possibility of its misuse' and 'the Legislature has a duty to safeguard the economic interest of the country.'

The court held that the amended section is not in violation of article 14 of the Indian constitution. Section 3(d) does not 'discriminate' against the pharmaceutical sector, it only makes a 'justified differentiation', given the specificity of salt forms in the sector. Other technology sectors such as mechanicals, electronics, etc., do not face such issues.

Several important issues emerge from the judgment. Firstly, the judgment clearly views the pharmaceutical sector as a sector which merits a justified differentiation for its ability to impact human life. In doing so, it draws an order of priority amongst competing entitlements and rules that acknowledge over TRIPS the imperatives of good health obligation. In referring the matter of TRIPS compliance to the dispute settlement board of the WTO, it clearly demarcates issues of patentability and health entitlements. It thus, provides a framework for evaluating the adequacy of a health safeguard in the light of the health imperatives of the country and, very significantly, the health imperatives of the global civil society, implying that there is need to conceptualize health rights in global-citizenship terms also.

Secondly, the section 3(d) provision provides a useful scheme for the courts to catalyze decisions, relating to drug patents, with added criteria of, what appears to be, a set of scientific, technical requirement. The intent of section 3(d) was, quite clearly, to prevent ever greening of drugs, for furthering patent claims. It was this intent which got reflected in the court's decision. It is this intent, more than the actual framing and wording of the provision (which has been quite widely adjectivized as vague, 'arbitrary',[75] nebulous, shoddy drafting'),[76] which functioned as a defense against internationally imposed mechanisms that constrain access rights. The court has been able to harness the full potential of this section in order to read in health related concerns into the very determination of

[75] Refer to the Novartis Petition in the High Court of Judicature At Madras (Special Original Jurisdiction) W.P. No. 24759 of 2006. Section 'Grounds' DVI.
[76] Shamnad Basheer, 2005, 'India's Tryst with TRIPS: The Patents (Amendment) Act, 2005', *The Indian Journal of Law and Technology*, 1, p. 21.

patentability of a substance. The court's role thus goes beyond the merely judicial, into the administrative—by making a policy matter—health outcomes—a part of its concern. It consciously adopted adjudicating on grounds of socio-economic (health) entitlements and in doing so, the court, in many ways, provides a lead and presets the grounds of future adjudications, both nationally and internationally. As a galvanizer, this judgment may lay the basis for health safeguards to prefigure actual legal-institutional outcomes.

The Drug Donation Argument

Novartis claims that this is a battle for protection of its intellectual property on grounds of principle.[77] GlivecIt asserts that Glivec was being distributed widely and successfully among the needy and poor through the Glivec International Patient Assistance Program (GIPAP) 'In 2006, our access-to-medicines program reached 33.6 million patients. Novartis spent US 755 million dollars last year alone. ... The Glivec International Patient Assistance Program (GIPAP) is one of the most far-reaching patient assistance programs every implemented on a global scale. In India, 99 per cent of patients who receive Glivec receive it free from Novartis [6,600 people]'.[78] It therefore insisted that the patent right for Glivec, does not conflict with health interests. Glivec Novartis alleges that there is virtually no commercial market for Glivec in India, and that it was distributing drugs free of cost to 99 per cent of CML patients in India. Its official website states that the price of Glivec is almost irrelevant in India as 99 per cent of the patients who need the medicine receive it free from Novartis through the GIPAP.[79]

The most obvious difficulty with these claims is the empirical veracity of the numbers. Novartis claims that most Indian CML patients (approximately 7000) are covered by the GIPAP. Centre for Trade and Development (CENTAD), an independent, non-profit organization, however cites the prevalence of about 27,000 new cases of CML every

[77] 'Novartis Concerned that Indian Court Ruling Will Discourage Investments In Innovation Needed To Bring Better Medicines To Patients.' Novartis Media release. 6 August 2007. Available at http://www.novartis.com/newsroom/news/index.shtml (last accessed on 7 November 2007).

[78] Quoted from Brook K. Bakerhttp, 7 February 2007, 'A deconstruction of Novartis's defense of its challenge to the India patent regime,' available at www.cptech.org/ip/health/c/india/hgap02072007.html (last accessed on 7 November 2007).

[79] Available at the Novartis website http://www.novartis.com/downloads/about-novartis/facts-vs-fiction-india-glivec-patent-case.pdf (last accesed on 7 November 2007).

year. Almost ten patients die every day from CML and the demand for this drug is nearly 30 lakh capsules per month.[80]

Novartis's GIPAP is fraught with inequities and irregularities as has been demonstrated by the cases in Brazil, Argentina, and Korea.[81] One of the first conflicts over Glivec occurred in South Korea when patients protested against the price of Glivec and the lack of insurance cover for the drug. The Ministry of Health and Welfare announced official Glivec price and official insurance coverage.[82] Novartis refused to comply with the official Glivec price and threatened to pull the drug out of the South Korean market; CML patients could not obtain Glivec because of supply instability.[83] Novartis reached a settlement with the Government after a long standoff. The government agreed to reimburse Novartis 80 per cent of the 'global average price' (US 27,000 dollars), and Novartis and the consumer were to each shoulder ten per cent of the cost of Glivec.[84] However, there are some patients who cannot afford even the proposed 10 per cent of the cost of the medicine. Generic versions of Glivec have not been given marketing approval by the South Korean government. South Korean law nevertheless has an exception called the 'personal use' exception, which allows patients to procure the generic drug individually. Nearly fifty South Korean patients are currently importing the generic version (Veenat) produced by Natco India Ltd at US 1 dollar per tablet as opposed to the US 20 dollars charged by Novartis. Not only does

[80] K.M. Gopakumar, 2007, 'The Novartis Case', CENTAD, Available at http://www.centad.org/focus_49.asp (last accessed on 16 September 2007). Also referred to in a speech by Y.K. Sapru, Chairman and CEO, CPAA, India, 24 January, Davos, Switzerland. Available at http://www.cpaindia.org/aboutus/PublicEyeAwards.htm (last accessed on 6 September 2007).

[81] For a brief synopsis of the issues at stake see, 'Charity for Monopoly Rights: Some Global Experiences of Drug Donation Programs of Pharmaceutical MNCs'. Draft Document (India: Care, 2007) 2007. Also see http://www.essentialdrugs.org/edrug/archive/200608/msg00070.php (last accessed on 6 September 2007).

[82] In wealthier countries like South Korea, Hong Kong and New Zealand, Novartis has encouraged patients who have received free drugs to become advocates for high priced drugs to be included in the insurance cover, pressing public health systems to pay high prices for the drug. See, 'Drug Maker's Vow to Donate Cancer Medicine Falls Short' *The New York Times*, 5 June 2003. Available at www.nytimes.com/2003/06/05/business/drug_maker_s_vow_to_donate_cancer_medicine_fall_short.html (last accessed on 8 December 2009).

[83] For details see Request for a Compulsory License from KIPO (Korean Intellectual Property Office) to grant a compulsory license for registered patent No. 261366 (Glivec patent) in accordance with article 107(1)(iii) of the Korean Patent Law.

[84] K.M. Gopakumar, Aditya Krishna, and Priti Radhakrishnan, 2006, 'India and the Glivec (Imatinib Mesylate) Patent: A Case Study', Internal Document, India: Oxfam India, p. 13.

the South Korean case highlight the irregularities of the drug donation programme but also underscores the importance of generic supplies from India which make treatments available and accessible to people across the world.

In India too the GIPAP has not been without contention. Novartis began its donations of Glivec with a warning that it would halt the programme if the government let local companies eat into its profits by selling generic versions of the drug.[85] Hundreds of Indian cancer patients got Glivec free, and commercial sales soared as well. However, in April 2003, after India had cleared generic versions of Glivec for sale, Novartis made good its threat, saying it would leave it to Indian companies to meet the needs of patients. It suddenly discontinued its free Glivec program without caring for patients depending on it. New York Times described the Glivec donations as both the promise and the perils of corporate philanthropy.[86] The drug donation program was resumed only after the EMR was granted in November 2003 which removed the generic versions from the market. The CPAA submission (dated 22 January 2007) in the Madras High Court, brought to light evidence of denial of access to Glivec, to many genuine patients in India. It specifically mentions the workers who have insurance coverage under the Employees State Insurance Scheme or the Central Health Insurance Scheme, but who are not reimbursed cost of treatment of diseases like CML.[87]

Philanthropy has been often used to generate pressure for an increase in intellectual property protection in developing countries. It has also been used, as in India, to lobby or pressurise a country not to use TRIPS safeguards or to introduce their own safeguards to protect public health, as was the case with section 3(d). Drug donation and discounted drugs become the legitimizing principle for patenting of drugs, which then eliminates the generic drugs from the market. Innovation, patenting, high pricing, and drug donation form a vicious circle of the corporate logic of pharmaceutical industries which deny access to essential drugs to millions of people in the least developed and developing countries. The politics of

[85] Stephanie Strom and Matt Fleischer-Black, 2003, 'Company's Vow to Donate Cancer Drug Falls Short', *New York Times*, 5 June. Also see, 'Novartis Stops Donation of Cancer Drug to India', *Silicon India News*. Available at http://www.siliconindia.com/shownews/Novartis_stops_donation_of_cancer_drug_to_India_nid-19721.html (last accessed on 20 October 2009).

[86] See note 82.

[87] Text of the petition filed by Novartis in Writ Petition.no.24759 of 2006 before The High Court of Madras (Special Original Jurisdiction) *Novartis AG & Another v. Union of India & Others*, pp. 28, 29.

drug donation is beyond the scope of this study but it would suffice to mention that philanthropy is often, in these cases, driven by commercial and vested interests.

The core issue being debated here is not the success or the failure of Novartis's GIPAP or even the merits and the flaws of corporate philanthropy and social responsibility (CSR).[88] The point being argued is that donations or forms of corporate philanthropy ought not to add weight to a patent claim—'What is the harm in granting a patent claim; after all 99 per cent of the patients are receiving the drug free of cost?'. Donations cannot become a cover-up argument against public interest infringement. Further, they cannot proxy for substantive rights. Drug donation is neither a viable nor a sustainable alternative to freely available generic drugs. There are many life-saving drugs like Glivec that need to be taken life long, sometimes instead of 400 mg per day, up to 600 or even 800 mg per day.[89] Few drug donation programs can sustain this. Moreover, corporate donations are not a sustainable solutions because: (1) they are frequently hard to access, (2) they are revocable, (3) they are not offered across the broad spectrum of patented medicines that poor people need, and (4) they may be designed to forestall generic competition by removing market incentives. The assumption that the issue of public health and access to drugs can be addressed through donations, philanthropy, and corporate social responsibility is fundamentally flawed in as much it does not even begin to see health as a human right or a right to life.

THE GLIVEC CASE IN A LARGER PERSPECTIVE

The issue of access to drugs is fundamental to the claim for health as a basic right. It is in this context that the Glivec case assumes importance, and for this reason that it has become the face of the global campaign to save generic production of drugs in India. India has been a very large player in the production and export of generic medicines the world over. The following figures compiled by MSF highlight the importance of India as a crucial player in access to affordable medicines.

1. 67 percent of medicines produced in India are exported to developing countries.
2. 75–80 per cent of all medicines distributed by the International

---

[88] For the successes of GIPAP see Roger Bate, 7 February 2007, 'India and the Drug Patent Wars India and the Drug Patent Wars', *Health Policy Outlook, AEI Online.*

[89] Joana D. Ramos, 'Cancer in Global Perspective', 3rd Annual Western Regional International Health Conference: Politics, Social Justice and Global Health. Available at http://ramoslink.info/ (last accessed on 10 January 2008).

Dispensary Association (IDA) to developing countries are manufactured in India.

3. In Zimbabwe, 75 per cent of tenders for medicines for all public sector health facilities come from Indian manufacturers. 90 per cent of the Anti Retroviral drugs (ARVs) used in Zimbabwe's national treatment programme come from India.

4. The state procurement agency in Lesotho, NDSO, states it buys nearly 95 per cent of all ARVs from India.

5. India ranks second on the list of countries from which United Nations International Children's Emergency Fund (UNICEF) purchases medical supplies. Belgium only ranks first because certain types of vaccines (for instance, combination vaccines) are not produced in India.

6. 80 per cent of the ARVs MSF uses are purchased in India, and are distributed in treatment projects in over 30 countries.

7. Over 90 per cent of all patients using AZT/3TC in MSF projects are on generic versions of the drug.

8. Globally, 70 per cent of drugs for the treatment for patients in 87 developing countries, purchased by UNICEF, IDA, the Global Fund to Fight AIDS, Tuberculosis and Malaria (GFATM) and the Clinton Foundation since July 2005 has come from Indian suppliers.

9. The US President's Emergency Plan for AIDS (PEPFAR), also purchases ARVs from India for distribution in developing countries, thus resulting in cost-savings of up to 90 per cent . 89 per cent of the generic ARVs approved by the US Food and Drug Administration for PEPFAR are from India.[90]

In recent times, the most striking success of Indian pharmaceutical companies has been their ability to provide access to HIV/AIDS drugs at affordable prices. In fact, the issue of access to drugs and the need to make cheaper drugs available arose primarily in the context of HIV/AIDS. India is the world's primary source of affordable ARVs, for HIV treatment as it is one of the few countries with the capacity to produce these newer medicines as generics. Therefore, all AIDS programs use India as their main source of products. A three-in-one cocktail pill introduced by the generic manufacturers substituted two pills for six pills per day. Thus the

[90] 'Examples of the importance of India as the 'Pharmacy of the World'. (Mediciens Sans Frontiers, Campaign for Access to Essential Medicines). Available at http://www. accessmed-msf.org/documents/Overview%20Jan%202007%20FINAL.doc (last accessed on 19 January 2007).

FDCs (Fixed Dose Combinations–AZT/3TC) increased the accessibility as well as availability of ARV drugs. The introduction of FDCs became possible only because of the absence of product patent protection in India. National treatment programs in India, Burkina Faso, Mongolia, Central African Republic, Malawi, Peru, the Republic of Kyrgyzstan, Cambodia, Ukraine, and Swaziland rely heavily on generic AZT/3TC. The availability of affordable quality generic versions of Combivir (AZT/3TC) and other anti-retroviral medicines has allowed developing countries to put more people on treatment and thus extend their lives.

Globally, life-saving drugs remain beyond the reach of the majority of people with HIV/AIDS. For instance, of the 6 million people worldwide who needed ARVs in 2003, fewer than 8 per cent were receiving them.[91] Many millions of people still cannot access existing vaccines and drugs for tuberculosis, malaria, cancer, neglected diseases, and many others. By excluding generic versions, essential-drug patents have the potential to undermine access to medicines for HIV/AIDS, for heart disease, diabetes, in fact for every new medicine needed by the poor in developing and poorer countries. In every case, generic prices present an opportunity for cost savings. A PEPFAR report states that in some cases, the branded price per pack of a drug is up to eleven times the cost of the approved generic version.[92]

TABLE 1: Price Differentials between Branded and Generic Drug Prices

Patented Brand Name—Generic Brand Name
Note: Brand name Generic version of the drug are marked with an asterisk
Mean Pack Price US dollars

	FY04	FY05
Stocrin—Efavirenz*	FY04	FY05
Stocrin 600mg (30 TAB)	32.50	32.76
Efavirenz 600mg (30 TAB)*	n/a	23.30
*Retrovir—Zidovudine**		
Retrovir 300mg	21.67	34.78
Zidovudine 300mg*	n/a	14.48
Zerit—Stavudine	FY04	FY05

[91] K. Attawell and J. Mundy, 2003, 'Provision of Antiretroviral Therapy in Resource-Limited Settings: A Review of Experience up to August 2003', Health Systems Resource Centre, Department for International Development, London. Available at http://www.who.int/3by5/publications/documents/en/ARTpaper_DFID_WHO.pdf (last accessed on 4 April 2005).

[92] 'Bringing Hope: Supplying ARVs for HIV/AIDS treatment'(PEPFAR, May 2006). Available at http://www.state.gov/documents/organization/66513.pdf (last accessed on 2 September 2007).

Zerit 15mg (60 CAP)	4.88	9.22
Stavudine 15mg (60 CAP)*	n/a	5.18
Zerit 1mg/ml	10.73	8.71
Stavudine 1mg/ml*	n/a	7.15
Zerit 20mg (60 CAP)	6.36	5.99
Stavudine 20mg (60 CAP)*	n/a	5.64
Zerit 30mg (60 CAP)	6.48	6.20
Stavudine 30mg (60 CAP)*	n/a	3.83
Zerit 40mg	6.60	6.14
Stavudine 40mg*	n/a	4.32
*Viramune—Nevirapine**		
Viramune 10mg/ml	24.81	24.30
Nevirapine 10mg/ml*	n/a	7.50
Viramune 200mg	50.23	59.86
Nevirapine 200mg*	n/a	5.79
Viramune 50mg/5ml	26.19	34.79
Nevirapine 50mg/5ml*	n/a	7.50
Epivir—Lamivudine		
Epivir 150mg	7.22	13.56
Lamivudine 150mg*	n/a	4.93
Epivir 10mg/ml	7.34	9.12
Lamivudine 10mg/ml*	n/a	5.35
*Combivir—Zidovudine/Lamivudine**		
Combivir 300/150mg	24.87	24.23
Zidovudine/Lamivudine 300/150mg*	n/a	17.51

Source: PEPFAR Report on Antiretroviral Drugs for HIV/AIDS Treatment. [93]

Besides price differentials, generics also impact pricing structures of patented drugs. Take the case of Cipla's aggressive pricing of its ARV drug, Triomune, in March 2001 at US 350 dollars per patient, per year. The offer by Cipla created ripples in the international drug industry because the prices of these drugs in the US and other developed countries are between US 10,000 dollars and US 15,000 dollars per patient per year. The Cipla offer (which was followed by counter offers from two other Indian pharmaceutical companies, Hetero and Ranbaxy) encouraged Merck, a US pharmaceutical company, to reduce the price of Crixivan, a protease inhibitor, to about the same price, which in turn caused Bristol Myers Squibb and Glaxo SmithKline to follow suit. Moreover, Abbott Laboratories, holder of patents over Kaletra, another HIV drug, came to

[93] Available at http://www.state.gov/documents/organization/66513.pdf (last accessed on 12 January 2008). Also available in this report are data and figures on the increasing role that generics have come to play in providing access to ARV drugs in LDCs and developing countries. And India plays a vital role in generic supplies.

May 2000–April 2004

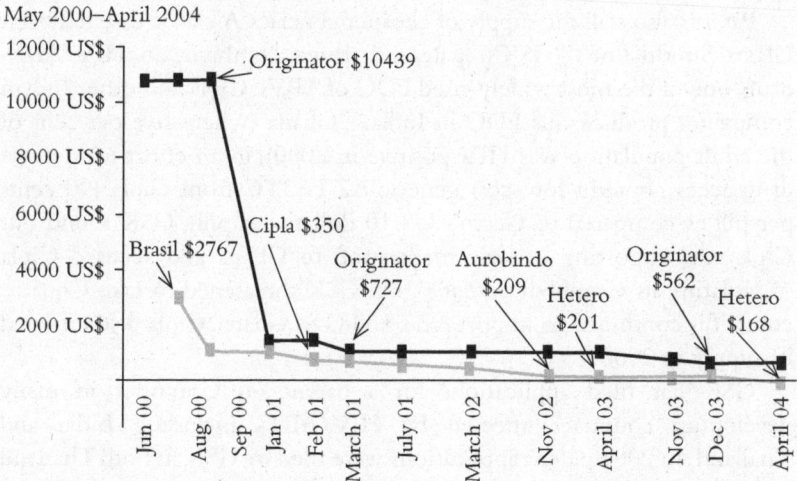

FIGURE 6.1: Effects of Generic Competition on ARV Prices

Source: TRIPS, R&D and Access to Medicines: A Guide to the Post 2005 World. External briefing document. Médecins Sans Frontières (MSF) Campaign for Access to Essential Medicines. January 18th 2005 presentation to Members of European Parliament. February 2005.

an agreement with the Brazilian government reducing the price by 30 per cent—a saving of US 10 million dollars per year.[94]

Table 1 is instructive in ascertaining the role that generic drugs play in assuring access to essential drugs. They have come to play a vital role in public health agendas with the realization that access can be affected at the practical level by the introduction of patents on medicines. Figure 1 similarly, shows the effect of generic competition on the price of first-line AIDS triple therapy.

Country case studies reveal the extent to which competition from non-patented drugs has driven down the cost of patented medicines. When Thailand ended the exclusive patent period for Fucanazole (used in the treatment of HIV-related meningitis) prices fell by 80 per cent in 6 months. In Pakistan, patented antibiotics used to treat childhood diarrhea cost eight times more than the non-patent equivalents made in neighbouring India. Patents clearly increase the cost of medicines.[95]

---

[94] See, Kavaljit Singh, 'Patents vs. patients: AIDS, TNCs and drug price wars', TWN. Available at http://www.twnside.org.sg/title/twr131c.htm (last accessed on 14 December 2007).

[95] 16 November 2001, 'Cutting the Cost of Global Health' Parliamentary Briefing, Oxfam, UK.

Patents also stall the supply of cheaper generics. A classic case has been Glaxo SmithKline's (GSK's) patented drug, Combivir, an HIV/AIDS drug, one of the most widely-used FDC of ARVs. Cipla and other Indian companies produce this FDC in India.[96] Ghana (where five per cent of the adult population was HIV positive in 2000), in an effort to increase drug access, bought low-cost generic AZT+3TC from Cipla (90 cents per pill as compared to Glaxo's US 10 dollars per pill), GSK found out Cipla was importing generic medication to Ghana and accused Cipla of violating its Combivir patent rights. GSK threatened to take Cipla to court if it continued to import AZT+3TC to Ghana. Cipla discontinued its supply in 2000.[97]

GSK has filed applications for a patent on Combivir in many developing countries affected by HIV/AIDS including India and Thailand. In 2006 patent applications were filed by GSK in both Thailand and India.[98] Patient networks and public interest groups, in both the countries opposed the multinational's patent application on Combivir in March 2006. People Living with HIV/AIDS in India and Thailand appealed to the government to refuse the patent and lodged a legal objection to GSK's patent application on the grounds that it is not a new invention but simply the combination of two existing drugs. GSK's patent application on Combivir was opposed in India on technical and health grounds by the Manipur Network of Positive People, under the aegis of the Indian Network of People Living with HIV/AIDS. In June 2006, GSK instructed its agents in Thailand and India to withdraw this patent application. This means that GSK has no patent protection on Combid/Combivir in Thailand or India, and is not seeking any.[99]

Globally, ARVs remain beyond the reach of the majority of people with HIV/AIDS.[100] There has been relative success in improving access

---

[96] Combivir has not been patented in India because India's patent law provides that you can't get a patent by simply combining two old molecules into a single product.

[97] Available at www.globaltreatmentaccess.org/content/camp/gsk/ghana.html (last accessed on 25 September 2007).

[98] See, 'GSK's Patent Application Endangers Availability of Essential Aids Drug,' *Business World Online*, New Delhi, 7 August 2006. Available at http://www.businessworldindia.com/issue/press_rel26.asp (last accessed on 11 November 2007).

[99] P.T. Jyothi Datta, 'GSK withdraws Combivir patent plea', *Business Daily* (last accessed on 21 August 2006).

[100] K. Attawell, J. Mundy, 2003, 'Provision of Antiretroviral Therapy in Resource-Limited Settings: A Review of Experience Up to August 2003', Health Systems Resource Centre, Department for International Development, London. Available at http://www.who.int/3by5/publications/documents/en/ARTpaper_DFID_WHO.pdf (last accessed on 4 April 2005); 'A Commitment to Action for Expanded Access to HIV/AIDS Treatment,'

to ARVs by countries like India and Brazil but it is vital that the second line treatment of HIV becomes cheaper and more accessible. Apart from HIV many millions of people still cannot access existing vaccines and drugs for tuberculosis, malaria, cancer, and for the few neglected diseases medicines that exist. Price constitutes a very important dimension of drug access. Novartis's defense of its cancer-drug patent today had the potential to undermine access to medicines for HIV/AIDS, for heart disease, for diabetes, in fact for every new medicine needed by the poor in developing and poorer countries. In addition, it may also skew R&D initiatives away from the 'diseases of the poor', NDs, to lifestyle diseases with high monetary demands. This is the reason many diseases have been termed 'neglected', for research gaps, and for drug availability and accessibility gaps. While they all have multiple contributing factors, patents constitute a vital connection.

The ramifications of this case are wide: they extend beyond India, and beyond the drug Glivec, bringing the ethics of patenting medical drugs into focus and questioning the fundamental basis of IPRS in medical field. The case also highlights the need to adopt a system of priority in adjudicating claims between competing rights, such as the right to health and life, and the right to intellectual property. Adjudication of these claims calls for clear, justiciable articulation of laws that protect and prioritize 'basic' or 'prior' rights like health before innovators' rights. While legal mechanisms are seldom sufficient tools for the delivery of rights, they do constitute necessary conditions. Significantly, it also brings into focus the right of a sovereign country to grant, uphold or delimit rights in consonance with its socio-economic imperatives.

The Glivec judgment is significant for three reasons, from the immediate to the larger. First, it ensures the availability of cheaper versions of Glivec to CML patients. Second, it has enabled Indian companies to make available generic medicines for leukemia (CML) at roughly one tenth of the Rs 1,25,000 a month that Novartis charges for Glivec. 'We fought for patients' rights and we are greatly relieved that the court has ruled in our favour and recognized that patients, more than patents, need protecting,' said Y.K. Sapru, founder and chairman of the CPAA.

Moreover, it sets a precedent for similar grounds of conflict between an Indian manufactured generic drugs and the patented drugs which

---

International HIV Treatment Access Coalition (Geneva: World Health Organization, 2002). Available at http://www.who.int/hiv/pub/arv/who_hiv_2002_24.pdf (last accessed on 4 April 2005); 'Treating 3 Million by 2005: Making It Happen The WHO Strategy', 2003, Geneva: World Health Organization. Available at http://www.who.int/3by5/publications/documents/en/3by5StrategyMakingItHappen.pdf (last accessed on 29 August 2007).

have been incrementally improved for a 're-patent' and whose 'enhanced efficacy' is not clearly demonstrable. What stands threatened by the Novartis case are the drugs which are not truly innovative.[101] Take the case for the patent filing made by Abbott Laboratories Inc. for Aluvia, an anti-HIV drug. Pre-grant oppositions have already been filed in the US on grounds that it a similar version of an old drug. In India, several patient groups stated that they were also contemplating following the example set by Initiative for Medicines, Access & Knowledge (I-MAK), which announced the filing of its objections in the Mumbai Patent Office, on 16 August 2007.[102] Sold under the brand name Aluvia by Abbott, the drug is a combination of lopinavir and ritonavir drugs, both of which are pre 1995 drugs and, hence, not admissible for patents. Aluvia is a heat resistant version of the original Kaletra which has the same drug combination but is in the form of soft gel capsules and is non-heat resistant. The combination, which is heat stable, does not deserve a patent by itself, says a drug access campaigner of MSF. Roughly 93,000 AIDS patients in India are on antiretroviral therapy and a tenth of them are estimated to require drugs similar to Aluvia.[103] Lawyers Collective, a group of advocates engaged in public health and drug access issues, has also challenged the grant of patents to several HIV drugs such as Merck's Efavirenz, Gilead Sciences's Tenofovir and Amprenavir, and also Roche's hepatitis drug Pegasys, contesting the incremental innovation claimed by the applicants.

[101] For a view that the majority of research conducted by industry is for higher-priced and similar versions of existing medicines ('me-too' medicines with little added therapeutic benefit), or monopoly extensions for new uses of old medicines, see H. Mintzberg, 15 August 2006, 'Patent Nonsense: Evidence tells of an industry out of social control,' *Canadian Medical Association Journal*, 175(4). Available at www.cmaj.ca/cgi/content/full/175/4/374 (last accessed on 6 September 2007). These medicines are rarely innovative: only 15 per cent of the new drug applications approved by the US Food and Drug Administration (FDA) from 1989 to 2000 were identified as clinical improvements over products already on the market. 'Changing patterns of Pharmaceutical Innovation' (National Institute for Health Care Management, May 2000). Available at http://www.nihcm.org/finalweb/innovations. pdf (last accessed on 6 September 2007). For a comparison of New Molecular entities inventions (NMEs) with incrementally modified drugs (IMDs) see, 'Changing Patterns of Pharmaceutical Innovation,' Research Report, The National Institute for Health Care Management Research and Educational Foundation, May, 2002. Available at www.nihcm. org/pdf/innovation/pdf (last accessed on 11 December 2007).

[102] A Summary of the patent challenge is available at http://www.i-mak.org/storage/ Kaletra%20Heat%20Stable%20Pre-grant%20Opposition%20Summary.pdf (last accessed 11 Deceiber 2007).

[103] Bhuma Shrivastava, 27 August 2007, 'Abbott Labs' bid for anti-HIV drug patent to face stiff challenge', *The Wall Street Journal*. Available at http://www.livemint.com/ Articles/2007/08/27001549/Abbott-Labs8217-bid-for-ant.html (last accessed on 31 August 2007).

Anand Grover, project director of the HIV/AIDS unit at Lawyer's Collective states that the group has filed 15 pre-grant oppositions against patent applications.[104] Of the 7000 applications pending in the 'mailbox' around 2000 drugs may come under section 3(d), which Novartis wanted deleted from patent laws.[105] There are 150 pre-grant oppositions which are likely to be affected by the Glivec ruling. Prominent among these 150 pre-grant oppositions are some that involve an AstraZeneca's lung cancer drug, a Pfizer treatment for fungal infections, Roche's Tamiflu for bird flu/swine flu, and Eli Lilly's erectile dysfunction drug.[106]

This case thus has huge implications for the supply of affordable medicines not just in India but in African countries and other parts of the developing world that rely on medicines exported from India. As Sarah Hiddleston evocatively writes: 'For the 32 million people in India suffering from diabetes, for the 36 million with coronary heart disease, the 5.2 million living with HIV, the 3.3 million with tuberculosis (TB), the 1.2 million with malaria, the 25,000 people diagnosed each year with CML, and for the government agencies, hospitals, non-governmental organizations (NGOs) and patient groups distributing medicines, the Madras High Court's 6 August 2007 rejection of Swiss pharmaceutical giant Novartis' challenge to the Indian government is significant'.[107]

There is a third and a larger issue under consideration here—the relationship between intellectual property, the proprietary knowledge system that it advances, and public health. The key question is whether medical patents necessarily conflict with the realization of health as a right. Patents function poorly for the pharmaceutical industry where a strong potential for the conflict is generated in populations unable to access existing medicines because of their high prices. Patents increase the threshold of accessibility and reduce the number of people who can afford them. Denial of access is denial of the right to health. The TRIPS framework does not provide much guidance concerning its links with other rights. The TRIPS agreement was adopted as a stand-alone

[104] See web site of the Lawyers' Collective at http://www.lawyerscollective. org/^amtc/^Patent_Oppositions/introduction.asp (last accessed on 23 December 2007).
[105] 'Industry Hails Novartis Decision,' *The Times of India* (last accessed on 8 August 2007).
[106] Pre-grant opposition allows a company or individual to oppose claims in a patent application before its granted. See, Sliverman (ed.), 'India's Glivec Ruling Is Bad News For Other Drugmakers Too', *Pharmalot*. Available at http://www.pharmalot.com/2007/08/indias-Glivec-ruling-is-bad-news-for-other-drugmakers-too/ (last accessed on 6 August 2007).
[107] Sarah Hiddleton, 11 August 2007, 'Patent Issues: Beaten Challenge', *Frontline*, 24(16).

agreement which makes no mention of the impacts it can have, for instance, in the field of health. Examples from South Africa, Brazil, and more recently India indicate that TRIPS agreement cannot be implemented in isolation. There are a number of other international obligations, in particular in the field of health as a human right. Intellectual property rights coexist with them with a great degree of unease and context dependent interpretations.

ACCORDING HEALTH RIGHTS PRIORITY

Both health rights and intellectual property rights have been accorded the status of human rights in the UN covenants.[108] Tensions inevitably arise in devising terms of adjudication as both rights claim universal application. One can argue that health rights are universal in a strong sense, that is, they apply in more or less the same way to all people everywhere, without there being large contextual variations. Intellectual property as knowledge rights are universal, if at all, in a far weaker sense. For one, they have strong contextual variations and interpretations. That knowledge creation and forms of ownership and use have large contextual variations has been discussed at length in Chapter 5 of this work. Most core normative considerations and fundamental cultural diversities in the construction and dissemination of knowledge limits applicability to all people in a similar manner. Of course even human rights that are universal in the strong sense, like health rights, will often require context-dependent interpretation. This will happen, for example, when a context either generates a conflict between the two rights in question or makes inadequate standard institutional efforts at securing some particular right. But morally the claim that 'universally' people ought to have access to justiciable health rights is a stronger claim than that people should have rights over their intellectual property. When two rights conflict, as in the Glivec case, between health rights and intellectual property rights, grounds of adjudication need to be based on a clear understanding of the potential that rights have in augmenting life conditions.

The moral claim to a right derives from its ability to enhance conditions of life and its prospects. When there are competing rights claims we need to establish that health care rights are special and that they should be accorded higher priority when adjudicating. In other words, I am arguing for a system of commensuration whereby it is possible for us

---

[108] Universal Declaration of Human Rights, Article 25; ESCR Covenant, Article 12; Intellectual property as a human right: Article 15(1) of the ESCR covenant; Article 27(2), Universal Declaration of Human Rights, 1948.

to designate health rights as having a higher moral claim than intellectual property rights. Health rights need to be connected to other central notions considered vital for justice. I consider the linkage to justice as important, since rights are delivery mechanisms of justice, an end-state which enhances conditions and quality of life.

The right to health implies freedom from disease in a way that it does not debilitate or terminate one's life. The moral priority of health care rights is determined by the fact that good health preconditions the enjoyment of all other rights. Secondly, as Norman Daniels states, good health is a fundamental element in the realization of equality of opportunity.[109] Disease and disability, by impairing normal functioning, restrict the range of opportunities available. Daniels' thesis is useful for it helps us to relate impairment of the normal opportunity range with the relative importance of health-care needs at the macro level. For the purpose of justice, the central moral importance of preventing and treating disease and disability derives from the protection that it grants to a normal range of opportunities. The right to health has the ambition to sustain people as participating citizens.[110]

Thomas Pogge argues that the strength of our moral reasons to uphold and prioritize health rights also derives from, 'relational factors'—the relationship between the medical condition people suffer and our material and causal relation with those conditions.[111] Here the focus is not on the distribution of health outcomes but on how these outcomes are produced. If they are produced, for instance through our material support of global institutional order like the TRIPS agreement, which reinforce adverse health conditions by making medicines inaccessible and unaffordable, the relational link between adverse medical conditions and the TRIPS regime tacitly supported by us would make it morally incumbent on us to prioritize the mitigation of medical conditions. The moral obligation therefore, comes to be grounded in not our positive obligation towards distributional aspects of health conditions—number of people affected, severity of the disease, cost of treatment, etc.—but comes to be grounded in our negative duties. '[The] moral reason to mitigate the injuries of an

---

[109] Norman Daniels, 1981, Health-Care Needs and Distributive Justice, *Philosophy and Public Affairs*, 10(2), pp. 146–79. Distributive Justice in Social and Political Philosophy.

[110] Rosamond Rhodes, M. Pabst Battin, Anita Silvers, 2002, *Medicine and Social Justice: Essays on the Distribution of Health Care Medicine and Social Justice: Essays on the Distribution of Health Care*, USA: Oxford University Press.

[111] For an explication of this thesis see, Thomas Pogge, 2004, 'Relational Conceptions of Justice: Responsibilities for Health Outcomes' in *Public Health, Ethics, and Equity*, Sudhir Anand, Fabienne Peter, and Amartya Sen (eds), Oxford: Clarendon Press, pp. 135–61.

accident victim is stronger if you were materially involved in causing his or her accident.'[112] An analogous point relating to institutions is that in 'in shaping an institutional order, we should be more concerned, morally, that it not substantially contribute to the incidence of medical conditions than that it prevent medical conditions caused by other factors.'[113] As the TRIPS regime does exacerbate medical conditions by limiting access rights, there is a moral claim of health rights which calls upon the obligations of global institutions. This places a greater moral responsibility on part of the duty holders than if we were to say that it is the duty of global institutions to help the poor and needy, without relating it to their material causality.

That health rights have prior moral claims, can be variously upheld. They call upon our positive obligation for just distribution of health goods as well as on our negative obligation to not contribute to situations that create medical conditions. Terms of adjudication need to be cognizant of the priority order that these two rights claim. Institutional efforts to secure health rights, particularly at national levels where health rights derive concrete articulation through justiciable rights, have been rather weak in comparison to institutionalization of intellectual protection. Health as a human right receives only its first level articulation in various declarations and international covenants, as statements of intent and guidelines for national health policies. Identifying human rights violations and adjudicating human rights claims, however, are incomplete unless these rights are enforced. While enforcement mechanisms are in place with respect to intellectual property, such is not the case with health rights. It is highly dependent on the ability, will, and capability of individual states to enforce mechanisms while being compliant with the TRIPS framework.[114]

The tensions between intellectual property and public health emerge not out of competing moral claims but out of competing institutional claims. As a moral claim, health rights far outweigh the claim of IPRs, which are more in the nature of economic entitlements or rewards for innovation. The institutional apparatus of health rights needs to be bolstered, as Ellen t'Hoen states, in order to 'outweigh full protection of intellectual property.'[115] The global extension of IPRs, especially patents,

---

[112] Ibid., p. 135.

[113] Ibid.

[114] The Glivec case clearly showed that non-compliance of a domestic legislative provision, section 3(d) with the TRIPS regime was a key complaint of the petitioner, Novartis.

[115] Ellen t' Hoen, 2002, 'TRIPS, Pharmaceutical Patents, and Access to Essential Medicines: A Long Way From Seattle to Doha', *Chicago Journal of International Law*, 3(1), p. 46.

and the enhanced powers conferred on title-holders have raised concerns about the extent to which the fundamentally commercial interests protected by intellectual property rights may be given primacy over other interests of society, such as those relating to public health. Medical patents constitute an important case study within the broader field of intellectual property rights because this constitutes an area where the industry is highly dependent on patents.

The existing TRIPS rules that restrict access to affordable medicines, even as they icentivise their production, are deeply problematic. The utility of intellectual property protection, even if that were to be its most powerful defense, cannot be judged in terms of the innovation generated.[116] Innovation is a means to an end: the end utility being the well-being of the people. If a third of the world's population does not have access to basic drugs, then clearly innovation is not meeting its desired objectives.[117] Access to drugs is a component of the human right to health and one that is severely restricted by patenting of drugs. Denial of access is denial of the right to health. Lack of access to basic health necessities can, at best, preclude a minimally decent and autonomous life or, at worst, prove to be fatal for the victims. From the victim's perspective, the object of this right is more important than that of many other traditional libertarian rights.

[116] Refer to Adam B. Jaffe, and Josh Lerner, 2004, *Innovation and Its Discontents: How Our Broken Patent System is Endangering Innovation and Progress, and What to Do About It*; Michele Boldrin and David K. Levine, 'The Case against Intellectual Property', (2002) *American Economic Review*, 92(2); and Sunil Kanwar and Robert Evenson, 2004, 'Does Intellectual Property Protection Spur Technological Change?' Center Discussion Paper No. 83, Economic Growth Center:Yale University.

[117] See United Nations Development Programme, 2003, *Human Development Report 2003*, OUP.

7 Farmers' Rights and Proprietary Claims in Agriculture
McFarling v. *Monsanto*

The concept of farmers' rights was developed in the context of extension of IPRs in agriculture. It was argued that the two concerned international agreements, the International Union for the Protection of New Varieties of Plants, 1991 agreement (UPOV 1991) and the TRIPS agreement, which had been set up to give crop plant breeders exclusive rights over the varieties they develop, disregard the traditional rights of indigenous and farming communities to their genetic resources and associated knowledge. These agreements granted greater recognition and protection through IPRs, to the breeders and inventors for what came to be referred to as the 'improved varieties'. They substantially broadened the gap between source materials and improved varieties in terms of value and ownership rights attached to them. However the UPOV and TRIPS agreement left the farmers (traditionally breeders and conservers), outside the domain of IPRs in agro bio-resources and associated knowledge. It was this omission that spawned the debate and the movement for a formal recognition and institutionalization of farmers' rights.

The addition of farmers' rights to the list of rights that were demanding attention and institutionalization added new dimensions to the rights discourse. The first reinforced what UPOV and the TRIPS agreement had already brought within the ambit of property rights—that genetic and biological resources are a domain that can be owned. Bringing farmers within the ambit was merely adjudicating who the legitimate owner of this resource could be. In a way, the farmers' rights-talk has brought some kind of a closure to the contentious issue of ownership of genetic resources with talks veering towards issues of democratization and citizenship and away from the extension of property rights into the realm of nature, constitutive of a further reification of property. Rights of farmers—those that would entitle them to control and access their genetic resources and to rewards and benefit-sharing, for use of their genetic resources—began to occupy greater international and policy attention; the collapse of distinctions between the biological, natural and man-made, that is created through propertization, began to be considered a settled debate.

Another dimension has emerged, though only at the level of conceptualization and still devoid of institutional or policy expression, the conception of community rights in agricultural practices and resources. Plant genetic resource and its knowledge has always been held communally by the farmers in most parts of the developing world. Traditional knowledge associated with diverse livelihoods agriculture, forestry, fishing, etc. seldom exists in the individual domain. It is held and exchanged communally, even when the end user is an individual. Rights in this context, therefore, began to be conceptualized as rights of communities.[1] Into the rights discourse was thus incorporated the conception of community rights,[2] which emerged as an alternative conceptualization of rights in the context of the push for individuated IPRs. In order to create spaces for the rights of local communities and indigenous peoples, to control and access their agro-genetic resources, it was argued that an alternative conception of rights, creatively based on the historical ways and systems of local communities,[3] needs to be devised and incorporated in the legal frameworks and instruments governing international exchange of bio-agro-genetic resources. Thus emerge conceptions of traditional resource rights (TRRs), traditional ecological knowledge rights (TEK), traditional indigenous knowledge rights (TIK), and so on. However, concepts of community rights remain devoid of both content and institutional expression, They continue to occupy the rhetorical spaces of, 'objectives', 'statements of intent', etc., in international instruments, lacking justiciability, and policy intent.

Concepts of farmers' rights, currently in the process of negotiations and re-negotiations in international forums, are subject to many different

[1] See, for instance Gurdial Singh Nijar, 1994, 'A Conceptual Framework and Essential Elements of a Rights Regime for the Protection of Indigenous Rights and Biodiversity', in *Biodiversity Convention Briefings*, Third World Network, Penang.

[2] Collective Rights finds a mention in the following international covenants: ILO Convention on Indigenous and Tribal Peoples; ICESCR 1976; International Covenant on Civil and Political Rights, 1976; Declaration on the Rights of Indigenous Peoples, 2007.

[3] The use of the wider concept of 'local communities' (including farmers and indigenous peoples) encompasses a large array of different organizational and cultural realities. It reflects very significantly, collective attitudes towards the ownership, use, custodianship, stewardship, sharing, and enjoyment of resources.

interpretations of their meaning and scope. A number of these interpretations are of course mediated by international trading and business interests and do not represent farmers' interests or participation. Amongst the many interpretations, this chapter adheres to the following understanding of farmers' rights, advanced by the Via Campesina's 1996 Intervention to the Food and Agricultural organization (FAO):[4]

... 2. *Farmers' Rights* include the right over resources and associated knowledge, united indivisibly, and mean the acceptance of traditional knowledge, respect for cultures and the recognition that these are the basis of the creation of knowledge;

3. The right to control, the right to decide the future of genetic resources, the rights to define the legal framework of property rights of these resources;

4. *Farmers' Rights* are of an eminently collective nature and for this reason should be recognized in a different framework from that of private property. (Emphasis mine)

This chapter aims to examine the issue of farmers' rights in the context of proprietary claims in agriculture as either patent rights or breeders' rights. I seek to argue that in the case of farmers' rights, the power that the right confers on the farmer ought to determine his capacity and power to sustain his life, not just as survival but as linked with dignity and well-being. Rights associated with life and livelihood form a stronger assertion for rights than those based on the principles of autonomy and economic entitlements. This chapter carries forward the previous chapter's basic understanding of rights in asserting that different rights carry different moral weights. Proprietary claims, like IPRs struggle as a moral claim as they challenge two basic premises of rights:

1) The 'like rights' of an individual—in this case, of a farmer to his intellectual property based on the 'equal respect' principle, that requires acknowledging the farmer as a rightful claimant to a fair share of social assets.

2) Rights as a guarantee for basic security and subsistence for the very poor. The central premise of farmers' rights is the conception that rights must include social provision for needs of members and moreover, that rights ought to honour, as Attracta Ingram states, 'the economic constitution of the people' who live under a rights regime.[5]

---

[4] Via Campesina is an international movement which coordinates peasant organizations of small and middle-scale producers, agricultural workers, rural women, and indigenous communities from Asia, Africa, America, and Europe. They are a coalition of over 100 organizations, advocating family-farm-based sustainable agriculture and were the group that first coined the term 'food sovereignty'. Their campaign material on farmers' rights is available at http://www.ukabc.org/gb3.htm#c1 (last accessed on 27 September 2009).

[5] Attracta Ingram, 1994, pp. 97–116.

I seek to argue that as necessary conditions the first premise is itself insufficient to help the realization of farmers' rights. When we argue that farmers are party to the exchange relationship dictated by the IPRs in plant varieties and, therefore, ought to be as much a subject of rights as breeders, we argue for their property rights and their like rights over the genetic resources that they control and use. However, the conception of farmers' rights needs to move beyond conceptualizing their rights as a counter to breeders' rights. They need to be conceptualized outside the language of property rights to include their developmental rights, rights which secure, protect and enhance livelihood, food and the knowledge rights of farmers. The idea of farmers' rights as property rights locates itself in the 'equal rights' principle which forms the bedrock of liberal democratic rights. As livelihood rights, farmers' rights move beyond the libertarian conceptions of autonomy and desert and locate themselves in conception of justice which upholds all rights that link with survival and livelihood as prior rights—prior to all rights that reward or compensate.

A case study of the legal proceedings in the *Monsanto Co.* v. *McFarling* (USA) case, has been undertaken to illustrate the conflict between IPRs and farmer's rights and to draw broader conclusions from it that relate to aspects of human rights and their realization. The *McFarling* case is instructive for it clearly illustrates the conflict between farmers' rights and intellectual property rights. However, issues of conflict between IPRs and farmers' rights get more complex as we move to illustrations from developing countries which bring livelihood concerns that are far more pressing. The attempt, therefore, would also be to cull out the implications of the inequitable rights distribution for farmers in developing countries. But before we move to the conflict zone it is important to understand the nature of rights that the chapter is concerned with, namely IPRs in plant varieties and farmers' rights; the issues of their compossibility will follow.

INTELLECTUAL PROPERTY RIGHTS IN PLANT VARIETIES

The policy goals of granting IPRs to plant varieties are grounded principally on an instrumentalist or utilitarian approach to IPRs. This is true both for patents and plant breeders' rights. Legal protection for the products of human intellectual effort and ingenuity is granted not because of a moral commitment to compensating creators or innovators, but rather because the products they create enrich a society's knowledge pool and thus increase its welfare. The grant of IPRs in plant varieties, following a utilitarian approach, is intended to provide adequate incentives for creators and inventors to invest intellectual capital and thereby create genetically engineered (GE) plant and seed varieties that could lead to greater productivity or enhanced nutritional value of foods, or to the elimination of destructive pests, weeds, and so on. They are the 'economic' motives behind the research required for genetic engineering in crops. Legal protection in the form of IPRs is largely to ensure that breeders receive adequate remuneration when they market the propagating material of those improved varieties. As a FAO document clearly states:

In the absence of a grant of exclusive rights to breeders, the dangers of free riding by third parties would be considerable. This is because the genetic material within plants that specifies their distinctive and commercially valuable features is naturally self-replicating, for example by reproduction of seeds or other propagating material. Self-replication makes innovations incorporating biological material particularly susceptible to exploitation by parties other than the innovator... It provides an incentive for private research and development into new breeding techniques, thereby reducing the need for government funding to subsidize these activities. It encourages the development of new and beneficial plant varieties for use by farmers and consumers. And it furthers the society's development of agriculture, horticulture and forestry.[6]

IPRs in plant varieties thus provide some assurance to breeders that they will be able to recoup the risks and costs of a value-added innovation that is based upon an underlying biological resource.[7] It is argued that strengthened IPRs would increase the flow of technology and products from the developing countries and provide new incentives for local research and innovation.[8]

For a long time in history no notion of ownership, property rights or sovereign rights over genetic and plant resources existed. What contributed to the emergence of property rights in plant varieties was the need to exploit the potential, particularly from the genetically rich global South, for commercial benefits in this area. The scope of patentable subject matter expanded, slowly and incrementally until it covered plants. In outlining the history of intellectual property and biotechnology, the French barrister and philosopher, Bernard Edelman indicates a move

[6] Laurence R. Helfer, 'Intellectual Property Rights in Plant Varieties International Legal Regimes and Policy Options for National Governments', for the Development Law Service, FAO Legal Office. FAO Corporate Document Repository. Section 1.2. Available at http://www.fao.org/docrep/007/y5714e/y5714e02.htm#bm2.2 (last accessed on 26 January 2008).

[7] W.H. Lesser, 1997, 'The Role of IPRs in Biotechnology Transfer under the Convention on Biological Diversity', *International Service for the Acquisition of Agri-biotech Applications (ISAAA) Brief*, 3, Ithaca, New York: ISAAA, pp. 8–10.

[8] T.M. Horbulyk, 1993, 'Intellectual Property Rights and Technological Innovation in Agriculture', *Technological Forecasting and Social Change*, 43(3/4), pp. 259–70.

from a strict prohibition against the patenting of nature towards a range of recent decisions allowing the patenting of living matter. He argues that there has been a progressive accommodation of biotechnology within the legal system, and summarizes the stages of this passage as follows:

> Life has been integrated into the market as easily as could be imagined because it has been a progressive process. It started with something that was symbolically far removed from mankind, the vegetable domain; from there it passed to the micro-organism, then to the most rudimentary forms of animal life, like the oyster. The whole of the animal kingdom is now targeted and we are on the verge of the human, weighed down with precedents which ensure the closure of the system and make any resistance difficult. The work of man, which must be remunerated, claims repayment from the whole realm of nature which has traditionally been free of any property claims.[9]

The rapid development of the biotech industry over the last couple of decades can be directly linked to the expanding scope of patents on life forms, in particular in the US, but also at the international level. Under Title 35 U.S.C. (United States Code), section 101 'A live, human-made micro-organism is patentable subject matter.' Although patents could be obtained as well for certain asexually reproduced plants covered by the Plant Patent Act of 1930, until the *Parker* v. *Bergy* case[10] (1978) no court had ever held that a living organism is patentable under section 101. In this case, however, a divided United States Court of Customs and Patent Appeals held that a living micro-organism was patentable under section 101.[11]

The year 1980 was another landmark in the history of development of life patents. The decision in the *Diamond* v. *Chakrabarty* case[12] triggered one of the most significant changes in the patent regimes in recent times. Under the US law, products of nature did not constitute patentable matter, although the Plant Patent Act did offer scope for patentability, as in the *Parker* case, by making a distinction between products of nature and man-made inventions rather than between living and inanimate things. This same distinction became the basis for the ruling in the *Diamond* v.

[9] Bernard Edelman, 1997, *Time and Commodity Culture: Essays In Cultural Theory And Postmodernity*, John Frow (trans.), Oxford: Oxford University Press, p. 197.

[10] 98 S. Ct. 3119, 1978

[11] For details see, Dianc Kay McDonald, 'The Patentability of Living Organisms under 35 USC S. 101: In Re Bergy', *Harvard Law Review*, 91(6) April 1978, pp. 1357–66.

[12] Genetic engineer Ananda Mohan Chakrabarty, working for General Electric, had developed a bacterium (derived from the *Pseudomonas* genus) capable of breaking down crude oil, which he proposed to use in treating oil spills. He requested a patent for the bacterium. It was denied intially by the patent examiner but was subsequently upheld by both the CAFC and the Supreme Court. 447 US 303 (1980) No. 79-136.

Chakrabarty[13] case. The Court ruled that: '*A live, human-made micro-organism is patentable subject matter under [Title 35 U.S.C.] 101. Respondent's micro-organism (Bacterium) constitutes a "manufacture" or "composition of matter" within that statute.*'[14] [Emphasis mine]

The *Chakrabarty* decision opened the door to patentability of microorganisms in the US. It laid the basis for patentability of genes and plant varieties. The decision of *Diamond* v. *Chakrabarty* determined that genetically engineered organisms are either a *manufacture* or a composition of matter and are, therefore, patentable. From single-celled organisms, the line then passes through genetically engineered plants to oysters and transgenic animals like the Oncomouse.[15]

The development of genetic engineering in the private sector is directly linked to the introduction of IPRs in life forms. Patents emerged as the legal tool to protect investments in research on genetic engineering. An understanding of the developments in the US is relevant because legal developments in patenting have there, in many ways, set the pattern for several multilateral intellectual property treaties.

Legal developments are rarely independent of larger social or economic movements. What is common in both instances is the link between the development of the patent regime and its association with economy and the requirements of industry. At one level, it is a structural story about the triumph and the compulsions of global capitalism, the collaboration between business and government, the increasing mobility of capital, ascendance of private capital in global governance which changed the character of IPRs as 'grants of privileges', that were explicitly recognized as exceptions to the rules against monopolies, to 'rights' upheld by law.[16]

[13] 447 US 303 (1980) No. 79–136. Argued 17 March 1980. Decided 16 June 1980, US Supreme Court.

[14] Ibid.

[15] The OncoMouse or Harvard mouse (Trademark: USPTO serial number 75797027) is a type of laboratory mouse that has been genetically modified using modifications designed by Philip Leder and Timothy Stewart of Harvard University to carry a specific gene called an activated oncogene. The activated oncogene significantly increases the mouse's susceptibility to cancer, and thus makes the mouse suitable for cancer research. The rights to the invention are owned by Dupont. OncoMouse(R) is a registered trademark. See, for instance, Fiona Murray, The Oncomouse that Roared: Resistance & Accomodation to Patenting in Academic Science (March 2006). Available at http://web.mit.edu/fmurray/www/papers/THE%20ONCOMOUSE%20THAT%20ROARED_FINAL.pdf (last accessed on 26 January 2008).

[16] For a discussion on the structural interpretation of patent legislations see, Susan Sell and C. May, 2004, 'Moments in Law: contestations and settlement in the history of IP', *Reviews of International Political Economy*, 8(3), pp. 467–500; for details of evolution and analysis of the universalization of TRIPS see, S. Sell, 2003, *Private Power, Public Law: The*

Plant Breeders' Rights

One of the earliest supranational agreements on IPRs in plant varieties was the Union for the Protection of New Plant Varieties (UPOV). UPOV was first adopted in Paris in 1960, and subsequently revised in 1972, 1978, and 1991. The objective of the convention was the protection of new varieties of plants through IP rights. By codifying intellectual property for plant breeders, UPOV aims to encourage the development of new varieties of plants for the benefit of society. The mission statement of UPOV states as its objective the need to protect innovation in new plant varieties: 'To provide and promote an effective system of plant variety protection, with the aim of encouraging the development of new varieties of plants, for the benefit of society.' According to the terms of the UPOV, 'Each contracting party shall grant and protect breeders' rights'. Plant varieties can be protected under UPOV if they fulfilled the criteria of novelty, distinctness, stability, and uniformity (for patents, the criteria are novelty, inventiveness (non-obviousness), utility, and reproducibility).[17] The concept of 'novelty' under UPOV is noteworthy because it differs from its equivalent under patent law. Under patent law 'novelty' signifies an invention; here 'novelty' refers to the earliest commercialization of a variety, that is, it has not been sold or otherwise disposed to others by, or with the consent of, the breeder. Two important developments in the 1990s further expanded the scope of plant variety protection (PVP)[18]— the 1991 UPOV revision and the TRIPS agreement in 1994.

The UPOV 1991 revision increased breeders' rights by including the notion of 'essentially derived variety' and extending protection to these varieties. An essentially derived variety is one that is predominantly derived from the initial variety itself which would, as per UPOV 1991, fulfill the normal protection criteria of novelty, distinctness, uniformity, and stability. It became the subject of protection in 1991 but can not be exploited without the authorization of the breeder of the protected (initial) variety.[19] As per the UPOV 1978 a protected variety could be

---

Globalization of IP Rights, Cambridge: Cambridge University Press, Chapters 1 and 7.

[17] International Convention for the Protection of New Varieties of Plants. 2 December 1961, as revised at Geneva on 10 November 1972, on 23 October 1978, and on 19 March 1991, Chapter II Article 2. Available at http://www.upov.int/en/about/mission.html (last accessed on 2 September 2007).

[18] For details on PVP Act, see, Janice M. Strachan, 'Plant Variety Protection: An Alternative to Patents', available at http://www.nal.usda.gov/pgdic/Probe/v2n2/plant.html (last accessed on 10 September 2007).

[19] Article 14(5), UPOV-1991. Available at http://www.upov.int/eng/protectn/derivatn.htm (last accessed on 11 March 2007).

modified in very limited respect and needed to be clearly distinguishable from the initial variety and was separately protected without any obligation to the breeder of the initial protected variety. The UPOV 1991 protects breeders from situations in which limited changes are made to their varieties and then exploited.

The UPOV 1991 also has implications for the scope of 'farmers' privilege'. It further restricts farmers' rights, which had already been curtailed by the grant of breeders' rights by UPOV 1961. UPOV 1978 allowed the farmer to reuse propagating material from the previous year's harvest and to freely exchange seeds of protected varieties with other farmers. UPOV 1991 limited this option—the 'farmers' privilege' which granted them the prerogative to save seeds was made optional for member countries. Thus under UPOV 1991, through the notion of 'essentially derived variety' the breeder could widen the ambit of what was ownable.[20] These changes made plant breeders' protection very strong and effective from the perspective of the same.

Patents in Plant Varieties

The TRIPS agreement was the second development that had a major impact on the expansion of plant breeders' rights and patents on life forms. With the conclusion of the GATT Uruguay Round and the agreement on TRIPS at Marrakech in 1994, developing countries found themselves under the obligation to provide some form of intellectual property protection on plant varieties. Article 27.3(b) of the TRIPS agreement imposes on all WTO member states, introduction of plant variety protection (PVP) through 'plant breeders' rights' (PBRs) either through patents or through an effective sui generis system or both as per article 27 (3) (b) of the TRIPS agreement.[21]

Broadly speaking, part (b) of paragraph 3 [that is, Article 27.3(b)] allows governments to exclude some kinds of inventions from patenting, namely, plants, animals, and 'essentially' biological processes (but micro-organisms,

---

[20] D. Rangnekar, October–December 1998, 'Tnp.png in Front of UPOV: Plant Variety Protection in India', *Social Action*, 48(4), pp. 432–51.

[21] Article 27.3(b) of the TRIPS agreement reads: 'Members may also exclude from patentability: (b) plants and animals other than micro-organisms, and essentially biological processes for the production of plants or animals other than non-biological and microbiological processes. However, Members shall provide for the protection of plant varieties either by patents or by an effective sui generis system or by any combination thereof. The provisions of this subparagraph shall be reviewed four years after the date of entry into force of the WTO Agreement. The provisions of this sub-paragraph shall be reviewed four years after the entry into force of the agreement establishing the WTO.' Available at www.wto.org/english/tratop-e/art27_3b_e.htm (last accessed on 2 February 2007).

and non-biological and microbiological processes are eligible for patents). However, plant varieties have to be eligible for protection either through patent protection or a sui generis system created specifically for the purpose), or a combination of the two. Four categories of patents on life-forms and living processes are covered by TRIPS agreement: Processes producing extracts of plants for medical or industrial/agricultural purposes; Naturally occurring micro-organisms, cell lines, genomes, and genes isolated from natural organisms; Transgenic techniques and constructs, and resultant transgenic organisms; Nuclear transplant cloning and other *in vitro* reproductive technologies.

While the TRIPS agreement grants some flexibility to nations in devising the form of protection by permitting sui generis protection, on the whole it promotes the fundamental idea of IPRs in agricultural genetic resources. Most developing countries are opposed to the idea of patents in biological resources. However, there has been constant pressure on the developing countries to choose plant breeders' rights as the governing framework, if they are opposed to patents. IPRs in this field exist as PBRs or as patents and are used to protect new varieties of plants by giving exclusive commercial rights to market a new variety or its reproductive material. A PBR provides the rights-holder the right to direct the production, sale, and distribution of the new variety, receive royalties from the sale of plants/seeds or with the right to sell their rights. The TRIPS agreement required developing countries to enact IPR legislation for plant varieties by the year 2000, while LDCs had until 2005 to enact the legislation. There is speculation that this novel sui generis option will become defined as plant variety protection (PVP), a soft patent system for seeds.

There were two main reasons why the patent system was seen as inappropriate. Firstly, plant material was not regarded as capable of meeting the requirements of novelty, inventive step, and disclosure. Secondly, it was not thought to be in the public interest to permit such an extensive monopoly over plant varieties, given their communal importance. Underlying this was the view that it was desirable to retain, in so far as it was possible, the tradition of free exchange of new plant material between plant breeding institutes. This would ensure the widest possible dissemination and use of new combinations of genetic information.[22]

Commercial interests, economic impulses, the need to generate newer profit seeking avenues changed the scenario gradually and IPRs

[22] Margaret Llewelyn, 1997, 'The Legal Protection Of Biotechnological Inventions: An Alternative Approach', *European IP Review*, 19(3), p. 115.

in plant varieties slowly started gaining legitimacy and acceptability. The legitimacy was never universal and the acceptability was, at least in the developing part of the world, almost always tempered by political and international political concerns. Perhaps this is the reason why these rights are still contested and their legitimacy still tenuous.

A PBR differs from a patent in that it has a different and more relaxed criterion for judging novelty and inventiveness. Conditions for the grant of Breeder's Right require the plant variety to be new, distinct, uniform, and stable.[23] 'Novelty' is determined by the fact that the variety has not been in commercial use prior to the date of filing (there are time stipulations for the territory of the contracting party and other territories. Refer Article 6 Chapter III). The variety shall be deemed to be distinct if it is clearly distinguishable from any other variety whose existence is a matter of common knowledge at the time of the filing of the application (Article 7). A major difference between the two is that PBRs do not extend to the use of a grower's crop (that is, the grower does not have to pay a royalty on the crop produced), nor do they extend to the use of the variety in plant breeding or retention by growers of seed for the production of another crop on their land. A patent, on the other hand, can cover the commercial use of that variety of seed in subsequent crops for up to 20 years for a standard patent (the innovation patent offers protection for up to eight years). Generally speaking, the patent system and the PBR system have tended to complement each other. A plant breeder is able to apply for protection under both the PBR framework and the standard patent system.[24]

The distinction between patents and PBRs is significant because the original intention was to exempt PBRs from the strict monopoly privileges that accrue under patents. PBRs were a recognition of the fact that the subsequent uses of naturally propagating material cannot be monitored and regulated in the same way as other non-life patents. However, the distinction between patents and PBRs is being applied more and more restrictively. The US Supreme Court has in fact recently confirmed that inventors of new plant varieties can apply for patents. In *JEMAg Supply, Inc* v. *Pioneer Hi-Bred*[25] the Court reasoned that Plant Variety Protection

[23] Article 5, Chapter III of UPOV, 1991.

[24] Apart from patents and PBRs there are other forms of IPRs that are recognized such as 'Geographical Indicators' (GI), Database Protection; Trade Secrets. For a brief summary of these refer to Kauser Abdulla Malik and Yusuf Zafar, 2005, 'IP Rights in Plant Biotechnology: A Contribution to Crop Biosecurity', *Asian Biotechnology and Development Review*, 8(1), pp. 9–10.

[25] *JEM AG Supply* v. *Pioneer Hi-Bred International*, Supreme Court of the US, 10 December 2001, 122 S Ct 593.

Act, 1970 (PVPA) does not preclude the possibility of protection through patents as the latter provides more extensive rights and protection. JEM argued that the Plant Protection Act, 2000 (PPA) and PVPA were the *exclusive* statutory means for protecting plant life. The US Supreme Court held that plants can also fall within the subject matter of the Patent Act, and neither the PPA nor the PVPA limits this coverage. PBRs can limit the use and sale of all reproductive material by farmers, depending on the particular interpretation of the latest UPOV. For example, in Europe, under the 1991 Act of UPOV, PBRs allow neither on-farm seed saving nor swapping grain for seed without compensating the breeder.

UPOV was, to begin with, a treaty negotiated between countries with relatively mechanized agricultural practices and systems. However, the introduction of PVP in the TRIPS agreement, article 27.3 (b) made it mandatory for member states to either adopt the UPOV-PBR model or patents or an effective sui generis model. A number of countries that had no PVP before 1994, turned to UPOV either to join it or, in most cases, to adopt its PVP framework. Though UPOV remains even today a treaty with modest membership (67 in 2009) its model of PBRs has been adopted widely and become the framework for PVP.[26] It is also in many ways the precursor to PVP in TRIPS which has led the era of life patents (plants and animals) in genetic engineering.

Farmers' Rights

The demand for extending intellectual property protection to agriculture in developing countries met with counter-claims for granting farmers' rights. Developing countries are in the process of attempting to fulfill these demands by evolving IPR regimes that simultaneously protect the rights of breeders and farmers. There have been many articulations and enactments at the national level in favour of sui generis legislation which protect the farmers and their plant varieties. For instance, India which did not have existing sui generis legislation developed its own version of PVP, recognizing both PBRs and farmers' rights through the same act, the Plant Variety Protection and Farmers' Rights Act, 2001.

There are persuasive arguments in favour of farmers' rights articulated at various levels. The starting point of the argument is that the biotechnology led innovations in plant varieties and animals did not happen spontaneously. It used, as a base, the knowledge of seeds and breeds

---

[26] For details on the terms of the UPOV convention see Phillipe Cullet, 2005, pp. 226–36.

and plant properties, generated, shared and exchanged over thousands of years. Farmers, in most developing countries, have been the main actors involved in saving seeds, cross-breeding to produce new varieties with better suited traits, biodiversity management, and so on. They have played the combined roles of producer, consumer, and conserver. They are thus the original rights holders of agricultural resources, especially in developing countries. This was the beginning of the conception that farmers are also IPRs holders in a similar, if not in a more forceful way, as the modern biotechnologically assisted plant breeders are. In sum, it was a recognition that while the commercial breeders were protected by either PBRs or through patents in plant varieties, the farmers' contributions as preservers and developers of the gene pool, on which was based much of the incremental changes that were made by commercial breeders, remained unrewarded and unprotected. There was no system for compensating or providing incentives for farmers.[27]

As breeders, conservers, and protectors of agricultural genetic resources for centuries, farmers never had any defined rights over their knowledge, or the genetic resources that they held. Commercial breeding, fuelled by biotechnological innovations in agriculture, transformed these farmers from owners of their gene pool to donors, who then received the commercially bred plant varieties and their seeds at a fee. For instance, under patent law, farmers replanting patented seed for the next season would be legally required to pay a license fee or a technology fee. Many of the most successful varieties available commercially are derived from stocks which have been carefully bred by farmers, especially so in the global South. But instead of being rewarded for their important contribution, both for developing the genes for desirable traits and the knowledge and skills required to use these, they may be required to pay the companies to use the products.

The inequity and exploitative implications of IPRs in agriculture, whether PBRs or patents, led into a recognition that farmers have a prior right to be adequately compensated for the resource they hold, in terms of both their knowledge and genetic pool, and that there is a need to devise and institute fair and equitable benefit-sharing mechanisms which would make farmers partners in biotechnological developments in agriculture, forestry, etc. There was also a growing understanding that patenting will seriously limit the access that farmers, poor farmers in particular, have to

[27] See, for instance, GRAIN, 1999, 'Plant Variety Protection to Feed Africa?', *Seedling*, 16/4 (2).

the genetic resources on which their livelihoods depend. The livelihood rights of the farmers thus needed to be protected by securing their access to the genetic resources under threat by patents and PBRs.

One of the first attempts to acknowledge farmers' rights was in the Agenda 21, adopted in Rio de Janeiro in 1992 at the UN Conference on Environment and Development (UNCED), and Convention on Biological Diversity (CBD), which was to serve as an instrument for the conservation and sustainable use of plant genetic resources and the fair and equitable sharing of the benefits arising from the use of such resources.[28] The Food and Agricultural Organisation's Global System on Plant Genetic Resources, which was prepared by FAO as a result of Agenda 21's commitment to the conservation of agricultural biodiversity, includes continued commitment to the implementation of farmers' rights.[29] These inclusions were in order to broaden the scope of farmers' rights and to assess it in the conservation of biodiversity.

The inequitable treatment between the owners of germplasm and the owners of technology spawned a debate these international forums. The result was the institutionalization of farmers' rights in the form of two main instruments:

a)   In 1983, the demand for farmers' rights formally got incorporated by the FAO as an International Undertaking on Plant Genetic Resources (IU).[30] The FAO as the central UN body dealing with agriculture has played an important role in setting the legal frame work for

[28] CBD was adopted at the Earth Summit in Rio de Janeiro in 1992. The Convention has three main goals: conservation of biological diversity (or biodiversity); sustainable use of its components; and fair and equitable sharing of benefits arising from genetic resources. In other words, its objective is to develop national strategies for the conservation and sustainable use of biological diversity. It is often seen as the key document regarding sustainable development. It entered into force on 29 December 1993 as part of the outcome of the decisions of the United Nations Conference on Environment and Development (UNCED) (Rio de Janeiro, Brazil, 1992). Article 8(j) of CBD on *in situ* conservation states: Subject to its national legislation, respect, preserve and maintain knowledge, innovations and practices of indigenous and local communities embodying traditional lifestyles relevant to the conservation and sustainable use of biological diversity and promote their wider application with the approval and involvement of the holders of such knowledge, innovations and practices and encourage the equitable sharing of the benefits arising from the utilization of such knowledge, innovations and practices; See also FAO Corporate Document repository, Title: IPRs in plant varieties. Section 1.3.5.3. *Convention on Biological Diversity ('CBD').* For full text of CBD see http://www.cbd.int/convention/convention. shtml. (last accessed on 26 September 2007).

[29] Chapter 14, Agenda 21, Report of the UN Conference on Environment and Development, Rio de Janeiro, 3-14 June 1992, UN Doc A/CONF 151/26/Rev1 (Vol. 1), Annexure II.

various activities linked with agriculture. The IU resolutions in 1989 were negotiated by the Commission on Plant and Genetic Resources and were unanimously approved by more than 160 countries in the FAO conferences in 1989 and 1991.[30] The resolutions recognized 'the enormous contribution that farmers of all regions have made to the conservation and development of plant genetic resources, which constitute the basis of plant production throughout the world, and which form the basis for the concept of Farmers' Right....'[31]

b)   The International Treaty on Plant Genetic Resources for Food and Agriculture (PGRFA treaty)[32] was drafted in November 2001. The PGFRA incorporated the new orientation given by the CBD and The FAO Conference (November 2001), and established legally binding rules to secure facilitated access to and exchange of plant and genetic resources within a multilateral system. To conform to the CBD, it also has effective provisions for benefit-sharing, including articles on funding and farmer's rights to benefit small farmers who have been the traditional custodians of plant genetic resources for food and agriculture (PGRFA), particularly in developing countries.[33]

The evolution of both the treaties reflects the journey that policy changes have made at the international level with regard to use of plant genetic resources for food and agriculture and with respect to the location of farmers' rights within the matrix of rights associated with the use of plant genetic material.[34] The IU was until 2001 the only international instrument which outlined the content of farmers' rights, albeit at a very general level. In contrast, PBRs were more clearly articulated and protected; farmers' rights were not precisely defined and remained at best a general recognition of farmers' contribution to food security the world over.[35] It recognized the contribution made by the farming community but stopped short of defining rights of farmers over their intellectual assets.[36]

[30] IU resolutions 4/89, 5/89 for Plant and Genetic Resource, Resolution 8/83, Text available at ftp://ftp.fao.o=rg/ag/cgrfa/iu/iutextE.pdf (last accessed on 15 November 2007).

[31] Resolution 4/89, p. 3.

[32] International Treaty on Plant Genetic Resources for Food and Agriculture Resolution 3/2001 ftp://ftp.fao.org/ag/cgrfa/it/ITPGRe.pdf (last accessed on 15 November 2007).

[33] International Treaty on Plant Genetic Resources for Food and Agriculture. Available at Ftp://Ftp.Fao.Org/Ag/Cgrfa/It/Itpgre.Pdf (last accessed on 17 October 2007).

[34] For details see, Philippe Cullet, pp. 89–110.

[35] Ibid., p. 106.

[36] Resolution 4/89, Agreed Interpretation of the IU Report of the Conference of FAO, 25th Session, Rome 11–29, November, 1989. Doc C89/REP.

The definition of farmers' rights under the IU reads as follows: 'Farmers' Rights mean rights arising from the past, present and future contributions of farmers in conserving, improving and making available plant genetic resources, particularly those in the centers of origin/diversity. These rights are vested in the International community, as trustee for present and future generations of farmers for the purpose of ensuring full benefits to farmers, and supporting the continuation of their contributions, as well as the attainment of the overall purposes of the IU.'[37]

At present, the PGRFA treaty provides the only existing recognition of farmers' rights in a binding instrument.[38] One of the main features of the PGRFA treaty is the focus on the situation of the farmers, their contribution to the conservation of agro-biodiversity and the rights they have over their physical assets, for instance, over seeds or their traditional knowledge. It gives broad guidelines to states concerning the scope of farmers' rights to be protected. The terms that should govern the content and scope of farmers' rights are however devolved to the states themselves. This includes protection of traditional knowledge, farmers' entitlements and benefit sharing arrangements, right to participate in the decision making processes concerning the management of plant genetic resources. However, the treaty is silent over a farmer's right to his plant acres; there is also no mention of property rights. The rights that are recognized are more residual ones like the right to use, exchange, and sell farm-saved seeds. The overall significance of PGRFA treaty, as outlined by Cullet and Koluru, is that this is the first treaty providing a legal framework which not only recognizes the contribution made by the farming community in the conservations and sustainable use of plant genetic resources, but also delineates a regime for access and benefit sharing and this process provides direct and indirect links to intellectual property instruments.[39]

The recognition and the incorporation of the concept of farmers' rights was a culmination of many divergent strands of thought. Most of them have dealt with the right of farmers to control seeds and propagating material they grow and to receive a fair and equitable share of the benefits arising from the commercial use of these genetic resources. Both these strands are based on a recognition that historically plant varieties have been developed and nurtured by farmers, small holders and subsistence

[37] Ibid. Resolution 5/89, Sections a, b and c of the resolution.
[38] Contained in the Preamble and in Article 9 on farmers' rights, and in provisions related to farmers' rights in Article 13 on benefit sharing, and Article 18 on financial resources.
[39] Phillippe Cullet and Radhika Koluru, 2003, 'Plant Variety Protection and Farmers' Rights: Towards a Broader Understanding', *Delhi Law Review*, 24 (2002), p. 4.

farmers playing a major role in developing and enhancing plant variety in consonance with the local environment.[40] However, by and large, farmers' rights have been incorporated as customary rights arising from the practice of farmers during the past ten thousand years to reuse and exchange seeds from their harvests, a point to which I will return later.

Part of the reason for the rather blurred definition has been that the development of farmers' rights has been contentious for a number of reasons. Firstly, farmers' rights have the potential to restrict the freedom of researchers and commercial breeders to use, what till now was freely available to them as, global commons. Secondly, if farmers were to be recognized as intellectual property holders it would directly compete with the IPRs of prospective breeders and restrict the domains available to them. Thirdly, any benefit sharing mechanism would also cut into the profits of the breeders. It was, therefore, only after intense negotiations and passionate support from the global South that farmers' rights were entrenched in the IU in 1991.

Another location of farmers' rights has been sui generis clause of TRIPS [article 27.3(b)]. In developing countries, hesitant to unequivocally grant IPRs over plant varieties, it took the form of a clause on 'farmers' privilege'. The latter allows farmers to re-use propagating material from previous year's harvest and to freely exchange seeds of protected varieties with other farmers.[41] In some developing countries, like India, it led to a formal recognition and institutionalization of farmers' rights. Farmers' privilege was allowed by breeders in the early years of UPOV and were limited to 'plant back rights' (right to save seeds from the harvest to sow in the next season) in varying degrees. In some UPOV member countries, France, for example, limited exemptions were granted to farmers, in others like Greece, these were more generous. Exemptions for farmers were retained till the 1978 version of UPOV. They have been considerably diluted since. After the last amendment in 1991, exemptions for farmers are no longer a matter of course. They have been made optional and are subject to the consent of the breeder.[42] Thus, like farmers' rights, the scope of farmers' privilege too has been left loosely defined and implemented, particularly in the developed countries. However, developing countries,

[40] See for instance, Jose Esquinas-Alcazar, 1996, 'The Realization of Farmer's Right', in *Agrobiodiversity and Farmers' Rights*, M.S. Swaminathan (ed.), New Delhi: Konark.

[41] For details see, Graham Dutfield, 2003, *Intellectual Property Rights and the Life Cycle Industries*, Aldershot: Ashgate, p. 189.

[42] Suman Sahai, 'Farmers' Rights and IPR' (Gene Campaign) Available at http://www.genecampaign.org/We%20stand%20for/Farmers%20rights&IPR.html (last accessed on 11 November 2007).

where traditional agricultural systems thrive, defined the scope of farmers' rights and privilege in more precise terms.

The African Model Legislation for the Protection of the Rights of Local Communities, Farmers and Breeders,[43] and for the regulation of access to biological resources, for instance, is based on the notion that the rights of local communities over their biological resources, knowledges and technologies are a priori rights which take precedence over rights based on private interests. Farmers' rights in this context include the right to the protection of their traditional knowledge relevant to plant and animal genetic resources; to obtain an equitable share of benefits arising from the use of these resources; to participate in making relevant decisions; to use a new breeders' variety protected under this law to develop farmers' varieties, including material obtained from gene banks or plant genetic resource centers; and to collectively save, use, multiply, and process farm-saved seed of protected varieties.

India, one of the first countries in the world to have passed a legislation granting rights to both breeders and farmers, enacted the Protection of Plant Varieties and Farmers' Rights Act, 2001 (PPVFRA), for the protection of farmers rights. The PPVFRA is an example of two ways in which proprietary claims to plant genetic resources may be made, namely PBRs and farmers' rights. According to the PPVFRA, in India 'In order to provide for the establishment of an effective system for protection of plant varieties, the rights of farmers and plant breeders and to encourage the development of new varieties of plants it has been considered necessary to recognize and protect the rights of the farmers in respect of their contribution made at any time in conserving, improving and making available plant genetic resources for the development of the new plant varieties.' India's PPVFRA not only upholds farmers' rights to save, use, and exchange seeds and propagating material but also attempts to enable farmers to claim special forms of IPRs over their varieties.

There is an inherently conflictual relationship implied in these two rights, that is, the breeders' rights and the farmers' rights. Farmers traditionally re-use the seed from their harvests and, therefore, come in direct competition with the breeders who develop plant varieties for commercial interests and then seek legal protection for the exclusive market exploitation of their varieties. Intellectual property regime takes away the traditional and community-centered control over

[43] OAU Model Law, Algeria, 2000—Rights of Communities, Farmers, Breeders'. Available at http://www.wipo.int/tk/en/laws/pdf/oau_modellaw.pdf (last accessed on 25 November 2007).

seed conservation and use, which has been the regular practice of farming communities all over the country. Outside of WTO, civil society organizations, cross-border networks, international treaties, and conventions all perceive a tension between PBRs on the one hand and farmers' rights and biodiversity on the other.[44] There are implications of establishing such a system of multiple rights on the utilization and exchange of genetic resources among various actors. These implications, in a large measure, have to do with the 'legal recourse capacity' of the two rights-bearing groups: the farmers and the corporations, the two groups that are owners of plant genetic resources. It is one thing for a legislation to grant rights and another for these rights to accrue to a community. Legislation does not automatically lead to the acquisition of rights which depends on a whole host of factors which have to do with the relative location of the rights bearer in the social, economic, and legal matrix.

The *McFarling* case is a fairly significant and representative example of the conflictual nature of the two rights and the asymmetrical way in which these rights play out. At the center of the conflict between these two rights are seeds which are literally and symbolically the germ of contention. Control over seeds translates into access and control of rights over both plant varieties and genetic resources. Transforming seed into property has enormous implications for genetic diversity, food security, and farmers' rights. Before the *McFarling* case is outlined, it is important to underscore the significance of seeds for the politics of farmers' and breeders' rights is, at the core, an issue of seed politics.

SEED AS PROPERTY

Whether something can be considered as property, depends on the possession of certain key traits or characteristics or upon being an entity of a particular kind. Traditionally, because seeds were freely reproducible, they defied the necessary criteria of property which are excludability and divisibility. A naturally propagating species was not amenable to be apportioned in the same way that a non-biological object was. There were no finite or boundary conditions, apart from those imposed by nature itself, on its availability. In that sense, it could not be labeled a scarce good, scarcity being a necessary condition for traditional property rights. Some goods like knowledge, water, forests are considered indivisible, because of which they cannot be apportioned and, therefore, are not considered truly

---

[44] See, for instance Gurdial Singh Nijar, 1996, 'In Defence of Local Community knowledge and Biodiversity: A Conceptual Framework and Essential Elements of a Rights Regime', Penang: TWN.

'appropriable' in the sense that house or a car is. Seeds present a similar case. It was not a classic 'commodity' with fixed embodiment. Each seed had the germ of the next. One time use does not prevent further or future use of the seed. It was, therefore, hard to own the seed as property because as a biological organism it carried within it the propensity to reproduce.

Described as the 'embodiment of life's continuity and renewability', the seed has been not only stated to be the source of history but also importantly, the ultimate symbol of food security.[45] The free exchange of seed among farmers has long been considered to be the very basis of maintenance of biodiversity as well as food security. Overall population active in the agricultural sector in least developed countries is 69 per cent and 54 per cent in developing countries, in 2004.[46] The figures would not be significantly altered now. This implies that an overwhelming majority of the rural people, most of who are directly or indirectly associated with agriculture, have strong incentives to sustainably manage their resource base. Seeds are a key component of this resource base. Any attempt to alter management and control of seeds will therefore necessarily impinge upon the livelihood and access rights of farmers.

The issue of seed and seed management assumes critical importance to farming and farmers, for seeds and seed management is vital to farmers' livelihoods. It is they who have traditionally been the backbone of seed management system. In India, 66 per cent to 85 per cent of the seeds, depending on the region and crop that are sown, are saved from the previous crop.[47] Inter-farmer sales of seeds account for 60 per cent of seed requirement of agriculture in India.[48] Added to this is the practice of exchange of seeds among farmers. The significance of seeds to a farmer's livelihood thus cannot be understated. The issue of seeds and control over them thus has huge economic implications for both the farmer and the country's agricultural production. It is vitally linked to farmers' livelihoods and food security. They are, as Jack Kloppenburg puts it, 'both a means

[45] V. Shiva, 2001, *Patents: Myths and Realities,* Delhi: Penguin, p. 69.

[46] UNCTAD, The Least Developed Countries Report 2004, UN Doc UNTACD/LDC/2004 (2004).

[47] C. Niranjan Rao, 21 February 2004, 'Indian Seed System and Plant Variety Protection', *Economic and Political Weekly*, 39(8), pp. 845–52. Percentage of the seed supplied by the seed industry vary widely according to the crop. See also V. Shiva, and Tom Crompton, 1998, 'Monopoly and Monoculture—Trends in Indian Seed Industry', *Economic and Political Weekly*, 33(39), p. 137.

[48] S. Sahai, 1993, 'Indian patents Act and TRIPS', *Economic and Political Weekly*, vol. 28, p. 1495.

of production as well as a product'.[49] The seed thus almost becomes a metaphor for the farmer's rights.

Traditional systems of farming are based on natural cycles of regeneration sustained through seeds. Open-pollinated seeds (that is, seeds other than hybrids), reproduce the traits of their parent seed with high fidelity. So once a farmer has even a small quantity of seed of a particular variety, he can obtain additional seeds simply by growing the crop and harvesting the grain, which is seed for the next planting. The seeds of desirable crop varieties have historically spread quickly from farmer to farmer. The incentive for private companies to invest in developing new plant varieties was limited because open-pollinated seeds are like a public good—once they exist it is difficult to prevent any farmer from using them (making them non-excludable), and because they self-reproduce, their use by one farmer does not compete with their use by another (making them non-rival).

The development of plant biotechnology, DNA-based techniques and their application to plants, has opened new possibilities for seed businesses. Plant biotechnology introduced hybrid genetically engineered seeds which were not self-regenerating, at least not with high fidelity. Hybrids became the primary driver of private investment in the seed business.[50] By creating GE crops with improved production traits that were attractive to farmers, companies built businesses based either on hybrid seeds or on genetically modified (GM) seeds.[51] GM seeds are not public goods because it is possible for companies to exclude farmers from reproducing their seeds by obtaining patent or PBRs over them. Thus the non-excludable and non-rival attributes of the seed got transformed and this provided a way to exercise property rights over seed varieties.

---

[49] Jack Kloppenburg, 1988, *First the Seed: The Political Economy of Plant Biotechnology 1492–2000*, Cambridge: Cambridge University Press, p. xiv.

[50] Hybrids are produced by crossing two distinctly different parental lines. Planting the seed harvested from a hybrid crop typically gives a range of different-looking, different-quality, different-maturity offspring.

[51] GE involves taking a gene from one organism, modifying it in a laboratory, and then inserting it into the target organism's genome to produce new and useful traits or phenotypes. Such GM organisms (GMO) are generally referred to as transgenics. Other methods of producing a GMO include increasing or decreasing the number of copies of a gene already present in the target organism, silencing or removing a particular gene or modifying the position of a gene within the genome. Genetically modified organism (GMO) is used to emphasize the intentional manipulation of genetic code. See, for instance, Matthew Stilwell and Brennan Van Dyke, 1999, *An Activists Handbook on Genetically Modified Organisms and the WTO*, Centre for International Environmental Law, 2nd edition. Available at www.ciel.org/Publications/GMO Handbook Second Edition.pdf (last accessed on 8 December 2009).

Modern biotechnology attempts to remove the biological and natural obstacles in many ways but the end result transforms the seed from a means of production and product into a mere raw material. There is a growing shift from self-regenerative seeds to seeds that are 'finished products', which in some cases means they are essentially 'inert', and non-reproducible. Environmentalist Vandana Shiva argues that these seeds cause ruptures in the natural cycle at two levels:

a) either they do not reproduce themselves or they are not permitted by patent laws to be used freely; from a renewable resource seeds are thus technologically turned into a non-renewable resource.[52]

b) they do not produce by themselves, as they need the help of inputs to produce, 'an external input into the ecological cycle of the reproduction of seed'.[53]

Jack Kloppenburg, in an interview to GRAIN[54] argues that one of the key features that has changed the direction of political economy of plant breeding is 'commodification'. He states 'It's hard to own the seed as property because it's a biological organism that wants to reproduce under all kinds of different circumstances. So industry pursued two routes of commodification—the social route, which has to do with legislation making the seed ownable, and the technological route, which is hybridization.'[55] Through hybridizations seeds were rendered inert and because they had the natural propensity to reproduce they were, as a result, rendered more 'ownable'. Once seeds are rendered 'ownable', scientific inputs into them, albeit based on a gene sequence already available to the researcher from nature, became intellectual property and a subject of IPRs under TRIPS or UPOV. The TRIPS regime provided the framework of a social legislation which would protect seed 'innovation' achieved through hybridization and genetic modification. There is thus a shift from the 'ecological process of reproduction to the technological process of production'.[56] This underlines the problem of ecological erosion and very

[52] Even when the seeds can be saved from a hybrid or a transgenic crop the seeds rendered are unstable and unreliable.

[53] Vandana Shiva, 1991, *Biotechnology, Biodiversity and Profits. Biodiversity: Social and Ecological Perspectives*, Penang: World Rainforest Movement, p. 52

[54] October 2005. GRAIN is a small international non-profit organization that works to support small farmers and social movements in their struggles for community controlled and biodiversity-based food systems.

[55] Interview of Jack Kloppenburg, *Seedling*, October 2005, available at http://www.grain.org/seedling/?id=414 (last accessed on 12 April 2007).

[56] Paul B. Thompson, April 1995, 'Conceptions of Property and the Biotechnology Debate', *Bio Science*, 45(4), p. 275.

importantly, the problem of dispossession of farmers. It is the latter that is the concern of this chapter.

The expansion of the western concept of IPRs has been instrumental in catalyzing the transformation of the ecological process of seed reproduction to a technological process of production. In a world increasingly dominated by trans-national, economic, free-trade conglomerates, the need for new commodities and markets becomes the driving force behind many national and international policy decisions. The market, propelled by the need to constantly grow and evolve new mechanisms to ensure growth, commodifies many aspects of life, rendering traditional life cycles (of both farmers and seeds) vulnerable.

Seed security forms an important dimension of farmers' rights. This chapter presents the *McFarling* cases as a case study and aims to argue that current biotechnology strategies, which are protected by intellectual property laws, should also be assessed in terms of the extent to which they protect or undermine farmers' rights. Farmers' rights here, as outlined earlier, refer to the capacity of the farmer to have control over seeds, the production process, access and knowledge of bio-resources, both of which would have a direct impact on land-productivity and the income of the farmer. This entails recognition of the farmer not just as a cultivator but also as a conserver of the gene pool and a breeder who has several successful varieties.

This chapter also concerns itself with IPRs in plant varieties, which enables seed manufacturers to genetically engineer seeds in order to imbue it with certain enhanced qualities, designed either to improve the nutritional content of the crop variety, its productivity or its resistance to pests, insects, weeds, etc. The focus here will not be to dwell on the success, failure and the ecological sustainability of genetically modified (GM) crops, but on the extent to which they enhance or undermine rights of farmers. The case of *McFarling* v. *Monsanto* has been selected to illustrate the linkages between IPRs in agricultural biotechnology and farmers' rights. The purpose would be to characterize the interests of the two rights bearers, in this case, McFarling, who represents the farmers, and the patent holder, Monsanto, who holds the patent for 'Roundup Ready' Soya, and thus throw some light on a debate that must take place between science and citizens, if biotechnology and the IPRs associated with it, is to align itself with human rights.

The attempt would also be to extend the implications of the *McFarling* cases to the livelihood rights of farmers in the developing parts of the world, for whom IPRs in agricultural resources not only threatens their claims over genetic resources but also their livelihood concerns and the culturally specific ways of negotiating nature and preserving agrogenetic resources. Rights over intellectual resources have little meaning if isolated from the rights of survival, where survival is defined in the larger framework of biological and ecological security within a highly diverse natural environment for the people concerned. Intellectual property law in agriculture is politically and socially significant because it represents an arena where the relation between nature, ecology, and culture are negotiated.

HOMAN MCFARLING V. MONSANTO COMPANY
Outline of the Case

Roundup-Ready soybean is based on a genetic modification developed by Monsanto, (a US based bio-technology corporation), which allows soybean plants to resist the broad-leaf herbicide. Monsanto developed a system for weed control that employs genetically modified crops that resist glyphosate herbicide. Upon planting such crops, farmers can spray glyphosate herbicide on their fields to kill weeds while sparing the resistant crops, a technique that allows for much more efficient weed control than is possible with unmodified plants. Monsanto sells the glyphosate herbicide under the trade name Roundup and sells seeds of the genetically modified soybeans under the trade name Roundup Ready.

Two patents, of importance here, protect aspects of Monsanto's Roundup Ready technology. First, Monsanto's US Patent No. 5,633,435 (the 435 patent) claims a patent for seed containing a DNA molecule that encodes a genetically modified enzyme that allows plants to survive exposure to glyphosate herbicide. Second, Monsanto's U.S. Patent No. 5,352,605 (the 605 patent) claims a plant cell containing a genetic promoter sequence that facilitates a plant's production of the modified enzyme.[57]

Monsanto distributes the patented seeds by authorizing various companies to produce the seeds and sell them to farmers. It required those seed companies to obtain a signed Technology Agreement from purchasers. Monsanto licenses its proprietary Roundup Ready technology through two interrelated licensing schemes. First, it licenses the patented gene to seed companies that manufacture the glyphosate-tolerant seeds that are sold to farmers. Under this license, seed companies gain the right to insert the genetic trait into the germplasm of their own seeds (which can differ from one seed company to another), and Monsanto

---

[57] United States Court of Appeals for the Federal Circuit, 05-1570, 1598. *Homan McFarling* v. *Monsanto Company.*

receives the right to a royalty or 'technology fee' of US 6.50 dollars
for every 50-pound bag of seed containing the Roundup Ready sold by
the seed company. Monsanto also owns several subsidiary seed companies
that comprise approximately 20 per cent of the market for Roundup
Ready soybeans.[58]

Second, Monsanto requires that seed companies execute licenses,
rather than conduct unconditional sales, with their farmer customers. It
required those seed companies to obtain a signed technology agreement
from purchasers. The 1998 version of this 'Monsanto Technology Agreement' between Monsanto and the soybean farmers using Roundup
Ready soybeans places several conditions on the soybean farmers' use of
the licensed soybeans. In exchange for the 'opportunity to purchase and
plant seed containing' the Roundup Ready technology, soybean farmers
agree, inter alia:

1.   To use the seed containing Monsanto gene technologies for planting
     a commercial crop only in a single season.
2.   To not supply any of this seed to any other person or entity for
     planting, and to not save any crop produced from this seed for
     replanting, or supply saved seed to anyone for replanting.
3.   To not use this seed or provide it to anyone for crop breeding, research,
     generation of herbicide registration data or seed production.[59]

Of special relevance here is that the farmers promised not to replant
seeds that were produced from the purchased seeds or to supply those
seeds to others for replanting. Those promises ensure that a farmer who
uses Roundup Ready seeds buys the seeds that he plants each year. The
technology agreement also contains a clause specifying damages in the
event of breach by the farmer: In the event that the grower saves, supplies,
sells or acquires seed for replant in violation of this Agreement and license
restriction, in addition to other remedies available to the technology
provider(s), the grower agrees that damages will include a claim for
liquidated damages, which will be based on 120 times the applicable
technology fee.[60]

In 1998, Homan McFarling purchased bought 1,000 bags of the
Roundup Ready soybean seeds from a seed company. He signed the

    [58] Lisa Sternoff Feldman, Spring/Summer 2004, 'Sow Complicated: *Monsanto Co.* v.
Homan McFarling'. *CASRIP Newsletter, Current Developments,* United States.
    [59] Monsanto Technology Agreement. Available at http://www.mindfully.org/GE/
Monsanto-Technology-Agreement-1998.htm (last accessed 21 November 2007).
    [60] Ibid.

technology agreement for that year and paid the required fees. When the farming season concluded, he evaluated his yield and saved 1,500 bushels of seed from his crop, enough to plant 1,500 acres. These included a genetically modified seed developed by Monsanto. He replanted these seeds in 1999. He then saved 2,075 bags from the next crop and replanted in 2000.[61] This was in violation of the license agreement—he saved seeds both from his 1998 soybean crop from his 1999 crop and planting them in 1999 and 2000 respectively. The saved seeds contained the patented genetic traits, but McFarling did not pay the license fee for the 1999 or 2000 growing seasons.

Monsanto v. McFarling in the District Court

The second generation seeds, grown by McFarling were genetically identical to the ones originally purchased and thus fell under the scope of the patents. Monsanto brought suit against McFarling after the farmer violated his agreement and saved second generation soybean seeds to replant his 5,000 acre farm. Monsanto argued that it had not sold the seed to McFarling but instead had only granted him a 'limited use license' to use the seed for one generation.[62]

The United States District Court for the Eastern District of Missouri ruled, in November 2002, against defendant Homan McFarling and in favour of Monsanto under Federal Rule of Civil Procedure 54(b). The courts found that McFarling's actions breached the license.[63] The district court held that, when McFarling replanted some of Monsanto's patented Roundup Ready soybeans that he had saved from his prior year's crop, McFarling breached the Technology Agreement that he had signed as a condition of his purchase of the patented seeds. The District Court ruled that McFarling violated a Monsanto-held seed patent and ordered him to pay the company, through a 120 multiplier in the liquidated damages provision of the Technology Agreement, US 7,80,000 dollars in damages, given his admission that he saved seeds after harvesting crops grown from Monsanto's patented Roundup Ready soybean seed.[64]

[61] Lisa Sternoff Feldman, 2004, 'Sow Complicated: *Monsanto Co. v. Homan McFarling*', Section IIB, *CASRIP Newsletter: Current Developments*, United States.

[62] *Monsanto Co. v. McFarling*, No. 4:00CV84 CDP (ED Mo 15 November 2002) (granting final judgment); (ED Mo 15 November 2002).

[63] Ibid.

[64] Monsanto sued to collect 120 times the actual amount of claimed damages, a total of 780,000 dollars. *Monsanto v. US Farmers.* A report by Center for Food Safety (CFS), 2004, pp. 47–8.

The Monsanto Co. v. Homan McFarling CAFC

McFarling brought his case to the Federal Circuit Court of Appeals (CAFC). Monsanto also moved in the district court for a judgment on some but not all of the pending claims—namely, the breach of contract claim, the claim of infringement of the '605 patent, and all of McFarling's counterclaims.[65] McFarling argued that the District Court's judgment on the breach-of-contract claim was erroneous on the following issues: (1) His patent-misuse defense: whether a patent holder could 'lawfully prohibit farmers from saving and replanting seeds as a condition to the purchase of patented technology?' (2) His antitrust counterclaim: 'Does obtaining patents on products which are subjects of licensing agreements, afford an absolute defense to any claim that the licensing agreement violates the Sherman Act?'[66] (3) His defense under the PVP Act invoking farmer's privilege, and (4) his defense that the 120 multiplier in the liquidated damages provision of the Technology Agreement is a penalty clause that is unenforceable under Missouri law.[67]

McFarling asserted that Monsanto's license impermissibly restricted the use of farmer-grown Roundup Ready soybean seeds. He also argued that Monsanto had committed patent misuse because Monsanto had impermissibly tied an unpatented product to a patented product. In McFarling's words, 'by prohibiting seed-saving, Monsanto has extended its patent on the gene technology to include an unpatented product—the germplasm—or God-made soybean seed which is not within the terms of the patent.' McFarling argued that he should be granted a compulsory license to use the patent rights in conjunction with the second-generation Roundup ready soybeans in his possession after harvest. 'We decline to hold that Monsanto's raw exercise of its right to exclude from the patented invention by itself is a "tying" arrangement that exceeds the scope of the patent grant'. What was fundamentally objectionable to McFarling was that the license controlled what McFarling could do with second-generation seeds—the seeds that McFarling 'made' using the seeds that he acquired under a strict license. McFarling argued that the prohibition in

---

[65] McFarling's petition for Writ of Certiorari to the US Court of Appeals for the Federal Circuit. *Monsanto Co. v. McFarling*, 03-1177 Fed. Cir. 9 April 2004.

[66] The Sherman Antitrust Act (Sherman Act, 2 July 1890, Ch. 647, 26 Stat. 209, 15 USC S. 1–7), was the first United States government action to limit cartels and monopolies. It is the oldest of all federal US antitrust laws.

[67] Refer to Mc Farling's petition. *Mosanto Co. v McFarling*, 03-1177 (Fed. Cir. 9 April 2004), Section IV and V.

the Technology Agreement on 'saving any crop produced from this seed for replanting' constitutes patent misuse.[68]

The CAFC rejected McFarling's petition and affirmed the district court's judgment in favor of Monsanto, upholding the validity of the technology agreement, which does not impose a restriction on the use of the product purchased under license but rather imposes a restriction on the use of the goods made by the licensed product. The Court of Appeals also rejected McFarling's counterclaims and defenses, including his patent-misuse defense, antitrust counterclaim, and defense under the PVP Act. 'We rejected that defense because the licensed and patented product (the first generation seeds) and the good made by the licensed product (the second-generation seeds) are nearly identical copies...given that the 435 patent reads on the first generation seeds, it also reads on the second-generation seeds'.

However, the court vacated the district court's judgment on liquidated damages and remanded for the district court to determine actual damages. On 9 April 2004, the Court set a major precedent when a federal Appellate Judge determined the 120 multiplier in the technology agreement to be unenforceable.[69] McFarling would no longer have to pay Monsanto the calculated amount of 7,80,000 dollars and would likely end up paying a significantly lower sum.[70] The Court held 7,80,000.00 dollars is grossly disproportionate to the loss that Monsanto actually suffered in loss of technology fees due to McFarling's replanting of saved seeds. Under Missouri law, however, the liquidated damages provision was not a reasonable forecast, and thus unenforceable as a penalty.[71] These damages ruled the court, 'is inimical to the compensatory nature of contract remedies: it sounds in deterrence, not compensation, and therefore suggests that the multiplier is in the nature of a penalty clause rather than a liquidated damages clause' (App. 136a). The CAFC then remanded to the district court for a determination of actual damages (App. 137a).[72]

The district court submitted the issue of damages to the jury. The jury returned a damages verdict of 40 dollars per bag[73] of saved seed, well

---

[68] Ibid.

[69] Summary Judgment, CFAC, 9 April 2004, *McFarling v. Mosanto Co.*, 363 F.3d 1336 (Fed. Cir. 2004).

[70] Robert Schubert, 2004, *Mississippi Farmer Gets Big Break From Appeals Court in Monsanto Biotech Seed Case, Crop Choice.*

[71] Summary Judgment, CAFC, 9 April 2004, *McFarling v. Mosanto Co.*, 363 F.3d 1336 (Fed. Cir. 2004).

[72] Ibid.

[73] Ibid.

in excess of the 6.50 dollars per bag for which Homan McFarling had argued, but substantially less than the 80.65 dollars per bag (for 1999) and 73.20 dollars per bag (for 2000) urged by Monsanto based on the analysis of its expert. Mr McFarling again moved to limit the damages award to what he contended was Monsanto's 6.50 dollars per bag established royalty for use of its patented technology. The district court denied the motion, adopted the jury's verdict, and awarded Monsanto approximately 3,75,000 dollars in damages. The district court also permanently enjoined Homan McFarling from future unauthorized use of the patented technology. McFarling argued that the damages should have been limited to the 'established royalty' for Roundup Ready seeds, *that is*, the Technology Fee of US 6.50 dollars per bag that Monsanto charged licensees who purchased Roundup Ready seeds under its Technology Agreement.[74]

Furthermore, the court noted that infringement damages could properly include (a) any harm felt by Monsanto as a result of the infringement, as well as (b) any additional benefits gained by McFarling. This included harm to Monsanto's reputation as a result of rogue planters, potential lapses in Monsanto's database of planting techniques, McFarling's increase in yield of 31–61 dollars per acre, as well as bargaining power. This decision by the CAFC changed the way patent infringement damages could be calculated and potentially make allowable damages significantly larger.

Writ of Certiorari in *Monsanto* v. *McFarling*

McFarling petitioned the Supreme Court for a Writ of Certiorari challenging the amount of the damages award.[75] He argued that the these damages were not based on procedures of 'established royalty' but on 'hypothetical royalty' on grounds that it was impossible to justify 40 dollars/bag damages through the 'established royalty'[76]. The 'established royalty method' could justify a royalty of up to 28.50 dollars per bag (the 6.50 dollars Technology Fee plus a 22 dollars Seed Company Fee). His contention was that 'The Federal Circuit has rewritten the patent-damages statute to provide patent owners with a remedy that far

---

[74] By statute, damages for patent infringement are to be 'adequate to compensate for the infringement, but in no event less than a reasonable royalty for the use made of the invention by the infringer, together with interest and costs as fixed by the court.' 35 USC Section 284.

[75] Petition for a Writ of Certiorari to the United States Court of Appeals for the Federal Circuit. Available at http://www.patentlyo.com/patent/McFarlingPetition.pdf (last accessed on 26 January 2008).

[76] Ibid. Clause IA, p. 11.

exceeds the amount "adequate to compensate for the infringement".[77] McFarling's argument was that patent damages are not intended to deter infringement—merely to compensate for it. The Supreme Court upheld the quantum of the damages: 'We therefore uphold the trial court's judgment as to the quantum of damages'. However, they made a concession by ruling that 'McFarling may plant Roundup Ready soybeans acquired from any lawful dealer, but to do so McFarling must sign any applicable technology agreement required by Monsanto.'[78]

What makes the McFarling case significant from an intellectual property perspective is not what the court focused on, but rather what they upheld. The McFarling judgment clearly explicates that transgenic varieties would enjoy patent protection, because a patented gene or a patented gene sequence has been added to them. The farmer's privilege,[79] and the breeder's exception could not apply under these circumstances. Consequently, breeders who used genetic engineering would have an advantage over those who used traditional methods of plant selection, because the latter can rely only on the PBR Act to protect their varieties.[80] In the ultimate analysis, what were upheld were the patent rights of a breeder and what was displaced was the right of a farmer to save and reuse seeds that he made/developed, conventionally akin to a natural right.

THE MCFARLING CASE AND FARMERS' RIGHTS

Monsanto is one of the few patentees that sues individuals for patent infringement. The infringers are individual farmers who allegedly save and replant Monsanto's patented genetically modified seeds violation of their Technology Agreement. In another high profile case, *Monsanto Co.* v. *Percy Schmeiser*[81] (1998), the Federal Court and the Federal Court of Appeal of Canada upheld the rights of Monsanto Co. to protect its patented GE seeds. The court ruled Saskatchewan farmer Percy Schmeiser infringed upon Monsanto's rights when he planted the company's

[77] Ibid.

[78] The SC judgment no. 04–31. Available at http://www.usdoj.gov/atr/cases/f209268. pdf (last accessed on 8 December 2009).

[79] Farmers' privilege finds an explicit mention in 11 countries. See Policy Brief: 'Lessons from a Cross Country Perspective'. Box 1. Available at http://www.ncap.res.in/ upload_files/policy_brief/pb11.pdf (last accessed on 25 November 2007).

[80] PBR is a weaker version of patents. PBR has incorporated the notion of 'farmers' privilege' which basically allows farmers to save seeds (different efficacy in different countries). Patents do not permit seed saving without payment of license fee.

[81] *Percy Schmeiser* v. *Monsanto Co.*, A-367–01 (T-1593-98) Federal Court of Appeal (On Appeal from the Federal Court-Trial Division). Available at http://www.percyschmeiser. com/Appellants'%20memorandum.pdf (last accessed on 8 December 2009).

patented herbicide resistant canola seeds without the company's permission. Schmeiser, however, contended that the seeds landed on his farm by accident (blew over from a neighboring farm resulting in cross pollination). Under Canadian patent law, as in the US and many other industrialized countries, it is illegal for farmers to re-use patented seed, or to grow Monsanto's GE seed without signing a licensing agreement. In *Monsanto Canada Inc.* v. *Schmeiser*, the Supreme Court held in a majority five-to-four decision that even though plants may not be patented in Canada, a patent relating to a plant cell or a modified gene in a cell gives its holder the right to decide what others may do with the plant in question, since each plant cell contains the modified gene.

The ruling against Schmeiser establishes an even more dangerous precedent because it means that farmers can be forced to pay royalties on GE seeds found on their land, even if they didn't buy the seeds or benefit from them. Schmeiser and his supporters, a coalition of consumers, environmentalists and farmers called the court ruling a huge setback. The National Farmers Union said it violates the long-standing right of farmers to harvest and develop their own seeds and effectively hands control of Canada's farms to giant multinationals.[82]

The case involving the 73 year old Percy Schmeiser became a rallying point for critics of genetically modified plants. While Canadian court decisions have no direct bearing on American law, or national PVPs of various countries, Andrew Kimbrell, executive director of the Center for Food Safety in Washington, said that the Canadian judgment could nonetheless have an impact on similar claims by Monsanto against farmers the world over. Almost 100 such cases have so far gone to trial in the United States, and farmers have paid penalties averaging 100,000 dollars each to Monsanto.[83] The Schmeiser case touched upon a long-standing issue that is not resolved globally: can technological manipulations of genetic composition of plants—a biological, naturally propagating species —be claimed as man-made innovation?

In the *McFarling* case, what eventually became the central issue of contestation was the quantum of damages. However, it points to a larger issue: the farmers' right to save seeds. Throughout the proceedings of the

[82] 'Monsanto vs. Percy Schmeiser: No Corporate Liability for Unsafe Sex and Bioserfdom'. RAFI. Available at http://www.cropchoice.com/leadstry2732.html?recid=283 (last accessed on 8 December 2009).

[83] Bernad Simon, 22 May 2004, 'Monsanto Wins Patent Case on Plant Genes', *New York Times*. Available at http://query.nytimes.com/gst/fullpage.html?res=9A01E5DA1F3F F931A15756C0A9629C8B63 (last accessed on 31 October 2007).

case, McFarling contended that the patent laws did not allow Monsanto to control the future use of seeds that were a natural product of the seeds that he had bought and planted. He argued that the technology agreement involved an unlawful misuse of Monsanto's patents by restricting use of 'god-made' second-generation seeds. The licensing agreement and the technology agreement jointly benefit Monsanto and the Soybean seed companies. This profit accrues to Monsanto and the seed companies year after year since the agreement prohibits the farmer from using his saved seeds. The scale of profits that accrue to Monsanto, and the part played by Roundup ready in those profits, is clear by the following report: 'Monsanto has grown to a massive company with over 4.5 billion dollars in sales in 2002 alone. Of these sales, 40 per cent came from Roundup and other glyphosate products and 34 per cent from seed and genomics'.[84] Profit that accrue to a company like Monsanto are part due to the license and technology fee that they receive from Roundup Ready and part also due to an increased use of the herbicide, glyphosate, which it manufactures.[85] The US Department of Agriculture statistics from 1997 show that expanded plantings of Roundup Ready soybeans have resulted in a 72 per cent increase in the use of glyphosate.[86]

IPRs in plant varieties reveal how the economic interests of the technology holders often take precedence over protecting the rights of the farmers. Rights and their regulatory frameworks are always vulnerable to being framed in terms of the knowledges and life-worlds of the contextually powerful. Contextual power resides in a particular science and its products. Thus seeds which have been reared by the farmer become a 'non-claimant' of protection as IP, than the seed that has been genetically engineered. The latter become the subject of not only intellectual property protection, through patents and plant breeders' rights, but also through private contractual and licensing agreements, clearly reflecting and buttressing the asymmetrical and non-consensual terms embedded in IPRs in plant varieties and biotechnological innovations.

[84] Monsanto Report, 'Selling Food Health Hope: the real story behind Monsanto Corporation', (MASIPAG, RESIST and PRESSURE POINT, June 2003.) Available at http://www.masipag.org/monsanto%20report.pdf (last accessed on 29 November 2007).

[85] Monsanto has major chemical manufacturing facilities in Argentina, Belgium, Brazil, and the US, and land parcels, manufacturing and agricultural facilities in Africa, Asia, Australia, Europe, North America, and South America. Ibid.

[86] 'Fields of Dream: Gene-tech Goes South', Seedling (September 1998). Available at http://www.grain.org/seedling/?id=120 (last accessed on 25 April 2007).

A significant development, which played a decisive role in determining the onus of liability, has been the pre-eminence of private contractual agreements which often run counter to the Plant Variety Protection Act of the United States specifically states that, it 'shall not infringe any right here under for a person to save seed produced by the person from seed obtained, or descended from seed obtained, by authority of the owner of the variety for seeding purposes and use such saved seed in the production of a crop for use on the farm of the person, or for sale as provided in this section.'[87] However this comes in direct clash with the technology agreements which the farmers voluntarily sign. The use of contracts to privately legislate control over goods that embody intellectual property often run counter to some publicly legislated grant of rights.

In a study done on plant variety rights in Australia it was reported that many farmers complained that PBR has facilitated the use of 'closed-loop contracts', where a farmer buys seed from an agribusiness company and is contractually obliged to sell the entire harvest back to that company. These contracts are often unwelcome to farmers, in that they feel that their autonomy is being restricted. The farmer becomes like an employee locked into a contract that may punish him for relatively minor infractions like having a few weeds in the field. Closed loop contracts can and do exist in the absence of PBR, but they are easier to enforce when the variety in question is PBR/patent protected.[88] Technology agreements, licenses, closed loop contracts, etc., are examples of privately legislated contracts used to augment public legislation by clarifying what restrictions are being placed on the intellectual asset. Licenses may also be used to circumvent public legislation by restricting the downstream use of a good, in a manner not commensurate with the scope of the patent. In either case, these forms of private legislation tilt the balance between the rights of owners and the rights of users towards owners by augmenting owners' rights, restricting users' rights.[89]

There is increasing recognition that the contribution of farmers to the conservation and development of plant genetic resources cannot be fully acknowledged and preserved through 'exceptions' to patents or plant variety protection. Private licensing and contractual agreements in any case plug these 'privileges' and 'exceptions'. Indeed, many believe that

[87] USC section 2543 (2000).

[88] Alexandra Andrew, and Frank Vanclay, 2004, 'Innovation, Exclusion and Commodification of Plant Types: A Social and Philosophical Investigation of Plant Types', *Rural Society (Aust.)*, 14(1), 46–56.

[89] Ibid.

referring to the traditional activities of farmers as a privilege, exception or exemption, is illustrative of the totally residuary and dispensable character that they come to be imbued with. Stripped to their bare minimum, when rights are clothed as privileges they are divested of the agency so vital for the realization of a right.

LIVELIHOOD DIMENSIONS OF ACCESS TO SEEDS

Recent controversies surrounding use of transgenic technology reveal that the issues that have acquired centrality are chiefly two: first, ecological and food safety; and second, socio-economic concerns relating to increased dependence on novel technologies that may be controlled by external actors. In the global North, some of the main debates have revolved around issues of environmental impacts and food safety. In the global South, these aspects are raised in conjunction with the socio-economic impact of transgenic technology in a society where majority of the population is engaged in agriculture. In the global North, the farmers as stakeholders are numerically much smaller than their counterparts in the South. Therefore, any talk of farmers' rights acquires a far greater potency when the reference is made to the farmers in the developing world.

The seed is one piece of the agricultural puzzle but a particularly powerful and a symbolic one. It produces not only new life forms but new forms of life as well.[90] For the breeder who engineers seed varieties it means economic control of present and future resources; for the poor farmer the very right to livelihood and subsistence. It is important to bear in mind the socio-economic profile of the farmers in developing countries like India, Asia, and Africa. The farm sizes are small; the bulk of the farmers, poor and marginal; and the nature of agriculture in large pockets, subsistence. In the two most populous countries of the world, namely, China and India, where more than one third of the world's population lives, the small holders account for more than 50 per cent of the farm households. In the Sub-Saharan Africa, small-holder population constitutes nearly 75 per cent of the rural population.[91] Two significant developments of plant variety protection (PVP) in developing countries has been the rising cost of protected seeds and loss of biologically diverse

[90] Sheila Jasanoff, 2005, 'Let them eat Cake: GM foods and the Democratic Imagination', in *Science and Citizens: Globalization and the Challenge of Engagement*, Melissa Leach, Ian Scoones, and Brian Wynne (eds), *Science*, London: Zed Books, p. 183.

[91] Ramesh C. Agrawal, 2000, *Perspectives for Small Farmers in Developing Countries: Do They have a Future?* Berlin: Centre for Advanced Training in Agricultural & Rural Development, Humboldt University.

solutions to seed and agricultural practices. These become crucial factors in restricting livelihood security of farmers.

Seed costs are central to the issue of revenue and livelihood for farmers. For instance, in the case of Bt cotton in India, the patent rights were exclusively held by the US-based Monsanto. From 2002 till 2005 the Monsanto varieties were the only approved varieties in India. In the absence of competition and allowance by breeders' rights, Monsanto used its power to fix the seed prices and royalty. In 2005, Bt cotton seed was sold in India Rs 1,650 per bag as against Rs 400 to Rs 450 per bag in the case of the usual hybrid seeds.[92] Of this price, Rs 1200 per bag is said to be the licence fee for the patent holder, Monsanto.[93] In other countries the seed cost of Bt cotton per hectare is 14 dollars (Rs 620), 32 dollars (Rs 1,380), and 58 dollars (Rs 2,500) in South Africa, China and Mexico respectively. However, it is 103 dollars (Rs 4,430), and Rs 4,625 in Argentina and India respectively.[94] G.V. Ramanjanyulu of Center for Sustainable Agriculture (CSA) argues that, 'In a few years, the seed firms have established a near monopoly and reduced the state to a party that fights a losing battle to lower the cost of Bt seeds, even make cotton seeds available. Imagine if this were the case with every crop'.

Given the higher Bt cotton seed prices a natural tendency of farmers would have been to switch to local non-Bt varieties. However, inputs dealers in Vidarbha (one of the poorest districts in Maharashtra, India) say that there is hardly any non-Bt hybrid variety available in the market this year (2007).[95] There are clearly mechanisms that ensure the non-availability and the gradual displacement of land varieties. Poor peasants of the global South cannot survive seed monopolies. The seed prices can push poor farmers into a debt trap leading to farmers suicides which has acquired worrying dimensions in parts on India, specifically in the cotton-growing belts of Maharashtra and Andhra Pradesh.

Bt cotton has been under scrutiny as far as debt traps leading to farmer suicides are concerned. In a study conducted by Tata Institute of Social Sciences (TISS), investigating causes of farmer suicides in Maharashtra

[92] Normally you have quoted the US price. Please do the same here also along with INR.

[93] Aniket Alam, 24 May, 6 June 2003, 'The Andhra Pradesh Experience', *Frontline*, 20(11).

[94] Aldas Janaiah, 'Why a Re-think on GM Crops is Needed', *Hindu Business Line*, 12 April 2006.

[95] See, Jaideep Hardikar, 'India Together', 2 July 2007. Available at http://www.indiatogether.org/2007/jul/agr-btvidarb.htm (last accessed on 30 September 2007). Also see P. Sainath, 'Farm Suicides in India, The Result of Profit Driven "Free Market" Reforms', *The Hindu*, 7 April 2007.

few central conclusions are significant. In Maharashtra the total numbers of suicides reported in Maharashtra, till December 2004, were 644, with most of the deaths occurring in the Vidharbha, Marathwada, and Khandesh regions of the state. Seventy per cent of the cultivators grew cotton as their primary cash crop.[96] The government of Maharashtra admitted to 1,447 farm suicides in 2006 alone and 350 farm suicides in first four months of 2007. These figures pertain only to six districts of the Vidharbha region—Just these six districts saw far more suicides in 2006 than the whole State did in 1995.[97] It is instructive to know that Vidarbha witnessed an almost 100 per cent Bt cotton season in 2007, a 60 per cent season in 2006.

In regions where income levels of farmers are precariously balanced and severely contingent on rainfall, any exposure to further risk is literally suicidal. High input costs are exactly that, Vidarbha Jan Andolan Samiti (VJAS) has been demanding complete ban on Bt. Cotton in west Vidarbha as now it is official that Bt Cotton has failed in rain-fed areas. Ninety-seven per cent of cotton grown in Maharashtra is unirrigated.[98] A new study has shown that the government's introduction of Bt cotton in Vidarbha, a rain-fed area, has added to farmers' debts in an area that already has a history of indebtedness. Seventy per cent of small farmers have already lost their landholdings as collateral for loans they can never repay.[99] The State government's own report informs us that in preceding seasons too, 'in rain-fed conditions, Bt cotton has not paid good returns.'

Eighty-three per cent of Andhra Pradesh, India, farmers (highest among all States) were in debt according to the report of the National Sample Survey Organisation (NSSO) based on farm household surveys (2003).[100] These figures are indicative of how high the risks are,

[96] 'Causes of Farmers' Suicides in Maharashtra: An Enquiry', Final Report submitted to the Mumbai High Court. 15 March 2005 by Tata Institute of Social Sciences. Available at http://www.tiss.edu/Causes%20of%20Farmer%20Suicides%20in%20Maharashtra.pdf (last accessed on 14 September 2007).

[97] P. Sainath, 7 April 2007, 'Farm Suicides in India, The Result of Profit Driven "Free Market" Reforms', *The Hindu*.

[98] Ibid.

[99] 'Bt Cotton Increased Farmers' Indebtedness in Vidarbha', Research study, Gene Campaign. Available online at http://www.infochangeindia.org/AgricultureItop.jsp?section_idv=10 (last accessed on 27 January 2007).

[100] National Sample Survey Organisation's 'Situation Assessment Survey of Farmers'. Available at http://www.mospi.gov.in/mospi-nsso-rept_pubn.htm (last accessed on 30 September 2009). Also see Devinder Sharma, 'Farm Incomes And Costs: Returns from Farming'. Available at http://www.foodpolicy.in/html/incomes/incomes.htm (last accessed on 30 September 2009).

especially for small farmers. While there is not one exact reason for the
suicides, mounting debt due to increased input costs of GM crops like
Bt cotton, low procurement prices, crop failure is seen as a primary
cause.[101] Given the higher Bt cotton seed prices a natural tendency of
farmers would have been to switch to local non-Bt varieties. However,
in 2007, inputs dealers in Vidarbha stated that there was hardly any non-
Bt hybrid variety available in the market. Seed dealers interviewed by a
news journalist stated: 'We get good margins on Bt from the companies.
Also, the companies haven't marketed hybrids this time around.' One
dealer frankly admitted, 'We are not keeping non-Bt seed, for it has no
future.'[102]

In two years of planting in Indonesia, Bt cotton increased pesticide
use and left farmers in a spiral of debt.[103] The government revealed that
more than 70 per cent of the Bt crop locations did not produce the
promised expected yields.[104] In a recent study of 481 cotton farmers in
five provinces of China, researchers from Cornell University found that
the early income gains that Chinese cotton farmers had achieved with Bt
cotton during the 2000–2001 season had completely disappeared three
years later.[105] In Makhatini, South Africa, often cited as the showcase Bt
cotton project for small farmers, 1,00,000 hectares were planted with Bt
cotton at the start of the project in 1998. By 2002, that had crashed to
22,500 hectares, an 80 per cent reduction in four years. By 2004, 85 per
cent of farmers who used to grow the crop had given up. The farmers
found pest problems and no increase in yield. Those farmers who still
grow the crop do so at a loss, continuing only because the South African

[101] See, 'Causes of Farmer Suicides in Maharashtra: An Enquiry'. Final Report
Submitted to the Mumbai High Court. 15 March 2005. Tata Institute of Social Sciences,
p. 21–4; Available at http://www.tiss.edu/Causes%20of%20Farmer%20Suicides%20in%20
Maharashtra.pdf. Also see Somini Sengupta, 'On India's Farms, a Plague of Suicide', *New
York Times*, 19 September 2006.
    [102] Jaideep Hardikar, 'India Together', 2 July 2007. Available at http://www.indiatogether.
org/2007/jul/agr-Btvidarb.htm. Also see, P. Sainath, 'Farm Suicides in India, The Result of
Profit Driven "Free Market" Reforms', *The Hindu*, 7 April 2007.
    [103] 'FAO declares war on farmers, not on hunger', *GRAIN*, 16 June 2004.
    [104] Friends of Earth International. Available at http://www.foei.org/en/publications/
link/gmo/40.html (last accessed on 26 January 2008). For testimonies and more details see
the web site of the Organic Consumers Association www.organicconsumers.org/ gefood/
IndonesiaCotton.cfm (last accessed on 11 July 2007).
    [105] Wang Shenghui, David R. Just, and Per Pinstrup-Andersen, 'Tarnishing Silver
Bullets: Bt Technology Adoption, Bounded Rationality and the Outbreak of Secondary
Pest Infestations in China', Selected Paper prepared for presentation at the *American
Agricultural Economics Association Annual Meeting* Long Beach, CA, 22–6 July 2006.

government subsidizes the project and there's a guaranteed market for the cotton.[106]

In general, IPRs in agriculture facilitate control over seeds and related knowledge by agri-business at the expense of especially small and subsistence farmers. In developing countries breeders' rights may not restrict a farmer's ability to save and replant seeds.[107] However there are limiting factors to the realization of the farmers' rights and institutionalization of farmers' rights may not always protect the farmer. In India, the same act grants both farmers' and breeders' rights, each having multiple claims over separate plant varieties.[108] This creates a number of possibilities in terms of negotiations that may be required for creating the product. It could pose problems of overlapping claims and result in complicated bargaining requirements for utilization of varieties.[109] It is often here that the lag between the rights available to the farmer and the ones accessed by him occurs. The terms of bargaining themselves are likely to be asymmetrical given knowledge about and access to legal measures that a common farmer has. For instance, the India Plant Variety Act does provide legal protection to the farmers within the narrow confines of a sui generis systems permitted by article 27.3b of the TRIPS agreement. However, it only deals with plant variety management from the point of view of its commercialization and fails to take into account the fact that commercial activity cannot be separated, either legally or in practice, from conservation of agricultural biodiversity and associated rights of the

[106] Elfrieda Pschorn-Strauss, 'Bt Cotton in South Africa: The Case of the Makhathini Farmers', *Seedling*, GRAIN. April 2005. Available at http://www.grain.org/seedling/?id=330 (last accessed on 10 November 2007).

[107] The Protection of Plant Varieties and FRs Act (PPVFRA) 2001 is an example of two ways in which proprietary claims to plant genetic resources may be made, Plant Breeders' Rights (PBRs) and FRs (FRs). The combining of the two rights has largely been governed by primarily two strands of thinking: (1) the recognition that farmers' traditional ways of farming, managing, and securing agricultural resources and biodiversity ought to be protected. There is also the understanding that FRs are crucial not just for the livelihoods of the millions who are dependent on agriculture but for the benefit of agricultural and food security. (2) A focus on ensuring access to technology and promoting economic development. Both these get reflected in the legislation in India governing PVP and FRs. Thus, India did establish IPR laws to protect the rights of innovators, but attempted to balance this with the need for access to resources.

[108] India's Act allows four types of varieties to be registered reflecting the interests of actors: New Variety, Extant Variety, Essentially Derived Variety, and Farmers' Variety. PVPFRA, 2001, Section 2.

[109] For details of the argument see, Anitha Ramanna, 'India's Plant and Farmers' Rights Legislation: Potential Impact on Stakeholder access to Genetic Resources', *EPTD Discussion Paper* No. 96, Washington, 2003.

farmers.[110] In developing countries of the global South, infringement of farmers' rights may only be an indirect consequence of a system that does not promote the realization of farmers' rights. It is the contention of this chapter that farmers' rights have been conceived and instituted more as a counter to breeder' rights and less as developmental rights designed to protect and enhance the domain of their rights to livelihood, food security, access to resources, etc.

The farmer continues to remain located outside the legal framework which has apparently been instituted for him. Law becomes the key location for conflicts because it provides groups with symbolic resources for framing of rights, and groups struggle within the field of law to gain control over law's normative and instrumental benefits. Engagement with law can influence a group's institutional architecture, discourse, and strategies. However, this engagement presumes the capacity of the right bearer to engage with law. Ownership rights are meaningless for a community of farmers whose engagement with law is severely constrained because of a whole host of factors like absence of functional literacy or legal literacy, awareness of bureaucratic/legal procedures, financial resources to name a few. Secondly, when two competing rights manoeuver for space within the same framework, the rights-holder is lowered down in the socio-economic matrix loses out, lending an implicit hierarchy to the domain of laws in general and plant variety rights in particular.

In developing countries like India, farmers' rights have emerged as insufficient mechanisms for the protection of the domain of these rights in the context of proprietary claims in agriculture. Farmers' rights have been incorporated within a conception of property rights based on the equal respect principle, in which intellectual property rule-setting defines the very formulation of another right. There is a deep integration of legal procedural measures that is required by the TRIPS regime, even when it allows for sui generis systems to be adopted. These sui generis systems which enable the provisions of farmers' rights are still located within the language of individual property rights. Response to proprietary rights in agriculture, when framed as counter or competing property rights, often fail to be realized because their realization is contingent on: a) the legal recourse capacity of the farmers, and b) on the peculiar *non-*exclusionary character of farmers' property rights. Farmers' rights focus on assigning property rights for the farmers' knowledge and resources

[110] Phillippe Cullet and Radhika Koluru, 2002 (2003), 'Plant Variety Protection and Farmers' Rights: Towards a Broader Understanding', *Delhi Law Review*, vol. 24, p. 7.

that give them the right to commercialize their knowledge rather than simply stop others from commercializing it.[111] In other words, it does not exclude others' use of it. Biotechnological formulations of 'derived varieties', and intellectual property protection for them (patents and plant breeders' rights) are predicated on the lack of exclusionary implications of farmers' rights. The assumption behind this formulation clearly was that farmers' rights have to, in the ultimate analysis, run alongside and not counter plant breeders' rights. As signatories of the WTO and consequently TRIPS, this was the only available format in which farmers' rights could be adopted in developing countries to safeguard their biodiversity and to protect vulnerable farmers and their plant varieties. Such an approach propels international and national legal formulations to run along parallel paths but inevitably adds a nebulous and a hierarchical order in the realization of farmers' rights. There is an ambiguity or, to use a phrase by Daniel Thorner, there is often a 'built-in depressor' in the very conception of the right which retards the realization of farmers' rights.

The conception of farmers' rights therefore emerges as one with mixed implications. On one hand, farmers' rights are a unique form of rights that may help transform conventions of intellectual property in ways that are better suited for registering and materially encouraging alternative forms of innovation, such as those offered by farming communities. On the other hand, farmers' rights have proven to have a notoriously indeterminate core which is masked by the language of farmers' rights and will continue to elude principles of substantive equality so long as they remain disconnected with the social justice agendas of the farming communities.

SEEDS, BIO-DIVERSITY, AND RIGHTS OF THE RURAL POOR

Every year new varieties of seed are produced with specific varieties developed for different climates and different growing environments. Some of these varieties will succeed, and some will fail. Therefore, to reduce the risk of low yield and profitability, rather than gamble on one variety of seed, farmers choose to plant their fields with multiple varieties. McFarling spent months reviewing seed descriptions and determining which varieties to purchase. At the end of each growing season, McFarling determined which variety had the highest yield and saved enough of that seed to plant roughly 50 per cent of his acreage the next

[111] Phillipe Cullet, 2005, p. 259.

year. He would plant the other 50 per cent with new varieties that he purchased.[112] Before the introduction of GM seed, this was the standard farming practice—selection of seeds through trial and error.

The shift from farm saved seed to corporate monopolies of the seed supply has very significant implications for the displacement of diverse bio-resources. Biotechnology development in essence is drawn out of the need to manipulate plant and animal species, through genetic modification, in order to evolve solutions to existing problems of disease, malnutrition, hunger; and so on. Golden Rice, for instance, is a genetically modified rice variety which claims to address issues of Vitamin A deficiency which is one of the main causes of blindness in poorer parts of Africa; or it may a modification in the seed variety to make it more high yielding, or pest resistance, as is the claim for Bt cotton varieties. Kloppenburg however warns that 'though the capacity to move genetic material between species is a means for introducing additional variation, it is also a means for engineering genetic uniformity across species.'[113] In essence therefore, there is a propagation of a solution that is uniform and consequently, in essence, is antithetical to diversity. Once diversity gives way to uniformity, says Gurdial Singh Nijar of TWN, only aged single species stand. In agriculture only species whose production can be optimized for commercial interests are advanced. Biotechnology in crops thus expedites the tendency towards monoculture as locally adapted strains or advantages of local planting techniques, geared towards maintaining diversity rather than productivity are replaced by protected genetically engineered crops.[114]

Monocultures and uniformity, which have been fostered by the dominance of genetically engineered solutions to world hunger and poverty, increase the risks of crop failure as diverse seeds adapted to diverse ecosystems are replaced by rushed introduction of unadapted and often ill-tested seeds into the market. In the state of Bihar, when farm saved corn seed was displaced by Monsanto's hybrid corn, the entire crop failed, creating losses of Rs 4 billion and increased poverty for already

[112] Based on a reference of an Interview with Homan McFarling, near Tupelo, Miss. (Jan. 2005). Quoted in Lisa Sternoff Feldman, 'Sow Complicated: *Monsanto Co.* v. *Homan McFarling.*' (CASRIP Newsletter, United States. Spring/Summer 2004)

[113] J. Kloppenburg, *Seedling* (2005).

[114] Gurdial Singh Nijar, 'In Defense of Local Community knowledge and Biodiversity: A Conceptual Framework and Essential Elements of a Rights Regime', in *The Movement for Collective Intellectual Rights*, Solomon Tilahun, and Sue Edwards (eds), Institute for Sustainable Development, Addis Ababa. The Gaia Foundation, London, 1996, p. 73.

desperately poor farmers.[115] The risk that the farmer faces in adopting a single crop cultivation model, that too of a plant variety which is alien both to their understanding and local conditions, is enormous. In another example, the District of Warangal in Andhra Pradesh used to grow diverse legumes, millets, and oilseeds. Seed monopolies created crop monocultures of cotton, leading to disappearance of millions of products of nature's evolution and farmer's breeding.[116] The failure of Bt cotton led to colossal losses to both farm revenue and farmers' lives. Today Bt cotton hybrid local varieties are faring better than the Monsanto Bt. Cotton introduced in 2002. Ronald Herring states that in Gujarat, farmers have adapted Bt varieties for their own conditions and created hybrid concoctions. These hybrids are cheaper and locally more adaptable; many farmers believe they work better than the approved Bt varieties, and they are spreading rapidly.[117]

The danger of displacement of local land varieties and loss of genetic diversity is all the more perceptible in case of higher potential or yield exhibited by the commercial variety. Higher yield and higher revenues, in the short run, might lead the farmer to abandon existing varieties. The loss of local varieties is in itself a loss of agro-biodiversity. Agricultural biodiversity, especially crop genetic diversity, has been recognized as an effective strategy to minimize risks and operates as a kind of an insurance cover against climate change, diseases, and pests.[118] Farmers tend to thrive on increasing biodiversity of their territories in which they live, as a strategy for increasing the variety of resources at their disposal and, in particular, reducing the risk associated with fluctuations in the populations of individual species. The land races, local species which have been bred by farming communities through a process of crossing and selection over hundreds of years, bred by the farming communities are the basis of the diverse gene pool that exists among local crop and species' varieties.

Genetic and agro-biodiversity are crucially linked to food and livelihood security for the rural poor. It has been estimated that about 60 per cent of the world's population, mostly in the Third World, depends, to some extent, on self-sufficiency for their food supply. This proportion

---

[115] Vandana Shiva, 5 April 2004, 'The Suicide Economy Of Corporate Globalization'. Available at http://www.countercurrents.org/glo-shiva050404.htm (last accessed on 11 October 2007).

[116] Ibid.

[117] 'Understanding the Bt Cotton Maze', Available at http://www.indiatogether.org/2006/jun/ivw-herring.htm (last accessed on 25 October 2007).

[118] Suman Sahai, November–December 2006, 'Access to Agrobiodiversity Means Food for the Rural Poor', *GeneNews*. 1(3), p. 22.

goes up to 80 per cent when considering those for whom medicinal plants constitute the backbone of their basic health care.[119] Most of the rural communities in the developing countries are farming communities with integrated production systems that provide not only food and medicines, but also fuel, shelter, organic fertilizers, and clothing, among other basic resources. Genetic resources are productive assets providing the basis for livelihood security. The ability of the poor to access and use diverse genetic resources has both long and short term implications for their agricultural productivity and food/ livelihood security.[120] Farmers tend to thrive on increasing biodiversity of their territories in which they live, as a strategy for increasing the variety of resources at their disposal and, in particular, reducing the risk associated with fluctuations in the populations of individual species. Any attempt to alter the chain of provisioning that these rural communities have devised and sustainably used, will adversely affect the poorer people to the extent that their livelihoods and food security might be seriously jeopardized. It would also at the same time, threaten important environmental and developmental concerns because it ignores, replaces, and destroys locally specific livelihood systems.

There are many strands in conservation of biodiversity. One of them connects biodiversity with self reliance and decentralization. Diversity in this perspective get incorporated into the production processes of agriculture. Diversity protects the livelihood niches of different communities.[121] There are a number of ways in which GM crops threaten the existence and conservation of land species. Contamination of organic crops by transgenic seeds;[122] pest resistance of land varieties to natural forms of pest control; elimination of those species which are not herbicide tolerant (GM crops are usually certified 'HT', that is, herbicide tolerant); elimination of weeds by herbicides which are an important source of livestock feed as well form a part of people's diet (for instance, 'chaulai' and 'bathua saag'). Plant genetic resource variety acts as the biological

[119] Marcus Colchester, 1993, 'The International Response: Policies of the International Agencies', in *The Struggle for Land and the Fate of the Forests,* Marcus Colchester, and Larry Lohmann (eds), London and Penang: Zed Books.

[120] For a report on growing food insecurity see, Per Pinstrup-Andersen, Rajul Pandya-Lorch, and Mark W. Rosegrant, 1997, *The World Food Situation: Recent Developments, Emerging Issues, and Long-term Prospects,* 2020 Vision Food Policy Report. IFPRI, Washington, DC.

[121] Vandana Shiva, 'Biodiversity, Biotechnology, and Profits', in *Biodiversity: Social and Ecological Perspectives,* V. Shiva, Anderson, *et al.* (eds) (World Rainforest Movement: Penang, Malaysia, 1991), p. 44.

[122] For details see, Samir Kumar Mohapatra, November–December, 2006, 'GE Contamination: A Global Scenario', *GeneNews,* Gene Campaign, 1(3), p. 9.

basis for livelihood security. The environment in which people pursue their livelihoods and their exposure to effects of the external environment determines the extent of their vulnerability to threats to livelihood security. Rights are closely linked to access to resources because these are the principal means by which people reduce their vulnerability. It is the access to resources, assets, and entitlements that together give people the capabilities to pursue livelihood strategies.

The connection between genetic diversity and the livelihood security of the farmer is significant in the context of the rights claims being made on plant varieties. Thus, there are patents on plant varieties and seeds, plant breeders' rights, farmers' rights all associated in some way with control over productivity in agricultural sector. While the former rights are rights over intellectual property, for farmers these are rights which secure their livelihood and their intellectual heritage. These rights have conflicting claims for ownership and control. The link between GM technology, IPRs in them; and agricultural productivity, loss of diversity, propagation of monocultures, is a multilayered and a contextual link. It has implications for environment, productivity, technology development, science and ethics, rights of farmers, IPRs to name only a few. An important dimension of this multilayered process has been the adverse impact that patented, protected GM crops have had on the various rights of the farmers. Biotechnology in the field of agriculture has twin declared objectives. Firstly, to increase productivity at lower costs, and secondly, to disburse benefits among the chief stakeholders, the farmers, especially the medium and small farmers whose livelihood crucially depends on the margins available to them at prevailing cost prices. IPRs in agricultural innovations have tended to jettison both these objectives.

LAW, SCIENCE, AND LIFE

The push for the extension of the IPRs has been greatly accentuated in the last few years by developments in biotechnology and genetic engineering. The development of genetic engineering has tremendous implications for agricultural, practices and rights of the people associated with agriculture, for it seeks to transform not just the way people practice agriculture but the space in which they thrive.

The adoption of the TRIPS agreement and a shift towards patenting of life forms constituted a very significant shift, almost paradigmmatic in nature, in the very conception of rights over IP. Expansion of property rights to include biological resources was not a simple expansion of IPRs in a new domain. What was significant was that this new domain was biological in nature, which by definition, is self-evolving and self-propagating. To claim inventive rights over a certain genetic combination or engineering constituted an important change in the very notion of what could be considered property. It could well constitute the third reification of property.

The first reification was represented by the physical externality and materiality of the object owned. Limited rights in land, revenue, or office gave way to absolute ownership rights in freely disposable goods. The disposal of land too was no longer constrained by virtue of its immobility. Earlier conceptions of property, whether in formal legal doctrine or elaborated in 'indigenous' theories, did not account for biotechnological manipulations of 'life'. It conformed to a distinction between life and things. Things were regarded as objects of propertization and persons, and other forms of life, were left outside the domain of propertization. In fact, the abolishment of slavery was predicated on the distinction between persons and things. The twentieth century, however, saw the ontological connection between property and things break down with property like status being attributed to knowledge, ideas, and other 'mental' outputs. This extension of property rights to intangibles like intellectual property represents the second reification of the concept of property. By granting the status of property to knowledge, IPRs do not make distinctions between tangibles and intangibles. Plant breeders' rights and patents in life forms take it a step further and do not make distinctions between biological and non-biological forms of property. It replicates the old form of jurisprudence to all forms of innovative activity, DNA, micro-organisms, which makes it possible to acquire IPRs over life forms which lack the basic criteria of man-made innovation. The original understanding of the patent law was that products of nature could not be patented and that patents should be restricted to products of human inventiveness. In a way, it was granting 'life' a form of legal immunity from commodification. However, science increasingly enmeshed itself with other social institutions, bringing about a third level of reification which has brought about the extension of property rights to naturally propagating biological species.

The dimension of 'life' or 'nature', that critiques of commodification seek to protect, is bound to a particular conception of legal power. Earlier conceptions of legal power were tied to the notion of sovereign power— one that preceded the notion of 'bio-power', a term coined by Michel Foucault to distinguish between the formal and the informal ways in which power is exercised, bio-power representing the latter.[123] Within the formal discourses available for politics it was the conception of sovereign power that reigned earlier, prior to the advent of capitalism and, more specifically, globalization. Its inception was tied to the exercise of formal monarchical powers. From its genesis in Hobbes, to its maturation in Steven Lukes, the concept of power is something that denies, forestalls, represents, and prevents. A classic feature of sovereign power is that it is employed only intermittently in discrete episodes; explicit power is mostly absent except when exercised. In a sense, sovereign power is distant from the civic body. This is not the case with bio-power which is deployed and finds expression, in everyday life. It normalizes through discursive formations of psychiatry, medicine, science and technology, education, and so on. The distinctive quality of bio-power is that it allows for the control of entire populations. Bio-power is literally having power over other bodies, 'an explosion of numerous and diverse techniques for achieving the subjugations of bodies and the control of populations'.[124]

The use of knowledge and technology to manipulate and commercialize aspects of life, the legal support granted to intellectual property in the form of TRIPS, UPOV, are all versions of bio-power which has led to a very profound transformation of the way global power is exercised. The transformation is one which shifts the level of the exercise of power from 'the juridical existence of sovereignty' to 'the biological existence of the population'.[125] One of the most important consequences of the shift to modern power has been a corollary shift in the juridical system of the law. Earlier forms of legal discourse conformed to the distinction between persons and things and were drawn more from a notion of sovereign power which based themselves on a fundamental distinction between law and nature, or between norms and the 'life' to which they referred. Bio-power in reinstituting law dissolves these distinctions. IPRs in agriculture thus not only re-institute property, but also re-institute law itself.[126]

---

[123] Bio-power was a term originally coined by French philosopher Michel Foucault to refer to the practice of modern states and their regulation and control of their subjects and their everyday lives. Bio-power in Foucault's conception is different from soveriegn power in both form and reach.

[124] Michel Foucault, 1998, *The History of Sexuality Vol. 1: The Will to Knowledge* [1976], London: Penguin, p. 140.

[125] Michel Foucault, 1998, p. 136.

[126] Alain Pottage, September 1998, 'The Inscription of Life in Law: Genes, Patents, and Bio-Politics', *The Modern Law Review*, 61(5), Human Genetics and the Law: Regulating a Revolution, pp. 740–65.

The dissolution of the distinction between persons and things, between law and the 'life' with which law concerns itself has another significant implication. Law installs life forms within the boundaries of property which considers commercialized science to be a better preserver of life. In doing so, it simultaneously affirms that life forms are given new dimensions by science; varieties of life forms become products of human inventiveness over which claims of intellectual property are made. New legal doctrine of patents dissolves this distinction by granting patent protection to life-forms and undoes the very distinction that made slavery illegal. As Alain Pottage argues, this is a somewhat conservative manoeuvre as distinctions between things and persons, objects and life were complicit in the earlier legal doctrines that abolished slavery.[127]

ISSUES IN OWNING LIFE

IPRs in life forms, like plant varieties, raises at least two issues. Firstly, there is the ethical question of the extent of private ownership that could be extended to life forms. The second dimension relates to the use of the idea of IP, and its appropriateness in the face of the larger dimension of rights on knowledge, their ownership, use, transfer, and dissemination.

Ownership of life forms has been made possible through interventions of biotechnology which render distinctions between the realm of the biological and social fuzzy such that it becomes possible to claim the former as 'man-made'. Current biotechnology strategies extend not only to legal protection of human intervention in nature but in establishing the 'very perspectival horizon within which such interventions are conceived'.[128] Today biotechnology patents are often understood as claims that breach the boundaries set by social-theoretical distinctions between law and nature, nature and culture. One could argue that the boundaries between the natural and social, between cultural, spiritual and the biological were always rather blurred in traditional societies. The subject which negotiated nature was never in a detached subject–object relationship. However, it is worth separating the substantive implications of blurred boundaries in the case of traditional societies, with the blurring that has been accomplished by science and biotechnology through law. The relationship between persons and things (animate/inanimate, biological/non-biological) in both the cases has two distinct genealogies, so distinct that they cannot be made to fit into one institutional or cognitive structure.

[127] Ibid.
[128] Ibid.

Ownership has been a key institution that has been central to thinking on personification and reification in modern rational systems. Ownership has nearly always been the context in which legal doctrine has worked out the relationship between *persons* in relation to things. It has also been vulnerable to social and technological developments. Biotechnological developments develop new attachments from which emerge a new set of claims. It is important to understand that the blurring of distinction between the realms of the natural and man-made are embedded in actualizing the claims made by individuals through the use of biotechnology. Herein lies the crucial difference between the two genealogies of blurred boundaries. In the case of traditional societies it is constitutive of their ontologies rather than a contingent element of ownership claims. It is the difference in convention and invention, the latter driving the fabrication of nature as a man-made construct, enabled by biotechnology and intellectual property rights. Thus, current biotechnology strategies not only extend legal protection to human intervention in nature but collapse the very distinctions on which property rights were predicated in the liberal era, which regarded certain realms as ownable and certain realms as non-ownable (land was ownable, slaves were not). It was the inherent characteristic of the realm itself which precluded ownership claims to be extended to it.

The use of biotechnology, especially in agriculture, is an extremely layered process with enormously diverse ramifications for the rights of agricultural communities. It is so because it is a process which begins with industry but seeks to transform the basis of agriculture and alter the space that the beneficiaries occupy in the agricultural matrix. A farmer like Mcfarling loses his right to save and use seeds. Biotechnology and ownership patterns recognized by the TRIPS regime exclude a farmer's property claims if they infringe patent claims. As an argument, if all seed varieties were to be biotechnological inventions, then there would be no property claims for the farmers at all. This complicity of law and science creates a new situation where land rights are rendered meaningless in the absence of seed rights.

In developing countries, the relationship between IPRs and farmers becomes more complex, as farmers are granted some sticks of the bundle of property rights. Granting farmers property rights over their species may not be a sufficient premise for their protection in the context of proprietary claims in agriculture. As issues of food security, livelihood rights, traditional knowledge rights, seed security gets linked to issues of patent protected bio-technological innovations, farmers become subordinate to the interests of capital with agro-input, processing, and retail sectors absorbing more of the food system's value.

Conceptions of farmers' rights have been a result of this realization and its institutionalization has been an attempt to protect farmers' traditional interests as well as to make them stakeholders in the biotech advancements. However, much of the farmers' rights discussion in the legal literature on intellectual property globalization so far has focused on the question of *procedural fairness.* The institution of farmers' rights, within the Indian Plant Variety Act is an instructive example: it is a measure to accord farmers rights in an attempt to procedurally balance out the rights given to breeders and farmers. It is in keeping with this principle of 'democratic property rights' that farmers' rights have been incorporated, where intellectual property rule-setting defines the very formulation of another right.

By and large, farmers' rights are posited as a new type of right within, as Borowiak would argue, the discourse on property.[129] These rights are a claim to a share of the material benefits that are based on adding value to farmers' seed varieties. Promotion of ownership, the farmer's right to save, use and sell seeds[130] hides other discreet processes which encroach upon farmers' rights. To give an example, these rights apply equally to open-pollinated and inbred plant varieties (the kinds developed by farmers) the seeds of which can be replanted over and over again. On the other hand, hybrid seeds are artificially cross-pollinated and are 'programmed' in such a way that seeds produced from hybrid plants lose their 'hybrid vigour' due to the concept of segregation; therefore, new seeds must be purchased every planting season. Hybrid seed production prevents farmers from saving, and replanting hybrid seeds (and these are plain hybrid seeds without the GURT technology). Being widely-marketed and commercially available, preference is given to hybrid seeds over open-pollinated seeds.[131] A clear indication of this was visible in the Bt cotton

[129] C. Borowiak, 2004, 'FRs: IP Regimes and the Struggle over Seeds', *Politics and Society*, 32(4,) p. 528.

[130] Under Section 39 (iv) of the chapter on farmers' rights (Plant Variety Protection and Farmers' Rights Act, 2001, India), the right to sell seed including protected seed, has been provided., 'provided that the farmer shall not be entitled to sell, branded seed of a variety protected under this Act'. This right to sell seed is crucial to maintaining the livelihood basis of the farming community and the nation's self-reliance in agriculture. The clause on the right to sell seed was the major bone of contention to the very end of the legislative process.

[131] Srinivasan notes that developing countries like India, Mexico, Brazil, Argentina that have opened up to foreign direct investment (FDI) in the seeds sector have witnessed a significant restructuring of the domestic seed industry in a relatively short span of time. For a number of strategic and economic reasons (Srinivasan: 2003, Morris: 1998), FDI in the

plantation which continued to proliferate despite failure, especially in the pre-2005 period. This weakens the genetic pool of open-pollinated varieties, which is the source of seeds for small farmers. Farmers' rights thus, get diluted with the developments in technology such as the hybrid, terminator, and other biotechnology-products.

Cast in the property language of intellectual property rights, farmers' rights are a claim to a share of the material benefits that are based on adding value to farmers' seed varieties. It pretends to be cast in a different language in as much it locates itself in diffuse communities, shared knowledge and traditional practices, the contributions of past generations, and so on. But the overall strategy is located in the 'equal respect principle' which grants a farmer rights over his varieties much in the same way as breeders get over their varieties. While this form of right has created a strategic site for symbolic as well as material recognition for farmers, in practice, issues such as the determination of the right holder, the obligated parties, and the particular actions that they should be performing need to be identified. In the context of farmers' rights, however, these remain unclear.

IPRs in agriculture transform the nature of agriculture, making it into a means for capital. In agriculture, capital encounters obstacles not found in other industrialized production processes because of the unreliability of nature-based farming (for instance, plant growth time, pest outbreaks, the weather, etc.). Capital seeks to dissolve these barriers with the aid of science and technology. Consequently, the farmer assumes less control over the crop system, often with deleterious consequences for both ecological and social systems and for the rights of farmers. [132] Science, with the help of institutional mechanisms like TRIPS and UPOV, helps the transformation of agriculture, where the relationship of the farmer to his farm and his produce is altered. The plant variety that is conserved, renewed or selected by farmers is separated from the social, economic and cultural systems in which farmers develop their production. The development of farmers' rights provides an opportunity to re-examine the entire issue of patents and breeders' rights as well as the issue of farmers' rights.

---

seeds sector has proceeded through acquisition of domestic seed companies by seed MNCs creating significant levels of concentration in market for hybrid seed varieties of important crops. For instance see, C.S. Srinivasan, 2005, 'The International Trends in Plant Variety Protection', *eJade* (electronic journal, FAO) 2(2), pp. 182–220, available at http:www.fao.org/es/ESA/ejade/Srinivasan.pdf (last accessed on 8 December 2007).

[132] R. Lewontin, July/August 1998, 'The Maturing of Capitalist Agriculture: Farmer as Proletarian', *Monthly Review*, 50(3), pp. 72–84.

8 Indigenous Knowledge Rights
Neem Patent Claims

It is often argued that the rights of the indigenous peoples are being violated when their access to resources and benefits from their contributions to science and technology are ignored. This has been attributed, in a large measure, to the intellectual property protection sanctioned by the TRIPS regime which recognizes and rewards innovative activity that is 'novel', 'non-obvious', and usually of some benefit to the society. It has been argued that what is regarded as innovation ignores the form and the kind of innovative activity undertaken by the traditional and indigenous communities. In doing so, the TRIPS regime becomes an international legal institution that fosters the intellectual dominance of the WMS and fails to acknowledge and grant epistemic parity to global intellectual pluralism.

This has become the background for varying claims: for the knowledge rights of the indigenous communities to be given parity within the TRIPS framework; for the protection of traditional knowledge systems (TKS); for an end to bio-piracy and the one-way genetic resource flow (reminiscent of the mercantile capitalist era); for the development of equitable benefit-sharing mechanisms; for community property rights, to name a few central ones. These are all rights which emanate from the central claim for knowledge rights of the indigenous/ traditional peoples which are as much aspects of their socio-economic rights as rights to food or health.

As in Chapters 6 and 7, this chapter seeks to locate knowledge rights in a case study—that of Neem—and outline the terms of conflict between intellectual property rights and knowledge rights of traditional-indigenous peoples. From there I draw larger conclusions about the inability of intellectual property rights to conjoin with knowledge rights of the traditional peoples which, I argue, are aspects of human rights as they are symbiotically linked with issues of subsistence and livelihood. I take forward one of the two central arguments of the book that rights need to be assessed in terms of the consequences—consequences which are rights-sensitive. Just as rights claims derive from deontological grounds of morality, so also do they derive from consequentialist grounds of morality through a valuation of outcomes. An assessment of outcomes invariably raises issues of *what* rights? And *whose* rights? Consequential analysis, therefore, needs be cognizant not merely of the inherent capacities of a right but also of its capacity to generate outcomes for certain individuals or groups of individuals. The same right could generate different consequences for different people. This chapter illustrates this point. Knowledge rights of the traditional peoples generate different consequences for the right holder than do knowledge rights of the intellectual property holders. It is on these consequences that, I argue, terms of adjudication between competing claims of *coequal* rights ought to be predicated. The stronger the relationship of the consequences with life-protecting, life-enhancing capacities, the stronger becomes its moral claim for a right. I argue, therefore, that the category of knowledge rights needs to be unpacked in terms of what the right protects and for whom? One set of knowledge rights is linked to a more fundamental claim for dignified existence and subsistence, and the other set to secured returns on capital investment. It is the former, that is, the right of traditional, indigenous peoples over their knowledges and associated resources, which stakes a claim as human rights. The right to life, and the rights which devolve from it, is most prior of all claims and have acquired an undisputed priority position in the lexical order of rights.

These two versions of knowledge rights are not just different but are also conflictual. Any attempt to club them together under a universal intellectual property system is likely to create epistemic hierarchies which threaten the domination of one by the terms of the other. Intellectual property rights infringe upon the traditional indigenous knowledge rights of vulnerable sections of society, whose sustainability is crucially linked to the sustainability of their economic and knowledge systems. It confronts the plurality and heterogeneity of knowledge systems, threatening to alter these in the image of western intellectual traditions. Finally, I argue that the threat that the current conception of intellectual property as individual rights poses to communally held knowledge rights, compels a re-thinking of the conception of intellectual property itself.

UNDERSTANDING TRADITIONAL INDIGENOUS KNOWLEDGE

Traditional indigenous knowledge (TIK)[1] is the information that people in a given community (who identify themselves as indigenous to a place, based on a combination of cultural distinctiveness and prior territorial occupancy relative to a more recently arrived population, with its own distinct and subsequently dominant culture[2]), based on experience and adaptation to a local culture and environment, have developed over time, and continue to develop. This knowledge is used to sustain the community and its culture and to maintain the genetic resources necessary for the continued survival of the community. TIK includes mental inventories of local biological resources, animal breeds, and local plant, crop, and tree species. It may include such information as trees and plants that grow well together, and indicator plants, such as plants that show soil salinity or that are known to flower at the beginning of the rains. It includes practices and technologies, such as seed treatment, storage methods, and tools used for planting and harvesting. TIK also encompasses belief systems that play a fundamental role in a people's livelihood, maintaining their health, and protecting and replenishing the environment. TIK is thus the totality of all knowledges and practices, whether explicit or implicit, used in the management of socio-economic, spiritual and ecological facets of life. Categories of these traditional knowledges include agricultural, meteorological, ecological, governance, social welfare, medicinal and pharmaceutical, legal and jurisprudential, music, architecture, sculpture, textile manufacture, metallurgy and food technology.[3] TIK is dynamic

---

[1] Some ethnographic studies prefer the usage of the term 'local'. For instance, according to Warren and McKiernan 'Indigenous Knowledge (IK) is local knowledge that is unique to a given culture or society' Maurial states 'Indigenous knowledge is *local* because it is the result of the quotidian interactions in indigenous people's territories' or in Dei et al.'s words, 'indigenous knowledges are those acquired by local peoples through daily experience'. See, Mahia Maurial, 1999, 'Indigenous Knowledge and Schooling: a Continuum Between Conflict and Dialogue', in *What is Indigenous Knowledge? Voices from the Academy*, Ladislaus M. Semali and Joe L. Kincheloe (eds), New York and London: Falmer Press, p. 63; George Dei, Jerry Sefa, Budd L. Hall, and Dorothy Goldin Rosenberg, 2000, *Indigenous Knowledges in Global Contexts: Multiple Readings of our World*, Toronto: University of Toronto Press, p.19.

[2] ILO, 1989: Article 1.

[3] For details on categories of indigenous knowledge see Odora Hoopers, 2004, *Culture, Indigenous Knowledge and Development*, Johannesburg: CEPD, Section 2. The UNESCO's World Intellectual Property Organization's definition of cultural heritage includes: Literary, performing and artistic works (including music, dance, song, ceremonies, symbols and designs); Languages; Scientific, agricultural, technical and ecological knowledge (including medicines and sustainable use of flora and fauna); All items of movable cultural property including burial artifacts; Indigenous ancestral remains; Indigenous human genetic material

in nature and may include experimentation in the integration of new plant or tree species into existing farming systems or a traditional healer's tests of new plant medicines. The term 'traditional' used in describing this knowledge does not imply that this knowledge is old or un-technical in nature, but tradition-based. It is 'traditional' because it is created in a manner that reflects the traditions of the communities, therefore not relating to the nature of the knowledge itself, but to the way in which that knowledge is created, preserved, and disseminated.[4]

Three features of TIK are important for our consideration here: a) that the development of TIK, covers almost all aspects of life of the holders and is a matter of survival for the people who generate these systems;[5] b) that TIK is often collective in nature and, therefore, eludes basic considerations (divisibility) for individuated property claims.[6] Such knowledge systems are cumulative, intergenerational, representing generations of experiences, observation, and trial and error experiments; and c) that TIK exists in a dialectical relationship with the ecology which sustains it. Perhaps that is the reason why some theorists have preferred the usage of the term 'traditional ecological knowledge' (TEK)[7] to any other because of the vital linkages that these knowledge systems have with their environment.[8] The relationship with and to nature, human agency and human solidarity underpins the knowledge system and the human existence around it. The unique cosmology and the world view of the traditional societies underline

---

(including DNA and tissues); Cultural environmental resources (including minerals and species); Immovable cultural property (including indigenous sites of significance, sacred sites and burials); Documentation of indigenous peoples' heritage in all forms of media (including scientific, ethnographic research reports, papers and books, films, and sound recordings).

[4] *Elements Of A Sui Generis System For The Protection Of Traditional Knowledge*, (WIPO, Intergovernmental Committee on IP and Genetic Resources, Traditional Knowledge and Folklore, 3rd Sess., 2002. WIPO/GRTKF/IC/3/8.

[5] Louise Grenier, 1998, *Working With Indigenous Knowledge: A Guide for Researchers*, Ottawa: International Development Research Center, p. 1.

[6] Exceptions like witchcraft, 'tantric' skills etc do exist where the form of knowledge is closely held by a family or a very small group of individuals.

[7] Firket Berkes writes, 'TEK represents experience acquired over thousands of years of direct human contact with the environment'. Firket Berkes, 1993, 'Traditional Ecological Knowledge in Perspective', in *Traditional Ecological Knowledge: Concept and Cases*, J.T. Inglis (ed.), Ottawa: International Development Research Centre, pp.1–9.

[8] Writing about the American Indians, Capra stated that ecological awareness arises 'only when we combine our rational knowledge with an intuition for the nonlinear nature of our environment. Such intuitive wisdom is characteristic of traditional, non-literate cultures, especially of American Indian cultures, in which life was organized around a highly refined awareness of the environment.' F. Capra, 1982, *The Turning Point: Science, Society and the Rising Culture*, New York: Simon & Schuster, p. 41.

all categories of their implicit and explicit knowledges making them non-individualistic, essentially communal, and non-amenable to propertization for any kind of proprietary rights to be legitimately claimed for them.

Without dwelling too much on the binaries of TIK and WMS it would suffice to assert, in this context, that TIK systems are fundamentally differentiated and different from WMS and that their respective alternate vocabularies render them incommensurable entities. Recent attempts to integrate TIK, it can be argued, renders them commensurable but all such attempts have tended to recast the TIK in the vocabulary of WMS, which does not make them commensurable but simply appropriable.

What has perhaps compelled a dialogue between the two, particularly in the post TRIPS era, has been the growing interest in alternate ways of healing, growing crops, alternate genetic sources, etc. A growing number of scientists and policy makers are aware of the contribution that TIK can make to a more sustainable development,[9] protection of biodiversity,[10] and as a starting point in the construction of a truly alternative agriculture.[11] TIK is being lauded as alternative wisdom relevant to a society which is increasingly confronting the limits of its science. That western science alone provides biological and ecological insights is no longer accepted unequivocally. As Berkes puts it, IK is being regarded as an 'alternative collective wisdom relevant to a variety of matters at a time when existing norms, values and laws are called into question'.[12] There is thus felt a pressing need to access this wealth so that the world at large can benefit from their wisdom and the resources. This initiated the intensified

[9] Viergever Marcel, 1999, 'Indigenous Knowledge: an Interpretation of Views from Indigenous Peoples', in *What is indigenous knowledge? Voices from the academy* M. Ladislaus Semali, and Joe L. Kincheloe (eds), New York and London: Falmer Press, p. 341.

[10] Masa Iwanaga, 1998, '*In situ* Conservation and the Development Process', in *Strengthening The Scientific Basis Of In Situ Conservation Of Agricultural Biodiversity On-Farm: Options For Data Collecting And Analysis.* Proceedings of a Workshop to Develop Tools and Procedures for In Situ Conservation On-Farm, 25–29 August 1997, Debra I. Jarvis and Toby Hodgkin (eds), International Plant Genetic Resources Institute, Rome, Italy, p. vi.

[11] Jack Kloppenburg (ed), 1988, *Seeds and Sovereignty: The Use and Control of Plant Genetic Resources*, London: Duke University Press; J. Kloppenburg, 1991, 'Social Theory and the De/reconstruction of Agricultural Science: Local Knowledge for an Alternative Agriculture', *Rural Sociology*, 56(4), pp. 519–48. Some agricultural research centers look at TIK as a key component of sustainable agricultural practices; others have been in charge of researching and cataloguing existing TIK. The Center for Indigenous Knowledge for Agriculture and Rural Development (CIKARD), established in 1987 at Iowa State University, is an example of the latter.

[12] Firket Berkes, 1993, 'Traditional Ecological Knowledge in Perspective', in *Traditional Ecological Knowledge: Concepts and Cases*, Luian T. Inglis (ed.), International Program on Traditional Indigenous Knowledge: International Development Research Center.

search for commercially profitable substances and resources among the ecosystems of indigenous peoples, in part compelled by the limits of the WMS.

INTEGRATION OF TRADITIONAL INDIGENOUS KNOWLEDGE

The intensification of interest in the commercial value of indigenous peoples' knowledge and resources and the subsequent institution of intellectual property rights, emergence of indigenous peoples as an economic possibility was predicated on a series of ideological and practical shifts in the contemporary world system. Among the more obvious reasons for the emergence of intellectual property rights and indigenous knowledge and resources was the increasing interest on the part of pharmaceutical companies in the collection and use of biological resources during the late 1980s and early 1990s.

The effort to source, integrate, exploit TIK systems has gradually acquired global and multi-industry dimensions. What began with pharmaceutical companies prospecting the rain forest resources and traditional knowledge bases for new therapeutic solutions now extends to exploring the local plant genetic resources, traditional/ local agricultural knowledge about crops, medicinal herbs, climatic requirements, ecology management, and so on. Recent advances in biotechnology have increased the ability of scientists to investigate organisms at the molecular and genetic levels and to find ways to commercialize products developed from these investigations. Prospecting for biological materials like plants with medicinal or other economically valuable properties like fibre or oil is becoming a dynamic and profitable enterprise. Benign biological products from the bio-diverse global South are being sought as substitutes for chemical products. For instance, the global market for herbal products, with its appeal ranging from pharmaceuticals, nutraceuticals and health foods to cosmetics, toiletries, and ethnic products is estimated to reach US 5 trillion dollars by 2020.[13] The wisdom and resources held by the traditional peoples of the developing countries forms the basis of a large part of the growing biotechnological boom.

In terms of the structuring of capital incentives within the biotechnological industry, one of the most significant events to occur

[13] Suman Sahai, *Commercialisation of Indigenous Knowledge and Benefit Sharing.* UNCTAD Expert Meeting on Systems and National Experiences for Protecting Traditional Knowledge, Innovations and Practices. (Geneva 30 October–1 November 2000). Refer point 15. Available at http://www.comunidadandina.org/desarrollo/6_India.pdf (last accessed on 15 December 2007).

during that time period was the 1980 United States Supreme Court ruling in the *Diamond* v. *Chakrabarty*[14] case, that a human-made strain of micro-organism, genetically engineered to improve its ability to degrade crude oil, could be considered a patentable product because the strain was not a naturally occurring composition of matter.[15] Prior to this ruling, it was generally recognized that living organisms and cells were 'products of nature' and thus were not patentable. In the United States, the Plant Patent Act, 1930 distinguishes between 'products of nature' and 'human-made inventions'. The Supreme Court's decision to allow the patenting of genetically engineered micro-organisms had both ideological and material effects. At an ideological level, the Court's decision substantially broadened the scope of what is human-made thus reordering what fell within the legal categories of nature and culture. Simultaneously, at the level of social practice, patent applications for products using genetic material rose by almost 200 per cent in the year 1981 following the Court's decision, and the cumulative equity invested in all types of biotechnology companies rose from 50 million dollars to over 800 million between the years of 1978 and 1981.[16] In fiscal year 1990 alone, the US government spent more than 3.4 billion dollars to support the R&D of biotechnological applications, most of it disbursed through the National Institutes of Health (NIH— 2.9 billion dollars).[17] The expansion of intellectual property rights in the United States to include microbiological material can thus be seen as an important motivation for global extension of intellectual property rights in biological/natural realm.

In addition to shifts in international and national intellectual property law, a series of technological advances within the pharmaceutical industry which helped to sustain support for natural product development, generated interest in the topic of intellectual property rights and indigenous peoples. Two technological developments in particular helped promote the biotech industry funding and operations: High Throughput

[14] 16 June 1980 447 US 303, 206 USPQ 193.

[15] Genetic engineer Ananda Mohan Chakrabarty working for General Electric had developed a bacterium capable of breaking down crude oil, which he proposed to use in treating oil spills. In a 5-4 ruling, the court ruled in favor of Chakrabarty, and upheld the patent, holding that a live, human-made micro-organism is patentable subject matter under [Title 35 USC] 101. Respondent's micro-organism constitutes a 'manufacture' or 'composition of matter' within that statute.

[16] Paul Rabinow, 1996, *Making PCR: A Story of Biotechnology, Diamond* v. *Chakrabarty,* 447 US 303, 206 USPQ 193. June, 1980, Chicago: University of Chicago Press, p. 27.

[17] *Biotechnology and IP Rights.* Available at http://www.acephale.org/bio-safety/IoC-ipr.htm (last accessed on 12 January 2008).

Screening (HTS) tools and the development of combinatorial chemistry and combinatorial biology. The advent of HTS, made possible the analysis of tens of thousands of plant samples per week. The development of combinatorial chemistry and combinatorial biology generated thousands of small molecular weight compounds for screening, thus creating the perfect match for HTS. HTS and combinatorial chemistry were significant steps in the development of the biotech industry.[18] The enhanced recourse to genetic screening and bioinformatics within microbiology caused a profound change in the organization of research and development of biotechnology. As a consequence of this, users and scientists became more interconnected in the innovation chain. The development of biotechnology proved to be the new driving force behind a particular segment of pharmaceutical industry and agro-based industries. A common feature of both these industries was their growing interest and reliance on indigenous knowledge and resources. The genetic resource rich South and the wisdom and the knowledge of local plant varieties proved to be the trigger for new innovations in biotechnology.

The third important event in this context was the United Nations Conference on Environment and Development (UNCED), which met in Rio de Janeiro in 1992 in order to consider the passage of the Convention on Biodiversity (CBD). The CBD fundamentally reconceptualized *to whom* biodiversity belonged. Specifically, it recognized that nation states had sovereign rights over their biological resources, and that the access and use of those resources should be determined by national legislation. Historically, biological resources were part of the 'global commons' based on the premise that they were the common heritage of mankind. The moral position taken by the United Nations FAO buttressed this position stating that, 'The major plants of the world are not owned by any one people [but] are [rather] quite literally a part of our human heritage from the past.' This meant, in other words, that plant genetic resources were free goods which entailed only the cost of collection. Free availability mandated unrestricted exchange of plant germplasm among plant breeders and other scientists. The norm of free exchange had been sufficient to maintain the relatively free international flow of plant genetic material stored in the gene banks across the world. The notion of state sovereignty over biological resources changed this. CBD might have had in mind the historical asymmetry in the flow of germplasm, which was

---

[18] Trish Appletion, 1999, 'Combinatorial Chemistry and HTS-feeding a voracious process', *Science Direct*, 27 August. Available at http:www.sciencedirect.com/science?-ob=Article URL&Udi=86764 (last accessed on 12 December 2007).

largely uni-directional from the South to the North, in vesting states with an opportunity to regulate access to plant resources and to deny that access if they considered it to be inimical to their national interests. State ownership of biological resources re-conceptualized these resources, and the knowledge embedded within them, as something that belonged to an entity (in the case of nation states) or to people (in the case of indigenous peoples or private owners). The very language of ownership, property, and hence compensation that the CBD introduced in relation to biological resources was essential to the emergence of both the notion of intellectual property rights in biological resources as well as to the emergence of the debate on the rights that indigenous people possessed—rights to, what now was considered, 'their resources' and 'their knowledge'.

The final defining legal event to be considered here is the TRIPS agreement which created international standards for intellectual property law and obligated member nations to commit to meeting these standards. A significant contributing factor is the high profitability of the biotech ventures which became the basis for patented innovations and which then ensured greater profits at monopolistic levels. The TRIPS framework became the driving force behind the spurt in industrial growth in this sector.

The relationship between the spurt in industrial growth and intellectual property protection is well documented. Steven Price, for example, argues that some form of monopolistic control has been found necessary to propel western economic development for the last 2,000 years: the progression of industrial society has co-evolved with the development of the patent system.[19] Calestous Juma has recognized the diminishing marginal productivity (or 'diminishing returns') of previous technologies and the surge that patent-protected biotechnology innovations have provided to the agro industries which has reorganized 'large sections of the industrial and agricultural sector'.[20]

Thus biotechnology is revolutionary in yet another sense—it has circumvented recurring diminishing returns, and has given a renewed push to industrial growth. Protected by intellectual property rights the biotechnology sector became one of the main reasons for export spurts in many western economies. Gadbaw and Richards estimate that the percentage of the US country exports with a high intellectual property

---

[19] Steven Price, 1992, p. 54. Quoted in *Biotechnology and IP Rights*, available at http://www.acephale.org/bio-safety/IoC-ipr.htm (last accessed on 12 January 2008).

[20] Calestous Juma, 1989, *The Gene Hunters: Biotechnology and the Scramble for Seeds*, Princeton University Press, p. 108.

content rose from 9.9 per cent in 1947 to 27.4 per cent in 1986.[21] Exports, as measured by royalties and licensing fees, amounted to about US 27 billion dollars in 1995, while imports amounted to only US 6.3 billion dollars.[22] With the legal infrastructure supporting the approval of patents on genetically engineered micro-organisms and with these patents operating as virtual monopolies, there began a continual search for sources of newer and greener fields which could yield newer avenues of innovation. Biological resources became very viable and profitable avenues for pharmaceutical and agro research and development. Indigenous communities participated in ethno-botanical projects, which used/use indigenous knowledge to help facilitate the collection of particularly efficacious genetic resources.[23]

The TRIPS regime had at least two far reaching effects in relation to the knowledge and resources of indigenous peoples. First, the agreement greatly altered how biodiversity was to be used and controlled. There was a shift in the ways and norms according to which nature was intercepted. Paul Rabinow remarks, writing about a particular kind of pharmaceutical technology, 'Biotechnology's hallmark lies in its potential to get away from nature, to construct artificial conditions in which specific variables can be known in such a way that they can be manipulated. This knowledge then forms the basis for remaking nature according to our norms'.[24] By conferring a property right to the biotechnological innovators, the tacit rights that local communities had over generations to their local environment and resources were transferred to a legal right that bio-prospectors could hold by freely accessing unprotected commons.

Secondly, the agreement greatly exacerbated the debate already raging between developed and developing countries over trade-related issues. It brought to fore the assumptions behind intellectual property rights and the dangers that it held for the food and ecological security of developing nations. Above all, it brought into focus the issue of the knowledge rights of indigenous peoples and the inequity or absence of benefit-sharing mechanisms.

[21] Graham Dutfield, 2000, *Intellectual Property Right, Trade and Biodiversity,* London: Earthscan Publications, p. 10.

[22] M. Ryan, 1998, *Knowledge Diplomacy: Global Competition and the Politics of IP,* Washington, DC: Brookings Institution Press.

[23] Ethnobotanical knowledge or resources is used to refer to a community's knowledge about medicinal and alimentary uses of plants. This distinguishes the knowledge of the plants from the plant matter itself. Rural Advancement Foundation International (RAFI), a Canadian advocacy organization (now called Action Group on Erosion, Technology, and Concentration (ETC), coined the term in 1994 as a spin on bio-prospecting. RAFI/ETC publishes annual 'Captain Hook awards' for notable achievements in bio-piracy.

[24] By Paul Rabinow, *Making PCR: A Story of Biotechnology,* p. 20.

The case study of Neem, which is dealt with later in this chapter, highlights the issues of inequitable terms of trade, non-existent or inequitable benefit sharing norms, and bio-piracy, all of which are outcomes of epistemic hierarchies implied and instituted by the TRIPS regime. The TRIPS agreement is one of the mechanisms that facilitates and provides incentives, in the form of patents and related intellectual property rights, for scientific innovation and adjudicates on what comprises science and innovation, which then become the basis for what comprises rights of ownership. Recognizing intellectual property of one kind and not recognizing the knowledge rights of the other—the one that exists in a 'non-scientific' domain—reinstates the cultural and cognitive status assumed by the West. As Pat Mooney of Rural Advancement Foundation International (RAFI) states, 'The argument that intellectual property is recognizable when performed in laboratories with white lab coats is fundamentally a racist view of scientific development.'[25] Dominant modes of cognition and knowledge generation, fostered and protected by TRIPS seek to integrate the relatively isolated but resource-rich traditional knowledge systems with global systems of biotechnology and intellectual property. It is the effort to integrate and the terms of this integration connect the knowledge debate with perspectives on human rights.

TRADITIONAL INDIGENOUS KNOWLEDGE AND THE TRIPS AGREEMENT

There are two important international conventions that have a bearing on intellectual property rights and traditional knowledge systems (TKS), namely, the TRIPS agreement and the CBD. The CBD is the only major international convention that assigns ownership of biodiversity to indigenous communities and individuals, albeit through the state and asserts their right to protect this knowledge. Two articles of this convention are particularly relevant:

1. Article 8 (j): State Parties are required to 'respect, preserve and maintain knowledge, innovations and practices of indigenous and local communities embodying traditional lifestyles relevant for the conservation and sustainable use of biological diversity and promote the wider application with the approval and involvement of the holders of such knowledge, innovations and practices and encourage the equitable sharing of the benefits arising from the utilization of such knowledge, innovations and practices.'

[25] RAFI has been tracking US patent data bases for controversial ownership claims. In 1985, Pat Mooney of RAFI developed the concept of farmers' rights as a counter weight to plant breeders' rights. See, 'The History of Farmers' Rights in the FAO: First use of Farmers' Rights'. *Farmers' Rights*, available at http://www.farmersrights/org/about/tr-history_Part1.html (last accessed on 8 December 2009).

2. Article 18.4: Contracting Parties should 'encourage and develop models of cooperation for the development and use of technologies, including traditional & indigenous technologies.'

Article 8(j) of the CBD recognizes communal knowledge, rights of indigenous cultures to preserve their knowledge and resources, clearly at odds with the individualistic conception embodied in the TRIPS agreement.[26] The US refrained from signing the CBD, a decision which was made largely due to the Convention's ambiguity regarding the IPRs.

The TRIPS agreement is a key international agreement promoting the harmonization of national IPR regimes.[27] The effect of this harmonization would be to provide minimum standards and to make national IPR regimes more similar to each other.[28] Although the TRIPS agreement covers four types of IPRs, namely, patents, geographical indications, undisclosed information (trade secrets) and trademarks, it does not acknowledge or distinguish between indigenous, community-based knowledge. Furthermore, it makes no reference to the protection of traditional knowledge. While there is mention of sui generis forms of protection in the TRIPS agreement (Article 27.3b), the agreement itself demands that sui generis provision ought not to run contrary to TRIPS.[29] Part of the rationale behind the sui generis provision is that the claims of indigenous knowledge holders are based on completely different socio-cultural norms, therefore, a system that is unique and rooted in local specificities should be used for the protection of indigenous knowledge.

According to Article 7 (Objectives) of the TRIPS agreement, protection and enforcement of IPRs, 'contribute to the promotion of technological innovation and to the transfer and dissemination of technology, to the mutual advantage of the producers and users of technological knowledge and in a manner conducive to social and economic welfare, and to the balance of rights and obligations'. This implies that national IPR regimes need not be modeled after that of the US, or any other country, so long as they comply with the minimum standards laid out in Parts II and III of the agreement. Article 1 (Nature and Scope of Obligations) makes clear that whilst members are required to implement the provisions of the

[26] Susan Sell, 2003, p. 144.

[27] By putting IPRs in the WTO agreements, members are obliged to respect other members' IPR commitments or, in case of non-compliance, to face trade sanctions by the WTO Dispute Settlement Mechanism.

[28] For details see Graham Dutfield, 2003, *Intellectual Property Rights, Trade and Biodiversity*, vol. 17. Box 3.1.

[29] For details, see Chapter 7, of this book.

TRIPS agreement, more extensive forms of protection and enforcement are not precluded. Therefore, as Graham Dutfield states, the absence of any mention of TIK does not disallow a member from enacting legislation to protect such a category of knowledge.[30] However, what is of significant importance is that the other WTO members are *not* required to recognize rights in other countries that go beyond the minimum standards established by TRIPS framework. Thus even when countries do undertake sui generis legislation to protect a category of knowledge it very often fails to get protected at the global level as there are no global commitments to these legislation outside the boundaries of the legislating country.

Intellectual property is a legal concept that deals with creations of human ingenuity. These creations, whether they are inventions, designs, trademarks or artistic works, are considered to be property and are protected for a certain period of time, provided that they meet the criteria of novelty, inventive step and utility. Although there is no reason why such categories of rights may not apply to various expressions of traditional knowledge,[31] there are several characteristics of traditional knowledge that create barriers to protection through the use of existing forms of IPRs.[32]

---

[30] G. Dutfield, *Intellectual Property Rights, Trade and Biodiversity: Seeds and Plant Varieties*, pp. 18–19. Kenya, for example, passed an Industrial Property Bill in 1989 that allows petty patents relating to traditional medicinal knowledge; Sui generis laws that have been passed in Panama in June 2000—Panama's Special System for Registering the Collective Rights of Indigenous Peoples, for the Protection and Defense of their Cultural identity and Traditional Knowledge, and Setting out other Provisions. According to WIPO 'the sui generis system of Panama actually constitutes the first comprehensive system of protection of traditional knowledge ever adopted in the world'. 'Review of existing IP Protection of Traditional Knowledge', Intergovernmental Committee on IP and Genetic Resources, Traditional Knowledge and Folklore, Third Session: Geneva, 13–21 June 2002. (WIPO Secretariat, 2002) WIPO/GRTKF/IC/3/7.

[31] For example, the knowledge of how certain plants within an indigenous group's homeland are used to treat fever would fall under IP rights. Likewise, particular understandings of the land, ecology, or environment of a certain area may also fall under IP rights. The key point is that IP rights refer to knowledge that otherwise would not be available. It is not knowledge gained through scientific experimentation, nor is it knowledge gained through empirical deductions. Rather, it is knowledge that is gained (some may say earned) through time, place, and experience.

[32] For a few cases of existing IP mechanisms, 'geographical indications, copyrights, trademarks and patents, that have been used to protect a few instances of TIK 'Review of existing IP Protection of Traditional Knowledge' Intergovernmental Committee on IP and Genetic Resources, Traditional Knowledge and Folklore, Third Session: Geneva, 13–21 June 2002. (WIPO Secretariat, 2002). Available at http://www.wipo.int/edocs/mdocs/tk/en/wipo_grtkf_ic_3/wipo_grtkf_ic_3_7.doc (last accessed on 10 January 2008).

Possession is probably the single most important basis of an intellectual property rights claim. A property is that which is capable of being delineated, with an identifiable author or inventor and is capable of being possessed or owned. Propertization is thus predicated on the divisibility of the object such that it can be delineated to an owner and on the location of the legitimate owner. On the basis of location, that is, who possesses it, knowledge may be categorized as individual knowledge, distributed knowledge, or communal knowledge, etc. According to Kibet A. Ng'etich's analysis, knowledge can exist in either of a combination of these, forms in all societies, including traditional societies. However, we also need to understand the peculiar nature of individually held knowledge in traditional societies 'the possession of knowledge by individuals... does not mean that such knowledge is perceived by communities as not belonging to them. Although, at any one time, knowledge may only be held by a handful of people with special roles in the community, in the course of the history of that community it becomes essentially communally held knowledge.'[33] This is because those with the special knowledge do not 'own' it as such, and many have obligations to share the knowledge within the community. There may exist, for instance, community standards for when the information must be passed, such as, during initiation rituals. They may hold the knowledge as trustees of the community.

Ownership here does not lead to standard exclusionary implications of the property language.[34] These features imply important differences between the meaning of individual property in Western culture, and knowledge held by individuals within a non-Western community context. The distinction between 'knowledge of communities' and 'of individuals within communities' does *not* get subsumed under the standard divide of private and public property. Privately held knowledge in traditional/ indigenous communities is not 'private' in the exclusionary sense. The residential connotations may not be implied here at all. In most cases of traditional and indigenous communities, a strong sharing ethos prevails, leading to an uneasy fit of any form of individualistic Western style appropriation as recognized and rewarded by the IPR regime.

---

[33] Kibet A. Ng'etich, *Indigenous Knowledge, Alternative Medicine and IP Rights Concerns in Kenya*. 11th General Assembly, Theme: Rethinking African Development: Beyond Impasse, Towards Alternatives (Maputo, Mozambique, 6–10 December 2005). Available at http://www.codesria.org/Links/conferences/general_assembly11/papers/ngetich.pdf (last accessed on 12 December 2007).

[34] Ibid.

Ownership patterns of TIK prevent rights claims over it within any framework of individualized rights, such as the TRIPS. In their recent study, political philosophers, Anthony Stenson, and Tim Gray argue that because TIK is primarily common knowledge and a product of collective experience without a individual act of creation, it gets precluded from being seen from the point of entitlement theory, as intellectual property.[35] The entire idiom of western legal practices and the vocabulary of intellectual property protection law carves out exclusive rights to an individual (either a natural person or a legal one) to exploit particular creations of human ingenuity. For example, a patent vests exclusive right in an inventor to develop, control, use, and market an innovative industrial process or product for a specified period of time. Trademarks extend protection to brand names that have a particular identity in the marketplace, while trade secrets protect confidential information often of commercial value to an industrial firm or person. Copyright covers literal and artistic works such as computer software, writings, and drawings. Generally, these forms of intellectual property protection do not provide the necessary protection for TIK, innovations and rights of indigenous and local peoples.[36] One of the prime reasons is that the locus of ownership cannot be clearly identified for knowledge systems that are essentially inter-generational and products of communal endeavour.

A necessary criterion that intellectual property must meet is that it must be considered non-obvious or 'novel'. Indigenous knowledge often falls short of this requirement as traditional knowledge is often orally transmitted, evolves gradually, the prime ambition being to respond to changing ecology and needs. It never actively endeavours to be 'novel' or distinct from nature. For example, in many indigenous communities, shamanic knowledge or medicinal products are believed to have come from natural or supernatural sources as opposed to being man-made or

[35] A. Stenson and T. Gray, 1997, 'Cultural Communities and IP Rights Check Title? in Plant Genetic Resources', in *Justice, Property and Environment: Social and Legal Perspectives*, T. Hayward and J. O' Neill (eds), Aldershot and Broof field: Ashgate Publishing, pp. 178–93.

[36] An exception is copyright law that accords a certain measure of protection for recorded or documented traditional knowledge. In Canada and Australia, copyright protection has been used by Aboriginal artists, composers, and writers of tradition-based creations. However, it is relatively expensive for holders of traditional knowledge to enforce their intellectual rights enshrined in copyright. It is important to also note that copyrights protect an expression and not necessarily the knowledge in that expression. A growing public policy debate is now whether traditional knowledge should be protected under other forms of IP law, particularly patent law.

invented.[37] In some Indian medical practices, certain medical potions acquire their potent properties only when they are blessed by the gods, again denoting a blur in the conception of natural and man-made. The extent of what constitutes natural and what is man-made differs from culture to culture indicating a difficulty in determining what should be considered an innovation (a product of human intervention and conceptualization) or simply a product of nature. This has an implication for intellectual property claims, unless a product is substantially different from one found in nature, and is thus the result of a 'non-obvious' human invention, the product or its knowledge cannot be considered a subject of intellectual property.

A third feature which prevents TIK from being regarded as intellectual property is the element of disclosure. Some traditional knowledges, especially in China and India[38] have, through history become disclosed as a result of codification (that is, formalization in written form), wide use, or through collection and publication by anthropologists, historians, botanists or other researchers and observers.[39] When TIK is disclosed it becomes publicly available and hence, under current IPR rules, lies in the public domain making it an 'obvious' form of knowledge that cannot be claimed as intellectual property. Kept in public access, these forms of knowledge acquire properties of public goods. Even the recent disclosure practices, a result of attempts by the Doha Declaration to align the TRIPS agreement with disclosure principles enumerated in CBD, sometimes find it difficult to locate the beneficiary, for the historical trial of cumulative knowledge is extremely fuzzy. Much indigenous knowledge is not traceable to a specific community or geographical area and is often classified as falling within the 'public domain'. The 'public domain' in intellectual property law consists of intangible commodities over which exclusive intellectual property rights cannot be claimed and which, therefore, become freely available to be used and exploited by any person. It is significant to note that the notion of the 'public domain' has been used to serve as a tool to not only deny the claims of TIK for intellectual property protection but also as a tool by the bio-prospecting

[37] N. Roht-Arriaza, 1996, 'Of Seeds And Shamans: The Appropriation of the Scientific and Technical Knowledge of Indigenous and Local Communities', *Michigan Journal of International Law*, 17 (919), pp. 919–965.

[38] D. Shankar, A. Hafeel, and T. Suma, 1999, 'Cultural Richness of Green Pharmacy', *Compass Newsletter*, 2, p. 10.

[39] M. Koning, 1998, 'Biodiversity prospecting and the equitable remuneration of ethnobiological knowledge: reconciling industry and indigenous interests', *Intellectual Property Journal*, 12.

corporations to legitimize the free appropriation of what has come to regarded as the 'global commons'.[40]

On the other hand, if forms of TIK are undisclosed as, for instance, amongst Kenyan traditional medical practitioners[41] and remain non-codified, they get termed as 'folk', 'rural', 'tribal' and 'indigenous', based on traditional beliefs, norms and practices, on centuries old experiences of trials and errors, and therefore cannot be classified as innovation or scientific and will not lend themselves to propertization. They also, it is alleged, exist in a 'non-commercial' form, valid and appropriate only for the people and geographical context in question. Thus, in order to improve their accessibility and wider applicability, they need to be repackaged in the language and form of a 'product', that can have a wider, perhaps universal, accessibility. TIK can, it is alleged, provide some useful leads or cues, 'sign posts' for the screening of natural products for therapeutic benefit. It may also be useful to confirm research results produced in the laboratory and complement scientific testing, including safety and efficacy. But in itself it does not exist in a form that can be accorded the status of intellectual property which is reserved for those innovative ventures that yield results and products that the market and global users can understand. This is the language of modern science. At play here is the ascendancy of scientific knowledge, first drawing out cognitive hierarchies, then homogenizing the 'other' in its own image.

A final barrier for TIK to become eligible for intellectual property protection is the prohibitive costs of registering and defending a patent or other IPR against a challenge or infringement. This effectively limits the availability of IPRs, depriving the vast majority of indigenous communities, primarily in developing countries. Apart from the costs

---

[40] Vandana Shiva, a vehement critic of the implications of global commons, argues that even though references are made to 'global biodiversity' and 'global genetic resources' biodiversity is not a part of global commons in the ecological sense in which the atmosphere or oceans are. Biodiversity has more the character of a 'local commons' around which communities subsist and in turn sustain the ecology that sustains them. She adds that a resource is common property when social systems exist to use it on principles of justice and sustainability. For details see, V. Shiva, 1994, 'Biodiversity Conservation, People's knowledge and IP Rights', in *Biodiversity Conservation: Whose Resources? Whose Knowledge?* Vandana Shiva (ed.), Delhi: INTACH, pp. 4–6.

[41] A significant part of traditional medicine remains secret. Knowledge held by bone-setters, midwives or traditional birth attendants and herbalists, including knowledge of healing techniques and properties of plants and animal substances, access is restricted to certain classes of people. For some instances of such knowledge in Africa see, Nyamwaya David, 1992, *African Indigenous Medicine*, Nairobi: KEMRI. Kibet A. Ng'etich, *Indigenous Knowledge, Alternative Medicine and IP Rights Concerns in Kenya*, p. 6.

involved, most of the carriers of TIK are well outside the domain and the levels of legal awareness required for registering a claim either for claiming or breach of their knowledge practices.

These barriers have kept the traditional/indigenous societies outside the 'loop' of the intellectual property rights protection. Modern day intellectual property law allows control over knowledge if certain socially, economically, and culturally determined conditions are met. A claim to legal control over knowledge will normally fail if there is no external manifestation or precise delineation, no identifiable author or inventor, and no novelty or originality. Indigenous knowledge often falls short of these requirements.

Do the criteria reflect an intellectual and cultural bias? Does TIK need to be validated according to the western intellectual property norms in order for its legal status to be formalized? What happens to customary rights when confronted by the entire legal apparatus of scientific innovation and property rules?[42] Does protection accorded under access and benefit sharing mechanisms ever offer them the protection that customary rights provided them tacitly? These are important questions for they relate to the complex interplay of issues of rights, ecology, culture, and justice. A process which begins with the limits of modern science, is turned on its head and ends as a project which hegemonizes modern science. The events that occur between these two end points are of crucial significance What and who is subverted or subsumed to enable this transformation? Is it a matter of amending and fine-tuning the intellectual property laws in order to make them more responsive to dimensions of TIK, or of re-conceptualizing the very notion of knowledge as property?

I seek to argue here that the very notion of intellectual property is a notion that is incommensurate with the intellectual traditions of indigenous or traditional peoples, and that any attempt to incorporate the knowledge rights of the traditional peoples within the terms of the TRIPS framework, even if democratized, is likely to result in rewriting the history of TIK in terms of western hegemonic intellectual and cultural traditions. Part of the process of 'democratization' is to strip rights (which offer protection to TIK, in this case) to their bare minimum so that they do not run contrary to the purposes of intellectual property protection in general. As a delegate

---

[42] Customary rights are not written into law but lie at the very heart of secure livelihoods and survival options, especially of marginal, tribal, indigenous, farmer communities. These customary laws have offered timeless protection to the traditional producer communities through their inalienable collective rights to resources, knowledge, markets, and livelihoods.

at a WIPO Round Table in Sydney stated: 'One should not attempt to amend Western laws to cater for indigenous peoples. Attempts to do so will be doomed, because the intellectual property system and the needs of indigenous peoples are too distinct'.[43] The terms of integration envisaged by the international conventions and institutions like the UPOV, TRIPS framework, and CBD are 'nothing less than controlled assimilation'.[44]

Demonstrating the epistemic and cultural hierarchies embedded in the notion and practice of IPRs is politics of Neem. The example of Neem, an emblematic of indigenous knowledge, provides a useful resource to understandsymbolic politics of knowledge. Politics over the Neem patent demonstrates the extent to which the IP regime attempts to frame and structure TIK is in accordance with the principles of modern science. It symbolizes the appropriation of traditional knowledge as intellectual property; and the infringement of knowledge rights of the traditional and indigenous communities. It short, it plays out the entire gamut of issues that interface of intellectual property rights and TIK has come to represent.

NEEM: A CASE IN KNOWLEDGE RIGHTS INFRINGEMENT
The Significance of Neem

Neem (*Azadirachta indica.*), labelled as the 'the wonder tree' is perhaps the most celebrated medicinal plant of India and finds mention in a number of *Puranic* texts as also in ancient Persian and Urdu pharmacopeias who called it a 'Blessed Tree' and the 'Village Pharmacy'. Parts of the tree provide effective ingredients for traditional and modern toothpastes, medicines, cosmetics, and insect repellents. Neem, also called Holy Tree, is native to India and Sri Lanka. India alone has more than 20 million trees.

The past five decades witnessed intensive investigation and a growing scientific interest in Neem and its diverse properties resulting in a large number of research publications, books, and conferences at national and international levels. In India, attempts in research and development of Neem began as early as the 1960s.[45] It led to isolation and identification

[43] WIPO Draft Report on Fact finding Mission on Intellectual Property and Traditional Knowledge (1998–9), Sydney, Australia, 18 June 1998. Cited in WIPO Draft Report on 'Fact finding Missions on IP and Traditional Knowledge'. (1998–9). 3 July 2000. Available at http://www.wipo.int/tk/en/tk/ffm/report/interim/docs/7-1.doc (last accessed on 11 January 2008).

[44] Andrew Gray, 1991, 'The Impact of Biodiversity Conservation on the Indigenous Peoples,' in *Biodiversity: Social and Ecological Perspectives*, V. Shiva, Patrick Anderson, *et al.* (eds), Penang, Malaysia: World Rainforest Movement, p. 71.

[45] For an exhaustive list of the research institutions and scientists involved in Neem research see Vandana Shiva, Radha Holla Bhar, K. Vijaylakshmi and K.S. Radha, 2006, *Neem*, Delhi: RFSTE, pp. 28–30.

of hundreds of the active compounds, from various parts of the plant with pesticidal, fungicidal, bactericidal, anti inflammatory, anti-tumor and other beneficial properties that found applications in the pesticide, medical, healthcare, and cosmetic industry all over the world. Worldwide attention based on evaluation and realization of the long-term benefits that Neem promises have resulted in a surge of commercial interest. The potential for industrial applications has, in part, triggered feverish research on the understanding of Neem chemistry.

The Sanskrit name, *Nimba*, meaning to bestow health, suggests the many therapeutic values of the tree and its various parts. Over 700 herbal preparations based on Neem are found in Ayurveda, Siddha, Unani, Amchi and other local health traditions. P. Pushpangadan points out that over 160 local practices are known in different parts of the country where Neem forms an important or sole ingredient in curing human ailments or disorders. What is of significance in the context of this chapter is the evidence provided at the World Neem Conference on the extent to which the knowledge about Neem lies in the public domain in India.[46] Knowledge residing in the public domain essentially prevents it from being patented, at least in India, where Neem products and processes to derive the products, would neither be 'novel' nor 'non-obvious'. In cases where the patenting of TIK is prohibited in the source country, such as in India, there is a possibility that the product, or a process, could be patented in the jurisdiction of another country. Consequently, there have been several attempts to patent Neem in other jurisdictions. Attempts to patent Neem is only one example of a practice that is pervasive.

Neem Patents

Neem has been patented widely.[47] There have been numerous instances of challenges to Neem patent applications which have been successful

[46] The Fourth World Neem Conference, was held at Mumbai in 2002. Issues covered included Environment and socioeconomic rights, animal and human health, chemistry, nematode control, fungus control, processing and product development, genetic improvement, and afforestation. Conference report on 'Neem 2002: World Neem Conference' held in Mumbai from 27–30 November 2002 and organized by Neem Foundation, Mumbai.

[47] For a list of patent claims on Neem refer to the Annexures in Vandana Shiva, Radha Holla Bhar, K. Vijaylakshmi and K.S. Radha, 2006, *Neem: Fight against Biopiracy and Rejuvenation of Traditional Knowledge*, RFSTE. Two other controversial US patents on Neem are US patent No 4946681—granted in 1990 for improving the storage stability of neem seed extracts containing azadirachtin; US patent No 5124349—granted in 1994 for storage of stable insecticidal composition comprising neem seed extract. Patents for Neem have been granted in India too—for details refer to the Neem Foundation website at http://www.neemfoundation. org/neem-articles/patents-on-neem.html (last accessed on 26 January 2008).

in revoking the patents granted, but a number of Neem patents still exist. Since the 1980s, many Neem related processes and products have been patented in Japan, USA and the European countries. The first US patent was obtained by Terumo Corporation in 1983 for its therapeutic preparation from Neem bark.[48] In 1985 Robert Larson, a US timber importer, obtained a patent for his preparation of Neem seed extract and the Environmental Protection Agency (EPA) approved this product for use in US market. In 1988 Robert Larson sold the patent on an extraction process to the US Company W.R. Grace (presently Certis). Having gathered their patents and clearance from the EPA, four years later, Grace commercialized its product by setting up a manufacturing plant in collaboration with P.J. Margo Pvt. Ltd in India and continued to file patents from its own research base in USA and other parts of world. In 1992, the US Patent and Trademark Office (USPTO) issued a patent to Grace which covered a method of creating a stabilized azadirachtin (the active pesticidal ingredient found in Neem tree extracts) in solution, and the stabilized azadirachtin solution itself.[49] Subsequently, the EPA registered Grace's stabilized azadirachtin solution for use on food crops under the name Neemix.

Apart from Grace, Neem based pesticides were also marketed by another company, AgriDyne Technologies Inc., USA[50] (US Patent No. 5.009,886 was granted in 1993 to Floss Products Corp., Illinois, for the development of a toothpaste using Neem roots and branches). The patent also covers the paste compound and the process of deriving micro-fibres from the branches and roots to include in the paste. Using Neem twigs to clean teeth is a common practice followed throughout India, over millennia. The use of Neem as a dentifrice is thus neither 'novel' nor 'different'. The paste is merely a minor modification of traditional use, and this minor modification is based on the traditional knowledge of the use of Neem fibres as a dentifrice. Besides, Neem has been commercialized in India since the 1960s, Neem based toothpaste being produced by both the

[48] US Patent No. 4,515,785 (Neem Bark Extracts); US Patent NO. 4,537,774 (Hot-water Extracts of Neem) Granted to Terumo Corporation (Japanese Corporation) in 1983.

[49] US Patent No 5,124,349, Storage Stable Azadirachtin Formulation (issued 23 June 1992).

[50] AgriDyne had established a joint venture with Aftaab Investment Co. Ltd of the Tata Group of India to manufacture and sell plant based bio-pesticides on the Indian market. For agricultural pesticides, the annual estimated value of the Indian market is US 495 million dollars, the 13th largest in the world. J. Kocken and G.Van Roozendaal, 1997, 'The Neem Tree Debate.' *Biotechnology and Development Monitor*, 30, p. 811.

cottage sector as well as by the domestic industry. Prior commercialization of product and common knowledge are two criteria which establish the fact that particular knowledges lie in the public domain and are therefore constitute evidence of 'prior art' or 'prior knowledge' which should be sufficient to defeat patent claims.

The ten-year period from 1985 to 25 April 1995 was marked by a deluge of US and European patents on Neem-related products. Twenty-eight patents were filed in that period in USA (of which 15 were filed in just the 16 months between January 1994 and April 1995—almost at the rate of one every month), 16 European and 9 Patent Cooperation Treaty (PCT) patents—a total of 53 patents,[51] all claiming to be 'new inventions' however nearly all related to the dentifrical and pesticidal/fungicidal properties of Neem, known and utilized in India for centuries. As on March 2005, sixty-five patents for products derived from the Neem tree have been filed with the European Patent Office (EPO) to date, of which 22 have been granted, 28 are 'dead' for various reasons, and 9 are currently being examined.[52] These include claims for insecticides, fungicidal effects, methods of extraction, and storage, stable formulations of one of the active ingredients, azadirachtin, contraceptive, and medical uses. It is important to note that the Neem patents do not involve a genetically engineered product; neither has the tree itself been patented, nor any of its parts.

An analysis of the type of patents suggests that majority of them are for crop protection applications (63 per cent), followed by health care (13 per cent), industrial (5 per cent), veterinary care (5 per cent), cosmetics (6 per cent), and others (8 per cent). This trend is also seen in country-wise granted patents. For example, in the US, out of 54 Neem patents granted, 31 were for crop protection, and the rest for healthcare, cosmetics, industrial, and veterinary applications. Patents ownership by organization indicates that the largest number are owned by Certis—W.R. Grace (49) followed by Rohm & Haas (36), CSIR-India (14), Trifolio (9), Bayer (8), and EID Parry (6).[53]

The Neem Foundation records that the largest number of patents is in USA (54) followed by Japan (35), Australia (23), India (14).[54] With

[51] See, 15 March 1996, *Down to Earth*, 4(20), p. 22.

[52] V. Shiva, *et al.*, *Neem*, 174, Conference Report on 'World Neem Conference 2002'.

[53] Pramila Thakkar, *Patents on Neem*. (31 October 2007). Available at http://Neemfoundation.org/index.php?option=com_content&task=view&id=26&Itemid=26 (last accessed on 31 January 2008).

[54] Ibid. For examples of some patents also see the Annexures in Vandana Shiva, Radha Holla Bhar, K. Vijaylakshmi and K.S. Radha, 2006, *Neem: Fight against Biopiracy and*

corporations holding nearly three-fourths of all patents on Neem-related products, research institutions take a distant second place with six patents or 17 per cent of all patents; individuals have four patents or 11 per cent of all patents. One particularly intriguing European patent (Patent No. 436257 dated 10 July 1991), titled Hydrophobic extracted Neem Oil, a Novel Insecticide and Fungicide, is held jointly by W.R. Grace and Co. and the US government. Although some Indian companies have claimed patents on the Neem, they are outnumbered by multinational corporations, such as the US pharmaceutical company Rohm & Haas and most infamously agrochemical giant W.R. Grace.

Two patents: (1) US Patent No. 5,124,349 for 'Storage Stable Azadirachtin Formulation' issued on 23 June 1992 and (2) European Patent No. 436257 for 'Hydrophobic extracted Neem oil' issued on 10 July 1991 are significant cases because on them converged the symbolic fight against appropriation of TIK made possible by the TRIPS laws. They became the focal point of the assertion of the right of the traditional indigenous peoples over their knowledge rights and their resources. The patent battles came to question the conceptual and moral premises of intellectual property rights which assert the primacy of one kind of knowledge right over another.

Opposition to the European Neem Patent

The patent application was filed by United States Department of Agriculture (USDA) and W.R. Grace on 12 December 1990 at the European Patent Office (EPO). On 14 September 1994, the EPO granted a patent for a particular method for controlling fungi on plants which comprised contacting the fungi with a Neem oil formulation and the process for obtaining Neem oil ('Hydrophobic extracted Neem oil').[55] This pesticide was claimed to have the ability to repel insects from plant surfaces, prevent fungal growth, and kill insects and fungal pests at various life stages.

Rejuvenation of Traditional Knowledge, Delhi: RFSTE. Two other controversial US patents on Neem are US patent No 4946681—granted in 1990 for improving the storage stability of neem seed extracts containing azadirachtin; US patent No 5124349—granted in 1994 for storage of stable insecticidal composition comprising neem seed extract. Patents for Neem have been granted in India too. For details refer to the Neem Foundation website at http://www.neemfoundation.org/neem-articles/patents-on-neem.html (last accessed on 26 January 2008).

[55] Patent No. 436257 dated July 10, 1991. The grant of a European patent was for 'A method for controlling fungi on plants comprising contacting the fungi with a Neem oil formulation containing 0.1 to 10 per cent of a hydrophobic extracted Neem oil which is substantially free of azadirachtin, 0.005 to 5.0 per cent of emulsifying surfactant, and 0 to 99 per cent water'.

The patent grant was indignantly opposed in India for the use of Neem oil to repel fungi, bacteria, insects is as old as history. A patent challenge was filed on 5 June 1995 by Vandana Shiva of Research Foundation for Science, Technology and Ecology (RFSTE) (India), Linda Bullard of International Federation of Organic Agriculture Movements (Germany) and Magda Alvoet, Health and Environment Minister of Belgium.[56] The main contention was that an invention needs to be novel and non-obvious and there should be no evidence of 'prior art/use', and further, that the invented product should be radically different in its formulation than the existing ones in the field. This was not the case with the Neem patent. The legal opposition filed by the three opponents was on grounds that the fungicidal effect of hydrophobic extracts of Neem seeds was known and used for centuries on a broad scale in India, both in Ayurvedic medicine to cure dermatological diseases, and in traditional Indian agricultural practice to protect crops from being destroyed by fungal infections. Since this traditional Indian knowledge was in fact ubiquitous in Indian culture from ancient times, they asserted that the patent in question lacked two basic statutory requirements for the grant of a European patent, namely 'novelty' (Article 54 of the European Patent Convention [EPC]) and 'inventive step' (Article 56, EPC in the US called non-obviousness).

In addition, the opponents charged that the patent was contrary to 'morality' (EPC, Article 53a) because the so-called inventors claimed monopoly property rights on a method which forms a part of the traditional knowledge base of India, in essence, stealing it and theft is regarded as immoral in European culture. Finally, they cited the formal grounds of 'insufficient disclosure' (Article 83 EPC) and 'lack of clarity' (Article 84 EPC) in calling for the revocation of the patent. Subsequently, the opponents requested an additional ground for opposition, namely, that the patent constituted de facto a monopoly on a single plant variety, which is barred by Article 53 (b) of the EPC.[57] On these grounds the opponents 'challenged Patent 0436257 B1 to establish that this patent, like others based on biopiracy, was nothing novel and did not involve an inventive step'.[58]

---

[56] The three partners joined forces to launch the Opposition: an organization from the country where the resource was stolen, an international organization representing organic users and producers of Neem products throughout the world, and an environmental political party, well positioned to pursue changes in the legal system itself to outlaw Biopiracy. And from within these organizations it was women who initiated the action and sustained it—an Indian, a Belgian, and an American.

[57] Linda Bullard, Freeing the Free Tree (2005)

[58] V. Shiva, November 1999, *Campaign against Biopiracy*, New Delhi: RFSTE.

Two expert witnesses from India were made to testify from the opposition bench: Udai Pratap Singh of Varanasi (Professor and Head Department of Mycology and Plant Pathology, Institute of Agricultural Sciences, Banaras Hindu University), widely regarded as India's greatest expert on Neem from the scientific community, and Abhay Dattaray Phadke of Pune, an agronomist who had commercialized a Neem product in India (without claiming patent protection). On the basis of testimony presented, the Opposition Division of the EPO ruled that the patentee's claim of novelty had been destroyed on the basis of clearly demonstrated prior public use. It ruled that even in amended form, the 'invention' was lacking an inventive step. Thus, the patent was revoked in its entirety.

The Opposition Division of the EPO accepted the opponents' argument that patents should not be granted for common traditional knowledge, but pointed out that this argument should be used for establishing 'prior art' and is not a question of morality under EPC, as the opponents had charged.[59] It was clear that the case was won on the basis of affidavits and testimony, and through them the establishment of 'prior use' and not on the basis of the moral claim.[60] The US government and W.R. Grace appealed to the next level within the EPO, the Technical Appeals Board, demanding that the decision of the Opposition Division be overturned and submitting yet another modified formulation of their original claim.

Five more years of submissions and filings ensued before the case once again reached the level of an Oral Proceeding at the EPO.[61] The five-member Technical Board of Appeals needed only two hours to reach its decision. On 8 March 2005[62] the Chairman announced, 'The Appeal is dismissed. The patent is revoked.' The reasoning of the Opposition Division was upheld, that the patent did not satisfy the requirements for novelty and/or inventive step. EPO struck down Patent No. 436257, jointly held by the United States Government and the multinational W.R. Grace.

[59] Article 53(a) EPC: 'Inventions the publication or exploitation of which would be contrary to 'ordre public' or morality, provided that the exploitation shall not be deemed to be so contrary merely because it is prohibited by law or regulation in some or all of the Contracting States'. Available at http://www.epo.org/patents/law/legal-texts/html/epc/1973/e/contents.html (last accessed on 20 January 2008).

[60] From 'Decision revoking the European patent 436257' of the EPO, ref. Neemfungicide, dated 13 February 2001, Application No./Patent No. 90 250 319.2-2117/0436257/01.

[61] WR Grace in the meantime was acquired, along with its patents, by Certis, a wholly-owned subsidiary of the Japanese company Mitsui & Co., which is now one of the largest providers worldwide of 'safe food' technologies. Throughout these business mutations, the United States of America has remained the constant 'co-proprietor' of the patent.

[62] Significantly on Women's Day the three opponents were women.

The EPO upheld that this patent was based on the piracy of existing knowledge systems and lacked novelty and inventiveness. Vandana Shiva described the battle, collectively waged and successfully won, as 'a major milestone ... crossed in the contemporary movement of freedom from biocolonialism and biopiracy'.[63] Linda Bullard, the other co-opponent wrote, 'legal history was made on March 8th, 2005 in Munich, Germany when the Technical Board of Appeals of the European Patent Office (EPO) revoked in its entirety a patent on a fungicide made from seeds of the Neem tree, concluding a ten-year battle in the world's first legal challenge to a Biopiracy patent.'[64] In a press release on 8 March 2005, the Green parties in the European Parliament cabled out to the world that the decision to uphold the revocation of a patent on the Indian Neem tree was 'a killer blow to biopiracy in Europe and around the world'.[65]

Challenge to the US Neem Patent

Another contested Neem patent was the US patent no. 5,124,349 held by W.R Grace, which concerned a process to extract and stabilize an azadirachtin based pesticide (Margosan-O) from the Neem seed. In 1995, a coalition of 200 nongovernmental organizations from 40 countries was established to protest Grace's patent. In September of that year, the initiators of this coalition, Jeremy Rifkin of the Foundation on Economic Trends (USA) and Vandana Shiva, president of the Research Foundation for Science, Technology and Ecology (RFTSE, India), petitioned the US Patent and Trademark Office (PTO) to revoke Grace's patent. Other key petitioners included: Dr M D Nanjundaswamy of Karnataka Rajya Ryota Sangha, a farm organization representing farmers throughout India; Linda Bullard, Vice-President of the International Federation of Organic Agriculture Movements in Brussels; and Martin Khor, Director of the Third World Network.[66] Once again the opposition was based on grounds that the patent was derived from knowledge and use that lay in the public domain. Rifkin argued that the patent gives Grace exclusive rights to formulations, which have been developed and used by Indian farmers for centuries.

[63] Vandana Shiva, Free Tree, *Hindustan Times*, India, 9 June 2000.

[64] European patent No. 0436 257 revoked, available at: http://www.european-patent-office.org/news/pressrel/2000_05_11_e.htm (last accessed on 26 August 2007).

[65] 'EPO upholds decision to withdraw 'free tree' patent: Greens celebrate Neem biopiracy victory', available at: http://www.greens (last accessed on 31 August 2007).

[66] For an edited version of the petition filed by the coalition of organizations in the US Patent and Trademark office see, TWN report available at http://www.twnside.org.sg/title/Neem-ch.htm (last accessed on 16 January 2008).

The central issue of the patent opposition was that the pesticidal extract in question has long been known to and used by the Indian people for protecting their crops. The knowledge of this was therefore available at the time of patenting, to any ordinary person and the difference between it and the patented product, if any, was 'obvious'.[67] This challenge was seen as a critical test of the intellectual property laws established by the WTO. As trans-nationals and other enterprises from the global North scout remote regions of the South for genetic resources to patent, a process now referred to as bio-prospecting, the battle between native peoples and multinationals is, in the words of Jeremy Rifkin, 'likely to be the critical to the North-South political and economic issue of the coming decade'.[68] In what was seen as the opening round in this confrontation, the Neem tree became the symbol of resistance against appropriation of knowledge and resources from the global commons.

The pivot of W.R. Grace's justification for patents, therefore, was the claim that these modernized extraction processes constitute a genuine innovation: 'Although traditional knowledge inspired the research and development that led to these patented compositions and processes, they were considered sufficiently novel and different from the original product of nature and the traditional method of use to be patentable.'[69]

Attacking the claims of novelty, Vandana Shiva asserted that the theory that azadirachtin was being destroyed during traditional processing is inaccurate.[70] The extracts were subject to degradation, but this was not a problem, because the product was used within a few days of production by Indian farmers. Therefore, there was no immediate need for a process of stabilizing the extract. The need for extract preservation only arises in case of mass production for broader and distant export markets. Moreover, she added that stabilization techniques had already been developed by

[67] 'In the late sixties we discovered the potency of not only ethanolic extract, but also other extracts of Neem ... Work on the Neem as pesticide originated from this division as early as 1962. Extraction techniques were also developed by a couple of years'. Vandana Shiva, The Neem tree—a case history of biopiracy. Available at http://www.twnside.org.sg/title/pir-ch.htm (last accessed on 26 June 2008).

[68] Quoted from TWN website http://www.twnside.org.sg/title/Neem-ch.htm (last accessed on 26 June 2008).

[69] Quoted from Vandana Shiva, 1999, 'A Case Study of Intellectual Property Rights and Traditional Knowledge', International Conference of the Council of Europe on Ethical Issues Arising from the Application of Biotechnology, 16–19 May, 2(2), p. 244.

[70] Vandana Shiva, The Neem tree—a case history of Bio-piracy, Third World Network. Available at http://www.twnside.org.sg/title/pir-ch.htm (last accessed on 28 December 2008).

Indian scientists in the 1960s and 1970s. Margosan-O is a simple ethanolic extract of Neem seed kernel.[71] The biologically active polar chemicals can be extracted using technology already available to villages in developing countries, stated Eugene Schulz, chair of the NRC (National Research Council, US) panel.[72] Existing Neem patents, therefore, apply only to methods of extracting the natural chemical in the form of a stable emulsion or solution, methods which are simply an extension of the traditional processes used for millennia for making Neem-based products. The discovery of Neem's pesticidal properties and of how to process it was by no means 'obvious', but evolved through extended systematic knowledge development in non-Western cultures. In comparison to this first non-obvious leap of knowledge, it is the subsequent minor derivatives that are 'obvious'.[73]

Under Sections 301 and 302 of the US Patent Code, any individual may file a request for the re-examination of an existing patent if the requester believes 'prior art' would have a bearing on the patentability of any claim of the patent. Prior art includes knowledge that was available to a person at the time of patenting. An invention is not patentable if the differences between it and the prior art would have been obvious at the time of patenting. Revocation of Patent No. 5124349 (W.R. Grace's patent for Neem oil extraction) was demanded because the company's method of extracting stable compounds was widely used prior to the patent's issuance, and because the extraction methods had been previously described in printed publications. In fact, common knowledge and common use of Neem was one of the primary reasons given by the Indian Central Insecticide Board for not registering Neem products under the Insecticides Act, 1968. The Board argued that Neem materials had been in extensive use in India for various purposes since time immemorial, without any known deleterious effects.

The patents granted to W.R. Grace in Europe and the US stirred up a lot of indignation in India and many felt that W.R. Grace had claimed as its own, knowledge which belonged to the people of India. An associated fear was also that bringing Neem products and, as a consequence, Neem seeds into the ambit of global market exchange would drive seed prices

[71] R.P. Singh of the Indian Agricultural Research Institute in a conversation with Vandana Shiva, cited in Vandana Shiva, *Radha Holla-Bhar, Piracy by Patent: The Case of the Neem Tree*. Available at http://www. icta.org/doc/shiva%20holla-bhar.pdf (last accessed on 26 January 2008).

[72] Eugene Schulz, 1992, *Science*, 17 January. Quoted from Vandana Shiva, *Radha Holla-Bhar*, ibid., p. 152.

[73] Ibid.

up, dislocating the traditional balance of exchange and production of Neem and its products. When both the producers and the end users are farmers the dependence on the global trade nexus raises legitimate concerns and fears.[74]

BIO-PIRACY AND KNOWLEDGE RIGHTS

The Neem patents are just one in a large catalogue of genetic resources originating in the global South, over which intellectual property rights are being asserted by a few multinational corporations belonging largely to the North. The Neem patent challenge was initiated in solidarity with the Neem Campaign of India, which was launched in 1993 by farmers in India who feared that their genetic resources and traditional knowledge were coming increasingly under foreign control through the legal mechanism of patents. The whole process can be likened to a modern form of 'enclosure of the commons', in this case, of course, it was not public land being privatized but rather public knowledge. The case study attempted to highlight the undisputed existence of prior knowledge and usage of Neem related products in India, which presents before us a classic case of bio-piracy by the transnational corporations. Neither the traditional extraction methods, nor the modern methods developed by Indian scientists were patented. The botanical and the commercial value of Neem both ensure that there is an ongoing process of not only attempts at commercialization, but also attempts to secure, by means of patents, monopoly profits. In India, over 70 patents have already been obtained by western (mainly North-American) corporations involving some part of the Neem plant whose wide-ranging medicinal and environmental properties have been used, at no cost, by indigenous people for over 4,000 years. Neem's properties ironically are being claimed by big businesses as patented inventions.[75]

Neem presents a case of bio-piracy replicated in many instances, the common feature being existence of prior knowledge which lies in the public domain of traditional and often poor societies. The protection of this domain becomes dependent on their governments or public institutions who alone have the legal and the financial wherewithal to challenge the infringing patent. Discussed below are some prominent cases which, though representative of the infringement of knowledge rights, are by no means exhaustive.

[74] Shayana Kadidal, 1996–7, 'Subject-Matter Imperialism? Biodiversity, Foreign Prior Art and the Neem Patent Controversy,' *IDEA The Journal of Law and Technology*, vol. 37, p. 371.

[75] Regina Jere-Malanda, *Biopiracy: Neem, the wonder tree* is a classic example of biopiracy from which Africa has a lot to learn is the blatant pirating of the Neem tree, dubbed by the UN as the 'tree of the 21st century'. New African, December, 2003.

Basmati

A US based company called RiceTec Inc. in Alvin, Texas, filed a patent in the US patent office for a product it had made and called Basmati. In late 1997, this company was granted a patent to call the aromatic rice grown outside India 'Basmati'. RiceTec Inc, was issued the Patent number 5663484 on Basmati rice lines and grains on 2 September 1997 by the USPTO. RiceTec had been trying to enter the international Basmati market with brands like 'Kasmati' and 'Texmati' with minimal success. With the patent rights, RiceTec would be able to not only call its aromatic rice Basmati within the US, but also label it as Basmati for its exports. This was likely to hit Indian exports of basmati rice badly. According to Vandana Shiva, the 'theft involved in the Basmati patent is threefold: a theft of collective intellectual and biodiversity heritage on Indian farmers, a theft from Indian traders and exporters whose markets are being stolen by RiceTec Inc., and finally a deception of consumers since RiceTec is using a stolen name Basmati for rice which are derived from Indian rice but not grown in India, and hence are not the same quality'.[76]

The Indian government put up a fight against the patent granted to RiceTec., following which a US court ruled that the company did invent new technologies and that the patent is valid. India then re-approached the issue as one of nomenclature and attempted to protect the name 'Basmati' as a geographic indicator (GI). In other words, basmati is a term that should be restricted to the product from this geographic location. For instance, only wine of a particular sort, produced in a particular region in France can be signified by the GI name 'Champagne'. Identical wine produced in the US cannot be called so; and hence is termed 'sparkling wine'. Geographic indicators are useful concepts since they protect native wisdom, technologies and traditional efforts from being hijacked. Articles 22–4 of the TRIPS agreement provide for the protection of GI's and prevention of their misuse. Under this, bio-resources traditionally nurtured by the local community inhabiting the particular region should be deemed as belonging to that region. After a prolonged legal battle, the Basmati patent was revoked in 2001. The Patent Examiner also changed the title of the patent from 'Basmati Rice Lines and Grains'—covering a broad general claim to invention of Basmati to 'Rice Lines Bas867, RT 1117, RT1121' which are restricted to the specific strains bred done by RiceTec. The original patent was open-ended and covered a wide range of plant height,

[76] Quoted from Ted Case studies; Basmati. Available at http://www.american.edu/ted/basmati.htm (last accessed on 28 December 2007).

grain size, aromatic quality, including but not confined to the qualities associated with basmati rice. The patent holder now could not claim the unique qualities of basmati rice nor the unique name 'Basmati'.[77]

Turmeric

Turmeric presents a similar case. Two researchers of Indian origin, based at the University of Mississippi Medical Center in Jackson applied for a US patent on the use of turmeric in wound healing. As per the conditions of patentability,[78] the 'prior art' clause is recognized if it is described in a 'printed publication'.[79] In this case, printed materials were available but not presented. The patent was granted in 1995 on the basis of limited searches for prior art which did not indicate that the claims were a part of public domain.[80] Subsequently, the patent was challenged by Council of Scientific and Industrial Research (CSIR) and the patent was revoked on the grounds that the alleged invention was actually a part of public domain knowledge in India.

The turmeric dispute again highlights the central issue of whether the use of turmeric in wound healing should have qualified as a patentable US product; whether it meets the legal criteria of novelty, non-obviousness, and utility; and what India's rights should be with regard to trading of the herb bilaterally? US patent law is criticized for discriminating against developing countries by failing to recognize products like turmeric as non-novel, despite the fact that this medicinal plant and other traditional agro-chemicals have been used in healing for thousands of years.

Ayahuasca

Inspired by the turmeric case, the Coordinating Body of Indigenous Organizations of the Amazon Basin (COCIA), which represents more

[77] For further details on the patent battle see, 'RiceTec Inc. a Texas-based US corporation has lost the Basmati Battle', *Navdanya*, 21 August 2001. Available at http://www.navdanya. org/news/01august21.htm (last accessed on 26 December 2007).

[78] 35 USC Section 102: Conditions for Patentability; novelty and loss of right to patent.

[79] Ibid, See 35 USC Section 102 Clause (a) One way it can be proven that an invention is not novel or new, is to show evidence of prior art, or prior knowledge of the invention. In the United States proof of prior art would be prior knowledge, use or invention. However, prior foreign knowledge, use and invention are all excluded from proof of prior art, if a foreign nation such as India were to challenge the patent on grounds of novelty. For a foreign nation such as India to prove prior art they would need to come up with a printed publication, a document related to the applicants own foreign patent, or some other persons foreign patent. That stipulation seems unfair on many counts.

[80] US Patent No 5,401,504, Use of Turmeric in Wound Healing (issued on 28 March 1995).

than 400 indigenous tribes in the Amazon region protested about a patent (US Plant Patent No. 5,751 issued in 1986) granted by the USPTO on a plant species native to the Amazon rainforest, called 'Ayahuasca' and its traditional medicinal uses. The petitioner specifically cited the case of revocation of the turmeric patent fought by India and asked for similar justice. On re-examination, the patent was also revoked by USPTO in November 1999. Interestingly, although the patent was granted in 1986, the case was fought only in 1999, after the success of the turmeric case in 1997.[81]

Maca

The patent row over the Peruvian Maca plant is another representative case in point which highlights the infringement of knowledge rights at a global level. For hundreds of years, Quechua Indians have grown 'maca', the frost-resistant root that thrives in these frigid Andean highlands, to boost stamina and sex drive. Riding the Viagra craze, in 2001 a New Jersey Comapany, Pure World Botanicals, received a US patent for exclusive commercial distribution of an extract of maca's active libido-enhancing compounds, which it branded as MacaPure.[82] Peruvian officials called the patent an 'emblematic case' of biopiracy. The Peruvian government identified several patents and patent applications relating to 'maca' (Lepidium meyenii), including claims on extracts,[83] 'macamides' and therapeutic methods and uses of the plant.[84] The Peruvian government expressed its concerns about the extent to which the patents granted[85]

[81] For details see Glenn M. Wiser, Center for International Environmental Law, November 1999. Available at http://www.ciel.org/Biodiversity/ptorejection.html (last accessed on 15 March 2008).

[82] US Patent No. 6,267,995—Pure World Botanicals Inc. Issued 31 July 2001 for Extract of Lepidium meyennii roots for pharmaceutical applications; US Patent No. 6,093,421—Biotics Research Corporation. Issued 25 July 2000 for Maca and antler for augmenting testosterone levels. US Patent Application No. 878,141—Pure World Botanicals Inc. Published on 11 April 2002, Compositions and methods for their preparation from Lepidium.

[83] See WIPO, Intergovernmental Committee on Intellectual Property and Generic Resources, fifth session, Geneva, 7–15 July 2003. Patents referring to lepidium meyenii (maca). See, Response of Peru-WIPO/GRTKF/IC/5/13. Available at http://www.wipo.int/edocs/mdocs/tk/en/wipo-grtkf-ic-5-13.pdf (last accessed on 8 December 2009).

[84] Details compiled from Carlos Correa, 2009, Trends in Intellectual Property and Genetic Resources for Food and Agriculture, Background Paper 49, October.

[85] Granted patents include US 6552206, 'Compositions and methods for preparation from Lepidium'; US 6428824. 'Treatment of sexual dysfunction with an extract of Lepidium meyenii roots'; US 6267995 'Extract of Lepidium meyenii roots for pharmaceutical applications'; US 6878731 'Imidazole alkaloids from Lepidium meyenii and method of usage'.

and pending applications in the USA could prevent exports of maca extracts from Peru,[86] and about the recognition of patent rights on genetic materials obtained 'unlawfully, contrary to the specific Decision 391 or even the rules in force for collecting and exporting biological materials.'[87] The Peruvian government stated that seven grounds of 'prior art' and said that the '...one question which arises as a result of the patents analysed is the degree of indigenous knowledge which was used to generate the claimed inventions'.[88] These patents 'are very questionable from a legal point of view'.[89]

The Maca dispute exemplifies yet another collision between indigenous people and commercial interests over so-called biological prospecting, the growing practice of scouring the globe for exotic plants, microbes, and other living things ripe for commercial exploitation. That has not stopped some of the world's poorest countries, which are also the richest pockets of natural biodiversity, from contesting patent claims based on their knowledge resources. India has been recently successful in persuading the European Patent Board of Appeals to invalidate a 1994 patent granted to US based W.R. Grace & Co. for an insecticide derived from Neem seeds. Turmeric, Basmati are two other well publicized cases where Indian interests have been recognized by courts of other jurisdictions.

Neem, along with Maca, Turmeric, Basmati, Ayahuasca, only exemplify a typical story of what has come to be referred to as bio-piracy. Shiva, one of the earliest to have coined the term bio-piracy, defines it as a process by which 'the biological and natural resources of communities and the country are freely taken, without recognition or permission, and are used to build global economies.'[90] The central criticism in the bio-piracy literature is that the big corporations are freely appropriating bio-diversity and ethno-botanical resources and traditional knowledge bases

---

[86] According to information supplied by PROMPEX (Commission for the Promotion of Exports), exports of maca have grown from US 1,056,287.79 dollars in 1998 to US 3,016,240.03 dollars in 2002.

[87] WIPO/GRTKF/IC/5/13, para. 117. In accordance with Peru's submission, '... six of the seven inventors mentioned in the patents of the United States of America and international applications analysed recognize that they obtained dry maca roots from Peru in 1998' (idem. para. 118. X [ii]).

[88] WIPO/GRTKF/IC/5/13, ibid. IX (ii).

[89] Ibid., X (i).

[90] Vandana Shiva, 1996, 'Biopiracy: The Plunder Of Nature And Knowledge. A New Partnership For National Sovereignty', in Solomaon Tilahun and Sue Edwards (eds), p. 62.

of the people, generally by means of patents without compensation to the indigenous groups who originally developed such knowledge. Once TIK is appropriated from unprotected commons, repackaged and made 'scientifically tested' and 'commercially accessible', the erstwhile TIK, divested of its essential identity, is claimed as an innovation and then as intellectual property. Critics argue that if patent, copyright, and trademark infringements are acts of intellectual piracy, then so is the failure to recognize and compensate the intellectual contributions of traditional peoples and communities who are the primary innovators.

Bio-piracy and patenting of indigenous knowledge is a double theft, argues Shiva, because first, it allows theft of creativity and innovation; and second, the exclusive rights established by patents on stolen knowledge steal economic options of everyday survival on the basis of indigenous biodiversity and indigenous knowledge. Biopiracy thus means not only a resource flow of diverse forms of flora and fauna, but mainly the appropriation and monopolization of traditional population's knowledge and biological resources. It results in the loss of control of traditional populations over their resources and can have implications for their livelihood and food security.

Appropriation of traditional knowledge is facilitated by the fact that this knowledge is communally held, feely exchangeable, and in the public domain. According to the stipulations of the patent laws that conform to the TRIPS agreement and other patent laws in the West, this ought to constitute 'prior art, prior use, or 'prior Knowledge'. However, in most of the developed nations like United States, prior existing knowledge is only recognized as such, if it is published in a journal or is available on a database, not if it has been passed down through generations of oral and folk traditions. This raises important questions about the vulnerability of TIK to patenting in non-source countries. In the turmeric and the Neem cases, the two things that resulted in the revoking of the patent was the presence of printed material which was later presented as proof of prior art and the institutional intervention by CSIR in the case of turmeric, and RFSTE in the case of Neem. What was in favour of these groups was that it had to undertake the challenge in a single country. The problems multiply exponentially when the challenge has to be undertaken by an individual in multiple countries. The problem of challenging patents reaches a dead end if there is no printed material available which documents the presence of the knowledge in the public domain. There are more instances of TIK residing in oral traditions than documented texts. These then become doubly vulnerable as they cannot furnish proof required for establishing prior use, prior art.

The irony here is that India has suffered even though its traditional knowledge, as in China, has been documented extensively. However, the documentation is available in languages which are not found to be easily accessible to international users. For instance, *Ayurvedic* texts are in Sanskrit and Hindi, *Unani* texts are in Arabic and Persian, and *Siddha* material is in Tamil language. Patent examiners, when considering the patentability of any claimed subject matter, use available resources for searching the novelty and appropriateness of the patent in question. Patent literature, however, is usually wholly contained in several distinctive databases and does not access prior art that may be buried somewhere in the many and diverse sources of non-patent literature.

Volumes of documentation reveal the extent to which commercialized patented products, a very large proportion of them being pharmaceuticals, stem from the traditional use patterns and knowledge bases of the traditional communities which ought to have been recognized as evidence of prior use in order to contest novelty or non-obvious claims for patents. Examples abound and a few of them have been cited here to highlight the extent to which these knowledge systems underlie a lot of research and innovative activity taking place in the west.

Table 8.1 shows some indigenous plants forming a part of the Indian traditional knowledge over centuries, which have been claimed as novel and patented.

TABLE 8.1: List of Indigenous Plants of India which were Patented in Other Countries

Common name	Botanical name	US Patent No.	Patentee	Purpose
Kumari	*Aloe barbadensis*	5652265	Michael Collins	Medicine
Amaltas	*Cassia fistula*	5411733	Toyoharu, Japan	Antiviral
Kala Jeera	*Cuminum cyminum*	5653981	Hilton, USA	Activates immune system
Pomegranate	*Punica granatum*	5411733	Toyoharu, Japan	Antiviral agent
Harad	*Terminalia chebula*	5529778	Surendra Rastogi, India	Ayurvedic importance
Aswagandha	*Withania somnifera*	5466452	Whittle, USA	Skin disorder

TABLE 8.2: List of Indigenous Plants of India Which were Patented in the US

Company	US Patent No.	Pirated Indigenous Knowledge Related to:
W. R. Grace 1750 Clint Moore Road Boca Raton, Florida, U.S.A. 33487-2707	[4556562] [4946681] [5124349] [5001146] [5405612] [5409708] [5411736][5397571]	Neem (Hindi); Margosa Tree (Eng.) Azadirachta indica
RiceTec Inc. SchlossVaduz FL-9490 Vaduz Liechtenstein	[5663484]	Basmati (Hindi & Eng.); Oryza sativa
Sabinsa Corporation 121 Ethel Road West, Unit # 6 Piscataway, NJ 08854, USA	[5536506]	Kali Marich (Hindi); Black Pepper (Eng.); Piper nigrum
Calgene(Subsidiary of Monsanto Co) 800 North Lindbergh Boulevard St Louis, Missouri 63167, U.S.A	[5510255] [547991] [5494790][5538868] [5475099] [5576428] [5558834]	Erand (Hindi); Castor (Eng.) Ricinus communis
Calgene(Subsidiary of Monsanto Co) 800 North Lindbergh Boulevard St Louis, Missouri 63167, U.S.A	[5463174] [5563058] [5512482] [5455167] [5420034]	Sarson (Hindi); Mustard (Eng.) Brsassica compestris
Pioneer Hi-bred / DuPont International Inc., Des Moines, IA, USA.	5638637] [5625130] [5470359]	Sarson (Hindi); Mustard (Eng.) Brassica compestris

Source: Navdanya Website release. Available at http://www.navdanya.org/earthdcracy/food/letter-biopiracy-and-wto.htm (last accessed on 26 January 2008).

Tables 8.1 and Table 8.2 indicate that appropriation of TIK includes patents on uses of Indian medicinal plants such as Kumari (*Aloe Barbadenis*), Shallaki (*Boswellia serrato*), Amaltas (*Cassia fistula*), Kala Jeera (*Cuminum cyminum*), Dudhi (*Euphorbia Hirta*), Garden Balsam (*Impatiens balsamina*), Jangli Erand (*Jatropha curcas*), Indian Mustard (*Brassica compestris*), Pomegranate (*Punica granatum*), Kali Marich (*Piper nigrum*), Bhu Amla (*Hyllanthus niruri*), Rangoon Creeper (*Quisqualis indica*), Arand (*Ricinus communis*), Black Nightshad (*Solanum nigrum*), Arjun (*Terminalisa arjuna*), Harad (*Terminalia chebula*), Guruchi (*Tinospora cordifolia*), Aswagandha (*Withania somnifera*), Karela (*Momordica charantia*),Vilayeti Shisham (*Sapium sebiferum*), Chhotagokhuru (*Tribulus terrestris*), Ritha (*Sapindus mukorossi*),

Ber (*Zizyphus jujuba*), Adarakha (*Zingiber officinale*), Latjira (*Achyranthes aspera*), Dhaya (*Woodfordia floribunda*), Kathal (*Artocarpus integrifolia*).[91]

The US patents office had already granted fourteen patents on mustard, seven on castor, four on amla, three each for cassia, and kumari, and two for bitter gourd, black cumin, jatropha and black nightshade for their various properties, says the report by Afsar H. Jafri, deputy director of RFSTE.[92] The report lists 22 medicinal and agricultural plants, including ritha, amaltas, kumari, pomegranate, balsam, and Rangoon creeper that have been patented in America and Europe. The US tops the list with the maximum number of patents for Indian plants, followed by Japan, Canada, France, Germany, and the UK, says Jafri. Other plants patented by these countries include arjun, harad, jangli, guruchi, vilayeti shisham, and chottagokhuru.

1. Studies have shown that as many as 74 per cent of the plant derived human drugs are used for the same purpose for which native people discovered their use.[93]
2. At least 7,000 medical compounds used in Western medicine are derived from plants. The value of developing-country germplasm to the pharmaceutical industry in the early 1990s was estimated to be at least US 32,000 million dollars per year. Yet developing countries were paid only a fraction of this amount for the raw materials and knowledge they contribute.[94]
3. US imports of Indian medicinal and cosmetic plants equaled US 37.8 million dollars in 2001, one-quarter of total US imports.[95]
4. 25 per cent of the US prescription drugs are said to have active ingredients from Indian plants. The sale of these drugs amounted to US 4.2 billion dollars in1980 and US 15.5 billion dollars in 1990. In the EU, Australia, Canada, and the US, the market value for both

---

[91] Vandana Shiva, *et al.*, 1997, *Enclosures and Recovery of the Commons,* RFSTE.

[92] Ibid; Also see Afsar H. Jafri, People's Commission on Biodiversity, Indigenous Knowledge and People's Rights: A Report, New Delhi: RFSTE.

[93] *Patents on Neem.* (Society for Research and Initiatives for Sustainable Technologies and Institutions) Available at http://csf.colorado.edu/sristi/papers/patentonNeem.html (last accessed on 20 March 2008).

[94] June 1994, 'Microbial BioPiracy: Initial Analysis of Microbial Genetic Resources Originating in the South and Held in the North', RAFI's Occasional Paper Series, 1(2); 'Declaring the Benefits: The North's Annual Profit from International Agricultural Research is in the Range of U.S $4–5 Billion', 1(3), October 1994. RAFI's Occasional Paper Series.

[95] J. Finger, Michael and Philip Schuler (eds), 2004, *Poor People's Knowledge: Promoting IP in Developing Countries.*

prescription and over-the-counter drugs based on Indian plants amounts to US 70 billion dollars.[96]

5. Vinod Kumar Gupta, who is leading the traditional wealth encyclopedia project and heads India's National Institute of Science Communication and Information Resources (Niscair), reckons that of the nearly 5,000 patents given out by the US Patent Office on various medical plants by the year 2000, some 80 per cent were plants of Indian origin. By one estimate, a quarter of the new drugs produced in the US are plant-based. [97]

It is, therefore, now undisputed that TIK has immense commercial value. Academic scholarship in this field is replete with examples of the commercial value exploitatively extracted from ethno-botanical knowledge. It is not just indigenous flora and plant varieties that have been 'pirated' but traditional knowledge as well which has become the basis for new generation drugs, herbicides, cosmetics, etc.[98] After all, TIK enables the first level of selection which indicates the value of a plant/herb. The resurgence of interest in TIK has ensured that TIK is increasingly becoming the 'technical lead' in bio-diversity prospecting. A number of pharmaceutical companies, for example, Shaman Pharmaceuticals, rely extensively (and some exclusively) on traditional knowledge of indigenous and local peoples in their screening activities.[99] At the centre of debate and controversy is no longer the commercial or the scientific benefits of the traditional resources and knowledge; the issue is that of sovereign rights that ought to accrue to the holders and preservers of these resources.

As the number of patents filed by large corporations, for native crops and genetic resources increases, there is a growing concern about the economic effects of these patents on indigenous people. The infringement

[96] Kerry Ten Kate and Sarah A. Laird, 'Bio-Prospecting Agreements and Benefit Sharing with Local Communities' in, *Poor People's Knowledge: Promoting IP in Developing Countries,* J. Michael Finger and Philip Schuler (eds), World Bank and Oxford University Press, p. 134. Available at http://www.wds.worldbank.org/servlet/WDSContentServer/WDSP/IB/20 04/04/09/000090341_20040409102946/Rendered/NDEX/284100PAPER0Poor0peop les0knowledge.txt (last accessed on October 2008).

[97] V.K. Gupta, 'Documentation of Traditional Medicine Knowledge: Digital Library of India,' Document No. 16, Regional Consultation on Development of Traditional Medicine in the South East Asia Region, Korea, 22-4 June 2005, WHO. Available at http://www.searo.who.int/LinkFiles/Meetings_document16.pdf (last accessed on 20 January 2008).

[98] J. Michael Finger and Philip Schuler (eds), 2004, *Poor People's Knowledge: Promoting Intellectual Property in Developing Countries,* Washington: Oxford University Press.

[99] N. Roht-Arriaza, 1996, 'Of Seeds And Shamans: The Appropriation of the Scientific and Technical Knowledge of Indigenous and Local Communities,' *Michigan Journal of International Law,* 17(919), pp. 919–65.

of knowledge rights begins a causal chain which may eventually lead to a loss of control over resources and actually infringe upon the livelihood and subsistence rights of those dependent on the resources in question.

Take the case of US Patent No. 5,894,079, the 'Enola bean' (yellow bean) patent. The patent was granted to John Proctor, the president of seed company Pod-Ners, LLC, after he brought the bean seeds back from Mexico. With the patent granted, Proctor had an exclusive monopoly over yellow beans and could exclude the importation or sale of any yellow bean exhibiting the yellow shade of the Enola beans. From this, Proctor made 6 cents per pound in royalties.[100] In Northwest Mexico, yellow beans like azufrado and mayocoba have been cultivated for centuries. These are the beans Proctor purchased in Mexico and are Enola's ancestors. Customs officials at the US-Mexico border are now inspecting beans, searching for any patent infringing beans being imported into the United States.[101] Because of this bean alone and the threat of being prosecuted for infringement, some export sales have dropped below 90 per cent, affecting the market for other non-yellow beans, and crucially affecting the farmers producing them.[102]

Agriculture is the primary source of employment and livelihood for 3 out of 4 people in poor countries. How does the patenting of their resources and knowledge affect these farmers? Farmers may be unable to grow the crops they have grown for generations without first paying royalties to patent holders. The extent to which the livelihood of farmers in poorer countries is secured depends in a large measure on the extent of monopoly control permitted in the market through compliance with patent laws. The greater the monopoly, the greater the dependence of farmers and other users on market mechanisms, and the greater their vulnerability. Indigenous peoples are vectors of indigenous knowledge. Their sustenance is compromised when their communal property is appropriated. It should be their right and not privilege to protect their cultural spaces and their subsistence livelihoods.

The controversy over who has the rights to the Neem tree, or turmeric or maca, raises a larger question: who has the sovereign rights

[100] 'A Bean of a Different Color', available at http://www.americanradioworks.org/features/food_politics/beans/5.html (last accessed on 25 February 2002).

[101] Gillian N. Rattray, 'The Enola Bean Patent Controversy: BioPiracy, Novelty and Fish and Chips', Duke L. and Tech. Rev. 0008, 2002, available at http://www.law.duke.edu/journals/dltr/articles/2002dltr0008.html (last accessed on 21 January 2008).

[102] 'Enola Bean Patent Challenged', available at http://www.etcgroup.org/article.asp?newsid=96 (last accessed on 21 January 2008).

over resources that are part of the global commons. As negotiations over access and benefit sharing, disclosure, clause inclusions dominate the centre stage of issues relating to TIK, the larger question of who possesses knowledge rights remains unanswered, in fact obscured by the talk about making the TRIPS regime more inclusive of traditional societies. In fact this talk legitimates an ideology which considers private property to be a better preserver and user of global commons. In many locales, the legal status of this ideology is unimpeachable.

A competing ideology, dating back to the Roman Empire, upholds the public trust doctrine, that David Takacs draws our attention to.[103] He states that the public trust doctrine preserves traditional ecological/knowledge system as a value system and an ethic, as its expression in law mutates and evolves. The doctrine, on which environmental human rights and knowledge rights of the traditional indigenous peoples have come to be based, upholds the simple moral principle that it is immoral, and that it ought to be illegal, for private parties to appropriate as property that which commonly belongs to the commons for general health and happiness. What kind of a rights claim does this moral claim translate into? Not all moral claims easily translate into legal rights, for legal inclusions still reflects the primacy of individuated rights which draw sustenance from premises of liberty or utility. This becomes the ideological premise of rights which by definition precludes rights that seem morally inviolable but are legally not cognizable for their collective, non-individualistic, non-utilitarian premises do not conjoin the principles of libertarian rights. Thus knowledge rights of the traditional indigenous peoples are human rights but enshrined in instruments of 'soft laws' with obligations that are derogable.

LIMITATIONS OF OVERLAPPING RIGHTS

It is fairly well-established that the intellectual property rules for protecting innovative/creative endeavor pose important challenges for considerations of an appropriate legal framework for the protection of biodiversity, genetic information, and associated traditional knowledge. It becomes difficult for the project of universal intellectual property rules to simultaneously be attentive to individual and collective rights; to intellectual property and traditional knowledge rights; to act as reward mechanisms and as protectors of sustainable ecological development. Not

[103] David Takacs, 2008, 'The Public Trust Doctrine, Environmental Human Rights, and the Future of Private Property', *New York University Environmental Law Journal*, vol. 16, p. 711.

only do the nature of rights conflict but the nature of rights-bearers too preclude easy resolutions of these conflictual demands. Of those challenges, the non-economic values often associated with the protection of animal and plant life, the timeless character of traditional principles that underpin conceptions of ownership, and an entirely different perspective on what constitutes 'property' or 'knowledge' stand out as significant limitations of existing global proprietary schemes. Also, the valuation of intellectual property rights is typically divorced from the substantive principles that govern protection.[104] These inherent tensions reflect themselves in the TRIPS agreement's patentability criteria in Article 27 and its sui generis provisions in Article 27.3 (b). Article 27.3(b) prescribes a review of itself with regard to the optional exceptions to patentability. This review was to take place four years after the WTO Agreement came into force, the first one falling in 1999.

One of the main ideas behind the review provision was to reassess the manner in which TRIPS agreement dealt with the commercial use of TIK and genetic material by those other than the communities or countries where these originate, especially when these are subjects of patent applications. The primary area of concern expressed by developing countries of the South, in the reviews of 1999 and 2003, was about the grant of patents or other IPRs covering TIK without the authorization of the indigenous peoples or communities, who have created, controlled, used, and lived in their knowledge systems for centuries, without proper sharing of the benefits that accrue from such use.[105]

At the WTO Seattle Ministerial Conference, the review of Article 27.3(b) in 1999 several South American countries,[106] together with India made the following submission:

'given that TRIPS Agreement requires countries with traditional and indigenous communities to provide intellectual property protection for a broad range of subject matters including new ones such as plant varieties, biological materials, lay-out designs and computer software, it is only equitable that traditional knowledge should be given legal recognition. Indeed, it is the responsibility of the international community to create

[104] Ruth L. Okediji, 'Access, Benefit-sharing and the Interface with Existing IP Systems: Limits and Opportunities', International Expert Workshop on Access to Genetic Resources and Benefit Sharing.

[105] Refer to Note by the Secretariat, WTO Council for TRIPS on 'The Protection of Traditional knowledge and Folklore'; Summary of Issues raised and points made. point. 2, point No. 7. Available at http://www.ige.ch/e/jurinfo/documents/IP-C-W-370.pdf (last accessed on 25 January 2008).

[106] Bolivia, Colombia, Ecuador, Nicaragua and Peru, IP/C/W/165; Cuba, Honduras, Paraguay and Venezuela, IP/C/W/166.

an egalitarian system for the availability, acquisition, maintenance and enforcement of intellectual property rights, which does not a priori exclude any section of the society'.[107]

It emphasized the need to reconcile provisions of the TRIPS agreement with international treaties and undertakings like the CBD, International Undertaking on Plant Genetic Resources, the model law of the Organization of African Unity (OAU), which recognize and protect the rights of local communities, farmers and breeders. Moreover, it was highlighted by these countries that the legal protection of traditional knowledge would improve confidence in the international intellectual property system.[108] Several African countries again reiterated that any protection of genetic resources and traditional knowledge will not be effective unless international mechanisms are found and established within the framework of the TRIPS agreement. Other means, such as access contracts and data bases for patent examinations, can only be supplementary to such international mechanisms, which must contain an obligation on members collectively, and individually to prohibit and take measures to prevent the misappropriation of genetic resources and traditional knowledge.

The review meet of WTO in 2003 highlighted the inadequacy of the system of intellectual property rights adopted by the WTO and its member nations in addressing issues of bio-piracy and protection of traditional knowledge. It also brought into focus the limitations of the prior art/ use clause which does not recognize information available to the public through use or oral traditions outside their domestic jurisdictions. Often TIK exists only in oral form or, if documented, is available in languages that the patent authorities are not familiar with. The language barrier could lead to insufficient screening for prior use. It could also mean that even when the country of origin does not grant patents on a claimed invention on grounds that the source of the invention lies in the public domain, it can be patented in other countries where this knowledge is not in the public use or domain.

Development of databases on traditional knowledge would ostensibly help resolve this problem. Documentation, as has been attempted by Traditional Knowledge Digital Library (TKDL) will, to a large extent, circumvent this problem and put up a case for prior knowledge, in patent

---

[107] India, IP/C/M/28, para. 128.
[108] EC, IP/C/M/35, para. 238-9, IP/C/M/30, para. 145.

challenges, specifically for those within the ambit of the document.[109] Oral traditions however, would continue to remain vulnerable.

This raises a vital question: Is the legitimacy and legal recognition of traditional knowledge based merely on documentation and developing databases on traditional knowledge, or is the issue of knowledge rights of peoples over their centuries-old knowledge systems a broader claim? What is being argued here is that the issue of patenting and the threat it poses to traditional knowledge ought not to be *only* a matter of whether or not a patent has been successfully challenged and revoked or whether there is ample protection through documentation of various traditional knowledges, whether there are sufficient disclosures and whether norms of equitable benefit sharing have ensued from disclosures. Rights have different sticks in their bundle, some being more important than others. The unimportant sticks of the bundle lack the power to *exclude*. For example, the right to benefit sharing does not *exclude* bio-prospectors from sourcing genetic resources and knowledges from the traditional communities. It simply makes the community in question a claimant of some compensation. Similarly, disclosures which are a necessary prelude to benefit sharing, does not foreclose a patent claim. Again it merely makes the distributional chain of benefits a condition for claiming patents.

Alternatively, establishment of prior art could lead to a revocation of patent claims as was the case with Neem and Turmeric. The challenge to a patent (pre- or post-grant) is a costly and an intricate legal process, linked to too many conditionalities which cannot be fulfilled by non-resourceful, non-legal societies. For instance, there ought to be demonstrable proof of prior art, failing which no legal claim contesting 'novelty' can be made. On the other hand, if a patent claim is proved as obvious, only the prior

---

[109] Initiatives have taken in India to document the wealth of its traditional knowledge heritage in a format recognizable and accessible by the international IP regimes and laws. An ambitious 2m dollars project, christened TKDL, an encyclopaedia of the India's traditional medicine was created in an effort to stop people from claiming them as their own and patenting them. The Indian library contains information on 36,000 formulations used in Ayurveda—India's 5,000-year-old system of traditional medicine. The information—presented in English, French, German, Spanish and Japanese—was created in a format accessible by international patent offices to prevent the granting of inappropriate patents. India's TKDL in fact became a model for other South Asian countries who are attempting a similar documentation. According to the Director of NISCAIR, V.K. Gupta data on 65,000 formulations in Ayurveda, 70,000 in Unani and 3,000 in Siddha had already been put in the TKDL. The data relating to only 7,000 formulations each in Unani and Siddha, and 1,500 postures in yoga remained to be included and expected to be included by December 2007. See, 'India to sign pacts with patent offices abroad', *The Hindu*, 30 June 2006.

existence of TIK in question is established. Even if there is a successful patent challenge, it does not establish the intellectual property rights of the community in question. It only ensures, *temporarily,* that the specific knowledge does not belong to a domain over which any individual or institutional rights claim can be established. The right to challenge, through establishment of prior knowledge/ use, is not a sufficient right to ensure either protection or to put knowledge rights claims at par with Western modern sciences.

'Benefit sharing' is a good example of the strategy of overlapping rights that has evolved from TRIPS agreement, albeit indirectly through other instruments such as the CBD and FAO (benefit sharing is a form of monetary compensation for the use of local people's knowledge). Overall, benefit-sharing constitutes a useful strategy to ease some of the adverse impacts of bio-piracy. Without benefit-sharing, such knowledge may be 'taken' from its current holders without any form of acknowledgement or compensation. However, benefit-sharing does not contribute to the definition of an alternative regime to patents. Indeed, while it seeks to limit the impact of the introduction of patents in the field of biological resources, it does not seek to provide any rights to current holders of knowledge. In this sense, it assumes that local people do not have intellectual property rights over their knowledge and that a monetary reward constitutes a sufficient compensation. Benefit-sharing supports the idea that the knowledge of farmers and local communities is not disposed towards fulfilling patenting criteria. There is no hint that the creators and holders of knowledge may be the owners of these resources and should thus have the right to determine whether they want to sell and at what price.

Intellectual property rights, like other property rights, are aggregates of different sorts of rights and rights-correlatives. The right to possess/ own is to be sharply distinguished from mere protection of possession which is what the 'prior art' clause or benefit sharing mechanisms seek to do. The right to possess, that is, to have ownership, is a claim right to have possession, not merely the liberty to keep. The currently employed protective mechanisms grant the TIK holder:

1. A right to challenge a patent claim through demonstration of prior art,
2. The ability to induce disclosures, again based on the demonstrable proof of its prior existence, and
3. A right to benefit sharing based on disclosures.

Once proof is demonstrated it places certain obligations on part of the patent holder. The primary right holder is then the patentee who, in some conditions, has a duty towards the original knowledge or resource holder. The *duty* does not establish the traditional holder's intellectual property rights claim. It only establishes that monopoly of use or possession cannot be granted to a present or potential patentee without downstream compensation for use.

Post/pre-grant opposition, disclosure requirements, benefit sharing mechanisms are actually proxies for traditional resource rights (TRRs); they function more like aspects of intellectual property rights which disburse benefits of successful intellectual property claims. These rights are, to use Becker's classification, secondary rights 'which are entailed by the existence of another right, and extinguished when the primary right is extinguished'.[110] They are together at best a specification of the conditions under which the patent holder's rights claim may be said to be sound and justified or may be justifiably overridden or may obligate him to share profits with the community of origin. It does not specify the conditions under which the traditional knowledge holder may claim his right—a right which says that this is ours and we refuse to part with it, 'benefits' notwithstanding.

Access and benefit sharing mechanisms are residuary rights which are akin to, to use Rosemary Coombe's phrase 'neo-liberal spaces of governmentality'.[111] They do, as she asserts, 'endow some social groups with new forms of negotiating skills [...] provide opportunities to assert new kinds of rights and to interpret universal rights through the lens of vernacular practices, obligations, commitments, and aspirations'. However, as they afford spaces of negotiation for rights and benefits (more like rights to benefits) they also further reinforce market subjectivites and global networks of influence.

The moral claim of TIK rights has not translated into legal claims within TRIPS agreement. Claims of benefit sharing have been acknowledged by TRIPS (for instance, by the Doha Declaration) but these are conceptualized in a manner that they *enable* the Intellectual Property system. Even as they run alongside CBD and 'share benefits' or 'disclose origins', their abiding commitment remains the protection

---

[110] Lawrence C. Becker, 1977, p. 7.

[111] Rosemary Coombe, Intellectual Property in Regimes of Neoliberal Governmentality: Locating Community Subjects and their Traditions. Submitted for inclusion in Mario Biagioli, Peter Jaszi and Martha Woodmansee (eds), *Contexts of Invention,* University of Chicago Press.

of intellectual property. In a sense then, TIK never evolves into counter rights claim which have the sustained capacity to deter infringements. Community property rights, traditional resource rights, community knowledge rights lack the legal power and juridical status that make them coequal to intellectual property rights. As Joel Feinberg states, 'the legal power to claim one's right or the things to which one has a right, seems to be essential to the very notion of a right. A right to which one could not make a claim would be a very "imperfect" right indeed!'[112]

KNOWLEDGE AS A HUMAN RIGHT

Since the adoption of the UDHR in 1948, intellectual production has been considered a fundamental human right of all peoples.[113] The relationship between human rights and contributions to knowledge is however arguably controversial. The International Covenant on Economic, Social and Cultural Rights (ICESCR) is in many ways the most crucial international instrument through which the relationship between the two can be examined.[114] On the one hand, it recognizes the rights to self determination (Article 1), food and clothing (Article 11), work (Article 6), physical and mental health (Article12) as fundamental human rights. The common feature of this cluster of rights is the right to 'human' conditions of living, in that they all emerge as implied rights of the most fundamental of all rights—the Right to Life. On the other hand, it recognizes in Article 15 individuals or groups that make intellectual contribution that benefit society. Although it does not mention or imply that these rights in any way refer to the cluster of rights related to the intellectual property regime, by implication these rights may be articulated in the form endorsed by the TRIPS regime.

The notion of knowledge as a human right may be appropriated as a justificatory premise for the claim of intellectual property rights. The right of the techno-scientific community to the fruits of their labour becomes

[112] Feinberg Joel, 1992, 'The Nature and Value of Rights', in *Rights*, Carlos Santiago Nino (ed.), NY: New York University Press, p. 194.

[113] Article 27 of the Declaration provides that: (1) Everyone has the right freely to participate in the cultural life of the community, to enjoy the arts and to share in scientific advancement and its benefits. (2) Everyone has the right to the protection of the moral and material interests resulting from any scientific, literary or artistic production of which he is the author. Available at http://www.un.org/Overview/rights.html (last accessed on 26 January 2008).

[114] Article 15 International Covenant on Economic, Social and Cultural Rights. Available at http://www.unesco.org/education/information/nfsunesco/pdf/SOCIAL_E. PDF (last accessed on 26 January 2008).

a powerful argument for libertarian rights in intellectual property. This poses a predicament for knowledge rights of traditional societies which also stake their claim as human rights—rights which are impossible to distinguish from livelihood rights, environmental human rights, farmers' rights, food security, and so on. In a sense then these are two coequal rights, both belonging to the genre of knowledge rights but drawing sustenance from two very diverse premises. One strategy could regard both as a species of human rights, as has been declared by the UDHR and state that the best possible outcome would be afford legal protection to both rights. But this strategy has its pitfalls as I have discussed in the last chapter. Coequal legal status is often not a sufficient condition for equity of outcomes if the right bearers are not coequal. When rights compete, so do the rights' bearers and the one who is better endowed, socially and economically, competes better. Rights need able, capacitated vectors or else they fail as justice mechanisms. As rights, not only do IPRs *not* meet the fundamental human rights criteria, they also infringe upon the fundamental rights of other peoples and communities, rights that are crucially linked to subsistence, survival, well-being of the people. They are able to do that first, because the right capacitates them to do so, and second, because their location in the socio-economic, global matrix endows them to be capacitated vectors of the right.

The other strategy, and the one I argue in favour of, is to demarcate these rights in terms of the consequences they generate for the right holders—the biotechnology enabled innovator, with IPR protection in one case, and on the other, the traditional communities. Demarcating rights in terms of their consequences draws up a priority order that has a sense of *whose* interests and *what* interests are served by a rights regime. There are consequences for innovators in the form of greater profits, and there are consequences for traditional communities which could be in terms of protection of livelihood, subsistence, biodiversity, etc. Which right is being served and which infringed ought to be a factor in adjudicating rights. Political morality needs to take cognizance the consequence aspect of rights.

Looking at consequences enables us to evaluate *what* is being protected. If protecting X right is less important than protecting Y, then regardless of the two rights being coequal the latter ought to be given both moral and juridical preference. What then would make TIK more of an ethical claim than IP? Codified as a knowledge right of traditional communities, it serves as a corollary to the fundamental inviolable right of life. Protection to knowledge, in the traditional community setting, rights clearly determines the extent to which these people enjoy their basic rights to life, health, adequate food, and traditional livelihood. Knowledge rights, farmers' rights, ecological rights, all inextricably linked, become aligned with the right to life for their ability to sustain livelihoods and subsistence among poor communities. The value that life attaches to the norms of rights makes life protecting rights non-negotiable.

On the other hand, IPRs as human rights claims, falter. First, unlike most human rights instruments they are not vitally linked to the protection of 'human condition'. The essence of human condition is an important baseline for the instrumentality of human rights and intellectual property rights, as mentioned earlier, as reward mechanism and an economic entitlement. They are bereft of the 'life' connection that most human rights link up with.

Second, because western intellectual property law is based on individual property ownership, its aims are often incompatible with, if not detrimental to, those of traditional communities. For many traditional communities, knowledge production is a means of developing and maintaining group identity and survival, rather than promoting individual economic gain. The emphasis of the existing western intellectual property rights regime on individual proprietary rights does not address the collective nature and the essentiality of traditional knowledge. Intellectual property rights raise a number of concerns with regard to their impact on the realization food, health and livelihood of traditional communities. There is therefore an apprehension that the realization of some human rights, far more basic and fundamental in nature, may be affected in countries that adopt or strengthen intellectual property norms based on their commitment to the TRIPS framework. The status of knowledge as a human right, therefore, needs to be qualified, perhaps re-examined. Some knowledge rights, that is, those that are linked to issues of survival, food security, livelihood rights, ecological sustainability, etc. have an unquestioned claim as a human right, while for intellectual property rights the claims are questionable and contestable on moral grounds. I make a crucial distinction between the knowledge rights of the traditional peoples and the knowledge rights in the form of IPRs to draw out distinction between two co-equal rights in the absence of which, one right struggles for content and space.

It is important to draw this distinction between the two knowledge rights in question so as to make a larger point that carries from the two preceding chapters. Rights are often conflictual in nature and may require adjudication in order to settle the conflicting claims being made. The terms of adjudication ought to be based on upholding and protecting prior rights like the right to life, subsistence, and livelihood, sustained and drawn from the knowledge rights of the traditional peoples.

Key arguments in this chapter also suggest that the prevailing notion of intellectual property rights establishes the primacy of WMS over the knowledge systems of the traditional and indigenous peoples. Contemporary critiques of intellectual property rights from the perspective of TIK are symptomatic of a more fundamental, broader questioning of universalized, essentialized, and singular notions of science and its projects. It has led to a fundamental questioning of the foundational principle of IPRs—the idea of scientific rationality. A regime like intellectual property rights in enwrapped in the vocabulary of modern expert science. This, as a number of critics have pointed out,[115] obscures attention to alternative knowledges, sciences, and forms of socio-ecological orders that may exist in the public realm. During the WTO Seattle Ministerial Conference for the review of Article 27.3(b), Bolivia, Colombia, Ecuador, Nicaragua, and Peru submitted a proposal, 'Protection of intellectual property Rights Relating to the Traditional Knowledge of Local and Indigenous Communities.' It stated: 'The entire modern evolution of intellectual property has been framed by principles and systems which have tended to leave aside a large sector of human creativity, namely the traditional knowledge possessed by local and indigenous communities.'[116]

Science and technology studies need to move away from the Durkheimian perspective that cultural and social situatedness is the mark of lower knowledge forms, and science is 'independent of any local context'.[117] Local epistemologies and their associated values have come to have bear upon the ways in which science is understood to be constituted. Critical questions have been raised in the last fifty years or so about the biases and categories that have shaped our visions of rationality, science, and progress in our everyday lives. For both intellectuals and social movements, the very idea of science as uncovering universal truths about objective reality and the idea of science as progress, has become problematic and, at times, suspect.[118]

---

[115] P. Caplan, (ed.), 2000, *Risk Revisited,* London; Pluto, B. Wynne, 1996, 'May the Sheep Graze Safely?: A Reflexive View of the Expert-Lay Knowledge Divide,' in *Risk, Environment and Modernity: Towards a New Ecology,* S. Lash, B. Szerszynski, and B. Wynne (eds), London: Sage Publications.

[116] 3 WTO IP/C/W/165, November, 1999.

[117] E. Durkheim, 1972, *Selected Writings,,* [1899] A Giddens (ed. and transl), Cambridge: Cambridge University Press.

[118] See, D.W. Brokensha, *et al.* (eds), 1980, *Indigenous Knowledge Systems and Development,* Lanham: University Press of America. A. Escobar, 1995, *Encountering Development: The Making and Unmaking of the Third World,* Princeton: Princeton University Press; J. Fairhead,

The conventional approaches to scientific endeavour and objectivity, which persist today in institutions like the TRIPS, have tended to reinforce simplistic dualities such as the 'modern' versus 'traditional' and 'scientific' versus 'non-scientific'. The traditional comes to be seen in this context as local and pre-scientific and the techno-scientific as the sole repository of rational ideas for progress. In offering protection to one kind of knowledge system, the TRIPS framework reinforces the binaries of epistemic projects.

TIK stands in complete contrast to WMS, in terms of conceptualizations, the residential and proprietary status, generation, and communication. It encompasses the beliefs, knowledge, practices, innovations, arts, spirituality, and other forms of cultural experience and expression that belong to indigenous communities worldwide. TIK, unlike common perceptions, incorporates its own explanations of the natural world and has its own distinct database, its own 'science'. Attempts to incorporate traditional or indigenous knowledge into the databases of WIPO or attempts to use TIK as database and information, are attempts to assimilate TIK in terms and forms that are commercially and globally acceptable and viable. These framings essentially attempt to codify and measure one system of knowledge by the intellectual and cultural standards of another. It is important to note that in the negotiations, benefit sharing and compensation, what gets lost is the broader negotiation of meanings and identities, which may not be an obvious area of dispute but is often an obvious outcome. Any attempt to legally recognize, compensate or protect indigenous knowledge using international patent law, highlights the difficulty of protecting one kind of cultural knowledge by the standards—legal, cultural—of another.

Cases of appropriation of traditional knowledge by way of patents which are granted on derived applications are numerous. They highlight the anomalies of trying to bring about heterogeneous knowledge systems under one intellectual property law system. The anomalies are related in some cases to the legal framework in place at the international level and in individual countries concerning traditional knowledge protection. In other cases, they are related to broader issues concerning sovereign rights over knowledge systems based on the recognition and advocacy for rights of the indigenous peoples over their knowledge and resources, and for the inclusion of equitable benefit sharing mechanisms where the indigenous / traditional peoples become equal partners in biotechnological developments. The issue of sovereign rights is, however, beyond that of

and M. Leach, 1998, *Reframing Deforestation: Global analyses and local realities—Studies in West Africa,* London: Routledge; also refer to Chapter 4 of this work for a discussion on sociology of scientific knowledge.

merely evolving equitable benefit sharing mechanisms. Evolving benefit sharing mechanisms is actually a process which fine-tunes the existing intellectual property laws in a manner that conflicting concerns and issues can be resolved within the existing system of TRIPS and which do not run contrary to the fundamental principles that govern the notion of intellectual property rights. In a way, attempts at democratization of the IPR regime shift attention from the innate confrontation between individualized knowledge rights and community rights over knowledge resources.

9 Issues in the Moral Grounding of Intellectual Property Rights

It has been the aim of this book to consider both the moral arguments that support, as well as those that deny the proposition that intellectual property rights, in their current conception, have a moral basis. Rights must necessarily have moral premises and moral dimensions for they address fundamental issues related to the human good, which in itself is an aggregate of a number of equally fundamental ethical aspects. Rights may be devised to secure and advance individual autonomy and interests and presuppose individuals as the sole bearer of these; rights, in another perspective, may presuppose individuals as parts of social attachments and ends, and uphold a notion of the social good; rights may be devised as universal or local or culturally specific, whatever the conception and the motivation, rights are in essence related to the advancement of 'good' and are strongly related to their capacities to produce or secure other ethical goals. Rights are therefore, moral goods. Their institution or claim ought to be based on firm moral grounds, in the absence of which they will always have the ability to impair other ethical goals.

Intellectual property rights are both claimed and contested from a rights perspective and therefore it becomes imperative to inquire into the 'justness' of their premises. The central question that the study sets out to raise is: What kind of moral claim does a proposition of intellectual property rights make? Because the classical conception of property did not exhibit the same identifying characteristics as intellectual property does, it becomes necessary to examine whether the traditional moral justifications of property rights hold good for Intellectual property rights as well. If they do not, as I have argued, we are in a position to state that *even* premises of the property discourse are not good enough to legitimate intellectual property rights. This kind of positioning, which uncritically accepts natural rights and utilitarian premises for near absolute property rights, is a strategy which enables us to evacuate intellectual property rights of the very moral premises which it draws its sustenance. Section II then takes it beyond this 'internal' critique to inquire into the justness of intellectual property rights. Both the premise and the consequence are important dimensions of any rights inquiry.

Central to this study on intellectual property rights are two issues; one, can knowledge constitute a property right? And second, if at all knowledge can legitimately be held as property, who ought to be the legitimate holder of this property right? While the first leads us to theoretical concerns which preclude an easy extension of the conventional justifications for property to intellectual property rights, the second leads us to pragmatic concerns and anxieties which stem from the non-compossibility of intellectual property rights with particular aspects of human rights such as the right to health, livelihood, subsistence, knowledge and so on. The fundamental premise of this book therefore is that rights ought to have strong moral justifications or strong reasons such as a combination of an intuitive moral sense (as to whether there are specific rights people ought to have) and good' consequences, consequences which are 'rights sensitive'. Any requirement of a right, in a modern context, makes one person's rights conditional on similar rights for all and therefore, makes consequence evaluation an important aspect of the morality of rights. I have argued fervently in Section II that rights ought to be established not merely on grounds of utility, intuition or morality but also for the effects that they may generate for other rights. A right which conjoins with other rights has a stronger claim than a right which infringes upon other rights. If we begin with the premise that rights are moral goods, and that they exist because they augment conditions of good life or conditions of justice, then it becomes very important for rights to *not* transgress either individual claims for autonomy and freedom, or conditions of justice. Rights which infringe either the individual domain or the social, or both (as in the case of intellectual property rights) are largely ungrounded in any conception of morality.

Alternative conceptions of property have been presented which permit several types of evaluation for claims and disputes arising over intellectual property. One type of evaluation is the examination of the narrow implications of each conception. However, if property and ownership rights comprise both philosophical beliefs and practical utilities, one would expect them to be applied in combination. To use Lawrence Becker's pithy phrase: 'an all things considered argument' or all inclusive justification is properly a *moral* justification.[1] Amartya Sen,

---

[1] Lawrence C. Becker, 1977, p. 23.

in a similar vein, argues that any valuation exercise would only be partial unless the libertarian priority to rights and processes that give rise to a specified set of rights, and the utilitarian approach that lays emphasis on the valuation of outcomes, are integrated rather than being independent of each other.[2] Violation or fulfillment of rights therefore become an important dimension in the valuation of outcomes in this study which adopts this integrated approach while critiquing, on moral grounds, the idea of intellectual property rights.

THE LIBERTARIAN LIMITATION

A moral justification of intellectual property would draw upon multiple themes in the following way.[3] It would first take into account the ontological criteria which are implicit in the thoughts and practices of many people and thus inform the intuitions that people bring to a discussion of property. These criteria have evolved from traditional practices and in the course of time become the explicit norms for recognizing property rights and ownership patterns. They inform the intuition of people regarding the implicit legitimacy of a certain right or a norm. Natural rights and labour theory are examples of ontological approaches which have been used as a basic assumption for intellectual property, as in the works of Locke or Nozick discussed in Chapter 2.

The study evaluates the libertarian claim, drawn from Locke and Nozick, that views rights as a species of moral property in one's person, personal powers and justly acquires external resources. Referred to as the principle of self-ownership, it is a powerful way of expressing the principle of individual liberty which claims that individuals have full 'property rights' over their body, skills, and labour, and anything, justly acquired, with which they mix these becomes theirs to own, exclude, use, and dispose freely. While this became the 'natural rights' claim for property rights in tangible/physical property, it falters when applied to intellectual property.

The intuition that people deserve the fruit of their labour is a powerful justification for all forms of property, including intellectual property. These form the intuitive arguments which people use for legitimating all forms of property and are a source of appeal when more explicit criteria, like utility, fail to provide ready answers. They also formed the initial bias for rights in intellectual property. If an individual's labour originates

---

[2] Amartya Sen, 2002, *Rationality and Freedom*, Delhi: OUP, p. 633.
[3] Adapted from Edwin C. Hettinger, Winter 1989, 'Justifying Intellectual Property', *Philosophy and Public Affairs*, 18(1), pp. 31–52.

a property, then appropriation without consent violates the individual's liberties and his natural right to property. This theory provides a strong claim for ownership in goods which are products of one's labour.

Intellectual property rights constitute a grant of exclusive rights over the domain of an idea and the objects that are a product of that idea. They therefore entail not just rights over the idea, but also over the physical output associated with this intellectual labour. It is here that the problem arises in extending the classical Lockean labour theory, from which labour theory justifications for forms of tangible property are drawn, to intellectual property rights. Knowledge permits concomitant simultaneous use without diminishing another's similar use. My 'ownership' of an idea does not automatically preclude another from a parallel, simultaneous use. While the intellectual labourer is entitled to the fruits of his own labour, this entitlement does not establish the terms of use or dissemination of this intellectual product by others. Given the non-excludable and non-rivalrous character of intellectual products, the terms of non-interference are not naturally implied as with physical goods.

The principle of self-ownership, when extended to the domain of Intellectual Property rights, becomes self-contradictory. Intellectual Property rights, as upheld by TRIPS, exclude from its domain, rights of those people who have not been first movers. For instance, I may have expended mental labour, mixed it with external objects, created something but am not accorded rights to the fruit of my intellectual labour because existing intellectual property rules take away these rights from me. Therefore, in this case, recognizing a dominion over an idea (in the form of IPRs) may actually curtail my self-ownership rights, that is, the rights that I ought to legitimately exercise over the fruits of my mental labour. Recognizing your dominion over an idea can inhibit my use or transfer of my physical property or what I could potentially make my property. Intellectual property would therefore even contravene the Nozickian defense of ownership because it interferes with the freedom to exercise the right of transfer. A copyright or patent owner can impose prior restraint, fines, imprisonment, and confiscation on those engaged in peaceful expression and the quiet enjoyment or transfer of their tangible property. It could thus be violative of others' rights to their property— both intellectual and physical.

One of the central reasons why the right to intellectual property is not 'naturally' implied by labour theory is that intellectual property rights in one's knowledge, becomes inconsistent with the principle of liberty. Property rights, in libertarian theory, have been interpreted to be a derivative of rights to liberty that all humans are entitled to. It follows logically then that property ought to be consistent with other liberties of other people, (liberty being, to use Lawrence Becker's phrase, the 'originating right').[4]

There is thus a great degree of unease expressed about the protection of intellectual property interests among those who purport to treat individual liberty as the highest good. Intellectual property rights, to use a Nozickean expression, do infringe upon the 'like liberties of others'. Property rights, even from the classical libertarian position, need to be consistent with a regime of personal liberty. Self-ownership thus, as an abiding principle of libertarian property defense, falters in its defense of intellectual property rights. Any principle which contradicts the premises that generate that principle (liberty in this case) is self-contradictory, as much as self-ownership is as a premise for intellectual property.

THE UTILITARIAN LIMITATION

Lacking 'natural' entitlement or claim, the intellectual property system of rights is then negotiated in a manner that ensures that these intellectual products attain the properties of excludability through statutory enforcement. It is here that a more explicit criterion like utility is employed. It is in the social negotiation of the system that utilitarian arguments gain relevance. Utilitarian arguments have a role to play in reinforcing the moral grounds for property rights. That people will be more productive if they have *incentives* is a widely shared argument used to project intellectual property rights as incentives or rewards for research and innovation. The expectation that intellectual property protection would lead to good consequences for the society as a whole has led to the codification of intellectual property rules and regulations.

The intellectual property rights as incentive argument invites the objection that G.A. Cohen put forward in his powerful critique of Rawls.[5] Rawls' 'difference principle' states that inequalities are justified if they work for the good of the least fortunate. In keeping with that, incentives can be defended on grounds that inequalities engendered by the intellectual property regime are defensible on grounds that they create incentives that are advantageous to the least fortunate. Cohen argues that incentives cannot matter to moral and political theory. For instance, if I

[4] Lawrence Becker, 1977, p. 39.
[5] G.A. Cohen, 2000, *If You are an Egalitarian How come you are so Rich*, Cambridge: Harvard University Press. Also see, David Estlund, 1998, 'Liberalism, Equality and Fraternity in Cohen's Critique of Rawls', *Journal of Political Philosophy*, vol. 6, pp. 99–112.

am morally obliged to take care of someone else's interest, that obligation holds on me regardless of how much I get paid for it. Whenever incentives are legitimized from the standpoint of the difference principle, there is a superior alternative: let the talented work at innovation and if the welfare of the society is at the heart of that effort, then greater welfare is derived when no monopoly prices are demanded for that service. The worst off may be better in one sense, that is, reaping the benefits of innovation, for example, a new effective drug but would be worse off in another sense, that is, in having to pay a premium on access to an innovated drug. Moral philosophy cannot justify incentive based inequalities. Cohen's 'egalitarian conscience' is vital to the upholding of a stronger version of Rawls' difference principle.

One of the central theses of utilitarian philosophy is to draw a distinction between specific cases and 'general equilibrium' arguments. So, for instance, we know from the scholarship on property, that one cannot make a case that every instance of the exercise of property rights is efficient. However, we can still make the case that overall a system of private property is more efficient. The response to the efficiency claim is presented in Chapter 4 but the *overall* efficiency argument needs further engagement. The term 'overall' is a tricky word. It hides the disaggregated components of what constitutes the term 'overall'. If it can be demonstrated that eighteen million human beings die prematurely each year from medical conditions that can be cured; If it can be demonstrated that neglected diseases cause an estimated 5,00,000 to 1 million deaths annually and cause a global disease burden equivalent to that of HIV-AIDS,[6] then is this good enough to constitute 'overall'. If it does, as these figures and suffering do, merit that status by any standards, then it stands that the intellectual property system does not work for the mitigation of these conditions. It does not have R&D outlays for NDs; it makes drugs unaffordable such that millions of AIDS, cancer, and other victims are denied access to them. To add to this list, examples can be drawn from Chapters 7 and 8, loss of livelihood of farmers, indigenous peoples in developing countries because of the causal chain that connects them to the proprietary claims in agriculture and knowledge systems. If we agree that this constitutes the 'overall', then one can establish that

[6] The George Washington University; Neglected Tropical Diseases Initiative; 'Developing New Health Products: (Drugs, Diagnostics, and Vaccines) To Control The Ancient Afflictions of Stigma and Poverty'. Available at http://gstudynet.org/docs/The%20GWU%20Neglected%20Tropical%20Diseases%20Initiative.doc (last accessed on 22 March 2007).

the intellectual property system does not lead to overall welfare. It leaves large, marginalized sections outside its welfare radar.

On the other hand, if it is argued that if a third of the population dies of neglect and lack of drug access, two thirds still live and therefore, the net aggregate welfare would be better served by orienting incentives for the latter, it would compel an alignment of utility with other moral concerns, for aggregate utility cannot simply be a calculation of numbers. It has aligned itself with the quality of suffering or pleasure and not just the quantum. The suffering of a cancer patient cannot be compared to the suffering of a bald person. Utilitarianism has a weak basis in comparing utilities. Monopoly of use and profits that precondition the operation of intellectual property rights are inconsistent with utilitarian consequentialism that favors a diverse set of consequences namely, greater availability through lower prices and expanded volume. The assumption of utilitariansm that only utility consequences ultimately matter (calculated on the basis of benefits minus costs equals net welfare) is totally contingent on the variables that are quantifiable, both those that are taken into account and those that are omitted. Assigning each of these costs and benefits a value which can be compared to every other cost or benefit is, if not impossible, at least arbitrary. This is not a simple calculation involving comprehensible quantities.

Utilitarianism falters when the overall welfare principle does not take into account unaccounted costs, or undervalued costs. For instance, it is found that in the most industrialized nations, plant monopoly rights lead to control of the food chain by the intellectual property rights-holders, impacting the food security of people associated with and linked to farming practices. In another example, there are grave consequences for those who cannot afford life saving drugs at high patented prices. These are costs which any utilitarian analysis ought to take into account and assign a value which belies simplistic quantification.

Undiscovered costs and benefits, the ever-changing and impermanent character of costs and benefits, make it imperative that the utilitarian justification of intellectual property rights needs to be informed by other moral premises of rights and justice. If morality is to be evaluated in terms of the consequences, the goodness of the outcome should be in conjunction with other principles of justice. Fulfillment and violation of rights have to become important dimensions in any valuation of outcomes.[7] Intellectual

---

[7] For a discussion on limitations of the utilitarian perception of 'welfare', see Amartya Sen, 2002, pp. 634–5.

property rights cannot be solely judged in terms of wealth maximization; efficiency cannot become the basis for the grant of a right.

As a stand-alone conception of property, the utilitarian view provides a highly questionable basis for recognizing rights in intellectual property. The absence of intuitive ontological premises of intellectual property and limitations of a consequence-dependent system of intellectual property rights indicate a weak moral claim for Intellectual property rights.

An integrated approach to rights, as adopted by Amartya Sen,[8] tries to take cognisance of both the ontological premises and the outcome of rights. Here rights are viewed as normatively important but need to be integrated with outcomes as well—a view that goes beyond narrowly conceived utility consequences to take into account violations and fulfillment of rights as well. Here consequences matter but they need to cohere with our moral beliefs. Our core intuitive, moral sense, admittedly, cannot become the basis of public policy, since our moral beliefs might be mistaken. However, any notion of morality derived from the optimality of consequences, fails to be justified if it cannot cohere with our moral beliefs. There is a need therefore, to acknowledge a system of rights that takes note of consequences of various types—'other' liberties and rights being extremely important consequences.

THE RIGHTS LIMITATION

Does the intellectual property regime take into account the consequences that intellectual property rights generate for other categories of rights? People have rights other than to the fruits of their labour. My patent rights, derived from my labour may conflict with my right to health in ensuring access to essential medicines or they may conflict with a farmer's rights to re-sow his seeds, that is, his right to liberty, livelihood, subsistence, etc.

Intellectual property rights do not easily cohabit with other rights, as seen in Chapters 6, 7, and 8. Serious infringements of rights have been documented and enumerated in these chapters. Where rights conflict, terms of adjudication need to be devised to determine the salience of a particular right over another. Liberal philosophy, the source of most civil and political rights in liberal democratic regimes,[9] regards two rights as

---

[8] Ibid.

[9] Lockean philosophy has remained the cornerstone of American thought which is behind original draft of the Declaration of Independence which outlined the 'inalienable rights' of all men as including 'life, liberty, and property'. Later property was changed to 'pursuit of happiness' reflecting the unease with granting property the same degree of

'originating' or 'source' rights: the rights to life and liberty The right to property is often regarded as a derivative of the right to liberty, or in some Lockean readings, as a derivative of the right to life.[10] Since intellectual property rights have their origins in the libertarian thinking, the moral terms of adjudication between them and competing rights ought to rest upon, at least, upholding the primacy of these two fundamental, inalienable rights. The three case studies undertaken in this thesis establish the infringement, by intellectual property rights, of the rights to health, livelihood, and knowledge rights of traditional peoples—all aspects of the human right to life. What distinguishes these rights from intellectual property rights? Some of these rights are group rights (farmers' rights, Chapter 7), some are individual (health rights, Chapter 6), while some have a strong collective and cultural character (knowledge rights of traditional peoples, Chapter 8). In comparison to intellectual property rights, these rights are distinguishable in terms of the salience they acquire by virtue of being closely associated with the life and liberty of collectives, individuals, and individuals within collectives. The right to higher profits or returns on investment is not as salient as the right not to die as a result of not being able to afford anti-HIV drugs, or as a result of starvation. Some rights are in the nature of, to use Rawls terminology, 'primary goods' primary to life and liberty.

Intellectual property rights do not necessarily protect livelihood, subsistence, or entitlements which are to do with the essential quality of life, or protect the innovation and creations of peoples whose life depends on them. They are at best economic entitlements which can be described as claims for reward on investment in research and innovation activities. They do not protect liberty either. The liberty to think, create, transfer ideas and other intellectual products are not constrained in the absence of intellectual property rights. Legally, there would be nothing stopping people from undertaking innovative activity even if intellectual property rights were withdrawn. Innovation after all took place even in the absence of these laws in socialist societies, traditional societies, and even in western societies in the pre-Intellectual property era. Acquiring and using unowned objects is part of an individual's liberty (core libertarian ideals); so also is the freedom to exercise one's choice autonomously. The

---

salience as life and liberty. A closer reading of Locke however reveals that the right to property was secondary to life and liberty. Refer Chapter 1 of this book for a more detailed discussion.

[10] Locke believed that the foundational right, the right to subsistence, would be better protected if individuals had exclusive possessions over some resources. See, Chapter 2 of this work.

absence of intellectual property rights does not curtail the liberty of a person to express, acquire, use or transfer objects or ideas. Even without the grant of intellectual property rights, individuals can continue to research, innovate, create, and claim ownership of that creation and use or transfer it on terms that could be a result of negotiation between the creator and the market.

The right to liberty is also a limited act to be exercised *without infringing on the similar rights of others*. Liberty therefore, can only be a right that justifies individual acts of acquisition, use, and transfer of ideas. It cannot be a guarantee for future and others' use of the product, a right that intellectual property rights seek. What intellectual property rights aim to do is to control the terms of further transfers and dissemination. This is then about the right to control the trade trajectory of an object or an idea and not about the liberty to create or to claim ownership in the object or idea created.

Furthermore, the benefits that accrue do not outweigh the costs, particularly when costs are measured in terms of the rights of other people. Classifying IPR then, as human rights is problematic at both the theoretical and policy levels, for human rights are understood as rights that are inalienable and part of universal entitlements that are not limited by time, and cannot be suspended or curtailed. IPRs, on the other hand, are limited-duration statutory rights given by the State. They can be curtailed in certain circumstances where they conflict with the larger interests of society. For example, a patent held by a pharmaceutical manufacturer over a medicine can be suspended under compulsory licensing, if the granting of the patent causes the price of the drug to escalate, putting it out of the reach of a large section of society. This highlights a fundamental condition on which human rights are predicated and which demarcate IPRs from aspects of human rights. This is the basic distinction between the knowledge rights of traditional peoples and intellectual property rights. While the latter fail the criterion of being rights fundamental to the liberty, autonomy, and well-being of individuals, the former are essential to the preservation of the lives and autonomy of both the individual and communities.

The study draws attention to the conflictual nature of the knowledge systems which are marked by an inherent lack of commensurability—western scientific systems protected by the TRIPS regime and TIK attempting and struggling for protection. Left to their own domains, they perhaps may not conflict. It is when the two systems interconnect under conditions of globalization, that the latent incommensurability of these rights become conflictual and non-compossible.

What therefore lies at the heart of the debate is the problem of how to devise standards of commensuration at the policy level which could translate into policies for conflict management, based on terms of arbitration that are fair and equitable. I propose that terms of adjudication ought to rest on which rights are 'prior' rights—prior in the sense of being entitlements to minimal standards of food, clothing, shelter, and health care. Some rights are weightier than others—the right to nutrition, the right to health, and knowledge rights of certain traditional communities, linked to their survival strategies.[11] Rights which are crucially linked to survival strategies encompassing conditions of dignified human existence, are the most fundamental and inalienable ones, and therefore, demand to be upheld as one with a prior claims to protection vis-à-vis intellectual property rights. Rights and freedom of peoples, competing values such as public health, public interest, national security or morals, and above all, right to dignified human existence, should given enough weight that they trump rights to intellectual property.[12]

Collective Rights within Liberal Theory

The terms of the debate surrounding intellectual property rights are frequently dominated by the fact that intellectual property rights belong to the domain of liberal democratic rights which are individualistic in nature and therefore, fundamentally conflict with the rights of the traditional people which are usually located in collectives. For instance, farmers' rights are group rights, as are indigenous knowledge rights. These rights are political claims which get their sense from the status of persons/communities as self-governing units. These self-governing members can belong to and claim allegiance to altogether different conceptions of rights, rooted in their own socio-economic and cultural milieu.

How do we assign rights to collectives? Who is to be the bearer of these rights? This is the dilemma of contemporary liberal philosophy which seeks to increasingly adopt and articulate the language of human rights in order to mitigate the sufferings and poverty that afflict a larger part of the global population. The liberal dilemma poses itself in international

[11] For an explication of this argument, see, for instance J.W. Nickel, 1987, *Making Sense of Human Rights*, Berkley and Los Angeles: University of California Press, pp. 131–46.

[12] For the inalienability and salience of economic and social rights see, ICESCR, Article 4.

charters and Conventions. The UDHR states that members shall promote human rights 'without distinction to race, sex, language, or religion', but is in a quandary over the proper response to groups identified by race, language, or religion that want differential treatment in order to preserve characteristics they cherish.[13] The absence of legally binding international instrument on farmers' rights and on knowledge rights of the indigenous peoples is perhaps an outome of this dilemma. The dilemma does not exist at the level of diagnosing that these collective entities have rights claims; they are well recognized and have become a part of the official rhetoric at various national and international levels. The dilemma exists in assigning them juridical expression which will entail a set of obligations on the duty bearers.

Rights that are essential to the pursuit of the most basic interests and the satisfaction of the most basic needs have a strong moral basis for being considered as rights. Liberal–democratic thought assigns this as the basis of individual rights. Liberal theory holds that the freedom of each individual to live according to his/her own conception of the good is, as Mill said, the 'only freedom which deserves the name';[14] or as Dworkin states, 'The basic idea of right-based theory is that distinct individuals have interests that they are entitled to protect'.[15] Ernest Barker goes a step further and demarcates the area of moral rights only for individuals for according to him 'in the moral world there are *no group persons*' [emphasis mine]—no group exists that has collective moral rights.[16]

Extending the argument further to test its implication for who the bearer of the right ought to be, it can be asked that if the objective of rights is to satisfy the interests and needs of the individuals, then is it implied that associated rights should be assigned to individuals only. It can be argued that there is no basis for assuming that individuals are the only significant units as repositories of rights. Sometimes, the associated right is better protected when located in a collective unit. For instance, a farmer's right to livelihood may be better protected through a collective

---

[13] Francess Stevensson, September 1979, 'Liberal Democracy and Group Rights: The Legacy of Individualism and its Impact on American Indian Tribes,' *Political Studies*, vol. 37, pp. 421–30; Kenneth D. McRae, December 1979, 'The Plural Society and the Western Political Tradition,' *Canadian Journal of Political Science*, vol. 12.

[14] John Stuart Mill, 1991, *On Liberty and Other Essays,* New York: Oxford University Press, p. 17.

[15] Ronald Dworkin, 1977, *Taking Rights Seriously,* Cambridge: Harvard University Press, pp. xi, 176, 188.

[16] Ernest Barker, 1951, *Principles of Social and Political Theory,* Oxford: Clarendon Press, p. 71.

right that the farming community has over its resources. States are collective entities, so are business corporations and both have rights. Some interests and needs are therefore better conceived as collective rather than individual. If *interests* govern rights then it does not preclude collectives from being claimant and repositories of rights. Collective rights, I argue, can be claimed on the same basis and within the same system as individual rights. Will Kymlicka argues, that certain 'collective rights' are consistent with liberal democratic principles.[17] When collective rights are not rights of a group to limit the liberties of its own individual members (internal restrictions) but refer to the right of a group to limit the economic or political power exercised by the larger society over the group, then these collective rights are consistent with liberal democratic theory.

The liberal-communitarian debate, which dominated much of the 1980s, reflected the concerns and issues posed today by conceptions of individual and collective rights. The liberals defended the rights of an individual against encroachment by the state and society and communitarians defended the particularity and cohesiveness of the community/society against the unrestricted choices of individuals. A part of this debate was also framed in terms of universalism and particularism, where the individualists defended universal principles of liberty and freedom, while the communitarians insisted that morality was always embedded and tied to shared local meanings.

The ubiquity of rights-talk very often is animated by a fundamental tension between the desire to establish universal rights, on the one hand, and the awareness of cultural differences on the other. This often becomes the basis for intense negotiation of space for different rights. Emerging pluralities are a challenge—at both theoretical and policy levels, notions of the 'universal', universal rationality, universal rights, conventional conceptions of citizenship and so on. However, principles of moral universalism abide, albeit in an increasing dialogue with local definitions and legal particularism.[18]

Following the later work of John Rawls, much of contemporary liberal theory is premised on the claim that there are no non-contestable premises about fundamental or universal values of human nature from which liberal justification could proceed. The fact of reasonable pluralism', prevails on premises of moral universalism, which Rawls argued is the

---

[17] For details see Will, Kymlicka, 1995, *Multicultural Citizenship*, Oxford: OUP, Chapter 3.

[18] For an elaboration of the thesis see, Thomas Pogge, 2002, 'Moral Universalism and Global Economic Justice', *Politics, Philosophy and Economics*, 1(1), pp. 29–58.

'inevitable outcome of free human reason'[19] and 'a permanent feature of the public culture of a democracy.'[20] Rawls explains that there are several distinct but mutually incompatible comprehensive doctrines, non-converging religious, moral, philosophical views and that 'a continuing shared understanding on one comprehensive doctrine can be maintained only by the oppressive use of state power'.[21] Thus, according to Rawls, any political order that is premised on the truth of a single comprehensive doctrine—even a decidedly *liberal* one—is ipso facto oppressive and therefore illiberal.

Rawls' pluralism is not regarded as the most radical of pluralisms,[22] but is sufficient to suggest that any conception of rights has to take cognizance of distinct and plural cultures, communities, moral doctrines, ways of life, and religious systems, etc. Plurality has to become a condition of liberal regimes and liberal conceptions of the good, rights, and justice. Galston, a radical political pluralist states that 'while the distinction between good and evil is objective, there are multiple goods that differ qualitatively from one another and that cannot be rank-ordered'. From this, it follows that 'there is no single way of life, based on a singular ordering of values, that is the highest and best for all individuals'.[23] Therefore, the state must provide and protect the political space in which each individual can make such choices as s/he sees fit. The freedoms and choices of each individual are upheld only when they are embodied within the institutions and traditions of particular political communities.

The basic justification for individual rights and collective rights (or human rights, the bearers of which are collectives) are the same. Dworkin's principle of the 'right to equal concern and respect' could well be used as a plausible theory of collective human rights and could trump any ordinary claims of common good based on aggregating individual good.[24] The right to equal concern and respect is grounded in the interest an individual has in the quality of his life, and an individual's quality of life may well be defined or protected through collective or group rights. Many individual rights may be understood as flowing from the

---

[19] John Rawls, 1996, *Political Liberalism,* New York: Columbia University Press, p. 37.

[20] Ibid., p. 36.

[21] Ibid., p. 37.

[22] Gray and Galston, adopt more radical and robust versions of political pluralism than Rawls. John Gray, 2000, *Two Faces of Liberalism,* New York: The New Press, p. 16; William Galston, 2002, *Liberal Pluralism,* Cambridge: Cambridge University Press; and William Galston, 2005, *The Practice of Liberal Pluralism,* Cambridge: Cambridge University Press.

[23] Wiilliam Galston, 2005, p. 2.

[24] David Beetham (ed.), *Politics and Human Rights,* Oxford: Blackwell.

community's right to self preservation. Groups, cultural, ethnic, religious therefore, may generate entitlements.[25] There are many philosophers today who argue that doctrines that recognize only individual rights are not universally relevant to contemporary political problems.[26] Many societies are characterized by radical cultural heterogeneity and can function only on the basis of collective rights.

The problem therefore is not of devising a basis for assigning rights to collectives but that once rights are assigned, these collectives become distinct political units or economic entities which have the potential to confront the dominant and existing political or economic entities. Just as groups may generate entitlements so also entitlements may generate political entities which may confront established rights and norms. In cases of conflict—as routinely occur between indigenous knowledge holders and claims for intellectual property rights, or between farmers' rights and breeders' rights—the intellectual property rights of the individual may be put in jeopardy; the rights of the group might always be held to prevail. Resisting collective rights might have therefore, practical considerations for societies based on individual rights system. The issue of collective rights, specifically in the context of knowledge rights, is therefore not merely conceptual, but also one of pragmatic assessment based on vested self-interests of corporations and countries.

In devising universal rules and norms for knowledge generation and use, the intellectual property rights regime essentializes social and cultural categories, fixes identities as a concomitant of its task of developing general principles to include all possible cases. This universalizing is not a product of moral ambiguities and ethical choices between individual subjects and collective identities. The conflict between intellectual property rights and traditional peoples' knowledge rights is not just about incompatible values, attitudes and practices, but relates to a fundamental aspect of *rights as power*. Intellectual property rights bestow on the rights-holders the

[25] Whether it is for the protection and preservation of individuals within these groups or for the collectivity per se is a matter of some debate. In one interpretation collectives matter only to the extent that they affect actual individuals and that beyond this they have no special moral primacy as cultural groups are fluid categories with no natural primacy like the individual. See, for instance, Chandran Kukathas, February 1992, 'Are There Any Cultural Rights?' *Political Theory*, pp. 108–13. However whether collective rights such as the farmers' rights accrue to the individual within the group or to the group per se is not of much concern to us here. Any right may be subject to varying degree of interpretations by its endorsers.

[26] See, for instance, Vernon Van Dyke, April 1977, 'The Individual and the State, and Ethnic Communities in Political Theory', *World Politics*, vol. 29, p. 369.

power to appropriate in newer, more secure, and profitable ways. It assigns
them the power to enter other domains of knowledge, other domains of
rights: the entry always restricting the choices of others and curtailing
their rights. Rights, as legal process, are a 'structuring discourse' which
shape how the world is apprehended. Intellectual property rights are
forms of legal protection that protect a certain basis for the deployment
of knowledge for appropriation while denying others.

CONCLUDING REMARKS

Indigenous communities create collectively, which would mean that in
an alternative conception of intellectual/knowledge rights, the entire
community would be deemed the rightful owner of such creativity or
innovation. Michael Brown states, 'A group's relationship to its cultural
productions constitutes a form of ownership. This ownership may be
literal—that is, based on some comprehensive definition of cultural or
IP—or metaphorical, reflecting universal recognition that a group "owns"
the ideas and practices that it holds dear'.[27] Literal or metaphorical, most
ownership claims of indigenous peoples have been dissociated from the
proprietary connotations of intellectual property claims. The identification
of inventiveness with the solitary pursuit of an individual cannot be easily
reconciled with the cultural productions of knowledge of indigenous
peoples.

But the global politics of intellectual property has become increasingly
complex. It can no longer remain content leaving the two ownership
patterns relegated to their respective domains. As arenas of contestations
and negotiations emerge, it is deemed increasingly necessary to
democratize the field of practice of intellectual property. In this context,
one can easily see the attraction of framing traditional indigenous
knowledge demands in terms of ABS as an expression of cultural and
collective practices of property—collectively the community becomes
the repository of the right to claim benefits when its knowledge is used
to create further commercial value. The temptation to make disclosures
and ABS the sole acknowledgement of the demand for collective rights
is based on a fairly intuitive perception: if indigenous people own their
knowledge, and if it is taken from them, then it should simply be a
matter of compensation. In the absence of exclusionary premises of
TIK ownership norms (both as per customary law and modern legal

[27] Michael Brown, April 1998, 'Can Culture be Copyrighted?', *Current Anthropology*,
39(2), p. 194.

frameworks), ownership requirements are served through access and arbitrarily derived compensation norms.

Modern jurisprudence on property rights has used the absence of proprietary and residential claims of property in traditional knowledge customary laws to construct a version of ownership rights for indigenous peoples which lack not just exclusionary abilities, but also the power of structuring social and economic conditions. This relates to a fundamental aspect of *rights as power*. While intellectual property rights have the ability to structure conditions, weak residuary rights vested in the communities' claim to benefits of weak rights that are themselves structured in relation to another right, enabling rather than impeding the realization of intellectual property rights. Their derivative status ensures that they eventually become a part of the structuring discourse of intellectual property rights.

Pragmatically, there is reason to believe that the reappearance of the 'local' within the discourses and practices of global governance has had a large impact on the way rights are conceptualized and have been reorganized in terms of newer generations of socio-economic, cultural, and human rights. 'Localism' and 'globalsim' are themes which resonate in the various conceptualizations of knowledge rights, such as the Traditional Resource Rights (TRRs) and Community Property Rights (CPRs). The 'alternative' quality of these systems is derived from the recognition that universal values of freedom and democracy can only be upheld and protected if knowledge rights are embodied within the traditions, culture, and institutions of particular communities. A model community intellectual rights act was suggested in a Third World Network discussion paper[28] as a means of bringing about the evolution of new criteria for claiming intellectual property rights that are compatible with cultural values and the practices of indigenous peoples. The re-conceptualization of knowledge rights is critically linked to the capacities of varied communities around the world to sustain themselves. Their human rights are at times linked to their knowledge rights and to this extent

---

[28] Nijar argues for two legal principles as the basis for vesting the custodianship rights of local communities producing an innovation: (a) Constructive Trust: 'when property has been acquired in such circumstances, then the holder of the title (to these rights) may not in good conscience retain the beneficial interest: equity converts him into a trusty.' (b) Higher Trust: The recognition in Biodiversity Convention of governments possessing sovereign rights vis-a-vis their resources creates a higher trust. This 'imposes on the government an obligation to honour it in relation to those it holds the rights in trust for (that is, the community)'. For details see, Gurdial Singh Nijar, 1994, 'Towards a Legal Framework for Protecting Biological Diversity and Community Intellectual Rights—A Third World Perspective', TWN Discussion Paper, TWN. Available at (last accessed on 16 January 2008).

the conceptualization of TRRs and CPRs are allied to a *de facto* self determination of traditional peoples. TRRs seek not only to protect the knowledge relating to biological resources but also to assert the right of peoples to self-determination, including territorial and human rights, and the right to safeguard 'culture' in the broadest sense of the term. Darrel Posey and Graham Dutfield in their support to TRRs state that TRR recognizes the inextricable link between cultural and biological diversity and between the human rights of indigenous and local communities, including the right to development and environmental conservation. [29]

It is important to bear in mind that rights to cultural property, TRRs, and CPRs had existed in the customary law and customary rights domain for centuries. The dramatic expansion of intellectual property discourses went a long way in displacing traditional and customary ways of *owning*. In many ways, the intellectual property discourse brings to center stage conceptualizations of alternative property regimes and replaces what should be extensive discussion on the moral implications of the intellectual property right itself.

The concern with understanding the moral dimensions of intellectual property rights has been greatly influenced by an understanding that sees rights as social products and their morality as derived from the purpose of according a politico-legal status to the needs and wants of people who differ in their substantive conceptions of the good. As human rights get aligned with issues of needs and culture, so do they with issues of justice. Their intuitive appeal lies in its appeal to our normative imagination. However, for these moral claims to be translated into legal claims located in cultural practices of the people, human rights need to be brought 'down from its pedestal',[30] as Upendra Baxi proposes, in our struggles against the monocultures of universal rights, to re-situate human rights 'amidst other significant cultural concepts which define a 'good life' in a pluriverse'.[31]

[29] D.A. Posey and G. Dutfield, 1996, *Beyond Intellectual Property: Toward Traditional Resource Rights for Indigenous Peoples and Local Communities,* Ottawa: International Development Research Centre; Posey Darrell and Graham Dutfield, 'Mind The Gaps: Identifying Commonalties and Divergences Between Indigenous Peoples and Farmers Groups'. Draft prepared for the 5th Global Biodiversity Forum. Buenos Aires, Argentina 1–3 November 1996 (Oxford Centre for the Environment, Ethics & Society. UK). Available at http://www.gbf.ch/Session_Administration/upload/Posey%20and%20Dutfield.paper.doc (last accessed on 12 February 2008).

[30] Upendra Baxi, 2007, *Human Rights in a Post Human World*, New Delhi: Oxford University Press, p. 1.

[31] Esteva Gustava and Madhuri Suri Prakash, 1998, *Grassroots Postmodernism,* London: Zed Books, pp. 118–19. Quoted in Upendra Baxi, 2007, p. 1.

Both, the conception of rights and the conception of what is human, are located in practices of power and hegemony, to draw from Foucault, which in their acts of inclusion violently exclude what they consider beyond the pale of rights and human. Foucault thus demands an 'insurrection of subjugated knowledges' which goes beyond the accepted formula of rights and definitions of human. Ethical absolutism would suggest that what constitutes human is beyond the realm of contingency; that there is something inviolable, a priori about what constitutes human rights. However, as Baxi argues, 'philosophical pragmatism would suggest that what constitutes human is a matter of contingent beliefs, always open to negotiation and change...'.[32] What emerges out of this negotiation determines what constitutes *human* and what constitutes a *right* for a given community. Negotiations may entrench existing conceptions—I have argued that 'disclosure' and 'benefit sharing' are two such negotiated spaces within intellectual property rights. Or, it may expand the category of rights and the conditions that classify as human. The spaces of collective and cultural rights could emerge as another such negotiated space.

A view of rights, located in the perspective of cultural relativism, would presuppose a commitment to autonomy—not just a commitment to individual autonomy in the libertarian sense but also as the freedom of different cultural and social entities to define their ontologies. Autonomy implies that the conditions of moral and cultural pluralism be met for rights to be consistent with the enterprise of justice and for them to be conceptualized in terms of human rights. While there is a shared basis for universalism of rights (that rights should exist), there is also a shared perception that particular rights need to be located in the cultural and contextual milieux of different societies. The danger of universal rights is that it encourages the imposition of dominant ideals and standards on other cultures, often through an implied cultural denigration and replacement of local customary ways of being in the world. To this extent, intellectual property rights represent a specific instance of a larger claim for intellectual and cultural domination. To this extent the counter hegemonic perspective of rights needs to be located in a 'pluriverse' and one which recovers the meaning of being and remaining 'human'.

---

[32] Upendra Baxi, 2007, pp. 21–2.

Select Bibliography

BOOKS

Arup, C., 2000, *The New World Trade Organization Agreements: Globalizing Law through Services and Intellectual Property*, Cambridge: Cambridge University Press.

Ashcraft, Richard, 1987, *Locke's Two Treatise of Government*, London: Allen and Unwin.

Barnes, Barry, 1988, *The Nature of Power*, Cambridge: Polity.

——— 1985, *About Science*, Oxford: Blackwell.

——— (ed.), 1972, *Sociology of Science*, Harmondsworth: Penguin.

Bauman, Zygmut, 1976, *Towards a Critical Sociology:An Essay on Common sense and Emancipation*, London: RKP.

Becker, Lawrence C., 1977, *Property Rights: Philosophical Foundations*, London: RKP.

Beetham, David, 1995, *Politics and Human Rights*, Oxford: Blackwell.

Bentham, Jeremy, 1970 [1789], *An Introduction to the Principles of Morals and Legislation*, J.H. Burns and H.L.A. Hart (eds), London: The Athlone Press. Available at http://www.econlib.org/library/Bentham/bnthPML.html (last accessed on 25 January 2008).

Bentham, Jeremy, 1843, *Principles of the Civil Code*. Reprinted in The Works of Jeremy Bentham, Edinburgh: William Tait.

Berger, P.L. and T. Luckmann, 1966, *The Social Construction of Reality:A Treatise in the Sociology of Knowledge*, NY: Anchor Books.

Blair, Roger D. and Thomas Cotter, 2005, *IP: Economic and Legal dimensions of Rights and Remedies*, Cambridge: Cambridge University Press.

Böhme, G., Stehr, N. (eds), 1986, *The Knowledge Society*, Dordrecht: D. Reidel.

Boldrin, Michele and David K. Levine, *Against Intellectual Monopoly*. Available at http://www.micheleboldrin.com/research/aim/anew.all.pdf (last accessed on 6 July 2008).

Bowring, J., 1843, *The Works of Jeremy Bentham*, Edinburgh: William Tait, vol. V.

Boyle, James, 1996, *Shamans, Software, and Spleens: Law and the Social Construction of the Information Economy*, Cambridge, MA: Harvard University Press.

Brandt, R.B., 1979, *A Theory of the Good and the Right*, Oxford: Oxford University Press.

Brokensha, D.D. Warren, and O. Werner (eds), 1980, *Indigenous Knowledge Systems and Development*, Washington, DC, University Press of America.

Chidi Oguamanam, 2006, *International Law and IK, Intellectual Property Right, Plant Biodiversity and Traditional Medicine*, Toronto: University of Toronto Press.

Christman, John, 1994, *The Myth of Property: Toward an Egalitarian Theory of Ownership*, New York: OUP.

Cohen G.A., 1995, *Self-Ownership, Freedom and Equality*, Cambridge: Cambridge University Press.

Cornish, W.R., 1981, *Intellectual Property: Patents, Copyright, Trademarks and Allied Rights*, London: Sweet and Maxwell.

Correa, Carlos, 2000, *Intellectual Property Rights, the WTO and Developing Countries: The TRIPS Agreement and Policy Options*, London: Zed Books and Penang: Third World Network.

Cullet, Philippe, 2005, *IP Protection and Sustainable Development*, Butterworths: Lexis Nexis.

D.A. Posey and G. Dutfield, 1996, *Beyond Intellectual Property: Toward Traditional Resource Rights for Indigenous Peoples and Local Communities*, Ottawa: International Development Research Centre.

David, Miller, 1989, *Market, State, and Community*, Oxford: Clarendon Press.

Dei, George, Jerry Sefa, Budd L. Hall, and Dorothy Goldin Rosenberg, 2000, *Indigenous Knowledges in Global Contexts: Multiple Readings of our World*, Toronto: University of Toronto Press.

Dunn, John, 1985, *Rethinking Modern Political Theory: Essays 1979–83*, Cambridge: OUP.

Dutfield, Graham, 2003, *Intellectual Property Rights and the Life Sciences Industries*, Aldershot: Ashgate.

Dutfield, Graham, 2000, *Intellectual property Rights, Trade and Biodiversity*, London: Earthscan Publications.

Dworkin, Ronald, 2000, *Sovereign Virtue: The Theory and Practice of Equality*, Cambridge: Harvard University Press.

———, 1977, *Taking Rights Seriously*, Cambridge: Harvard University Press.

Edelman, Bernard, 1997, *Time and Commodity Culture: Essays in Cultural Theory and Post-modernity* (trans. by John Frow), Oxford: Oxford University Press.

Escobar, A., 1995, *Encountering Development: The Making and Unmaking of the Third World*, Princeton: Princeton University Press.

Finger, J. Michael and Philip Schuler, 2004, *Poor People's Knowledge: Promoting Intellectual Property in Developing Countries*, Washington: Oxford University Press.

Freeden, Michael, 1998, *Rights*, Delhi: WorldView Publications.

Fritz Machlup, 1962, *Production and Distribution of Knowledge in the US*, Princeton: Princeton University Press.

Galston, William, 2005, *The Practice of Liberal Pluralism*, Cambridge: Cambridge University Press.

Grunebaum, James, 1987, *Private Ownership*, New York: Routledge & Kegan Paul.

Halevy, Elie, 1928, *The Growth of Philosophical Radicalism*, London, Faber and Faber.

Hawore, A.M., 1961, 'Ownership', *Oxford Essays in Jurisprudeace*, A.G. Guest (ed.), Oxford: Clarendon Press.

Haworth, Alan, 1994, *Anti-libertarianism: Markets, Philosophy and Myth*, London: Routledge.

Hayek, Fredrich Von, 1944, *The Road to Serfdom*, Chicago: University of Chicago Press.

Hegel, G.W.F., 2001, *Philosophy of Right* (trans. by S.W. Dyde), Ritchener: Bateche Books.

Hillel, Steiner, 1994, *An Essay on Rights*, Oxford: Blackwell.

Hoopers, Odora C., 2002, *Indigenous Knowledge and the Integration of Knowledge Systems*, Claremont: New Africa Books.

Hunt, E.K., 2003, *Property and Prophets—The Evolution of Economic Institutions and Ideologies*, New York: M.E. Sharpe.

Ingram, Attracta, 1994, *A Political Theory of Rights*, Oxford: Clarendon Press.

Jaffe Adam B. and Josh Lerner, 2004, *Innovation and Its Discontents: How Our Broken Patent System is Endangering Innovation and Progress, and What to Do About It*, Princeton University Press.

Jagtenberg, Tom, 1983, *The Social Construction of Science*, Boston: D. Reidel Publishing Co.

Jasanoff, S. *et al.* (eds), 1994, *Handbook of Science and Technology Studies*, Beverly Hills, CA: Sage.

Joel, Feinberg, 1970, '*Justice and Personal Desert*', *Doing and Deserving*, Princeton, NJ: Princeton University Press.

Johannes, R.E. (ed), 1989, *Traditional Ecological Knowledge: A Collection of Essays*, Switzerland and Cambridge: IUCN.

Juma, Calestous, 1989, *The Gene Hunters: Biotechnology and the Scramble for Seeds*, Princeton University Press.

Kant, Immanuel, *The Philosophy of Law: An Exposition of the Fundamental Principles of Jurisprudence as the Science of Right 1887* (trans. by W. Hastic), (HTML and PDF files at libertyfund.org).

Kloppenburg, Jack, 2000, *First the Seed: The Political Economy of Plant Biotechnology 1492–2000*, Cambridge: Cambridge University Press.

——— (ed.), 1988, '*Seeds and Sovereignty: The Use and Control of Plant Genetic Resources*', London: Duke University Press.

Knorr Cetina, Karin, 1999, *Epistemic Cultures: How the Sciences Make Knowledge*, Cambridge: Harvard University Press.

———, 1981, *The Manufacture of Knowledge: An Essay on the Constructivist and Contextual Nature of Science*, New York: Pergamon Press.

Kymlicka, Will, 2002, *Contemporary Political Philosophy*, Oxford: OUP.

———, 1995, *Multicultural Citizenship*, Oxford: OUP.

Landes, William M. and Richard Posner, 2004, *The Political Economy of Intellectual Property Law*, Washington D.C: The AEI Press, http://www.aei.org/docLib/20040608_Landes.pdf (last accessed on 10 July 2008).

Laslett, Peter (ed.), 1968, *Two Treatise of Government*, Cambridge, Cambridge University Press, 1960.

Latour B., 1987, *Science in Action: How to Follow Scientists and Engineers through Society*, Cambridge, MA: Harvard University Press.

Leach, M., I. Scoones and B. Wynne (eds), 2005, *Science and Citizens: Globalization and the Challenge of Engagement*, London: Zed Press.

Lessig, Lawrence, 2001, *The Future of Ideas: The Fate of the Commons in a Connected World*, New York: Random House.

Long, R.D., 1979, 'Bentham on Property', in *Theories of Property: Arintoth to the Present*, Anthony Parel and Thomas Hanagan (ed.), Waterloo: Willfrid Laurier University Press.

MacPherson, C.B., 1973, *Democratic Theory: Essays in Retrieval*, Claredon: Oxford.

Doyle, McCarthy, E., 1996, *Knowledge as Culture: The New Sociology of Knowledge*, London: Routledge.

Meja Volker and Nico Stehr (eds), 1984, *Knowledge and Society: Contemporary Perspectives on the Sociology of Knowledge*, Transaction Books.

Milson, S.F.C., 1969, *Historical Foundation of the Common Law*, London: Butterworths.

Moore, Adam D., 2004, *Intellectual Property and Information Control: Philosophic Foundations and Contemporary Issues*, London: Transaction.

————, 1997, *Intellectual Property: Moral, Legal, and International Dilemmas*, A. Moore (ed.), Lanham, Md.: Rowman & Littlefield.

Munzer, Stephen R., 1990, *A Theory Of Property*, New York: Cambridge University Press.

Nelson, Richard (ed), 1962, *The Rate and Direction of Inventive Activity*, Princeton, NJ: Princeton University Press.

Nickel, J.W., 1987, *Making Sense of Human Rights*, Los Angeles: University of California Press.

Nordhaus, William D., 1969, *Invention, Growth, and Welfare: A Theoretical Treatment of Technological Change*, Cambridge: MIT Press.

Nozick, Robert, 1974, *Anarchy, State, and Utopia*, New York: Basic Books.

Olivecrona, Karl, 1971, *Law as Fact*, London: Stevens.

Parel, Anthony and Thomas Flanagan (eds), 1979, *Theories of Property: Aristotle to the Present*, Wilfred Laurier University Press.

Pels, Dick, 1998, *Property and Power in Social Theory*, London: Routledge.

Penner, J.E., 1997, *The Idea of Property in Law*, Oxford: Clarendon Press.

Pieterse, Jan Nederveen, 2001, *Development Theory: Deconstructions /Reconstructions*, London: Sage.

Pocock, J.G.A., 1985, *Virtue, Commerce and History: Essays on Political Thought and History Chiefly in the 18th Century*, Cambridge: Cambridge University Press.

Pollock, F., 1896, *Land Laws*, Third edn, London: Macmillan.

Rand, Ayn, 1967, 'Patents and Copyrights', in *Capitalism: The Unknown Ideal*, New York: New American Library.

Rawls, John, 1996, *Political Liberalism*, New York: Columbia University Press.

————, 1971, *A Theory of Justice*, Cambridge: Harvard University Press.

Reeves, Andrew, 1986, *Property*, London: Macmillan.

Ritchie D.G., 1952, *Natural Rights*, London: Allen and Unwin.

Rorty, Richard, 1979, *Philosophy and the Mirror of Nature*, New Jersey: Princeton University Press.

Rosenblum, Nancy, 1978, *Bentham's Theory of the Modern State*, Cambridge: Harvard University Press.

Rothbard, Murray, 1982, *The Ethics of Liberty*, Atlantic Highlands: Humanities Press.

————, 1978, *For a New Liberty, The Libertarian Manifesto*, revised edition, New York: Libertarian Review Foundation.

Ryan, Alan, 1987, *Property*, Milton Keynes: Open University Press.

Ryan, M., 1998, *Knowledge Diplomacy: Global Competition and the Politics of Intellectual Property*, Washington, DC: Brookings Institution Press.

Scherer, F.M. and David Ross, 1990, *Industrial Market Structure and Economic Performance*, 3rd edn, Boston: Houghton Mifflin.

Sell, Susan K., 2003, *Private Power, Public Law: The Globalization of Intellectual Property Rights*, Cambridge: Cambridge University Press.

Sen, Amartya and Bernard Williams (eds), 1982, *Utilitarianism and Beyond*, Cambridge: CUP.

Sen, Amartya, 2002, *Rationality and Freedom*, Delhi: OUP.

Shapiro, Ian, 2004, *Moral Foundations of Politics*, New Delhi: Sakar Books.

————, 1986, *The Evolution of Rights in Liberal Theory*, Cambridge: Cambridge University Press.

Shiva, V., November 1999, *Campaign against Biopiracy*, New Delhi: RFSTE.

———— (ed.), 1994, *Biodiversity Conservation: Whose Resources? Whose Knowledge?*, Delhi: INTACH.

Shiva, Vandana, Radha Holla Bhar, K.Vijaylakshmi and K.S. Radha, 2006, *Neem*, Delhi: RFSTE.

Steiner, Hichl, 1994, *An Essay on Rights*, Oxford: Blackwell, pp. 231–35.

Tully, James, 1980, *A Discourse Concerning Property: John Locke and his Adversaries*, Cambridge: Cambridge University Press.

————, 1979, *The Political Thought of John Locke*, Cambridge: Cambridge University Press.

Vallentyre, Peter and Hillel Steiner (eds), 2000, *Left Libertarianism and its Critics: The Contemporary Debate*, London: Palgrave.

Wagner, Roy, 1981, *The Invention of Culture*. Revised edition, University of Chicago Press.

Waldson, Jeremy, 1990, *The Right to Private Property*, New York: OUP.

Wood, Neal, 1984, *John Locke and Agrarian Capitalism*, Berkley: University of California Press.

ARTICLES, BOOK CHAPTERS AND OTHER DOCUMENTS

Arrow, Kenneth J., 1962, 'Economic Welfare and the Allocation of Resources for Invention', in *The Rate and Direction of Inventive Activity*, Richard Nelson (ed.), Princeton, NJ: Princeton University Press.

Attawell, K. and J. Mundy, 2003, 'Provision of Antiretroviral Therapy in Resource-Limited Settings: A Review of Experience Up to August 2003', Health Systems Resource Centre, Department for International Development, London. Available at http://www.who.int/3by5/publications/documents/en/ARTpaper_ DFID_WHO.pdf (last accessed on 15 July 2008).

Bell, Tom W., 'Indelicate Imbalancing in Copyright and Patent Law', in *Copy Fights* Published Paper. Available at http://www.tomwbell.com/writings/Indelicate.pdf (last accessed on 5 January 2008).

Berkes, Firket, 1993, 'Traditional Ecological Knowledge in Perspective', in *Traditional Ecological Knowledge: Concept and Cases*, J.T. Inglis (ed.), Ottawa: International Development Research Centre.

Block, Walter, 2003, 'Toward a Libertarian Theory of Inalienability: A Critique of Rothbard, Barnett, Gordon, Smith, Kinsella, and Epstein', *Journal of Libertarian Studies Journal of Libertarian Studies*, 17(2).

Boldrin Michele and David K. Levine, 2002, 'The Case against Intellectual Property', *American Economic Review*, 92(2).

Boyle, James, 2003, 'The Second Enclosure Movement and the Construction of the Public Domain', *Law & Contemporary*, 66(33).

————, 1992, 'A Theory of Law and Information: Copyright, Spleens, Blackmail and Inside Trading', *California Law Review*, vol. 80.

Brenkert, George G., 1998, 'Self-Ownership, Freedom, and Autonomy', *Journal of Ethics*, no. 2.

Brown, Michael F., April 1998, 'Can Culture Be Copyrighted?', *Current Anthropology*, 39(2).

Burri, Von Christian, April 2004, 'High Time to Take Action: Research on Neglected Diseases', *Bulletin von Medicus Mundi Schweiz* Nr. 92. Available at http://www.medicusmundi.ch/mms/services/bulletin/bulletin200401/kap01/08burri.html (last accessed on 2 January 2008).

Carrier, Michael, October 2004, 'Cabining Intellectual Property through a Property Paradigm', *Duke Law Journal*, 54(1).

Chandra, Rajshree, 'Intellectual Property Rights: Excluding Other Rights of Other People', *EPW*, XLIV(31).

Christman, John, February 1991, 'Self-Ownership, Equality and the Structure of Property Rights', *Political Theory*, 19(1).

————, 1988, '*Entrepreneurs, Profits and Deserving Market Shares*', *Soc. Phil. & Policy*, 6(1).

Changing Patterns of Pharmaceutical Innovation. A research report by The National Institute for Health Care Management Research and Educational Foundation. May, 2002.

Cohen, G.A., 1983, 'Self-Ownership, World Ownership and Equality, Part II', *Social Philosophy and Policy*, 3(2).

Costo, *Journal of Libertarian Studies*, 15(4).

Cullet, Philippe, 27 October 2001, 'Patents Bill and the Right to Health', *Economic and Political Weekly*, XXXVI/43.

Cullet, Phillippe and Radhika Koluru, 2003, 'Plant Variety Protection and Farmers' Rights: Towards a Broader Understanding', *Delhi Law Review*, 24(2002).

'Cutting the Cost of Global Health', 2001, Oxfam Parliamentary Briefing. November 16.

Demsetz, Harold, 1969, 'Information and Efficiency: Another Viewpoint', *Journal of Law and Economics*, vol. 12.

————, May 1967, 'Toward a Theory of Property Rights, '*The American Economic Review*, 57(2).

Drahos, Peter, 2004, 'The Regulation of Public Goods', *The Journal of International Economic Law*, 7(2), p. 321.

————, 2002, *Global Intellectual Property Rights: Knowledge, Access and Development*, Oxfam GB: Macmillan.

————, 1997, 'Thinking Strategically about Intellectual Property Rights', *Telecommunications Policy*, 21(3).

'Drug Patents under the Spotlight—Sharing Practical Knowledge about Pharmaceutical Patents.' Médecins Sans Frontières (MSF), June 2004.

Esquinas-Alcazar, Jose, 'The Realization of Farmer's Right', in *Agrobiodiversity and Farmers' Rights*, M.S. Swaminathan (ed.), New Delhi: Konark, 1996.

Evans, Peter B., 'The Eclipse of the State? Reflections on Stateness in an Era of Globalization', *World Politics*, 50(1).

Feinberg, Joel, 1992, 'The Nature and Value of Rights', in *Rights*, Carlos Santiago Nino (ed.), NY: New York University Press.

Fisher, William, 2001, 'Theories of Intellectual Property', in *New Essays in the Legal and Political Theory of Property*, S. Munzer (ed.), Cambridge: Cambridge Univ. Press.

————, 1999, 'The Growth of Intellectual Property: A History of the Ownership of Ideas in the United States'. Available at http://cyber.law.harvard.edu/people/tfisher/iphistory.pdf (last accessed on 15 January 2008).

Galvão, J., December 2002, 'Access to Antiretroviral Drugs in Brazil', *Lancet*.

Garris, Joel, 1996, 'The Case for Patenting Medical Procedures', *American Journal of Law and Medicine*, 22 (1996).

Global Burden of Disease and Injury Series, Harvard School of Public Health on behalf of the WHO and World Bank, Harvard University Press. Available at http://gstudynet.org/docs/The%20GWU%20Neglected%20Tropical%20Diseases%20Initiative.doc (last accessed on 15 January 2008).

Gupta, V.K., 'Documentation of Traditional Medicine Knowledge: Digital Library of India', Document No. 16, Regional Consultation on Development of Traditional Medicine in the South East Asia Region, Korea, 22–4 June

2005, WHO. Available at http://www.searo.who.int/LinkFiles/Meetings_document16.pdf (last accessed on 20 January 2008).

Harsanyi, J. 1977, 'Morality and the Theory of Rational Behaviour', *Social Research*, 44(4).

Helfer, Laurence R., 'Intellectual Property Rights in Plant Varieties International legal regimes and policy options for national governments.' For the Development Law Service, FAO Legal Office. *FAO Corporate Document Repository*. Available at http://www.fao.org/docrep/007/y5714e/y5714e02.htm#bm2.2 (last accessed on 15 January 2008).

Hettinger, Edwin C., 1989, 'Justifying Intellectual Property', *Philosophy and Public Affairs*, 18(1).

Hoen, Ellen 't., 'TRIPS, Pharmaceutical Patents, and Access to Essential Medicines: A Long Way From Seattle to Doha', *Chicago Journal of International Law*, 28(3).

Hohfeld, W.N., 1919, 'Fundamental Legal Conceptions', *Yale Law Journal*.

Honoré A.M., 1961, 'Ownership', in *Oxford Essays in Jurisprudence*, A.G. Guest (ed.), Oxford: Clarendon Press.

Hountondji, P.J., 2002, 'Knowledge Appropriation in a Post-Colonial Context', in *Indigenous knowledge and the Integration of Knowledge Systems: Towards a Philosophy of Articulation*, Odora Hoppers (ed.), Claremont: New Africa Books.

Hughes, Justin, 1997, 'The Philosophy of Intellectual Property', in *Intellectual Property: Moral, Legal and International Dilemmas*, Adam Moore (ed.).

Jaffe, A.B., 2000, 'The U.S. Patent System in Transition: Policy Innovation and the Innovation Process', *Research Policy*, vol. 29.

James de Long, 'Defending Intellectual Property.' Available at http://www.pff.org/issues-pubs/books/020701defendingip.pdf (last accessed on 8 July 2008).

Kauser, Abdulla Malik, Yusuf Zafar, 'Intellectual property Rights in Plant Biotechnology: A Contribution to Crop Biosecurity.' *Asian Biotechnology and Development Review*, 8(1).

Kernohan, Andrew, 1990, 'Rawls and the Collective Ownership of Natural Abilities', *Canadian Journal of Philosophy*, vol. 20.

Kerry Ten Kate and Sarah A. Laird, 'Bio-Prospecting Agreements and Benefit Sharing with Local Communities', in *Poor People's Knowledge: Promoting Intellectual Property in Developing Countries*, J. Michael Finger and Philip Schuler (eds), World Bank and Oxford University Press.

Khor, Martin Patents, 'Compulsory License and Access to Medicines: Some Recent Experiences'. TWN, February 2007.

Kinsella, N. Stephen, 2001, Against Intellectual Property', *Journal of Libertarian Studies*, 15(2).

———, 1998–9, 'Inalienability and Punishment: A Reply to George Smith', *Journal of Libertarian Studies,* 14(1).

Kitch, E.W., 1977, 'The Nature and Function of the Patent System', *Journal of Law & Economics*, 20.

Kloppenburg, J., 1991, 'Social theory and the de/reconstruction of agricultural science: local knowledge for an alternative agriculture', *Rural Sociology*, 56(4).

Koning, M., 1998, 'Biodiversity prospecting and the equitable remuneration of ethnobiological knowledge: reconciling industry and indigenous interests.' *Intellectual Property Journal*, No. 12.

Lamont, Julian, 2004, 'Distributive Justice', in *Handbook of Political Theory*, Gerald F. Gaus and Chandran Kukathas (eds), New Arizona University: Sage.

————, 1994, 'The Concept of Desert in Distributive Justice', *The Philosophical Quarterly*, 44(994).

Lanoszka, Anna, 2003, 'The Global Politics of Intellectual Property Rights and Pharmaceutical Drug Policies in Developing Countries', *International Political Science Review*, 24(2).

Lerner, Josh, 2002, '150 Years of Patent Protection', *American Economic Review, Papers and Proceedings*, vol. 92, May.

Lewontin, R., July/August 1998, 'The Maturing of Capitalist Agriculture: Farmer as Proletarian.' *Monthly Review*, 50(3).

Long, R.D., 1979, 'Bentham on Property', in *Theories of Property Aristotle to the Present*, Anthony Parel and Thomas Flanagan (eds), Waterloo: Wilfrid Laurier University Press.

Maurial, Mahia, 1999, 'Indigenous Knowledge and Schooling: a Continuum Between Conflict and Dialogue', in *What is Indigenous Knowledge? Voices from the Academy*, Semali, Ladislaus M. and Joe L. Kincheloe (eds), New York and London: Falmer Press.

McRae, Kenneth D., December 1979, 'The Plural Society and the Western Political Tradition', *Canadian Journal Of Political Science*, vol. 12.

Michael, Mulkay, 1984, 'Knowledge and Utility: Implications for the Sociology of Knowledge', in Volker Meja and Nico Stehr (eds), *Knowledge and Society: Contemporary Perspectives on the Sociology of Knowledge*, Transaction Books.

Mossoff, Adam, 2001, *'Rethinking the Development of Patents: An Intellectual History, 1550–1800'*, *Hastings L.J.*, 52(1255).

Nance, Dale A., 1990, 'Foreword: Owning Ideas', in 'Symposium: Intellectual Property', *Harvard Journal of Law & Public Policy*, 13(3).

Nelson, Richard D. and Mazzoleni, 1997, Roberto. 'Economic Theories about the Costs and Benefits of Patents.' http://www.nap.edu/readingroom/books/property/3.html

Paine, Lynn Sharp, 1997, 'Trade Secrets and the Justification of Intellectual Property : A Comment on Hettinger', in *Intellectual property: Moral. Legal and International Dimensions*, Adam Moore (ed.), Oxford: Rowman and Littlefield.

Palmer, Tom G., 1997, A Non-Posnerian law and Economics Approach, in Adam D. Moore (ed), *Intellectual Property: Moral, Legal and International Dimensions*, New York: Rowman and Littlefield.

————, 1990, 'Are Patents and Copyrights Morally Justified? The Philosophy of Property Rights and Ideal Objects', in 'Symposium: Intellectual Property', *Harvard Journal of Law & Public Policy*, 13(3).

Posey, Darrell A., October 1996, 'Protecting Indigenous Peoples' Rights to Biodiversity', *Environment*.

Posner, Richard and William Landes, June 1989, 'An Economic Analysis of Copyright Law.' *Journal of Legal Studies*, 17.

Pottage, Alain, September 1998, 'The Inscription of Life in Law: Genes, Patents, and Bio-Politics', *The Modern Law Review*, 61(5).

Pufendorf, Samuel, 1991, *On the Duty of Man and Citizen According to Natural Law, On the duty of man and citizen, Cambridge Texts in the History of Political Though*, James Tully and Michael Silverthorne (eds), Cambridge: CUP.

Rand, Ayn, 1967, 'Patents and Copy rights,' in *Capitalism: The Unknown Ideal*, Ayn Rand (ed.), New York: New American Library.

Rangnekar, D., October–December 1998, 'Tripping in front of UPOV: Plant variety protection in India', *Social Action*, 48(4).

Rao, C. Niranjan, 21 February 2004, 'Indian Seed System and Plant Variety Protection', *EPW*, 39(8), pp. 845–52.

Replogle, J., 2004, 'Central American Trade Pact May Limit Access to Generics', *Lancet*, vol. 363.

Riley, Jonathan, 1989, 'Justice Under Capitalism', *Markets and Justice*, John W. Chapman (ed.), New York: New York University Press.

Roht-Arriaza, N., 1996, 'Of Seeds and Shamans: the appropriation of the scientific and technical knowledge of indigenous and local communities', *Michigan Journal of International Law*, 17(919).

S. Sahai, 1993, 'Indian patents Act and TRIPS', *EPW*, 28(1495).

Sainath, P., 7 April 2007, 'Farm Suicides in India, The Result of Profit Driven "Free Market Reforms"', *The Hindu Global Research*.

Sell, Susan and C. May, 2001, 'Moments in Law: contestations and settlement in the history of intellectual property', *Reviews of International Political Economy*, vol. 8.

Shapiro, Ian, February 1991, 'Resources, Capacities, and Ownership: The Workmanship Ideal and Distributive Justice', *Political Theory*, 19(1).

Sharrock, W.W., 1974, 'On Owning Knowledge', in *Ethnomethodology*, R. Turner (ed.), Harmondsworth: Penguin.

Shavell, Steven and Tanguy van Ypersele, October 2001, 'Rewards versus Intellectual Property Rights', *Journal of Law and Economics*, vol. XLIV.

Shiva, V. and Tom Crompton, 1998, 'Monopoly and Monoculture—trends in Indian Seed Industry', *EPW*, 33/39, A-137.

Singh Nijar, G., 1994, 'A Conceptual Framework and Essential Elements of a Rights Regime for the Protection of Indigenous Rights and Biodiversity', in *Biodiversity Convention Briefings*, Third World Network, Penang.

Stenson, A. and T. Gray, 1997, 'Cultural communities and intellectual property rights in plant genetic resources.' in *Justice, Property and Environment: Social and Legal Perspectives*, T. Hayward and J. O' Neil (eds), Aldershot and Bloom field: Ashgate Publishing.

Stevensson, Frances, September 1979, 'Liberal Democracy and Group Rights: The Legacy of Individualism and its Impact on American Tribes,' *Political Studies*, vol. 37.

Stiglitz, Joseph, 'Knowledge as a Global Public Good', in Kaul, Grunberg and Stern. Available at http://www.worldbank.org/knowledge/chiefecon/articles/undpk2/index.htm (last accessed on 28 July 2007).

Taylor, Robert S., 2005, 'Self-Ownership and the Limits of Libistrarianism', *Social Theory and Practice*, 31(4).

Thompson, Paul B., April 1995, 'Conceptions of Property and the Biotechnology Debate', *Bio Science*, 45(4).

Trouiller, P. *et al.*, 2002, 'Drug development for neglected diseases: a deficient market and a public-health policy failure', *Lancet*, 359.

Tully, James, 1979, 'The Framework of Natural Rights in Locke's Analysis Of Property: A Contextual Reconstruction', in *Theories of Property: Aristotle to the Present*, Anthony Parel and Thomas Flanagan (eds), Wilfred Laurier University Press.

Van Dyke, Vernon, April 1977, 'The Individual and the State, and Ethnic Communities in Political Theory', *World Politics*, vol. 29.

Varells, Marcelo Dias, 2004, 'The WTO, Intellectual Property and Aids—Case Studies from Brazil and South Africa', *J World Intellectual Property*, 7/4(523).

Vogel, Ursula, 'When the Land belonged to All: the Land Question in 18th C Justifications of Private Property', *Political Studies*, vol. 36.

Waldron, Jeremy, 1993, 'From Authors to Copiers: Individual Rights and Social Values in Intellectual Property,' *Chicago Kent Law Review*, 68(841).

Waldron, Jeremy, 'Locke, Tully, and the Regulation of Property', *Political Studies*, vol. 32.

Waltercheid, Edward C., 'Inherent or Created Rights: Early views on IP Clause', *Hamline Law Review*, vol. 19.

Warren, D. Michael and Gerard McKiernan, 1995, 'A global approach to documenting indigenous knowledge for development', in *The Cultural Dimension of Development: Indigenous Knowledge Systems*, Warren, D. Michael, L. Jan Slikkerveer and David Brokensha (eds), London: Intermediate Technology Publications.

Weinstock, Neil, 'Copyright and a Democratic Civil Society', *Yale Law Journal*, 106(283).

DOCUMENTS

Agenda 21, UN Division for Sustainable Development, Available at http://www.un.org/esa/sustdev/documents/agenda21/english/agenda21toc.htm (last accessed on 25 January 2008).

Commission on Intellectual Property Rights, Innovation and Public Health (CIPIH) Report on Public Health, Innovation and Intellectual Property Rights, Geneva, April 2006. Available at www.who.int/intellectualproperty/documents/thereport/en/index.html (last accessed on 5 July 2008).

Convention on Biodiversity (CBD).Available at http://www.cbd.int/convention/ convention.shtml (last accessed on 5 July 2008).

FAO, International Undertaking for Plant and Genetic Resource (IU), Resolution 8/83. Available at ftp://ftp.fao.org/ag/cgrfa/iu/iutextE.pdf (last accessed on 15 July 2008).

http://www.justice.gov/atr/cases/f209200/209268.htm (last accessed on 2 January 2008).

http://www.patentoffice.nic.in/ipr/patent/patAct1970-3-99.html (last accessed on 5 February 2009).

International Covenant on Civil and Political Rights (ICCPR), Draft Declaration on the Rights of Indigenous Peoples.

Madras High Court Decision in the Glivec Case: Writ Petition—W.P. Nos.24759 and 24760 of 2006. Available at http://judis.nic.in/chennai/ qrydisp.asp?tfnm=11121 (last accessed on 5 December 2009).

Monsanto Co. v. Homan McFarling, 03-1177 (Fed. Cir. Apr. 9, 2004) – CAFC Decision. http://bulk.resource.org/courts.gov/c/F3/363/363.F3d.1336.03-1228.03-1177.html (last accessed on 5 December 2009).

Monsanto Co. v. Homan McFarling. No 4 of 31. Supreme Court of The United States.

Monsanto Technology Agreement. Available at http://www.mindfully.org/GE/ Monsanto-Technology-Agreement-1998.htm (last accessed on 12 January 2009).

Novartis Petition—The High Court of Judicature at Madras (Special Original Jurisdiction) w.p.no.24759 of 2006.

Report of the Conference of FAO, 25th Session. Available at http://www.fao. org/Unfao/Bodies/RegConferences/erc25/erc25_en.htm (last accessed on 15 January 2008).

Sources and Prices of Selected Drugs and Diagnostics for People Living with HIV/AIDS, UNICEF-UNAIDS-WHO/HTP/MSF (May 2001). Available at http://www.who.int/hiv/topics/arv/en/who_edm_par_2002.pdf (last accessed on 28 June 2008).

USC S 101—The Patentability of Living Organisms under 35 USC S 101.

United Nations, Agenda 21, UN Division for Sustainable Development. Available at http://www.un.org/esa/sustdev/documents/agenda21/english/ agenda21toc.htm (last accessed on 5 July 2008).

UPOV,1991.Available at http://www.upov.int/en/publications/conventions/1991/ pdf/act1991.pdf (last accessed on 12 July 2009).

USPTO—35 USC 102—Conditions for patentability; novelty and loss of right to patent.

Via Campesina Text on Farmers' Rights. Available at http://www.ukabc.org/ Via_Camp.html (last accessed on 15 July 2008).

WHO—Commission on Intellectual Property Rights, Innovation and Public Health (CIPIH) Report on Public Health, Innovation and Intellectual Property Rights, Geneva: April 2006 WHO—Doha Health Declaration

Implications of the Doha Declaration on the TRIPS agreement and public health (WHO/EDM/PAR/2002.3).

WIPO, Intergovernmental Committee Report on Intellectual Property And Genetic Resources, Traditional Knowledge And Folklore, 3rd Session, 2002.

WIPO/UNEP, The Role of Intellectual Property Rightsin the Sharing of Benefits Arising from the Use of Biological Resourcesand Traditional Knowledge – Selected Case Studies (Geneva: WIPO/ UNEP, 2002).

WTO Council for TRIPS—Proposal, titled 'Elements of the obligation to disclose evidence of benefit sharing under the relevant national regime' (IP/C/W/442), was submitted by Bolivia, Brazil, Colombia, Dominican Republic, Ecuador, India, Peru and Thailand. 8–10 March, 2005.

WTO Council for TRIPS—IP/C/W/370/Rev.1. Secretariat Summary: 'the Protection of Traditional knowledge and Folklore.' 9 March 2006. Available at http://www.ige.ch/e/jurinfo/documents/IP-C-W-370.pdf (last accessed on 15 January 2008).

WTO Council for Trade-Related Aspects of Intellectual Property Rights— IP/C/W/370/Rev.1. Secretariat Summary: 'the Protection of Traditional knowledge and Folklore', 9 March 2006.

Submissions by Bolivia, Colombia, Ecuador, Nicaragua and Peru, IP/C/ W/165; Cuba, Honduras, Paraguay and Venezuela, IP/C/W/166.

Index

commensuration 140, 166, 176, 226, 341
   TRIPS as a system of 158, 165
common property xvi, 21, 33, 55, 62, 95n10, 296n40
common good 32, 36, 99, 102, 344
communitarian 434
community rights 3
   in agricultural practices 231, 330
   See also oral traditions
compulsory license 194n26, 199, 200, 201, 205
   in the *McFarling* case 256
   See also Patent Act 1970
compulsory licensing 190, 194n28
   and Doha Declaration 197, 198, 200, 340
   in Brazil 196
   in South Africa 194
   in Thailand 200
   and India 202
   in August 30th decision 199
communal knowledge 291, 293
   and CBD 291
context of discovery 152, 153, 157
context of justification 152, 153, 157, 173
   See also Bruno Latour
contingency 14, 154, 349
   socio-cultural and historical 152, 154
control rights 48, 59, 75, 76, 78–80, 84
convention of biodiversity (CBD) 243n28, 244, 287, 288, 290–1
   and TRIPS 168, 295, 298, 321, 324
   and benefit sharing 243, 323
copyright xiv, 6, 10, 17, 70, 87, 101, 104
   and exclusion 123–4, 127, 137, 334
   and traditional knowledge 294, 313
   Anglo-American copyright laws 7, 62, 92
   Posner on 106–7
   Lockean reading of 89

Cornish, W.R. 12
Cullet, Phillippe 245
culture 140, 166, 173, 174, 276
   knowledge as 141–3, 145, 295
   and rights 183, 347, 348
   and science 161, 169, 171
   and traditional knowledge 164, 282
cultural rights 3, 167, 349
customary rights 246, 297, 348

D'Arcy, Eric 134
Dasgupta P. and J.E. Stiglitz 110–11
De Long, James 89n62
Demsetz, Harold 93, 104
Desert 63, 70, 71, 73, 74, 233
   See also Munzer
development, cultural turn in 140, 142, 176
development discourse 149, 177
Diamond v. *Chakrabarty* case 130n109, 235, 236
difference principle 45, 85, 86, 335–6
   See also John Rawls
disclosure 122, 138, 168, 169, 295, 303, 319, 324, 349
   See also prior informed consent, prior art, prior knowledge
Doha Health Declaration 196, 198, 203, 208n60
Doyle, McCarthy 146
drug donation 214, 217
   of Glivec, in Korea 216
   of Glivec, in India 216
Drahos, Peter 9n16, 15n39
Durkheim, E. 148
Dutfield, Graham 292, 348
Dworkin, Ronald 44–46, 71, 76, 81, 342

efficacy standards 206
   See also Section 3d
egalitarian conscience 86, 336
   See also Cohen, G.A